D0914593

The Critical Response to Katherine Mansfield

Recent Titles in
Critical Responses in Arts and Letters

The Critical Response
to Katherine Mansfield

Edited by
Jan Pilditch

Critical Responses in Arts and Letters,
Number 21
Cameron Northouse, Series Adviser

Greenwood Press
Westport, Connecticut • London

Library of Congress Cataloging-in-Publication Data

The critical response to Katherine Mansfield / edited by Jan Pilditch.
     p.   cm.—(Critical responses in arts and letters, ISSN
1057–0993 ; no. 21)
  Includes bibliographical references and index.
  ISBN 0–313–29064–4 (alk. paper)
  1. Mansfield, Katherine, 1888–1923—Criticism and interpretation.
2. Women and literature—New Zealand—History—20th century.
3. Women and literature—England—History—20th century.
I. Pilditch, Jan. II. Series.
PR9639.3.M258Z623 1996
823′.912—dc20   95–23548

British Library Cataloguing in Publication Data is available.

Library of Congress Catalog Card Number: 95–23548
ISBN: 0–313–29064–4
ISSN: 1057–0993

First published in 1996

Greenwood Press, 88 Post Road West, Westport, CT 06881
An imprint of Greenwood Publishing Group, Inc.

Printed in the United States of America

∞

The paper used in this book complies with the
Permanent Paper Standard issued by the National
Information Standards Organization (Z39.48–1984).

10 9 8 7 6 5 4 3 2 1

Copyright Acknowledgements

The editor and publisher gratefully acknowledge permission for use of the following material:

Extracts from the works of Katherine Mansfield, and various extracts from Katherine Mansfield's Stories, Poems, Letters, Journals and Scrapbook, reprinted with permission from the Society of Authors as the literary representative of the Estate of Katherine Mansfield. Extracts from *The Short Stories of Katherine Mansfield*, © 1937 and renewed 1965 by Alfred A. Knopf Inc. reprinted by permission of the publisher.

West, Rebecca, review, 1922: Reprinted with permission © *The New Statesman*, London, U.K.
Aiken, Conrad, "The Short Story as Colour" 1922. © Conrad Aiken, reprinted by permission of Brandt & Brandt, New York.
Mortimer, Raymond, review 1923: Reprinted with permission © *The New Statesman*, London, U.K.
Woolf, Virginia, "A Terribly Sensitive Mind" 1927, reprinted with permission from the Society of Authors as the literary representative of the Virginia Woolf Estate.
Wagenknecht, Edward, 1928, reprinted with permission of *The English Journal*, London.
Pritchett, V.S., review of *Novels and Novelists* in *The Spectator*, 1930, reprinted with permission of *The Spectator*.
Schneider, Elisabeth, "Katherine Mansfield and Chekhov", 1935. Reprinted from *Modern Language Notes* with permission of The Johns Hopkins University Press., Baltimore, USA.
Daiches, David, "Katherine Mansfield" reprinted from *New Literary Values (Studies in Modern Literature Series)*, 1936, with permission of David Higham Associates.
Sewell, Arthur, extracts from "Katherine Mansfield, a Critical Essay" 1936, reprinted with permission of William Sewell, the author's son.
Porter, Katherine Anne, "The Art of Katherine Mansfield" 1937. Reprinted with permission from *The Nation* magazine. © The Nation Company, L.P.
Anonymous article "Katherine Mansfield's Stories"1946, reprinted with permission © *The Times Literary Supplement*, London, U.K.

Murry, John Middleton, "Katherine Mansfield" 1949, reprinted with permission from the Society of Authors as the literary representative of the Estate of John Middleton Murry.

Hynes, Sam, "Katherine Mansfield: The Defeat of the Personal", 1953, reprinted with permission of *The South Atlantic Quarterly*, S2:4. © Duke University Press, 1953. Reprinted with permission.

Bowen, Elizabeth, "A Living Writer" ©1956 Elizabeth Bowen reproduced with permission of Curtis Brown, London.

Gordon, Ian A. "The Editing of Katherine Mansfield's Journal and Scrapbook" 1959, reprinted with permission of the author, © Ian Gordon.

Bateson, F.W. & B. Shahevitch, "Katherine Mansfield's 'The Fly'", 1962, reprinted from *Essays in Criticism* by permission of the editors of *Essays in Criticism*.

Brophy, Brigid, "Katherine Mansfield's Self-Depiction", 1966, reprinted with permission of *Michigan Quarterly Review*.

Mortelier, Christiane, "The Genesis and Development of the Katherine Mansfield Legend in France", 1970, reprinted from *AUMLA* with permission of the author.

Baldeshwiler, Eileen, "Katherine Mansfield's Theory of Fiction" *Studies in Short Fiction*. 7 (1970): 421-32. © 1970 by Newberry College. Reprinted with permission of the editor of *Studies in Short Fiction*.

Scott, Margaret A. "The Extant Manuscripts of Katherine Mansfield" 1973, reprinted with permission of the author.

Beachcroft, T.O."Katherine Mansfield's Encounter with Theocritus", 1974, reprinted with permission of The English Association, University of Leicester, U.K.

Mantz, Ruth Elvish, "Katherine Mansfield—Tormentor and Tormented" 1975, reprinted with permission of Harry Ransom Humanities Research Center, The University of Texas at Austin, U.S.A.

O'Sullivan, Vincent, "The Magnetic Chain: Notes and Approaches to K.M." 1975, reprinted with permission of the author.

Stead, C.K. "Katherine Mansfield and the Art of Fiction" 1977, reprinted from *The New Review*, with permission of the author. © C.K. Stead.

Meyers, Jeffrey, "Katherine Mansfield's 'To Stanislaw Wyspianski'", from *Modern Fiction Studies*, p.178© 1978 by Purdue Research Foundation, West Lafayette, Indiana 47907. Reprinted with permission.

Hankin, Cherry, "Fantasy and the Sense of an Ending in the Work of Katherine Mansfield", 1978, reprinted with permission of the author and *Modern Fiction Studies*.

Alpers, Antony, extract from *The Life of Katherine Mansfield*, Reprinted by permission of John Johnson Ltd., London and by Viking Penguin, a division of Penguin Books USA Inc. ©1980 by Antony Alpers.

Gubar, Susan, extract from "The Birth of the Artist as Heroine: (Re)production, the Künstlerroman Tradition, and the Fiction of Katherine Mansfield" from Heibrun, Carolyn G., Margaret R. Higonnet (eds.) *The Representation of Women in Fiction: Selected Papers from the English Institute, 1981*, The

John Hopkins University Press, Baltimore/London, 1983. Reprinted with permission of The John Hopkins University Press.

Gurr, Andrew, "The Question of Perspectives in Commonwealth Literature" 1984, reprinted with permission of the author.

Tomalin, Claire, "What is going to happen to us all?" from *Katherine Mansfield: A Secret Life*, 1987, reprinted with permission by Penguin Books Ltd. UK, and Alfred A. Knopf Inc. USA. ©1987 Claire Tomalin.

Arvidson, K.O.A. "Dancing on the Hand of God: Katherine Mansfield's Religious Sensibility" 1988, reprinted with permission of the author.

Dale, Judith, "Performing Katherine Mansfield" 1989, reprinted with permission of the author.

Gong, Shifen, "Katherine Mansfield: A Chinese Perspective", from an unpublished doctoral thesis, reprinted by permission of the author, © Shifen Gong 1993.

Ihimaera, Witi, "Dear Katherine Mansfield" from *Dear Miss Mansfield*, 1989, published by Penguin Books New Zealand, reprinted with permission of the publisher.

Every reasonable effort has been made to trace the owners of copyright materials in this book, but in some instances this has proven impossible. The editor and publisher will be glad to receive information leading to more complete acknowledgements in subsequent printings of the book and in the meantime extend their apologies for any omissions.

FOR

JOHN LEE PILDITCH

Contents

III New Approaches

IV Consolidation

V One Hundred Years On

Series Foreword

Critical Responses in Arts and Letters is designed to present a documentary history of highlights in the critical reception to the body of work of writers and artists and to individual works that are generally considered to be of major importance. The focus of each volume in this series is basically historical. The introductions to each volume are themselves brief histories of the critical response an author, artist, or individual work has received. This response is then further illustrated by reprinting a strong representation of the major critical reviews and articles that have collectively produced the author's, artist's, or work's critical reputation.

The scope of *Critical Responses in Arts and Letters* knows no chronological or geographical boundaries. Volumes under preparation include studies of individuals from around the world and in both contemporary and historical periods.

Each volume is the work of an individual editor, who surveys the entire body of criticism on a single author, artist, or work. The editor then selects the best material to depict the critical response received by an author or artist over his/her entire career. Documents produced by the author or artist may also be included when the editor finds that they are necessary to a full understanding of the materials at hand. In circumstances where previous isolated volumes of criticism on a particular individual or work exist, the editor carefully selects material that better reflects the nature and directions of the critical response over time.

In addition to the introduction and the documentary section, the editor of each volume is free to solicit new essays on areas that may not have been adequately dealt with in previous criticism. Also, for volumes on living writers and artists, new interviews may be included, again at the discretion of the volume's editor. The volumes also provide a supplementary bibliography and are fully indexed.

While each volume in *Critical Responses in Arts and Letters* is unique, it is also hoped that in combination they form a useful, documentary history of the critical response to the arts, and one that can be easily and profitably employed by students and scholars.

Cameron Northouse

Preface

The work of Katherine Mansfield carries with it an appeal which knows no geographical boundaries. All of it is in print and she is widely read, taught, and anthologized throughout the world and her work has been translated into a number of languages and the language of critical essays about her work is similarly diverse. Despite the international flavour of Mansfield criticism, however, the critical response to her work in this volume is represented, in the interests of lucidity, by those essays written in English, which form the bulk of any Bibliography. Included are some essays which indicate Mansfield's links with Europe, and the part played in her critical history by European, particularly French and German criticism, and by Asian critics. These inclusions can be reinforced by consulting the Select Bibliography, as can information of the complete publishing record of Mansfield's work which is not given in the Select Chronology. The essays in this volume, it is hoped, represent the diversity of the critical response to Mansfield's life and work over a period of some hundred years. Those wishing to know more are similarly urged to consult the Select Bibliography at end of the book.

Acknowledgements

As always, my first thanks must go to to Marshall Walker, who generously read the manuscript and advised. I owe a debt of gratitude to the staff of the National Library, London; the Bodleian Library, Oxford; the Newberry Library, Chicago; the Alexander Turnbull Library, Wellington; and to the staff at the Library of the University of Waikato, particularly Adrienne Ridley. I am grateful to K.O. Arvidson and Vincent O'Sullivan for their help and encouragement, to Sonia Wells, for the preparation of the manuscript, and to my family for their patience. I would like to thank the Research Committee of the University of Waikato for making the project financially possible, and finally, my thanks must go to Cameron Northouse, series adviser, for his advice and his commitment to the project.

Select Chronology of Mansfield Works

1898-1905   "Enna Blake" in *High School Reporter* (September1898)
"A Happy Christmas Eve" in *High School Reporter* (April 1899)
"Die Einsame" in *Queen's College Magazine* (1904)
"About Pat" in *Queen's College Magazine* (1905)

1907   "Vignettes" in *Native Companion*, (October), Melbourne, Australia.
"Silhouettes" in *Native Companion*, (November)
"In a Café" in *Native Companion*, (December)
"In the Botanical Gardens" in *Native Companion,* (December).
[The first three are signed 'K. Mansfield', the last signed 'Julien Mark'.]

1908-1910   "The Tiredness of Rosabel" (posthumous).
"The Education of Audrey", *The Evening Post*, (January 20, 1908), Wellington, New Zealand.
"The Lonesome Child", *The Dominion*, (6 June, 1908),Wellington, New Zealand.
"Why Love is Blind", *The New Zealand Freelance*, (20 June 1908).
"Study: The Death of a Rose", *The Triad* (July 1908), New Zealand.
"A Day in Bed", *Lone Hand*, (October 1909), Sydney, Australia. [Signed 'K.M. Beauchamp'].
"November", *The Daily News*, (November 3rd 1909), London.
"A Fairy Story", *OpenWindow* III, (December 1910), [Signed 'Katherina Mansfield'].

1911   *In a German Pension*, London: Stephen Swift.

1913   "Floryan Nachdenklich", *The Dominion*, Wellington, New Zealand,
            March 3, 1913. (Poem).
            "Old Tar", *Westminster Gazette* (London) October 25, 1913, (repr.
            in *The New Zealand Times*, December 11, 1913).

1918   *Prelude*, Richmond: Hogarth Press, (July). Edition of 300 copies
            printed by Leonard and Virginia Woolf.

1920   *Je ne parle pas français*, Hampstead: Heron Press.
            Bliss and Other Stories, London: Constable.

1921   *Bliss and Other Stories*, New York: Knopf.

1922   *The Garden Party and Other Stories*, London: Constable, (New
            York: Knopf).

1923   *The Dove's Nest and Other Stories*, ed. J.M. Murry, London:
            Constable.
            Poems, ed. J.M. Murry, London: Constable, (2nd edition 1930).

1924   *The Dove's Nest and Other Stories*, ed. J.M. Murry, New York:
            Knopf.
            Poems, ed. J.M. Murry, New York: Knopf (2nd edition 1931).
            Something Childish and Other Stories, ed. J.M. Murry, London:
            Constable, (published as *The Little Girl and Other Stories*,
            New York: Knopf).

1926   *In a German Pension*, New York: Knopf.

1927   *The Journal of Katherine Mansfield*, ed. J.M. Murry, London:
            Constable (New York: Knopf).

1928   *The Letters of Katherine Mansfield*, ed. J.M. Murry, London:
            Constable, (2 volumes).

1929   *The Letters of Katherine Mansfield*, ed. J.M. Murry, New York:
            Knopf (1 volume, including the letters to Murry).

1930   "The Aloe", ed. J.M. Murry, London: Constable (New York:
            Knopf).
            Novels and Novelists, ed. with introduction by J.M. Murry, London:
            Constable (New York: Knopf, repr. Boston: Beacon Press,
            1959).
            Stories: A Selection by J. Middleton Murry, New York: Knopf.

1937   *Stories by Katherine Mansfield*, New York: Knopf.
"To Stanislaw Wyspianski" (poem), privately printed (London).
The Scrapbook of Katherine Mansfield, ed. J.M. Murry, London: Constable (New York: Knopf).

1940   *The Scrapbook of Katherine Mansfield*, ed. J.M. Murry, New York: Knopf, (repr. New York: H. Fertig, 1974).

1945   *The Collected Stories of Katherine Mansfield*, London: Constable.

1951   *Katherine Mansfield's Letters to John Middleton Murry, 1913-1922*, ed. J.M. Murry, London: Constable (New York: Knopf).

1954   *Journal of Katherine Mansfield* (Definitive Edition), ed. J.M. Murry, London: Constable.

1970-79   "The Unpublished Manuscripts of Katherine Mansfield", trans. and ed. by Margaret Scott in *Turnbull Library Record*, vols. 3-7 and 12, Wellington, New Zealand.

1972   Scott, Margaret, ed. "Brave Love", in *Landfall*, XXVI pp. 3-29. Previously unpublished, written January 1915.

1974   *Undiscovered Country, The New Zealand Stories of Katherine Mansfield,* ed. Ian A. Gordon, London: Longman, 1974.

1977   *Katherine Mansfield: Publications in Australia 1907-1909*, ed. with intro. by Jean Stone, Sydney: Wentworth Books.
The Letters and Journals of Katherine Mansfield: A Selection, ed. C.K. Stead, London: Allen Lane.

1978   *The Urewera Notebook*, ed. with introduction by Ian A. Gordon, Wellington: Oxford University Press.

1982   *The Aloe, with Prelude*, ed. with intro. by Vincent O'Sullivan, Wellington: Port Nicholson Press.

1984   *The Collected Letters of Katherine Mansfield: Vol. I 1903-1917*, ed. Vincent O'Sullivan and Margaret Scott, Oxford: Clarendon Press.
The Stories of Katherine Mansfield, Definitive Edition, ed. Antony Alpers, Auckland: Oxford University Press.

1987   *The Critical Writings of Katherine Mansfield*, ed. and intro. by
            Clare Hanson, London: Macmillan (New York: St. Martin's
            Press).
            The Collected Letters of Katherine Mansfield: Vol. II 1918-1919,
            ed. Vincent O'Sullivan with Margaret Scott, Oxford:
            Clarendon Press.

1988   *Poems of Katherine Mansfield*, ed. Vincent O'Sullivan, Auckland:
            Oxford University Press.
            Letters between Katherine Mansfield and John Middleton Murry,
            ed. Cherry Hankin, London: Virago.
            Katherine Mansfield: Dramatic Sketches, ed. David Drummond,
            Palmerston North: Ngaere Press (First published in *The New
            Age* between 1911-1917, and also printed in Alpers, *The
            Stories of Katherine Mansfield*, 1984).

1990-91   *Letters Between Katherine Mansfield & John Middleton Murry*,
            Hankin, Cherry. (ed.) New Amsterdam Books, New York.

            "My Potplants" and "His Ideal", Alexander Turnbull Library MS.
            Papers 119. Unpublished.

1993   *The Collected Letters of Katherine Mansfield: Vol. III*, ed.Vincent
            O'Sullivan and Margaret Scott, Oxford: Clarendon Press.

This Chronology has been confined to first editions of Mansfield's work and to
major subsequent editions. Those wishing to see a more complete publication
record should consult the bibliographic volumes indicated in the Select
Bibliography.

Introduction

In July 1908, Katherine Mansfield left New Zealand for the second time. She was nineteen-years-old and, convinced that she could make her way in the world as a writer, she exchanged the security and comfort of her Wellington middle class home and family for the difficult, some might say treacherous, society of London. The act presaged a restlessness that persisted throughout her life. Her pregnancy and subsequent miscarriage during her first months of freedom, her two marriages, her ambiguous sexuality, and her endless movement characterised a life spent garnering experience. Her most significant friend, Ida Baker, known as LM, remained with her throughout her life, but there was a wide and changeable circle of acquaintance which included most of the major literary figures of the day. She, and her second husband John Middleton Murry, the writer, editor, and critic, numbered among their friends T.S. Eliot, D.H. Lawrence, Virginia and Leonard Woolf, Bertrand Russell, Aldous Huxley, and Lady Ottoline Morrell, to name but a few. It was one of the most innovative and exciting intellectual and literary circles of the day, but there was also loneliness and the death of her only brother in 1915, when she was already suffering from tubercolosis, and possibly gonorrhea, and her final years which were spent searching Europe for relief. Mansfield died in January 1923, at the Gurdjieff Institute for the Harmonious Development of Man, Fontainebleau-Avon.

Mansfield had begun to publish professionally before leaving Wellington. At first the substance and treatment of her early work was questioned by the Australian editor of the Melbourne based *Native Companion*, Brady, to whom she sent it, because he thought it too sophisticated to be the writing of a girl of eighteen. He wondered whether Frank Morton, a more established New Zealand writer, was 'putting one over'. Later, he was to note, he regarded Katherine Mansfield as *the* literary find of his distinguished editorial career. In London the critics, with reservations, were no less interested. In *The New Age* (Dec. 21, 1911), an anonymous review of her first collection of short stories, possibly written by Beatrice Hastings, describes the qualities of some of her stories as those "definitely belonging to the make-up of one of the most promising of young writers". (p.188) In the years following this review Mansfield published poems, critical pieces, and *Prelude* in 1918. Three further volumes of short stories followed, *Je ne parle par français* was published in 1920, as was *Bliss and Other Stories*, the latter was also published in America by Knopf in January 1921. Malcolm Cowley thought it one of those books which it is very hard to forget, despite having reservations about the subject matter. Mansfield, he observed in the *Dial* (Sept. 1921), had "got hold of a new and necessary form" (p.365). Her work enjoyed similar recognition in France and Germany, so that by the time of her death in January 1923, with only *The Garden Party and Other Stories* (1922) added to the list of works published in her lifetime, her death attracted widespread notice across Europe, America, and of course in her native Australasia.   The early critical response to her work was testimony to her promise, but her varied life and her tragically early death from tubercolosis ensured that the growth of her reputation was tempered by the growth of a legend.

The legend, like those of Chatterton, Keats, or Shelley, concentrated on the beauty and brilliance of a mind misunderstood in a harsh world. Her husband, Murry, in a poem published in Mansfield's memory in *The Adelphi* (Jan. 1924), wrote that:

> . . . she was wondrous beautiful,
> And some one with a wizard pen at birth
> Had drawn her brows, from some enchanted pool
> Had brimmed her eyes, trembling with deeper mirth,
> Nearer to profound tears than any of this earth. (p.663)

Edith Sitwell's essay "Three Women Writers", which appeared in the popular London journal *Vogue* in the October of 1924, was a genuine attempt to assess what Mansfield actually did, but nevertheless describes her as "exquisite, flawless, narrow, sweet, poignant, ·and contained within her own limtations". What Mansfield gives us, Sitwell insists: "is the thing we have known, but have hidden, for fear it should be spoiled." These comments, like much early French criticism, are typical of those made in the years following her death. While laudatory, they endow Mansfield's work with an ethereal other-worldly quality, and with a fragility as limiting as the intended compliment. Such publications drew attention away from Mansfield's work, and toward the facts of her life and, of course, toward the untimely tragedy of her death. There were numerous articles written by those who had known, or thought they had known, some portion of the Mansfield story. The stories circulated were odd mixtures of fact, fiction, and idealization, and often related in the sort of devotional tones usually reserved for the Saints. Conrad Aiken's short story "Your Obituary, Well Written", which appeared in *Costumes by Eros* published by Jonathon Cape in 1929, was among the less flamboyant, but Olgivanna, (Mrs Frank Lloyd Wright), who had been in Fontainebleau-Avon, and was at the Gurdjieff Institute when Mansfield died, could still describe her last days in *The Bookman* (Mar.1931) with a heady mixture of love, idolatry, and outright mysticism: "She stood in the doorway of our main dining-room and looked at all and at each with sharp, intense, dark eyes. They burned with the desire and hunger for impressions. . . I asked whose that wonderful face was." (p.6) Some stories were not merely exaggerated, but downright inaccurate. Mansfield's father, Harold Beauchamp, was driven to protest on more than one occasion that, contrary to popular belief, he had not kept his daughter hungry and penniless. To *The Saturday Review of Literature* (Sept. 30, 1933) he wrote:

Sir: In *The Bookman* of January last, there was published an interesting article written by Margaret Bell, entitled "In Memory of Katherine Mansfield." My object in writing is to point out that the author of that article is quite wrong in stating that my daughter had a hard struggle for existence in the early stages of her literary career, in fact from what Margaret Bell says, one would imagine that she was in a condition of abject poverty. That statement has been made on more than one occasion, for what reason I cannot divine, but to prove its inaccuracy, I should like to give you a copy of a letter which was written to *T. P.'s & Cassell's Weekly* on 28th May 1927 . . . (p.144)

The included letter, from Alexander Kay who had acted as Beauchamp's agent and attorney in the matter of his daughter's allowance, vigorously asserts Beauchamp's generosity to, and his affection for, his daughter.

Legends, however, are more easily created than destroyed and the interest in Mansfield's life was kindled by the publication of works such as Francis Carco's *Montmartre à vingt ans* (Paris 1938), and, of course, by Murry's own editing and subsequent publication of *The Journal of Katherine Mansfield* (1928), *The Letters of Katherine Mansfield* (1929), *The Scrapbook of Katherine Mansfield* (1939), and *Katherine Mansfield's Letters to John Middleton Murry 1913-1922* (1951). In 1933 *The Life of Katherine Mansfield* by Ruth Elvish Manzt and John Middleton Murry was published, further fuelling the interest in Mansfield biography. That work ended with the year 1912 so that the French translation was called, more accurately, *La Jeunesse de Katherine Mansfield*. Murry finally published what he called the 'definitive edition' of *The Journal of Katherine Mansfield* in 1954. By now far the greater part of Mansfield's work in print consisted of letters and incidental writing never intended for publication. Thus even as late as 1957 Christopher Isherwood, in *Great English Short Stories*, began his introduction to a Mansfield short story by commenting, quite rightly, that a good half of her writing had been published posthumously and, he goes on:

The more important half in some respects, for it revealed the personality of Mansfield herself-and it is as a personality, quite apart from her stories, that many readers have come to admire and love her. I myself felt a strong personal love for her at one time in my life, and it seems a little strange to me, even now, that we never actually met. She was so very much one of my circle of friends. (p.233)

The publication of the *Journal* and the *Letters* had made public a large body of intimate detail about Mansfield which distracted critics from Mansfield's work for some thirty years after her death, and led them to an engagement with sensitivity, passion, courage, and other like qualities. In the first decade after her death the Mansfield legend had become a cult.

All cults, of course, have their reactionary element. Both Murry and Mansfield were subject to attack as successive volumes of the *Journal, Letters,* and *Scrapbook* appeared. Murry, it was said, was exploiting his dead wife, while the relentless publication of much that might have remained private inevitably exposed Mansfield's vulnerabilities, as woman and as artist. The most famous of these attacks was the biting satire perpetrated by Aldous Huxley with his portrait of Burlap and his wife in *Point Counter Point* (1928). More helpfully, however, some critics, in conjuction with their interest in biographical material, did attempt to assess the work. Edward Wagenknecht, also in 1928, impatient with fruitless speculation about what Mansfield might have done had she lived, insisted that what she did do was beyond dispute. Being quite unlike any of her British contemporaries, Galsworthy, Wells, or De La Mare, she had, Wagenknecht remarks, moved the art of the short story "to the highest point of perfection it has yet attained."(p.273) Wagenknecht's placement of Mansfield within this group of Edwardian writers is some indication of her achievement. *The Garden Party*, like Joyce's *Ulysses* and Eliot's "The Waste Land", was published in 1922, and it is the writers of the Modern Movement with whom she is most often associated by today's readers. It is easily forgotton that *Bliss* first appeared in 1920, and that its impact on readers accustomed to the authorial point of view and narrative based form of the Edwardians, must have been immense. Raymond Mortimer remarks in a review of Mansfield's work in *The New Statesman* (July 7,.1922) that, for him, there are moments (and even months) when the influence of Chekhov on writers in England seems positively disastrous:

> In all Mansfield's work there is hardly an opinion or sentiment which is frankly her own and uncoloured by the mind of any of her characters. One penalty of the method is that it makes so difficult that affectionate relationship of reader to author which ties us to many of the great writers of the past. (p.394)

An affectionate relationship between Mansfield and her readers was forged, but via the more intimate medium of her *Letters* and *Journal*. The stories made new demands upon the critics. Thus Willa Cather's essay, "Katherine Mansfield", which appeared in *Not Under Forty* (1936), while mainly concerned with biography, nevertheless marks the two New Zealand stories, "Prelude" and "At the Bay", as being among Mansfield's finest, but, she goes on, the first writers and critics on reading Mansfield's work, "must have felt that here was a very individual talent." (p.151) As the more objective assessment of Mansfield's work began, attempts to characterise its difference varied.

Early Mansfield assessment was of its time and place, often taking a canonical approach by comparing Mansfield with other writers. Arthur Sewell, one of Mansfield's earliest New Zealand critics, noting the lyricism and density of Mansfield's work found it more akin to that of the English poets than the English prose writers. Keats, in particular, was used as a benchmark for this kind of assessment. Murry compared what he called Mansfield's spontaneity with that of Keats, suggesting that in these two the writing self was not entirely distinguishable from the living self, a view reiterated in his Preface to the American edition of *The Short Stories of Katherine Mansfield*. Such criticism, while giving consideration to Mansfield's art, tended to reinforce a legendary view of the writer as one who had only to wait for inspiration to strike. It was a view already losing its popularity. "Even today", wrote an exasperated Katherine Anne Porter, in a review appearing in *The Nation*, "he [Murry] can write that 'her art was of a peculiarly instinctive kind' I confess I cannot understand the use of this word." (p.435) Porter was attempting to extricate Mansfield's accomplishment from that of the life and legend. David Daiches also attempted to deal with the work rather than the woman. He considered Mansfield's close observation of detail, and her desire to embody the truth of reality in her art. His points of comparison were, perhaps more usefully, with Conrad and Joyce. The essays earnt the respect of Murry for the careful account taken of Mansfield's style, and it was with style, and with her contribution to form of the short story, that Mansfield's 'place' as part of the Modern Movement was beginning to be identified

As a concentration on style and form began to dominate Mansfield criticism, it gave rise to an unfortunate tendency, especially among English critics, to undervalue what had been achieved. C.K. Stead remarks in his essay, "Katherine Mansfield: The Art of Fiction" (*In The Glass Case*, 1981):

> In England art is seldom valued for its own sake; it is a vehicle, like a coal truck; and from Dr Johnson to Dr Leavis the English critics have almost without exception seen their primary task as being to check the quantity and quality of the coal. (p.29)

Virginia Woolf had reported in her diary of August 7, 1918 that she had thrown down her copy of *Bliss* saying that Mansfield was ". . . done for! Indeed I don't see how much faith in her as woman or writer can survive that sort of story." Q.D. Leavis's view, as Heather Murray has pointed out in her essay "Katherine Mansfield and Her British Critics: Is There a 'Heart' in Mansfield's Fiction?" (*Journal of New Zealand Literature, 6* 1988), was that the work of both Woolf and Mansfield displayed a deficiency in value and character which put them outside of the humanist 'Great Tradition'. Nor was criticism of this kind entirely absent in the American journals. Sam Hynes' essay, "Katherine Mansfield: The Defeat of the Personal", in *South Atlantic Quarterly*, asserts that: "The Horatian dichotomy - pleasure and instruction - still defines in the simplest possible terms the way art works and the way we as critics must approach it."(p.555) He concludes that Mansfield's work fails to provide the requisite Horatian blend and, therefore, ultimately fails as art. Further, the effort to define the origins of Mansfield's style had led Elizabeth Schneider, in an article of 1935, to make particular comparison between the Mansfield story "The Child Who Was Tired", which appeared in *In a German Pension* (1911), and a story by Chekhov called, in its English translation, "Sleephead" or "Sleepy". She demonstrated a similarity too great to be ignored, especially when viewed in terms of Mansfield's own wish, for a variety of reasons, never to reproduce that early volume of stories. Schneider concluded that there had been some unconcious imitation of Chekhov, of which literary history afforded many examples. The issues raised by her article, however, were still being debated in the correspondence of *The Times Literary Supplement* of October 1951, in the course of which Antony Alpers, in Mansfield's defense, pointed to her intense dislike of the youthful, and sometimes facile, satire in parts of *In a German Pension* as her reason for refusing to re-publish. He suggested Mansfield's own early story, "The Tiredness of Rosabel", was the true starting point for "The Child Who Was Tired".[1]

Mansfield criticism was still dogged by biographical considerations but 1951 saw the publication, by Yale University Press, of Sylvia Berkman's balanced appraisal, *Katherine Mansfield: A Critical Study*. Berkman had not been wholly dependent on the *Journal* and *Letters* for her impressions of Mansfield and, in her introduction, comments with some unease on Murry's justifiable, but indiscriminate publication of Mansfield material. She had drawn, in addition to the *Letters* and *Journal,* upon the resources of G.N. Morris, the New Zealand collector of Mansfieldiana, the help of Mrs Mackintosh Bell, Mansfield's family, Frieda Lawrence, and Dorothy Brett, among others. Then, when her work was in page proof, her path crossed that of Antony Alpers. In her own words:

> Mr Alpers has very generously let me read a draft of his manuscript. His careful research throws light on a number of obscure portions of Miss Mansfield's life, particularly the period between 1908 and 1912. My own account has not been invalidated by this fuller knowledge, however. It therefore stands intact, except for the revision of a few factual details. (*Katherine Mansfield: A Critical Study*, p.9-10)

Early biographical data had relied heavily on Murry's publication of Mansfield's letters and journals so that the work of Berkman and Alpers represented a more independent approach by critics. Katherine Mansfield's notebooks and papers were eventually sold at auction by the estate of the late John Middleton Murry. In 1959 the recent aquisition of her papers by the Government of New Zealand on behalf of the Alexander Turnbull library gave scholars the opportunity to study Mansfield's papers firsthand. The results were startling. Ian Gordon, in his article for *Landfall,* "The Editing of Katherine Mansfield's Journal and Scrapbook", recognized that the hetrogeneous mass of material aquired by the New Zealand Government was in fact the *Journal.* It was also the *Scrapbook* and the 1954 expanded edition of the *Journal* which Murry had called the 'definitive' edition. In all Murry's editing, Gordon says:

> he invariably referred to *the* Journal, the implication being that there was such an entity. I can find little trace of it in the extant documents. The *Journal* is a brilliant piece of literary synthesis and editorial patchwork by Murry, based on pieces taken from some forty notebooks and diaries and a few hundred single scraps of paper. (p.62)

The Mansfield of the *Journal* had proved, to say the least, to be an unreliable entity. Alper's fuller biography, *Katherine Mansfield: A Biography*, as described by Berkman, had been published in 1953, but was replaced, rather than revised, by his great work, *The Life of Katherine Mansfield*, in 1980. That work remains the most valuable of all Mansfield's biographies, although others, such as Jeffrey Meyers' *Katherine Mansfield: A Biography* (1977), which takes a more modern view, Gill Boddy's *Katherine Mansfield: The Woman and the Writer* (1988), which forms a useful introduction to the writer and her life, or Claire Tomalin's *Katherine Mansfield: A Secret Life* (1987), offer different, and also valuable, interpretations of Mansfield's life. A definitive edition of *The Stories of Katherine Mansfield* edited by Antony Alpers was published in 1984, while volumes one to three of the five volume edition of *The Collected Letters of Katherine Mansfield*, edited by Vincent O'Sullivan and Margaret Scott, were published in 1984, 1987, and 1993 respectively.

Critics began to rid themselves of the Mansfield legend. Brigid Brophy's article, "Katherine Mansfield's Self-Depiction", which appeared in the *Michigan Quarterly Review* , begins:

Once upon a time a sensitive soul was born in New Zealand, took the name Katherine Mansfield and came to Europe, where she wrote evocative fragments, loved delicately, and died young - technically of pulmonary tuberculosis but really because life was too gross for her. Fortunately, this banal person never existed. (p.89)

It, like Sally Brown's later essay "Hundreds of Selves: The British Library's Katherine Mansfield Letters" which appeared in *The British Library Journal* (Autumn, 1988), presented Mansfield the actress and, for Brophy at least, this element of Mansfield's personality tainted her work. Such critics, interpreting Mansfield's personality in this light, found ample evidence in the letters for their point of view, although later O'Sullivan, in his Introduction to *The Collected Letters of Katherine Mansfield, Vol. I*, (1984), marked a differing interpretation of Mansfield role-playing, that must be allowed:

She also told her cousin on 23rd December 1903: 'They call me false, and mad, and changeable. I would not show them what I was really like for worlds.' . . . From her adolescence, self-defence was almost inseperable from the way she behaved. (p.ix)

New approaches to Mansfield's life and personality were accompanied by new approaches to her work. F. W. Bateson and B. Shahevitch published their article "Katherine Mansfield's 'The Fly': A Critical Exercise" in *Essays in Criticism* (Jan. 1962). The sense of poetry in Mansfield's work had been suggested by H.E. Bates in *The Modern Short Story: A Critical Survey* (1941) among others, but Bateson and Shahevitch wished to demonstrate that, granted the difference in genres, the same kind of 'close analysis' critical procedure was as useful an approach to realistic fiction, as to a poem. The article prompted considerable correspondence in the journal, but, on the whole, that correspondence questioned interpretation rather than method. Mansfield's work responded well to the new critical practice, including feminist critical practice, and a process of consolidation began.

Several full length critical studies followed, including Saralyn Daly's *Katherine Mansfield* (1965), Nariman Hormasji's *Katherine Mansfield: An Appraisal* (1967), and Marvin Magalaner's *The Fiction of Katherine Mansfield* (1971). The importance of Mansfield's distanced imaginative use of her New Zealand background was affirmed, and complexity entered discussion about the relationship beween life and text, as it did in the matter of literary influence. Numerous and substantial journal articles were published, including Philip Waldron's more extended article on Murry's editing of the Mansfield Journal in *Twentieth Century Literature* (No.20, 1974), Vincent O'Sullivan's notable account of Mansfield's sexuality, and his assessment of the influence of Wilde and Pater in *Landfall* (No.114, 1975), and C.K. Stead's excellent account of Mansfield's style and form in *New Review* (no.42, 1977). Jeffrey Meyers' "Katherine Mansfield: A Bibliography of International Criticism, 1921-1977" was published in the *Bulletin of Bibliography and Magazine Notes* (vol.34, 1977). This was updated in a special edition of *Modern Fiction Studies* (no.24 1978) devoted entirely to Mansfield scholarship. Meyer's biography *Katherine Mansfield* (1978), and the new Alpers's biography *The Life of Katherine Mansfield* in 1980, mentioned previously, confirmed Mansfield's stature by the end of the decade. These were followed by Clare Hanson's and Andrew Gurr's *Katherine Mansfield* (1981), Cherry Hankin's *Katherine Mansfield and her Confessional Stories* (1983), Kate Fullbrook's *Katherine Mansfield* (1986) and Claire Tomalin's *Katherine Mansfield: A Secret Life* (1987) among others. Mansfield's work, as a major innovator in the art of the short story, and as an indispensable part of the development of modernism was now beyond question.

One hundred years after her birth the Mansfield Centenary in 1988 was celebrated throughout the world. In China and Japan, where her work is the subject of continued study, in America, throughout Europe, Australia, and in the place of her birth, Wellington, New Zealand, scholars gathered to discuss her work. Special editions of her stories appeared. Beyond the critical sphere her popularity is undiminished. Mansfield has always been a writers' writer. Her life and work have inspired numerous dramatic adaptations for television, radio, and stage. These continue to engage a general audience while in Patrick D. Morrow's *Katherine Mansfield's Fiction* (1993) an attempt is made to analyse Mansfield's fiction by concentrating on the themes, issues and the radical change in point of view that she accomplished in her lifetime. More recently, in *Katherine Mansfield: In From the Margin* (1994), edited by Roger Robinson, a new assessment has begun. In that work scholars from three continents concur in locating Mansfield as "a substantial and crucial figure" in twentieth century culture. The essays range from a consideration of Mansfield's "ambivalent colonial and European identity" to the first full assessment in English of Francis Carco, Mansfield's "indiscreet" Parisian lover. But the story will not end there. "It is always", as Mansfield wrote to Ottoline Morrell (July 24, 1921), "the next story which is going to contain everything, and that next story is always just out of reach."

NB: All essays and articles mentioned in this Introduction can be found in the
    Select Bibliography at the rear of the book.

---

[1] The correspondence surfaces again in Claire Tomalin's biography, *Katherine Mansfield: A Secret Life* (1987), where it is reproduced.

The Critical Response to Katherine Mansfield

I

The Early Years

Anonymous review of *In a German Pension*

When Miss Mansfield gets quite clear of the lachrymose sentimentality that so often goes with the satirical gift, she will be a very amusing and refreshing writer; but the publisher's comparison of her with Turguénieff she would probably be the first to ridicule. Her work is totally different from the vast, epic order of "Fathers and Children." She is a sketch artist, and very expert in producing vignettes that contain every necessary detail, if sometimes more than is necessary. Her unquenchable humour gives to the work an atmosphere dry and sparkling, very valuable in our swampy age. The advance made from the morbidistic "Child who was Tired" to "The Modern Soul," a triumph of humour, makes one wonder how she came to include the former in this collection, or the baldly conventional "Blaze", which hundreds of modern souls could pen between tea and dinner. "The Luft Bad," "A Birthday," and "Lehmann's," prove that the "Modern Soul" was no tour de force, but definitely belonging to the make-up of one of the most promising of young writers.

The New Age, December 21, 1911, p.188.

J.W.N. S[ullivan], "The Story-Writing Genius"

The critic who is given to "analysis" is the last person in the world who is likely to take his occupation with undue seriousness. He speedily becomes aware of the fact that there are two kinds of literature: there is the kind that with considerable plausibility, he can account for on his methods, and there is another kind whose essence seems to be quite unanalysable. It is, of course, this latter kind for which the critic has most respect: he refers it to "genius" a word indicating the complete breakdown of his critical apparatus. The essence of a good Tchehov story has this kind of elusiveness, and so has this story by Miss Katherine Mansfield. It is true that Miss Mansfield's story lends itself to description more than does a typical Tchehov story, it has more of a definite "subject," but any such description would not touch on that quality which makes us use the word "genius." In fact, it is at the very opening of the story, before the wheels begin to turn at all, that we are most conscious of this quality. The dirty little Parisian café becomes, in four pages, a chamber of initiation. It is a different universe, a different reality, a different set of values, to which we are introduced. The illusion of reality is so complete that it is, in truth, a new experience that we are being called upon to live through. We see everything through the eyes of the young French "literary" man and *procurer* Raoul Duquette who tells the story, and the fact that we can do so shows that he is completely realized, that the universe through which he guides us is, in its way, a complete universe. The story may be regarded as an exposition of this man's world. The exposition is made clearer by the introduction of two English lovers and the Frenchman's reaction towards their tragedy. This second "theme," however, is made almost too interesting; one's attention runs some risk of being diverted from the proper centre of the story. One nearly succumbs to the weakness of wondering what happened afterwards. . . . We think this is due to a slight weakening of Miss Mansfield's concentration; the effect is as if the patient on the operating-table became a vivid, suffering, appealing human being, with, conceivably, a life quite outside the hospital walls.

We are recalled to the "case" point of view, however, with a clean brutality. The episode assumes the perspective which belongs to it in this new world. It takes its place—a not unimportant place—amongst the other things that have occurred in this Frenchman's life. That is why the incident exists, that is why every incident in the story exists, to take its place in the world of Raoul Duquette. This way of presenting a character—by presenting the world in which the character fits, instead of by contrast with the reader's own world—will remind the reader of Dostoevsky's "Letters from the Underworld." Indeed, the pedigree of Miss Mansfield's story is pretty clear. Both Dostoevsky and Tchehov can be found amongst her ancestors, although she takes after the former more than the latter. But in her liking for a definite point, for "solid" materials, she remains English or, perhaps, French. It would be possible to investigate her relations to these and other writers more fully; it would, indeed, be a grateful side-path for the critic to wander down. But this would be for the critic to shirk his real task. As we have admitted, this is what we propose to do. We do it by saying that "Je ne parle pas Français" is a story which possesses genius.

The Athenaeum, April 2, 1920, p. 447.

Anonymous review of "Prelude," *Bliss and Other Stories*

The pervasive incentive of "K.M.'s" work as a critic of fiction is her creative penetration. She invariably endeavours to pierce behind her author's achievement to his conception, to compare what is done with what there was to do, the given representation of life with life itself as witnessed to in her own experience. But, as Dryden says, "till some genius, as universal as Aristotle, shall arise, who can penetrate into all arts and sciences, without the practice of them, I shall think it reasonable that the judgment of an artificer in his own art should be preferable to the opinion of another man." And here, in Miss Katherine Mansfield's collection of stories, we see K.M. as artificer at work in her own art. It is an art that is a kind of divination, and justifies or validates her criticism, for she can no more help "making things up" than she can help making things come alive. One glance at a face, and its secrets are hers; at a scene, and her mood responds to it. Without fear, without favour, though not without predilection, she accepts, explores, makes herself at home in the chosen phase of reality. Her consciousness is as clear, it is only *apparently* as indiscriminating, as a looking-glass. The spirit that surveys its field is delicate yet intrepid, fastidiously frank. To her very finger-tips she is in love with beauty, and securely so because her love springs out of her devotion to truth. ". . . but I tell you, my lord fool, out of this nettle danger, we pluck this flower, safety."

Whatever the actual medium of her story, whether that of general observer, so to speak, in "Prelude," or "Feuille d'Album," or in "Escape," or of that "true Parisian," Raoul Duquette, skipping and grimacing along the border of insanity, or of the eager, trustful "little governess," a grand-niece of Jane Eyre, or of that flimsy popinjay Mr. Reginald Peacock, or of that nursery Adam and Eve, "Sun and Moon," or of the intensively neurotic Monica in "Revelations," or of poor battered Miss Moss, the pitch of mind is invariably emotional, the prose lyrical. None the less that mind is absolutely tranquil and attentive in its intellectual grasp of the matter in hand. And through all, Miss Mansfield's personality, whatever its disguises, haunts her work just as its customary inmate may haunt a vacant room, its *genius* a place. For this very reason, perhaps, her finest pieces of characterization are such "ordinary" people as the clean-cut young Englishman Ian French, the guardian of "the little boy" in "Psychology," the epicure of "Dill Pickle," the young "Man without a Temperament" who in torture of soul and body scarcely utters one unusual syllable, except, perhaps, *"Tres* rum," and the vigorous Harry in "Bliss."

"The aforesaide Rosamond had a little coffer scarcely two foote long, merueylous artificially wrought, wherein gyauntes seeme to fight, beastes do startle and stirre, and fowles fliying in the ayre, and fishes swim in the water, without any mannes mouyng or helpe." So with these stories. The giants in them may barely seem to win their semblance of a fight, but the stirring beasts startle to some purpose, the fowls fly high, the fishes swim deep, and Rosamond gazes on, engrossed in every conceivable manifestation of the depicted problem, Life; whose answer - to go on with - is merely its indefatigable insistence on itself, its defiant momentum. Not one of Miss Mansfield's vile ones, (however steep the glimpses we get of the glissade) comes to a bad *end*, not one of her meek, cheated, enduring ones inherits the earth (it is doubtful, even, if Fate ever succeeds in hatching Ian French's egg). Their heaven is out of sight, deep, illimitable, within themselves. Yet whatever this unflinching contemplation and acceptance of life may perceive and reveal, what is left over for the reader, his reading done, is a gentle, champagne-like shimmering of delight. The world of this book, despite human abuse of it, illumined by human realization of it, remains never else than lovely and significant.

If perhaps we ask, Significant of what? Miss Mansfield does not answer, outright. "The pear tree was as lovely as ever and as full of flower and as still."

In spite of shock and disillusionment, in spite of the seemingly wanton destruction of faith, vision, or happiness, whether Sun's; or Bertha's in "Bliss"; or the little governess's,; or Mouse's in "Je ne parle pas Français"; we are left believing (sipping maybe meanwhile from a little privy bottle of sentimentality, *not* supplied by the author) in human virtue and integrity.

As for Miss Mansfield's craftsmanship, her sense of construction, the precise, concise progress of her stories—to watch them in action is an æsthetic pleasure not less rare than that bestowed by her coming-alivedness. She steps lightly on from saliency to saliency, everything in its exact apt aspect (in "Bliss," for outstanding instance), though the journey is apparently as smooth as Blondin's on a tight-rope. In the usual sense, her style is not "style" at all. She hesitates at no awkwardness, at no short cut:

> She looked at him; she saw herself looking at him in the white kimono like a nun. "Is there something the matter here? Has something happened?" But George gave a half shrug and a grimace. "Oh, no, Madame. Just a little occurrence." And he took up the piece of hair again. But, oh, she wasn't deceived. That was it. Something awful had happened . . . . Where was she going now? . . .
>
> George took a brush. "There is a little powder on your coat," he murmured. He brushed it away. And then suddenly he raised himself and, looking at Monica, gave a strange wave with the brush and said: "The truth is, Madame, since you are an old customer-my little daughter died this morning. A first child" - and then his white face crumpled like paper, and he turned his back on her and began brushing the cotton kimono. "Oh, oh," Monica began to cry. She ran out of the shop into the taxi. The driver, looking furious, swung off the seat and slammed the door again. "Where to?"
>
> " 'Princes'," she sobbed. And all the way there she saw nothing but a tiny wax doll with a feather of gold hair, lying meek, its tiny hands and feet crossed.

It will not be a waste of time to ponder for a moment over the *here*, the *occurrence*, the *piece of hair*, the *took*, the assonance and Biblical rhythm of *gave a strange wave with the brush and said*, the *since*, the *began's*, the *feather*, the *lying meek*. These minute strokes disclose the method of this writer, and prove that her imaginative gaze is fixed on the object. Spontaneity, impulse - their services are as indispensable as they are fortuitous, and genius, like mercy, droppeth as the gentle dew from heaven. But what captivates the intelligence in such work, what in itself is an emanation of the moral, and a tribute to the ultimate reasonableness of life, is the discipline and self-sacrifice, the restraint, the economy, the endless pains of so true an artist.

Her vision casts far its beams, illuminates a naughty world; and we may be content merely to scrutinize the world in its light. Hardly less precious to any true observer is the experience of watching the conscience in deliberation behind the eyes. That experience in these stories—of a promise certainly no less manifest than their achievement—is one of the rarest of lessons, the most secret of joys.

The Athenaeum, January 21, 1921, p. 67.

Malcolm Cowley, "Page Dr Blum!": *Bliss*

Bliss is one of those books which it is very hard to forget. Yet *Bliss* is not at all a likable book; Katherine Mansfield is impressed too much by people she dislikes and is more apt to write about them than about people she finds agreeable to her. Such at least is the evidence of these stories. In them the disagreeable people far outnumber the sympathetic; her likable characters, indeed, are usually introduced as a foil. Most of them are men and only two or three of them receive full-length portraits. Those figures which she draws in most carefully are women; they are selfish, weak, cultured, irritable, and conceited. *Bliss* in one sense is a book of neurotics; a literary corridor of the psychopathic ward.

But with what a vigour does she depict these neurotics. Typical of them is Monica Tyrrell, who suffered from nerves every morning from eight o'clock till about half-past eleven, "suffered so terribly that these hours were—agonizing, simply." There is Monica's male counterpart, Mr Reginald Peacock; fourteen pages are devoted to a venomously meticulous account of a day from his life. There are Linda Burnell and her sister Beryl from the first story. Most horrible of all is the woman in "The Escape", with her refrain of:

> "Oh, why am I made to bear these things? . . . Oh, to care as I care-to feel as I feel, and ever to be saved anything-never to know for one moment what it was to . . . to ."

From this treatment of Katherine Mansfield one might think that she was no more than a literary specialist in nervous disorders. The idea is mistaken; only about a third of the stories in her volume deal specifically with neurotics. It is simply that her handling of them is so vivid that they overshadow most of the other characters.

Yet these other characters are by no means lifeless. Her observation of people is extensive and accurate, and wherever her sympathy does not lead her to understanding, her hate does. Her style fits accurately to her matter. She has borrowed just enough from the new experiments in prose without trying to swallow them whole. In her punctuation she shows a positive genius. The result of all this is that her best descriptions are final and perfect; one must fight back the temptation to quote whole pages of them.

The form of her stories shows usually a certain amount of experiment; this carries her, in most of her work, to about the same stage as Chekhov. I do not mean to make any comparison of excellence with Chekhov; I mean simply that, like him, she has come to a point where she writes most of her stories around a situation instead of around a plot. Sometimes she goes farther. She has written one story around two themes instead of around a situation; she approaches here to the construction of music.

If you analyze "Je ne parle pas Français" conventionally for its plot, you will find very little. It is the story of how an Englishman ran off to Paris with a girl and left her there alone on account of his greater love for his mother. Implication of Freud. It covers some forty-four pages but the plot as stated is disposed of in less than twenty; the rest of the space is taken up with the divagations of Raoul

Duquette, the narrator. According to the standards of the Committee of Award of the O. Henry Memorial Prize Stories, it is badly and extravagantly constructed.

But abandoning all idea of plot, let us analyse the story for its themes. The little English girl, Mouse, is one of them, with her helpless refrain of *Je ne parle pas français*. Dick, the big Englishman, is the second theme. "He gets drunk slowly," says the narrator, "and at a certain moment begins to sing very low, very low, about a man who walks up and down trying to find a place where he can get some dinner. . . . How extraordinarily English that is . . . I remember that it ended where he did at last 'find a place' and ordered a little cake of fish, but when he asked for bread, the waiter cried contemptuously in a loud voice: 'We don't serve bread with one fish ball.'" That ridiculous song is repeated almost every time Dick enters the story; it serves as his motif.

With these two themes in mind, the construction of the story becomes clearer. The first theme is introduced; that takes eight pages, and not a word is wasted. Then an interlude on Raoul Duquette. Second theme: Dick. *Waiter, a whiskey . . . We don't serve bread*, et cetera. Re-entry of first theme in counterpoint with the second: twenty pages. And in these pages only is there any suggestion of a plot. Finally, the Coda, in which the Mouse theme is universalized:

> ". . . Evenings when I sit in some gloomy café and an automatic piano starts playing a "mouse" tune (there are dozens of tunes that evoke just her) I begin to dream things like . . .
>
> "A little house on the edge of the sea, somewhere far, far away. A girl outside in a frock rather like Red Indian women wear, hailing a light, barefoot boy who runs up from the beach.
>
> ". . . The same girl, the same boy, different costumes-sitting at an open window, eating fruit and leaning out and laughing.
>
> "All the wild strawberries are for you, Mouse. I won't touch one.
>
> ". . . A wet night. They are going home together under an umbrella. They stop at the door to press their wet cheeks together.
>
> "And so on and so on . . ."

Analysed in this fashion, the story appears as handled with a sense of form both strong and delicate. Merely because I have used certain musical terms in my discussion, it should not be confused with music. "Je ne parle pas français" is not an imitation of a sonata. Its form is purely literary, but it has the suppleness and some of the abstractness of music.

In one part of the story Raoul Duquette speaks of discussing the modern novel. For him this discussion was equivalent to stating "the need of a new form, or the reason why our young men appeared to be just missing it." Katherine Mansfield has got hold of that new and necessary form. So far she has used it only in a short story, but there is no reason why she should not meet with the same success if she applied it to a full-length novel.

The Dial, September 1921, vol. 71, p. 365.

Rebecca West, "The Garden Party"

Supposing, Katherine Mansfield's new book makes one speculate, a frozen earth should ever ring under the heels of visitors from another star, clad in a kind of Thermos armour to preserve the necessary heat, who earnestly set themselves to discover what manner of beings built these cities that they find, how puzzling a guide they will find in literature! Their scholars will master human languages and will arrange the books of the world chronologically, and their critics will read these and try to tell of what sort of life this art was an expression. They will be baffled as a general who receives two incompatible reports from two trusted scouts. Here, century after century, is the testimony of prose that man is a reasonable being, completely understandable, going about his business on the solid earth on two solid legs. Here, on the other hand, is the testimony of poetry that man is a wild and passionate and utterly unreasonable being, whose legs are not in the least solid, but sometimes bend at the knees so that he kneels in prayer to that of whose existence he has no certificate, and sometimes fail him altogether so that he falls on his face in a despair that is preposterous when there is still food to be eaten and wine to be drunk, and sometimes rise about the earth so that he treads the high airs of ecstasy. These critics of another star will incline towards the belief that poets were a kind of lunatic who were regarded as sacred and whose writings were preserved as charms and amulets. This conclusion will be immensely fortified when they come to the eighteenth century, for it will seem to them as if a body of sane men had taken over poetry and had tried to make it an instrument of the same reasonable view of life that inspired prose. But the next hundred years will bring them misgivings, for not only does the old madness return to poetry, but, far worse than that, prose begins to confirm it. By the end of the century the greatest novelists hold it; and at the point of time where we now stand they will find that a writer who did not subscribe to it could hardly hope to be considered as an artist. And one cannot believe that the future which we do not know will disprove that it is poetry which is the truth, and that the simple view of life which shaped yesterday's prose was anything but a myth invented by man to help him before he felt strong enough to face life's lack of simplicity.

One result of the conquest of prose by the logic of poetry is that many writers who would in any past age have written verse are now just as pleased to say what they want to in prose; and Katherine Mansfield is one of these. There is at the end of "At the Bay" something that in any other age would have been a lyric, where the young girl, dreaming desperately of love in her moonlit room, hears a call from the wood beyond the garden that sends her, still half dreaming, out into the moonlight to answer it; where she encounters such an unpleasing substitute as the world often offers to such dreamers, from which only her young strength rescues her, but afterwards it does not seem to matter, in spite of the ugliness, in spite of the disappointment, because there are still the clouds and the moon in the sky, and the deep sound of the sea. How one admires Miss Mansfield for conceiving that moment, as well as for insisting on working under conditions that make it possible for her to conceive such beauty. For "At the Bay" is a continuation of "Prelude", that section of a work of genius which was the best thing in *Bliss*. In other words, Miss Mansfield is writing a novel, but it is coming to her slowly. There is, after all, no reason why creation in art should take only an infinitesimal fraction of the time that is taken by creation in life. Abandonment to the leisurely rhythm of her own imagination, and refusal to conform to the common custom and finish her book in a year's session, has enabled her to bring her inventions right over the threshold of art. They are extraordinarily solid; they have lived so long in her mind that she knows all about them and can ransack them for the difficult, rare, essential points. Thus she produces such attenuated yet powerful sketches as the scene in the garden, when Linda thinks of her husband with love and disgust and fatigue and at the same time is forced by the personality of her new baby, to whom she thought she was indifferent, to recognise that she loves it. And to deal with those visions born of her deliberations she brings a technique that has been sharpened on the products of her swifter and more immediate work. Her choice of the incident that will completely and economically prove her point is astonishing, and only not invariable because she is occasionally betrayed into excessive use of her power of grotesque invention. (There is a passage in "The Daughters of the Late Colonel" which has strayed out of *Charley's Aunt*.) For instance, "Marriage à la Mode" with its picture of the ordinary but loving and fine-natured husband and his silly little wife, who turns from him to a rabble of sponging sham poets and painters, might very easily have appeared as the lesser tragedy of the shattering of an illusion. It might quite well have appeared that Isabel was a minx who was showing her quality, and that William was only losing what he had never had when he noticed it. But with extraordinary ingenuity Miss Mansfield invents an incident which convinces one that this is the greater tragedy of the shattering of a beautiful reality, that before her debauchment by this greedy, chattering horde she had been the miracle of kindness and loveliness that William thought her. "When he had been a little boy, it was his delight to run into the garden after a shower of rain and shake the rose-bush over him. Isabel was that rosebush, petal-soft, sparkling, and cool." To exhibit the drama of her decline, Miss Mansfield shows Isabel on the lawn among her horrid friends, receiving a desperate love-letter from William, who has returned to town after a week-end, during which he has not succeeded in being alone with her. One measures the extent of her ruin when she reads it aloud to them: "God forbid, my darling, that I should be a drag on your happiness." But one measures from what heights she has fallen when she suddenly runs from the giggling circle of her friends and runs to her own room and throws herself down on the bed. "But she felt that even the grave bed-room knew her for what she was, shallow, tinkling, vain. . . ." It is an excellent invention, though not more dazzling, perhaps, than the monologue at the end of the book in which "The Lady's Maid" artlessly betrays herself the predestined victim of the predatory egotist, or the curious study of spiritual jealousy and the hostility of a gross man for grim uncomfortable things in "The Stranger".

One of the results of Miss Mansfield's poetic temperament is that beauty is the general condition of her story. Most of her tales are laid in the glowing setting of the sub-tropics: "Marriage à la Mode" is acted in a midsummer countryside: even the miserable "Miss Brill" sits in a pleasant springtide day. Even in the lamentable "Life of Ma Parker" there is a kind of sensuous beauty in the description of the love of the old charwoman for her grandson. The mind takes pleasure in merely moving in such an atmosphere, apart from the meanings it may find there. That is where the writer who is a poet like Miss Mansfield scores over a writer who is not a poet.

The New Statesman, March 18, 1922, vol. 18, p. 678.

Conrad Aiken, "The Short Story as Colour"

Miss Katherine Mansfield's *Bliss,* a volume of short stories published a year or so ago, attracted, and deserved, a great deal of attention. It was at once recognized that Miss Mansfield was a short-story writer of unique sensibility—sensibility in the modern, not in the pre-Victorian sense—and exquisite deftness. If her stories suggested the influence of Chekhov, notably in their repeated use of what might be termed the completeness and charm of the incomplete, the suggestion was fleeting and unimportant: method is, after all, not a copyrightable affair, and all we have the right to ask of the borrower of a method is that he shall not permit it to cloud his own personality, or to supplant it. In the case of Miss Mansfield there could be no question of this. If one thing was arresting in her work, it was the evidence, luminous, colourful, and resonant everywhere, of a tactilism extraordinarily acute and individual. One was inclined to question, even, whether this perpetual coruscation, this amazing sensitiveness to rhythms and sounds and almost shuddering awareness of texture, was not symptomatic of a sort of febrility which would, sooner or later, impose on Miss Mansfield's work its very definite limitations; limitations already quite clearly implied. "Exquisite! yes— this song of sensibility," one might then have commented "this poetry of the eyes, the ears and hands a little feverish; but is it, ultimately, quite enough?"

It depends, of course, on what one means by enough. Clearly, this sort of febrility, clairvoyant and clairaudient, *is* enough, if one wants, in one's fiction, only and always an ecstatic awareness. How admirably such a tone adapts itself to the case of, say, a neurotic young woman, Miss Mansfield has several times triumphantly demonstrated—notably in "The Man Without a Temperament". It lends itself superbly, too, to description of the adolescent—what could possibly be better, more brilliant, than the portrait of "The Young Girl" in Miss Mansfield's new collection of stories? Equally applicable is it, again, to descriptions of children, whose minds may be said to exist wholly in their five senses—no contemporary writer has given glimpses of the bright, disintegrated, peripheral consciousness of the child as exquisitely true as those Miss Mansfield gives us in "Sun and Moon" or portions of "Prelude". But it is precisely here that one reaches a suspicion that if Miss Mansfield does these things beautifully it is because in these things she is freest to speak her own language; that her choice of these things is a dictated choice; and that her failure to step often out of this small charmed circle, and her relative failure when she does step out, are failures that we should quite expect.

What we get at is the fact that Miss Mansfield goes to the short story as the lyric poet goes to poetry—Miss Mansfield's short story is, in essence, an essentially "subjective" thing, far more subjective than one is accustomed to expect a short story to be. Of course the distinction between subjective and objective is relative. One may reasonably claim that Chekhov's short stories are "subjective" also, that they represent in the case of Chekhov a psychic compulsion just as unaccountable and uncontrollable as that indicated by Miss Mansfield's "Garden Party". That is perfectly true, and it compels us to see that the difference between the so-called subjective method in art, and the so-called objective method, is at bottom nothing whatever but a difference in range. Chekhov's range was enormous. He was as tremendously "rooted" in life, perhaps, as Shakespeare. His sensibilities, and therefore his curiosity, were not merely of one sort, but led him everywhere, gave him joy, pain, understanding everywhere, were both sensitive and tough. The world of consciousness (and of subconsciousness) with which he was thus by experience gradually endowed, and the language of associations which he spoke, were not merely intensely individual (independent of the literary) but, by comparison with the language of associations of the average writer, infinitely various. This is what leads us to think of Chekhov as a superlatively "objective" artist, and it is the reverse of this that leads us to think of Miss Mansfield as—just as superlatively?—a "subjective" artist. For Miss Mansfield's sensibilities, if clearly individual, are remarkably limited, and the language of associations which she speaks is, if brilliant, extremely small. The awareness, the personality of the larger artist is an infinitely more divisible, and therefore infinitely less recognizable thing; but the personality of the smaller artist is recognizable everywhere.

Thus, in Miss Mansfield's short stories, as in the poems of a lyric poet, it is always Miss Mansfield's voice that we hear, it is always Miss Mansfield that we see. How it is that limitations of this sort impose themselves on an artist, in childhood or infancy, we leave psychology to discover. Why did Miss Mansfield's extraordinary sensibilities find, as it were, so little to feed on? That is the question we must ask, whether or not we answer it. Did she lack the requisite "toughness"? At all events, her awareness is a very special and limited sort of awareness; the circle of her consciousness is small and bright, and we soon know its outermost limits. Miss Mansfield's new book confirms our speculations in this regard. If one makes the reservation that "Prelude" in the earlier book is the best thing she has written, then one can say that the second volume is just as good as the first. But the limitations are here again, and now seem more striking. We are not so easily deceived a second time, and we perceive too clearly that it is all a beautiful, an exquisite, a diabolically clever masquerade, with the protean Miss Mansfield taking now the part of Beryl, now that of "The Young Girl", now that of both "Daughters of the Late Colonel", now that of Miss Brill; achieving quite extraordinary ventriloquistic feats as Mr. Neave or Mr. Hammond—though she seldom attempts the masculine; and shining out beautifully, with not even the pretence of a mask, as Kezia. Yes, these people are all Miss Mansfield, all speak with her voice, think as she thinks, are rapidly, ecstatically aware, as she is aware; share her gestures and her genius; and represent, in short, not so many people or lives, but so many projections of Miss Mansfield's mind and personality into other people's bodies and houses. How exciting to disguise oneself, for a morning, as Ma Parker, or, for an afternoon, as the singing teacher! And Miss Mansfield's dexterity in the matter is extraordinary. She almost completely deceives us, and even when she has ceased to deceive she continues to delight.

The secret of this legerdemain is simply in Miss Mansfield's mastery of local colour, of twinkling circumstance, of the inflection of the moment. It is the song of a sensibility ecstatically aware of the surfaces of life. Her people are not real people, in the sense of being individual, of appearing to have, as Chekhov's characters have, whole lives, apart from the particular story, which the author does not touch on; but they give the illusion of reality; first, because Miss Mansfield endows them all with her own supersensitive and febrile (and perhaps sentimental) awareness, and, second (which follows from the first) because, therefore, the small circumstances of mood and scene are thus given to us with the feverish vividness of objects seen under lightning. Miss Mansfield puts a kitchen before us with her mention of the gritty soap in the sink; she desolates us, when, describing the bare floors of an abandoned house, she notes the carpet-tacks with their shreds of wool. She sees everything, sees miraculously, feels textures where the less sensitive would see only a smooth surface, hears rhythms and intonations where others would only note the persistence and dullness of a sound. Yes, it is the scene, the scene as apprehended by the hungriest of sensibilities, that Miss Mansfield above all gives us. Must we content ourselves with this? For if Miss Mansfield has little skill at characterization—substituting for "character" a combination of vivid externalities and vivid mood—one must also observe that even in "mood" her range is very small. In a sense the mood *is* the scene—it is the eternal responsiveness to scene. Whether the particular state of mind to be presented is gay or melancholy, bitter or resigned, capricious or saturnine, whimsical or cruel, hardly seems to matter. For the psychological process by which her people are gay or melancholy, bitter or resigned, is always, for Miss Mansfield, the same; the content may change but never the *tempo*. Everything is staccato and exclamatory, everything is intense, even grief is somehow sibilant. If one may use a metaphor which will not bear close psychological scrutiny, but nevertheless conveys one's impression, one may say that Miss Mansfield, instead of submerging herself in her characters, submerges her characters in herself. They come up shining, certainly, and peacock-hued; they burn and glisten in the bright air, shed fine plumes of flame; but they are all just so many Mansfields.

Well, this sort of vividness is something to be profoundly thankful for. The short story created in this manner approaches the poetic in proportion as its theme is largely and emotionally significant, and the colour thereby patternized. When the theme is slight, the story tends to become merely a triumph of colourism. In "Prelude", and in one or two other instances, Miss Mansfield has given us poetry; but mere cleverness—cleverness to the point of brilliance—too often betrays her into giving us a colourism which, for all its vividness and verisimilitude, is comparatively empty. The delight that many of these stories afford on the first reading is intense; it wanes a little on the second, and we notice the cleverness—

fatal sign! And on the third reading—but is there a third? One can not dine on the iridescent.

The Freeman, June 21, 1922, vol. 5, p. 357.

Raymond Mortimer, Review of *The Dove's Nest and Other Stories*

The lamentable death of Miss Katherine Mansfield at the age of thirty-four added one more shelf, possibly an important one, to the tragic library of unwritten books. Round the ceiling of this library are written in great mosaic letters many names that are unknown to us, for its catalogue records the works of those that never waked to ecstasy the living lyre. There, too, are the plays of Marlowe's maturity, the real masterpieces of Collins, the more important writings of Keats and Shelley, the poems Coleridge never finished, and those that Rimbaud never began. That Katherine Mansfield's work would have improved seems likely— she was always a conscientious artist, and one whose eyes remained intensely young and alive to every sight they met. The newly published posthumous volume contains six finished and fifteen unfinished stories. There is no new weakness in them, and they will be read by every admirer of her writing; but it is not, I think, possible by comparing them with her earlier work to discover in what direction, if any, her talent was developing. Upon the thirty stories contained in *Bliss* and *The Garden Party* her rank as a writer of fiction must now always depend, and I cannot believe that her artistic reputation will ever stand higher than it does at present. The detail of her observation, the sharpness of her phrase, and the play of her fancy are remarkable, and must give pleasure to most of those who care about writing. But the peculiar characteristics of her art were her use of Tchekhov and her gift for seeing others as they see themselves. That Tchekhov was a very great story-writer and the greatest of modern dramatists seems to me as certain as any aesthetic judgment of contemporary work can be. But there are moments, there are even months, when his influence on English writers appears positively disastrous. If the members of the London Group all began painting in the manner of Gontcharova and Larionoff the result would hardly be more unfortunate. Of course, this confession would enable counsel to challenge my presence on any jury sitting on the work of Katherine Mansfield. But the criticism of fiction being unluckily so much more a matter of personal judgment than is the criticism of historical or scientific work, it is unfair, if not impossible, to hide one's prejudices. In any case the critic is not really a juryman so much as a counsel for those with similar feelings to himself. And there must be many who admire Tchekhov and yet deplore the use of his methods, save in very few cases, by Western Europeans. Tchekhov was endowed with a miraculous sensibility, rather like the "touch" of a great painter, which made of every dab he used to compose his stories a thing of beauty and significance. Even so he depends to a perilous extent in his plays upon the actors, and in his stories upon the readers. But in his hands, so exquisite was his touch, masses of detail spring together to make a satisfying whole. Too often when used by others this method makes outrageous demands upon the reader, who is left to impose order where no order is. Critics complain that Ben Jonson's personages are in only two dimensions. But will Volpone take on more solid flesh in our imagination if we are told that he is left-handed, that he has a strawberry-mark on his ankle, that he cannot pronounce his "r's," or that his grandmother was fond of sucking eggs? By distortion and juggling with perspective a genius like Tchekhov can accomplish his design in literature as in painting. But most of his followers have loaded their stories with much that is arbitrary and irrelevant.

The other principal characteristic of Katherine Mansfield's art, I suggested, was her ability to put herself in other people's skins. All her stories are written in a sort of *oratio obliqua*. Every thought, every feeling, and even many of the turns of phrase in the narrative parts of the stories belong to the characters; sometimes to the same character throughout the story, more often to the one who is at the moment in the foreground. No one ever pushed this method further. The skill with which she managed it, the variety she thus gave to her work, and the sympathy with her characters, which she thus established are most admirable. Few writers have better described the unorganised flow of thoughts and feelings that continually move through the different layers of human consciousness, and specially the distorting influence of egotism upon the whole individual outlook. But this oblique method makes it extraordinarily difficult to discover the real colour of the author's mind. In all Katherine Mansfield's work there is hardly an opinion or a sentiment which is frankly her own and uncoloured by the mind of any of her characters. One penalty of the method is that it makes so difficult that affectionate relationship of reader to author which ties us to many of the great writers of the past. Obviously Miss Mansfield was an artist full of pity and tenderness, but no Parnassian can be more elusive. Her stories of the Burnell family, "Prelude" and "At the Bay", seem to be written most fondly, and it is, I think, likely that in these one comes nearest to her personality. Even then the writing of them is so deeply soaked in the atmosphere she describes that you cannot be sure at what points she is speaking directly and unmasked. These stories, however, do provide the crucial test for her readers, and I believe there are many, like myself, who cannot be comfortable with them. Katherine Mansfield had a beautiful *flair* for whatever is good in the worst of us, but so much occupied was she with this that she never, I think, portrayed a really agreeable person - the sort of person, I mean, with whom one would like to stay or to travel. Having failed to find a proper explanation, I can only report a fact which admiration for Miss Mansfield's skill cannot alter, and for which dislike merely of her methods cannot account: and that is that the personality behind her work, in so far as it can be isolated, is to some temperaments anything but *sympathique*.

The New Statesman, July 7, 1923, vol. 21, p. 394.

Edmund Blunden, "A Prose-Writer's Poems"

Though the prose writings of Katherine Mansfield revealed qualities which might identify her as a writer of poetry also, she chose to waive any public ascertainment upon the "might". It looked probable that so perceptive and innovative an interpreter of life would be given to experiments in verse, but only a small circle can have known that it was the fact. Why this secrecy? Even the most austere and other-worldly poet gives the ass of a public something to know him by. But it was not, apparently, an admirable if lofty view of poetry as holy ground which held Katherine Mansfield's poems from us. 'I remember her telling me,' we now read, 'when first we met, that the beautiful pieces now gathered together as *Poems, 1911-1913* had been refused, because they were unrhymed, by the only editor who used to accept her work. He wanted her to write nothing but satirical prose. This treatment made her very reserved about her verses.'

Standing in ignorance of that editor's name, the present reviewer makes bold to respect him for the stated reason of rejecting those contributions. I am far from girding, let me add quickly, at unrhymed verse as a whole. Apart from the Miltonic and Keatsian, I would go down to the deep repeating my steady delight in those English worthies Isaiah and Job, and, provided the subject be not too wonderful, modern *vers libre* finds me willing. May it grow like a green bay tree! But I comprehend the aforesaid editor; he briefly summed as 'unrhymed' what was in general undirected; his word was the innocentest hint of a 'can't make much of this' verdict:

> Across the red sky two birds flying,
> Flying with drooping wings,
> Silent and solitary their ominous flight.
> All day the triumphant sun with yellow banners
> Warred and warred with the earth, and when she yielded
> Stabbed her heart, gathered her blood in a chalice,
> Spilling it over the evening sky.
> When the dark-plumaged birds go flying, flying,
> Quiet lies the earth wrapt in her mournful shadow,
> Her sightless eyes turned to the red sky
> And the restlessly seeking birds.

Where is the potent word, though to be sure there are words enough for a fancy so unattached? What clear vision controls these thin metrical wanderings? The evening, to be sure, is not that which Collins sang and man sees; but grant invention—this is chimerical, pallid, and toyish. It is not the choice spirit of Katherine Mansfield.

Nor, at that period, is it evidenced that the use of a regular form, with its tendency to crystallize and impower the thought of the writer, assisted to distinguish her poetry. The sonnet "Loneliness" might have appeared in almost any tasteful volume of verses:

> Through the sad dark the slowly ebbing tide
> Breaks on a barren shore, unsatisfied.
> A strange wind flows . . . then silence. I am fain
> To turn to Loneliness, to take her hand,
> Cling to her, waiting, till the barren land
> Fills with the dreadful monotone of rain.

But the present collection must not be judged by its earlier pages, which are, after all, almost *juvenilia*. With the advance of time Katherine Mansfield's verse, although never finding the true region of final phrase and deeply founded simplicity, advanced in confidence and sequence. By 1914 she could give such a vigorous and incisive character as that of "Countrywomen" in a terse and ingenious form, with the sharp rhymes of epigram. The group of "Poems at the Villa Pauline", 1916, written by way of recreation on themes deliberately chosen, approach still nearer to the fusion of thought and tune, and we see in them more definitely the emotional fineness peculiar to their author. "Voices of the Air" is perhaps their most accomplished expression of a delicate joy, when above all Nature's grander tones are heard:

> the bee, the fly,
> The leaf that taps, the pod that breaks,
> The breeze on the grass-tops bending by,
> The shrill, quick sound that the insect makes.

From 1917 to 1919 Katherine Mansfield wrote ten more poems, which, even these last, are uneasy in their cadence, as they are fascinating in their lights and shadows of mood. "The Wounded Bird" closes them with unforgettable pathos:

> At night, in the wide bed
> With the leaves and flowers
> Gently weaving in the darkness,
> She is like a wounded bird at rest on a pool.
> Timidly, timidly she lifts her head from her wing.
> In the sky there are two stars
> Floating, shining. . . .
> O waters—do not cover me!
> I would look long and long at those beautiful stars!
> O my wings—lift me—lift me!
> I am not so dreadfully hurt. . . .

Criticism, which holds its peace in such a place, must return to its business. The total effect of these poetical gleanings is, to quote the introduction, 'not quite poetry'; may it be surmised that the acuteness of their author, recognizing their general incompleteness, was at least one factor in keeping them during her lifetime from the public gaze?

The Nation and The Athenaeum, January 26, 1924, vol. 34, p. 609.

Virginia Woolf, "A Terribly Sensitive Mind"

The most distinguished writers of short stories in England are agreed, says Mr. Murry, that as a writer of short stories Katherine Mansfield was *hors concours.* No one has succeeded her, and no critic has been able to define her quality. But the reader of her journal is well content to let such questions be. It is not the quality of her writing or the degree of her fame that interest us in her diary, but the spectacle of a mind—a terribly sensitive mind—receiving one after another the haphazard impressions of eight years of life. Her diary was a mystical companion. 'Come my unseen, my unknown, let us talk together', she says on beginning a new volume. In it she noted facts—the weather, an engagement; she sketched scenes; she analysed her character; she described a pigeon or a dream or a conversation, nothing could be more fragmentary; nothing more private. We feel that we are watching a mind which is alone with itself; a mind which has so little thought of an audience that it will make use of a shorthand of its own now and then, or, as the mind in its loneliness tends to do, divide into two and talk to itself. Katherine Mansfield about Katherine Mansfield.

But then as the scraps accumulate we find ourselves giving them, or more probably receiving from Katherine Mansfield herself, a direction. From what point of view is she looking at life as she sits there, terribly sensitive, registering one after another such diverse impressions? She is a writer; a born writer. Everything she feels and hears and sees is not fragmentary and separate; it belongs together as writing. Sometimes the note is directly made for a story. 'Let me remember when I write about that fiddle how it runs up lightly and swings down sorrowful; how it *searches*', she notes. Or, '*Lumbago.* This is a very queer thing. So sudden, so painful, I must remember it when I write about an old man. The start to get up, the pause, the look of fury, and how, lying at night, one seems to get locked.'

Again, the moment itself suddenly put on significance, and she traces the outline as if to preserve it:

> It's raining, but the air is soft, smoky, warm. Big drops patter on the languid leaves, the tobacco flowers lean over. Now there is a rustle in the ivy.
> Wingly has appeared from the garden next door; he bounds from the wall. And delicately, lifting his paws, pointing his ears, very afraid the big wave will overtake him, he wades over the lake of green grass.

The Sister of Nazareth 'showing her pale gums and big discoloured teeth' asks for money. The thin dog. So thin that his body is like 'a cage on four wooden pegs', runs down the street. In some sense, she feels, the thin dog is the street. In all this we seem to be in the midst of unfinished stories; here is a beginning; here an end. They only need a loop of words thrown round them to be complete.

But then the diary is so private and so instinctive that it allows another self to break off from the self that writes and to stand a little apart watching it write. The writing self was a queer self; sometimes nothing would induce it to write.

'There is so much to do and I do so little. Life would be almost perfect here if only when I was *pretending* to work I always was working. Look at the stories that wait and wait just at the threshold. . . . *Next day.* Yet take this morning, for instance. I don't want to write anything. It's grey; it's heavy and dull. And short stories seem unreal and not worth doing. I don't want to write; I want to *live.* What does she mean by that? It's not easy to say. But there you are!'

What does she mean by that? No one felt more seriously the importance of writing than she did. In all the pages of her journal, instinctive, rapid as they are, her attitude toward her work is admirable, sane, caustic, and austere. There is no literary gossip; no vanity; no jealousy. Although during her last years she must have been aware of her success she makes no allusion to it. Her own comments upon her work are always penetrating and disparaging. Her stories wanted richness and depth; she was only 'skimming the top—no more'. But writing, the mere expression of things adequately and sensitively, is not enough. It is founded upon something unexpressed; and this something must be solid and entire. Under the desperate pressure of increasing illness she began a curious and difficult search, of which we catch glimpses only and those hard to interpret, after the crystal clearness which is needed if one is to write truthfully. 'Nothing of any worth can come of a disunited being', she wrote. One must have health in one's self. After five years of struggle she gave up the search after physical health not in despair, but because she thought the malady was of the soul and that the cure lay not in any physical treatment, but in some such 'spiritual brotherhood' as that at Fontainebleau, in which the last months of her life were spent. But before she went she wrote the summing-up of her position with which the journal ends.

She wanted health, she wrote; but what did she mean by health?

'By health', she wrote, 'I mean the power to lead a full, adult, living, breathing life in close contact with what I love—the earth and the wonders thereof—the sea—the sun. . . . Then I want to *work*. At what? I want so to live that I work with my hands and my feeling and my brain. I want a garden, a small house, grass, animals, books, pictures, music. And out of this, the expression of this, I want to be writing. (Though I may write about cabmen. That's no matter.)'

The diary ends with the words 'All is well'. And since she died three months later it is tempting to think that the words stood for some conclusion which illness and the intensity of her own nature drove her to find at an age when most of us are loitering easily among those appearances and impressions, those amusements and sensations, which none had loved better than she.

The New York Herald Tribune, September 18, 1927, vol. 125, p. 716.

II

Towards Assessment

Edward Wagenknecht, "Katherine Mansfield"

I

She came and went, Katherine Mansfield, across the horizon of our contemporary letters; before we had quite accustomed ourselves to the thought that she belonged to us, she was gone. There was ever something a little uncanny about her, for all her thrilling human warmth. Where did she get her wisdom—this girl—her almost Shakespearean subtlety, her terrifying power to read bare the human soul? Certainly not from her contemporaries, in England at any rate. She is not even remotely like any of them, and it was the foremost among them—Galsworthy, Wells, De La Mare—who hurried to bear wondering testimony to her power.

She died in 1923, in the first flush of her fame. Yet nothing could be more fatuous than to treat Katherine Mansfield, as a type of unfulfilment. It is true, she came to the end of her life feeling that all the stories she had written were vain. "There is not one," she said, "that I dare show to God." In conversation with her friend Mr. A.R. Orage, she explained both her dissatisfaction with her past achievements and her plans for the future. "I've been a selective camera, and . . . my slices of life have been partial, misleading, and a little malicious. Further, they have had no other purpose than to record my attitude which in itself stood in need of change if it was to become active instead of passive." By way of remedy she planned: "To widen first the scope of my camera, and then to employ it for a conscious purpose—that of representing life . . . as it appears to another and different attitude, a creative attitude."

For the purpose of this paper I confess myself unable fully to accept this judgment of Katherine Mansfield's upon herself. What those *different* stories would have been like we cannot tell nor to what new heights they might have carried her, any more than we can tell what Keats might have done had he gone on into his fifties instead of being carried off as he was at twenty-six. But what Keats *did* do is beyond disputing, and it is on this basis that he lives in literature. So Katherine Mansfield, judged only by the books she left us, remains a great artist, one of the finest stylists in the long record of English prose. To many of us it seems that she carried the art of the short story to the highest point of perfection it has yet attained.

II

The biographical data for Katherine Mansfield are not extensive. She was born, Kathleen Beauchamp, in New Zealand, October 14, 1888. Of her formal education little is recorded save her own lament that though her college years were rich in *impressions*, they brought her little in the way of formal learning. When she was twenty-one years old, her first book, *In a German Pension*, was published in England. The critical reception was not over-kind: indeed Katherine Mansfield did not begin to be widely known until 1919 when, having meanwhile been married to Middleton Murry, she took over the reviewing of fiction for the *Athenaeum*. Before this, however, her creative writing had gained inspiration from a great personal bereavement. In October, 1915, her adored younger brother, Leslie Heron Beauchamp, was killed in France, barely a week after his arrival at the front. Katherine Mansfield had promised to write him a book, and though at first she was simply crushed by his death, she remembered her promise as "a sacred debt" to her brother and to New Zealand. She felt she must go on living "Because I have a duty to perform to the lovely time when we were both alive. I want to write about it and he wanted me to." Fulfilment came gloriously in "Prelude," written in 1917 and privately printed. Here a great writer first fully revealed herself: here she turned back to the country of her childhood, writing always with that "sense of mystery," that "afterglow" which she felt she must have if her writing were at all adequately to reflect the beauty of her brother's soul. In 1920 "Prelude" and other stories were collected under the title *Bliss*. This was followed a year later by that even more wonderful volume, *The Garden Party*.

The Garden Party was the last book Katherine Mansfield ever saw in print. She had been for several years a victim of consumption. In February, 1922, she was forced to seek health on the Continent. She spent the summer in Switzerland; in October she went alone to Fontainebleau where she entered the Gurdjieff Institute, hoping not only for an improvement in her physical condition but, much more definitely, for that readjustment of personality, that shifting of the current of her life to deeper channels without which further literary progress seemed to her impossible. At Fontainebleau she remained until the new year, and it was here, on January 9, 1923, when she was believed to be mending, and just at the moment when she felt she had gained the spiritual victory for which she had so long contended that she was taken suddenly with a hemorrhage and died instantly.

III

Thanks to Katherine Mansfield's *Journal*, and to the reminiscences of her husband and of Mr. Orage a very clear impression of her personality has been preserved for us. It is deeply to be regretted that the journal is so fragmentary: in human interest and self-revelation it quite equals the diary of Marie Bashkirtseff or of Josephine Preston Peabody. But it has more than a personal interest. There is so much technical originality in the work of Katherine Mansfield that many considerations of her have begun and ended just here. Now that the journal has been printed, it must be clear even to the most obtuse that all such considerations are unjust and unfair. Katherine Mansfield was absolutely at one with Milton in his conviction that "He who would write well hereafter in laudable things ought himself to be a true poem." She knew that it was utterly hopeless ever to try to write anything greater than her own soul. It was not art for art's sake that held her but art for life's sake, and if ever she was tempted to worship technique for itself, she triumphed over the temptation and crushed it beneath her feet. It was the spiritual aspect of her work in which she was primarily and overwhelmingly interested, and she kept her astonishing and original devices as mere cunning tools toward the achievement of something that was beyond them, something greater than life itself.

Her spirit was one of profound sincerity, of deep religious consecration. She prays: "Lord, make me crystal clear for thy light to shine through." She speaks of her aspiration "To be 'simple' enough as one would be simple before God." In October, 1921, she wrote:

> I wonder why it should be so difficult to be humble. I do not think I am a good writer; I realize my faults better than anyone else could realize them. I know exactly when I fail. And yet, when I have finished a story and before I have begun another, I catch myself *preening* my feathers. It is disheartening. There seems to be some bad old pride in my heart; a root of it that puts out a thick shoot on the slightest provocation . . . . . This interferes very much with work. . . . . Oh, God! I am divided still, I am bad, I fail in my personal life. I lapse into impatience, temper, vanity, and so I fail as thy priest.

It must not be forgotten that Katherine Mansfield's temper was severely tested, first by poverty and then by illness. When she is tempted to self-pity she brings herself back thus: "It is only by acknowledging that I, being what I am, had to suffer *this* in order to do the work I am here to perform—it is only by acknowledging this, by being thankful that work was not taken away from me, that I shall recover. I am weak where I must be strong." And it was under this strain and in these conditions that she experienced her final rebirth of personality and magnificently recharactered her conception of art!

What then was this final vision of Katherine Mansfield's? She had begun like most young writers, without any clearly reasoned or settled convictions on the subject of literary art. She was evidently committed to the realistic point of view; she was unmindful of traditional, "well-made" forms, determined that she would not force her fresh materials into alien molds. Her success she owed to her understanding of character, her fresh, unhackneyed presentation, her ability to observe and to chronicle an astonishing amount of astonishingly real detail which apparently nobody had observed for literary purposes before her. Some of her early stories, however, are mere transcripts of experience: even the great pieces about the Burnells have a certain autobiographical element in them. From all this, she turned away at the end. The new idea was clear to her but she had some difficulty explaining it to others. Briefly, she felt that there was something beyond writing to which writing might perhaps be made to serve as a means of approach. "There is something wanting in literary art even at its highest. Literature is not enough." Even if she could write as well as Shakespeare, still, she felt, there would be something lacking:

> The greatest literature is still only mere literature if it has not a purpose commensurate with its art. Presence or absence of purpose distinguishes literature from mere literature, and the elevation of the purpose distinguishes literature within literature. That is merely literary which has no other object than to please. Minor literature has a didactic object. But the greatest literature of all—the literature that scarcely exists—has not merely an esthetic object, nor merely a didactic object, but in addition a creative object; that of subjecting its readers to a real and at the same time illuminating experience. Major literature, in short, is an initiation into truth.

Katherine Mansfield did not have time to test out her theory in practice and the loss to the world is great. Yet surely among the pieces that she has left us, there are many which have served for us as "an initiation into truth." Let us examine certain features of these stories.

IV

Perhaps the first of Katherine Mansfield's qualifications for writing was her great faculty of observation. Examples might be chosen almost at random. Of the naked children braving the water "At the Bay" she observes that "The *firm compact* little girls were not half so brave as the *tender, delicate-looking* little boys." To the Burnell children the mirror in Aunt Beryl's dressing table is "very strange; it was as though a little piece of forked lightning was imprisoned in it." Sometimes, as in the case of Geraldine's cat in "Widowed," the detail is so vividly presented that it is unforgettable.

With this faculty for observation she had extraordinarily keen sense impressions. When Beryl goes bathing it is not enough that she puts on her bathing suit: rather, "she drew on the *limp, sandy-feeling* bathing-dress *that was not quite dry* and fastened the *twisted buttons*." So, when Kezia goes with Pat to see the duck beheaded: "She put her hand in his *hard, dry* one." Inevitably the apparently slight addition makes the thing live. When "Sun and Moon" come down to be slobbered over by their parents' eccentric guests, they observe "a skinny old lady *with teeth that clicked*." But the passage I like best of all is the description of Fenella in "The Voyage," trying to prepare for bed in the cabin of a ship: "The hard square of brown soap would not lather, and the water in the bottle was a kind of blue jelly. How hard it was, too, to turn down those stiff sheets; you simply had to tear your way in."

Very characteristic of Katherine Mansfield's psychological interest is her penchant for transferring sense impressions or even for attributing physical properties to the immaterial. She speaks of the music which "breaks into bright pieces, and joins together again, and again breaks, and is dissolved. . . . ." Of a cruel laugh she records, "It had a long sharp beak and claws and two bead eyes," while a "weak worn old voice" suggests "a piece of faintly smelling dark lace."

In "Six Years After" the *thoughts* of a selfish lazy husband, having come to a point where further reflection would be inconvenient, *feel the need of a cigar!*

It must be obvious that with such gifts Katherine Mansfield is a wonderful descriptive writer. How could a whole chapter enable us to see more clearly than this sentence the terrible "Woman at the Store." "Looking at her, you felt there was nothing but sticks and wire under that pinafore—her front teeth were knocked out, she had red pulpy hands, and she wore on her feet a pair of dirty Bluchers." Her child is equally vivid in one sharp, unlovely attitude: "A mean, undersized brat, with whitish hair and weak eyes. She stood, legs wide apart and her stomach protruding."

Of Katherine Mansfield's longer descriptive passages I like best the picture of early morning at the beginning of "At the Bay" and the psychological portrait of the horrible Mrs. Harry Kember in the same story. It is worth noting how she begins in the first instance—"Very early morning"—with a perfect study of still life. On page 2, when the sheep enter, the picture begins to stir, but it is not fully awake until Florrie the cat appears on page 4. As for Mrs. Kember she surely is one of the most convincingly horrible women in literature!

Yet much more striking than Katherine Mansfield's ability to see and to chronicle detail is her power to use it suggestively, to give us the implications of a whole character in a single reaction or a single gesture. When the temperamental Stanley Burnell leaves the house of a morning in a bad mood, he rushes out to catch the coach, shouting meanwhile to his wife, "No time to say good-bye." Katherine Mansfield comments cruelly, "And he meant that as a punishment to her." Is not the character of Stanley fixed in our minds for good and all? In "Marriage à la Mode", when we hear that "It was over a year since Isabel had scrapped the old donkeys and engines and so on because they were so 'dreadfully sentimental' and 'so appallingly bad for the babies' sense of form',", we understand at once just what it is that has been happening to Isabel, and we are prepared for the domestic tragedy which follows.

Katherine Mansfield is sometimes accused of trite themes and of artificial development. She realized the danger of artificiality and struggled hard against it. Her loyalty to truth was absolute: she would always rather abandon a story than force what seemed to her a not wholly inevitable development upon it. Yet it seems to me that even so famous a story as "Bliss", interesting as it is, quite fails to be convincing. The wife's deception is too thoroughgoing, there is not sufficient preparation for the outcome, it startles like a trick ending in an O. Henry story. The revelation of the husband's perfidy, coming after the wife's day of bliss, is indeed strongly ironical, but it is almost as definitely a piece of coincidence as the return of Paula's old love in *The Second Mrs. Tanqueray*.

As to the triviality, that is another matter. It is undeniable in many of the early stories, but I do not find that the mature Katherine Mansfield was ever trivial. Chances are that those who bring this charge against her do not understand what she is doing. Her avoidance of plot was intentional; she did not see life arranging itself into plots; so why should she arrange her stories in that way? Often when she seems at first glance most trivial, she is really most profound. She has learned from the psychologists that there are no little things. The human soul is what she is after and whatever reveals that soul is to her important, be it a handclasp or an avalanche. Take for example "The Fly", that marvelous story of her last days. Actually nothing happens in "The Fly" save that a man kills an insect by dropping ink on it. But the implications of the story go to the very roots of life. Humanity is symbolized twice in that story: in the fly—its pitiful struggles, its helpless heroism in the face of a power that has doomed it from the start; and again in the man—its thoughtless cruelty, its strange combination of sentimentality and callousness.

An interesting technical device in the writing of Katherine Mansfield is her tendency to shift, frequently and without warning, from the conscious to the subconscious. The women at the Bay are sure that some day Harry Kember will murder his wife: "Yes, even while they talked to Mrs. Kember and took in the awful concoction she was wearing, they saw her, stretched as she lay on the beach; but cold, bloody, and still with a cigarette stuck in the corner of her mouth." Similarly, disregarding time-order, Katherine Mansfield shifts from the present to the past and back again. As she remarks in connection with "The Weak Heart," "What I feel it needs so peculiarly is a very subtle variation of tense. . . ." Certainly she well understood how to manage such shifting. She writes as the mind works: so why should it not be clear? Excellent illustrations occur in "The Man Without a Temperament" and "Life of Ma Parker"; perhaps the best of all are in "The Daughters of the Late Colonel" and the two long stories about the Burnells—"Prelude" and "At the Bay." Here Linda thinks of her father, of her childhood days in Tasmania, and at once we are off with her mind as it lives over again those experiences she had with him. A careless reader must surely wonder where Linda's father came from and how he happened so suddenly to enter the story.

The development of Katherine Mansfield's skill in story-telling is a subject worthy of careful study. Indeed it seems to me that only those who know the early stories—*In a German Pension* and *The Little Girl*—can fully appreciate the wonder of the later collections—*Bliss, The Garden Party*, and *The Doves' Nest* —or can fully understand what Katherine Mansfield achieved and how unusual was her development. It is not primarily a question of mere writing in the earlier stories, not only a matter of technical immaturity, in, for instance, the all-important matter of exposition. It is rather a journalistic touch, a cynical exaggeration, a delight in smart cleverness for its own sake, all of which was later very definitely outgrown. Many of the *Pension* stories are told in the first person. "I" is a somewhat aloof, superior, cynical young person who, for example, considers child-bearing "the most ignominious of all professions." Later Katherine Mansfield's ideal was purely objective. As she says in her journal, "I can't tell the truth about Aunt Anne unless I am free to enter into her life without self-consciousness."

Katherine Mansfield's literary allusions are few and generally not significant or unusual. Whether this means that her reading was not extensive or simply that she drew directly from life and not through the intermediary of books when writing her stories, I do not pretend to say. Her symbolism is skilful but not extensive: perhaps the best example is the personification in "Prelude" of Stanley Burnell as a Newfoundland dog. Her impressionism is more characteristic. A stove has "the appearance of a headless cat with one red all-seeing eye in the middle of its stomach." In "Poison" a series of incidents and scraps of conversation are strung together, not to reproduce what actually happened but simply to give the flavor of the life that the characters have been living.

Her skill in the dramatic monologue deserves special attention. Her methods here are distinctly varied. Some of the stories—for example "The Lady's Maid" and "The Canary"—are monologues in the strictest sense: they contain no word that is not spoken by the character whose soul is being unveiled. Here, as often in Browning's dramatic monologues, the presence of a listener is assumed and his questions and comments are inferred. Such pieces as "An Ideal Family" and "Life of Ma Parker" are less strictly monologues: they give what passes through the mind rather than what actually finds its way to the lips. The latter has even a certain amount of narrative. It is, I believe, a rather fine achievement. Nothing happens in this story save that an old woman cleans a room. As she works, her mind runs back over her past experiences. The story is not sentimental, but the tragedy of a whole lifetime is there.

Many of Katherine Mansfield's descriptive passages have a decidedly Dickensian flavor. The eighth section of "At the Bay"—the interlude of Alice and Mrs. Stubbs—is quite in the Dickens tradition. She had Dickens' ability effectively to "tag" a character through the description of some single characteristic action. Thus little Else Kelvey in "The Doll's House" goes through life, "holding on to Lil, with a piece of Lil's skirt screwed up in her hand." In "The Dove's Nest" Prodger complains that it is so difficult to live in a hotel where you cannot get a hot plate by ringing for it. "Mother, though outwardly all sympathy, found this a little bewildering. She had a momentary vision of Mr. Prodger ringing for hot plates to be brought to him at all hours. Such strange things to want in any numbers."

The most Dickensian of all Katherine Mansfield's products is the unfinished "Married Man's Story." Here examples occur on almost every page. By all means the best is the boy's impression of his father at the mother's funeral:

> That tall hat so gleaming black and round was like a cork covered with black sealing-wax, and the rest of my father was awfully like a bottle, with his face for the label—Deadly Poison. And Deadly Poison, or old D. P. was my private name for him from that day.

Again, in "Mr. and Mrs. Williams" we have the description of Aunt Aggie:

> As a matter of fact it was Mrs. Williams' Aunt Aggie's happy release which had made their scheme possible. Happy release it was! After fifteen years in a wheel-chair . . . she had, to use the nurse's expression, 'just glided away at the last.' Glided away. . . . It sounded as though Aunt Aggie had taken the wheel chair with her. One saw her, in her absurd purple velvet, steering carefully among the stars and whimpering faintly, as was her terrestrial wont, when the wheel jolted over a particularly large one."

How Dickens would have loved that!

Dickens is, of course, sadly "mid-Victorian" and out of fashion these days. Some day an intelligent critic who knows his Dickens will come along and demonstrate that all the astonishing "new" devices of the ultra-modernists were effectively employed by Dickens long before any of them were born.

V

So much for the technique: what now of the spirit of Katherine Mansfield's work? What is the use of possessing marvelous powers of revealment if the only soul you have to reveal through their agency has been coarsened and shrivelled before you begin to write? Here was one of the most original, most uncannily skilful of writers who understood as the poets do and who thirsted after righteousness with the saints.

And if she had sensitiveness to the things of the spirit, she had also what should always go with it, tenderness for the human beings through whom so much of the life of the spirit is conveyed. Especially with children is Katherine Mansfield's sympathy charming and pervasive. The pictures of the little Burnells are nothing short of marvelous: they are such vitally real, delightsome darlings! There is no touch of sentimentality in her treatment of them, yet somehow they bring a lump into the throat. I do not know anything in literature that has quite the mingled tenderness and gaiety of the conversation on death between Kezia and her grandmother in the seventh section of "At the Bay," and no words of mine shall attempt to describe the picture of Linda's argument with her baby which immediately precedes it. Indeed Katherine Mansfield's children generally are lovely, sensitive innocents, striving pitifully and vainly to adjust themselves to a coarse world, constructed by adults to suit themselves. In "The Garden Party" it is only Laura who perceives the heartlessness of going on with the plans for the party after the workman has been killed. In "Sun and Moon" the unspoiled purity of children, their sensitiveness to beauty, is used to pass judgment on the coarse commonness of their elders. When her children are not sympathetic, as in "A Married Man's Story," it is not the child who is to blame: we see the bad results of loneliness and neglect. In "The Doll's House" the children are democratic and kindly-mannered as long as they follow their own inclinations; they become insolent little snobs only when these same naturally benevolent impulses are overruled by the purse-proud snobbishness, the petty class-consciousness of their elders.

Tenderness is extended to dumb creatures also. I have already cited the enormous sympathy implied in "The Fly," and "The Canary" is almost equally sympathetic. The description in "Prelude" of the beheading of the duck is a terrible piece of realistic writing: it is significant that this too is used by Katherine Mansfield to reveal the sympathy, the horror of cruelty in the heart of a sensitive child.

Extreme youth and extreme age seem to have a certain sympathetic comprehension of each other: witness the lovely "Indian Summer of a Forsyte" in *The Forsyte Saga*. Perhaps both are closer to the spiritual world than men and women in their prime, absorbed with the cares and passions of the present hour. So it is not surprising that Katherine Mansfield who loved children should have also a beautiful, comprehending tenderness for old age. The finest examples are the father in "An Ideal Family" and the sweet, pathetic figure of "Miss Brill".

Katherine Mansfield's shallow women are likely to be young, and her treatment of them is absolutely merciless. Such stories as "A Cup of Tea" and "Marriage à la Mode" are consummate in their revelation of the utter selfishness, shallowness, and affectation of certain types of fashionable women: they say simply all that there is to be said. The men Katherine Mansfield admires are simple, gentle, loving, sometimes a little absurd, but endearingly absurd. The selfish, pretentious, self-centered man she can pillory just as ruthlessly as she pillories his feminine counterpart.

When a writer has been so much influenced as was Katherine Mansfield by psychoanalysis and the new psychology, I think it worthy of special mention as all the more remarkable that she should be so completely and so consistently on the side of the angels. She is not in line with the usual trend of writers of this school, not preoccupied with the darker side of existence. She is after truth, and when evil enters her picture she faces it unblushingly but she does not go out of her way to find it. She is not ashamed of life and its processes. A euphemism, a round-about way of referring to one of the basic facts of life seems to her not modest but rather unclean: consequently she sometimes permits herself to use words which are not generally current among modern writers. This proves no impurity in her but rather an exceptional cleanness and honesty of spirit. Sexual hunger and perversion, that favorite theme of so many psychoanalysts, she hardly touched, save in "Je ne parle pas Français," and here it is handled so subtly and delicately that, as Mr. Murry himself remarks in a wholly different connection, hardly anybody has ever completely understood the story. Katherine Mansfield's work is an important testimony that psychoanalysis in the fiction of the future will not necessarily imply any impurity: when the writer's own spirit is essentially noble, he will bring up pearls and not slime from his excursions into its depths.

That such a spirit with such endowments should be taken away from humanity so quickly is an incomparable loss to which no amount of philosophy can completely reconcile us. Yet where so much has been given it is perhaps ungracious to ask for more. The spirit of modernity is sometimes considered simply a spirit of shallowness, of irreverence or destruction. Here is a modern of the moderns whose work is distinguished for precisely the opposite qualities, and who has been well-nigh universally accepted, by the moderns themselves, as a great exponent of their attitude. Katherine Mansfield helps us to remember in days of small things and petty cynicisms that God can still give genius to humanity, that great souls can live in the modern world, and that it is possible for great art to be worked out under the inspiration of modern ideals. She is an incomparably gracious demonstration that the Spirit of Life is stronger than any current fashion of living or manner of speech.

The English Journal, April 1928, 17: pp. 272-284.

V. S. Pritchett, "Toy Balloons": *Novels and Novelists*

Before getting to work with the reviewer's knife upon this volume one hesitates, remembering the phrase with which the Victorian novelists tantalized us when they dangled their heroines' unopened love-letters before our eyes, "But they were meant for the eyes of one person alone." The eyes now in question being those of the fortunate subscribers to the *Nation* in the year 1919-1920, when Katherine Mansfield's reviews of fiction appeared. Surely such ephemeral confidences, rages and appraisals ought not to be submitted so long after their occasion to the curious stare of the book-borrowing public. And what business has an interloping reviewer in reviewing a reviewer's reviews? Is this not the inmost circle of perversion?

One is, however obliged to put these austere feelings aside, because the persistent interest of anything Katherine Mansfield wrote, easily masters them. Her book disposes once more of the gibe that critics are artists who have failed. In criticism, indeed, she was an artist, never dully making a balance sheet of a book's virtues and defects or a Baedeker to its story; but, with much cunning, creating an appropriate atmosphere and letting the story rise or fall in it like a toy balloon. And this atmosphere had a peculiar quality of spiritual fineness, in which certain authors - Mr Walpole, and Mr. Galsworthy, for example,—sank with an ugly thump while, to one's immense surprise, a Blasco Ibañez, no doubt secretly importing the influence of exotic Spanish ether, sailed in the majesty of commendation. Mrs. Virginia Woolf went up gay and high, indeed, almost out of sight, carrying the reviewer away with her. Conrad and Tomlinson had a steady place in the heavens. But there was a host of novels which never went very far. They maintained an unsteady, wobbling existence until her sharp, amusing claws pricked them and slowly they shrivelled up, sank to limbo and expired. It was all done very prettily, intimately, and, in spite of the claws and gambols, was rarely kittenish. This weekly despatch of coloured balloons was a delight to the intelligence.

Like many sensitive artists who turn to criticism and whose judgments are intuitive, Katherine Mansfield demanded above all in her fellow-artists an intense spiritual austerity, a fastidiousness in feeling. To those who preserved other virtues and neglected this, she was uncertain. This inevitably alienated her sympathy from a moralist like Mr. Galsworthy, whom she seemed contemptuously to regard as a man who had got art "into trouble" and was worried about it. Craftsmanship was not enough for her, though she was more than generous to the fine craftsmanship of H.M. Tomlinson. One must have seen the vision and felt the initial passion, and because this initial passion seemed to her to be lacking, *Esther Waters*, for all its perfection of detail, was not a great novel.

> "All is as cold and toneless as if it were being read out of that detective's notebook. It is supremely good evidence . . . but we forget it as soon as it is read for we have been given nothing to remember."

Again, her quarrel with Mr. Walpole is that he is animated by "determination rather than inspiration, strength of will rather than the artist's compulsion." With great labour and skill he can bring his horses to the mysterious water—but they will not drink for him. It is instructive to turn from her opinion of Mr. Walpole to that of Louis Couperus, whose *Old People* and *Things That Pass* were translated into English in 1919. Here was another novelist of family life who knew his creatures and who is not, as one frequently feels with Mr. Walpole, all the time trying to get hold of them. The Dutch novelist's people are seen in relation to life - "not to a part of life, not to a set of society, but to the bounding horizon, life." And neither is life made to "fit" them. The novelist who attempts to "fit" life to his characters "will find himself cutting something that gets smaller and smaller, finer and finer, until he must begin cutting his character next to fit the thing he has made."

In the rightness of these words one senses the limitations of Katherine Mansfield's austerity. The ready affinity of her sharp spirit with that of the Russians alienated her from the genial or the polite English tradition. What her spirit had in terrifying penetration it lacked in confident magnitude. She was essentially a creature of our age. One thinks of her intelligence as one thinks of feline claws, a sharp and beautiful mechanism, sliding out of their subtle velvet, now playfully, now with luxurious motion, now passionately, but always private in their impulse.

The Spectator, September 6, 1930, vol. 145, p. 315.

Elisabeth Schneider, "Katherine Mansfield and Chekhov"

The influence of Chekhov on Katherine Mansfield has often been remarked. She herself freely expressed admiration and a feeling of kinship for her Russian predecessor. Her husband, Mr. J. Middleton Murry in his edition of her *Journal*, however, says that critics over-estimate her debt to Chekhov, and that her literary development would have been much the same had she never read his stories.

This may well be true. Yet a remarkable parallel is to be found between one of her early short stories, "The Child-Who-Was-Tired" from the volume *In a German Pension*, and a story of Chekhov's called, in its English versions, "Sleepyhead" or "Sleepy."[1] In *The Life of Katherine Mansfield* by R.E. Mantz and J. Middleton Murry [2] the inception of her story is described: "Superficially, it is a realistic story of peasant life; but in essence it is nothing of the kind."

"The Child who was Tired" is indubitably herself in the summer of 1909—the Katherine wearied with pain and crying in vain for rest —'the frightened child lost in a funeral procession.' The peasant household is not any peasant household that Katherine experienced—actually the Bavarian peasants were kind to her, and she liked them—but merely a symbol of her experience of life.

Yet the similarity between the two stories is too great for us to suppose them entirely independent. The central idea of Chekhov's tale would be unlikely to occur of itself to another writer. It is briefly, and so is Katherine Mansfield's, the story of a servant girl, who, overworked all day, is compelled to stay awake at night to rock the baby. Crazed by fatigue and lack of sleep, she strangles the child and at once falls asleep.

The period of time covered by the action in Katherine Mansfield's story is slightly shorter: she begins in the early morning when the girl is aroused by a blow, while Chekhov begins during the preceding night with the girl's desperate efforts to stay awake. Both end the following night after the mistress's final command to rock the baby. But the likeness of the two stories does not end with the outline; the mood, and even much of the detail, are the same. At the crisis of both stories the girl's stupefied mind seizes with a feeling of great discovery upon the idea that it is the baby who prevents her sleeping. She thinks of strangling it; without any question or moral conflict, she laughs with pleasure at the thought; and when she has finished she lies happily down upon the floor and falls fast asleep. The action of the preceding day, the account of a servant girl's daily work, would naturally be much the same—splitting wood, lighting the oven, "heating" the coffee (or the samovar), washing the floor (or the steps), peeling potatoes—these details one would expect to find, and one does, in both. But there are others. In Chekhov's story there is a recurrent picture or motif which appears when the child in spite of herself has fallen asleep in the night and dreams of "a broad high road covered with liquid mud," with people and wagons, and tall hills on either side. This is repeated after she has been wakened by a "sharp slap behind the ear," and it recurs the next night before she thinks of killing the baby. Katherine Mansfield's story has a similar recurring motif introduced in the first sentence: "she was just beginning to walk along a little white road with tall black trees on either side . . . where nobody walked at all, when a hand gripped her shoulder, shook her, slapped her ear." This vision too recurs at the same points in the story, once soon after she has got up and again just before the crisis as well as at other moments during the day. The sensations of sleepiness and fatigue are on the whole rather different, but in both the child's neck aches, and objects seem to grow large before her eyes: in Chekhov's story it is the master's golosh which as she is cleaning it, "grows, swells and fills the whole room"; in "The Child-Who-Was-Tired" the man and his wife sitting at supper seemed to "swell to an immense size as she watched them, and then become smaller than dolls." The day's work in both stories is prolonged by the arrival of visitors in the evening with further parallel commands to "set the samovar" and to "put on the coffee."

There are other rather minute likenesses; there are differences as well. The most important of the latter is one which shows the increasing tendency of the more modern writer toward concentration of time, scene, and interest. I have said that the Russian story begins earlier on the night before the crisis. The interval is occupied by the child's half-waking dreams of her early life, by means of which Chekhov gives us rather a complete picture of her past. In the story of Katherine Mansfield we are kept more strictly to the present scene, the child's past being suggested only by a few words of the mistress which she overhears.

The explanation that I suggest for the similarity, which amounts almost to a reproduction of the same story, is offered only tentatively. In spite of the very close parallel there was probably no deliberate plagiarism on the part of Katherine Mansfield. It seems unlikely, too, that, if she were experimenting to see what she could do with the same plot, she would have published it without acknowledgment. Only a less exigent egoism than hers would be likely to seek, or find, satisfaction by an accomplishment not really her own. It seems more probably a case of unconscious memory, a phenomenon common enough in matters of detail, though not common in such complete instances. This is, of course, only surmise. But the interpretation is somewhat strengthened by another resemblance which I think is not fanciful, though it is scarcely susceptible of definite proof, of one of Katherine Mansfield's later stories to a novel of Henry James.   The fragment called "The Dove's Nest," which is about a girl named Milly, suggests, in something more subtle than its title and heroine's name, certain parts in the latter half of James's *The Wings of the Dove*. Something of the spirit—the color of the air, one might call it, in the two houses (one in the south of France, the other in Italy), the two women living in each of them—much in the heroine herself, and in the author's unspoken attitude toward her, a delicate, romanticized, veiled portrayal, though it is quite indefinable, seems distinctly similar. In this case a writer who was deliberately borrowing an atmosphere would hardly have taken care to point the indebtedness by the use of the reminiscent title and a heroine with the same name. There is no similarity here of action or of situation, and the whole is typical of those vague, unconscious reminiscences of which literary history affords any number of examples. If I am right in drawing this parallel, the probability that the earlier story was an unconscious imitation of Chekhov is somewhat strengthened. One feature of a certain type of imaginative mind is the power of taking in that which appeals to it with so much activity of its own, so little of mere passive appreciation, that the memory afterward will seem to bear the stamp of its own imagination. Whether this interpretation is correct or not, the case itself is an interesting one - how interesting, only those who read the four stories together, and then read Katherine Mansfield's letters and Journal, can know.

Modern Language Notes, June 1935, 50:6, pp. 394-397.

---

[1] This had appeared in an English translation by R.E.C. Long in 1903. "The-Child-Who-Was-Tired" was published originally, with the additional title of "Bavarian Babies" in *The New Age* for February 24, 1910.

[2] London, 1933, p. 326.

David Daiches, from "Katherine Mansfield"

I

The short stories of Katherine Mansfield, though not many in number, contain some of the most sensitive writing in our literature. "Sensitive" is a much-abused critical term, but here it is the only one appropriate: there is in these stories a delicacy of response to life, a fine insight into the given situation, combined with a mastery of communicative phrase, that set them apart, almost as a unique species of writing. Where else can we find such a preference of reality to art together with such a perfect moulding of art to fit reality? Katherine Mansfield's stories are not large-scale studies of the ways of man, or narratives intended to illustrate conventional values, nor are they descriptive sketches merely, studies in style, or fine treatment of language for its own sake. They are imaginative studies of situation, attempts to get "the deepest truth out of the idea," as she herself wrote in her journal. She dealt always with the single situation, the single idea, and the whole purpose of the story with its carefully chosen setting and detailed description was to bring out the meaning of this—meaning, significance, not in terms of anything external but with reference only to the truth of experience. She approached human activity from the angles provided by the isolated instance, the single combination of circumstances; she did not approach life directly at its most exuberant, in its richest and most crowded moments, but sought to illuminate it by so presenting the aspects she selected as to bring out the "deepest truth of the idea," the reality and therefore the *relevance* of the short sequence of events she chose to isolate and present.

It is not the most obvious way of telling a story, nor is it the easiest. To make the content so dependent on the form, as it were, by relying on the method of presenting the situation in order to make it a situation worth presenting, without distorting the facts to meet the idea and without any comment, is to risk complete failure. There can be no half-success with this method; the critic cannot say, "A thoroughly well-told story, though a little pointless," because the point is so bound up with the telling that if it cannot be brought home the telling has no purpose—indeed, no separate existence—at all. This does not apply to some of the earlier stories, many of which are only descriptive sketches, or to those later stories where Katherine Mansfield deliberately takes a holiday from her normal method, but it is true of nearly all her work after *In a German Pension*. She has imposed upon herself a much severer discipline than the majority of story-tellers dare to do; she writes only to tell the truth—not the truth for the outsider, for the observer who watches the action from the street corner, but the truth for the characters themselves and so the real meaning of the situation.

A situation can have "meaning" from many different points of view. The point of view may be ethical, or æsthetic, or dependent on any scheme of values the author wishes to apply. Katherine Mansfield consciously and deliberately avoided any such external approach. For her the meaning of the situation meant its potentialities for change in the lives of the characters, in so far as such a change had reference to aspects of experience known and appreciated by feeling and suffering beings in general. There is always this ultimate reference to life in its wider aspect, though it does not take the form of the description of the most impressive or superficially the most "significant" elements in life. It is not the course of the action itself that has this connection, but, in so many cases, this element of *change* which links up her stories with general human activity. The varying and unstable qualities of human emotions and the very essence of these qualities are illustrated by the point, the dynamic element in the story which is brought out in the presentation. It is a point the mere *observer* would miss—some subtle change of emotional atmosphere or realisation by the characters of something new, something different and cogent, though they might not themselves be aware of what it is. Thus the "truth of the idea" meant to Katherine Mansfield the meaning of the situation for those concerned in it, and this had implications far beyond the individual instance, though these implications were not stressed or commented on: this meaning she nearly always saw as involving some kind of change.

The identification of the point of a story with change can best be understood by reference to some examples. It is not, of course, an invariable feature of Katherine Mansfield's stories—some of her best are without—but it is sufficiently predominant to be worth examining as a feature of her work. We see it in her very earliest work, e.g. in "The Sister of the Baroness", the second sketch in *In a German Pension,* but here the treatment is comparatively crude and immature. The "point" of the story is quite superficial; it is the old theme of the lady's maid masquerading as the lady and successfully imposing on a boarding-house full of people. The change comes suddenly, at the end, as in so many of Katherine Mansfield's later stories:

> "But where is my maid?" asked the Baroness.
> "There was no maid," replied the manager, "save for your gracious sister and daughter."
> "Sister!" she cried sharply. "Fool, I have no sister. My child travelled with the daughter of my dressmaker."
> Tableau grandissimo!

It is an obvious and mechanical change here, with no attempt to extract "the greatest truth out of the idea" and, further, we have what in the more mature stories we never have—comment. To underline the fact as is done with the comment "Tableau grandissimo!" gives the reader no further insight into the reality of the situation; it merely stresses the obvious. But the story is interesting as illustrating at this early stage the beginnings of what was to be one of the most important features of Katherine Mansfield's technique.

Later examples of this "peripeteia" are abundant. In "The Garden Party" the story rests on the change from the party atmosphere to the atmosphere of sudden death in the carter's cottage, and the *meaning* of that change. All the other elements, the description, the dialogue, the character sketching, are subordinated to this. In "Her First Ball" the point of the story lies in the change of mood:

Leila gave a light little laugh, but she did not feel like laughing. Was it—could it all be true? It sounded terribly true. Was this first ball only the beginning of her last ball after all? At that the music seemed to change; it sounded sad, sad; it rose upon a great sigh. Oh, how quickly things changed! Why didn't happiness last for ever? For ever wasn't a bit too long.

And the story concludes with a change back to the original mood.

"The Singing Lesson" is perhaps the most obvious example of all—a little too obvious to be really effective. The story describes first the mood of a singing teacher giving her lesson in school after receiving a letter that morning from her fiancé breaking off the engagement, and concludes with her sudden change of mood after receiving a telegram telling her to pay no regard to the letter. Here the change comes right at the end, and that is its usual place in the stories. "The Stranger" describes an impatient husband waiting for the entrance into harbour of the liner which brings back to him his wife after she has been away for ten months. His longing to possess her again and his anticipation of a blissful reunion is perfectly conveyed—and then comes the change when, once they are in the hotel together, she tells him how one of the passengers had died on board the previous night:

"Oh, it wasn't anything in the least infectious!" said Janey. She was speaking scarcely above her breath. "It was *heart*." A pause. "Poor fellow!" she said. "Quite young." And she watched the fire flicker and fall. "He died in my arms," said Janey.

And the story ends:

"You're not—sorry I told you, John, darling? It hasn't made you sad? It hasn't spoilt our evening—our being alone together?"
But at that he had to hide his face. He put his face into her bosom and his arms enfolded her.
Spoilt their evening! Spoilt their being alone together! They would never be alone together again.

This stress on the significance of change comes in again and again. "Revelations" depends on the change wrought in Monica's mood by the death of her hairdresser's little girl. In "Bliss" the change comes at the very end, when Bertha's mood of glorious well-being, which has been the theme of the story up to the last page, collapses like a burst balloon as a result of what she sees in the hall when her husband is showing out the guests. Even in her unfinished stories we see the stage set for the peripeteia. In "The Dove's Nest" everything is there but the final change to give point to the story, and this is true also of "Father and the Girls", "Honesty", and "Second Violin". In "Widowed" and "Susannah" the change has already come.

The uniqueness of Katherine Mansfield's method of giving point to what has gone before by the sudden twist at the end can be best appreciated by comparing her technique with that of some other short-story writers. A really illuminating comparison is that of James Joyce's story "The Dead" (the last in *Dubliners*) and Katherine Mansfield's "The Stranger", the conclusion of which has already been quoted. Both have similar themes—the change produced in a man who is longing passionately to be alone with his wife on learning that her mood is the result of something quite unconnected with himself, something that has reference to an experience he does not share and which he feels is coming between them and their love. In Joyce the development of the story is much slower, much more deliberate, and the final point emerges gradually in the course of the narrative. But with Katherine Mansfield much more depends on the actual presentation of the story. Neither she nor her characters make lengthy comment; the meaning of the situation is never *stated,* but implied. Her endeavour is to put the story in a position to illuminate itself; the parts throw light on the whole and the whole throws light on the parts so that, for example, the change at the end puts new meaning into what has gone before, putting everything into a new perspective which we had not been aware of until we arrived at the end. Joyce's method is more discursive, less economical, though quite as effective in its own way. But this difference in technique must not blind us to the many points of similarity between Joyce's *Dubliners* and Katherine Mansfield's stories. "Ivy Day in the Committee Room", though so different in theme, is similar in "texture" to that little masterpiece "The Daughters of the Late Colonel", one of the more static of Katherine Mansfield's stories. Both have that quiet observation and penetrating selection of detail so effective in creating atmosphere. Joyce's story "A Painful Case", shows at once the points of resemblance and the points of difference between the two writers. Comparison of this kind could be prolonged indefinitely.

Katherine Mansfield seems to have been always on her guard against any lapses from the ideal of strict self-restraint which she imposed upon herself in dealing with emotional crises. Mr Middleton Murry tells us in his introductory note to *Something Childish and Other Stories* that "Sixpence" was excluded from *The Garden Party and Other Stories* by Katherine Mansfield because she thought it 'sentimental.' After describing an imaginary scene—"The New Baby"— in her journal, she adds:

> You ought to keep this, my girl, just as a *warning* to show what an arch-wallower you *can* be.

That she had a tendency in this direction is shown by occasional false touches throughout her work. "Miss Brill" for example, the pathetic story of the governess out for her weekly walk in the park wearing, after a long interval, her beloved fur, which is audibly described by a giggling girl as looking "exactly like a fried whiting," concludes thus:

> But to-day she passed the baker's by, climbed the stairs, went into the little dark room—her room like a cupboard—and sat down on the red eiderdown. She sat there for a long time. The box that the fur came out of was on the bed. She unclasped the necklet quickly; quickly, without looking, laid it aside. But when she put the lid on she thought she heard something crying.

Here the emotion seems to be stressed in the wrong place. The "truth of the idea" lies in the change of mood when Miss Brill, in the midst of her exultation, the feeling that she is an actor among fellow-actors in this bright morning scene, suddenly learns the truth from the chance remark of a girl. As a rule Katherine Mansfield manages to bring out the significance of a situation with greater economy and a surer touch. In "The Man without a Temperament" there is the same suggestion of sentimentality in the ending, but here it is adequately balanced by the facts, as it were; the contrast between the Englishman abroad as he appears to the foreign observers and the Englishman alone with his wife is the whole point of the story; it is a case where the truth itself is sentimental:

> . . . He went over to the washstand and dipt his fingers in water. "Are you all right now? Shall I switch off the light?"
>
> "Yes, please. No. Boogles! Come back here a moment. Sit down by me. Give me your hand." She turns his signet-ring. "Why weren't you asleep? Boogles, listen. Come closer. I sometimes wonder—do you mind awfully being out here with me?"
>
> He bends down. He kisses her. He tucks her in, he smooths the pillow.
>
> "Rot!" he whispers.

Sentimental, perhaps, but there is no other way of doing it—except to tell a different story.

Objective truth was always Katherine Mansfield's aim in her stories. She wished to become the supreme recorder, free from all personal bias and even interest. "I can't tell the truth about Aunt Anne unless I am free to enter into her life without self-consciousness," she wrote in her journal in 1921. She was reproaching herself for not being calm enough when writing. "Calm yourself. Clear yourself. And anything that I write in this mood will be no good; it will be full of *sediment*. . . . One must learn, one must practise to *forget* oneself." Yet sometimes the reader is left a little in doubt whether the story is told in terms of the thought of the observer or the observed. The meaning of the situation is the meaning for those concerned in it, but occasionally we find the writer herself entering into the situation for an instant. In the beginning of "The Doll's House" she is describing the emotions of the children on receiving the present of a doll's house:

> The hook at the side was stuck fast. Pat prized it open with his penknife, and the whole house front swung back, and—there you were, gazing at one and the same moment into the drawing-room and dining-room, the kitchen and two bedrooms. That is the way for a house to open! Why don't all houses open like that? How much more exciting than peering through the slit of a door into a mean little hall with a hatstand and two umbrellas! That is—isn't it?—what you long to know about a house when you put your hand on the knocker. Perhaps it is the way God opens houses at the dead of night when He is taking a quiet turn with an angel. . . .

In the last two sentences of this paragraph Katherine Mansfield has substituted her own mind for that of the children. The thought at the end is not a child's thought; it is her own. From describing the working of a child's imagination she has slipped almost imperceptibly into giving an example of the working of her own. We find this occasionally throughout the stories—the spectator becoming too interested to hold aloof and allowing her own consciousness to enter. It is just because her approach is usually so objective that we notice those occasions where, only for a moment, she allows the subjective element to enter. Of course, in pure description the author must talk to some extent in her own person, but once the characters are set going and the story is told in terms of *their* minds any intrusion by the author is dangerous. There are few authors who intrude so rarely as Katherine Mansfield, who, when she does intrude, does it in this almost imperceptible way, substituting her own imagination directly just for a sentence or two; and perhaps to note those occasions when she lapses from her own rule is cavilling criticism. Certainly it needs an eagle eye to spot the examples, and "The Doll's House" remains one of her most perfect stories in spite of this brief intrusion. But we can imagine how effective a *child's* simile might have been in that passage, especially one created by Katherine Mansfield, one of whose greatest qualities is her insight into the child mind.

It is always difficult, in describing the significance of a situation for those concerned in it, to avoid letting one's own sense of significance intrude unconsciously. It requires such a high degree of imagination to tell the truth. Only in her less successful moments does Katherine Mansfield give us some notion of the difficulty of the achievement involved in her successful work. Her writing at its best has a purity rare in literature. She never attempted to put into a story more than "the truth of the idea" warranted. "The truth is one can get only *so much* into a story; there is always a sacrifice," she wrote in her journal. It was a sacrifice she was constantly making. She always kept her eye strictly on the object, trying to probe to its inner meaning and reality by sheer intensity of observation. She wrote no more than she saw, but she saw so much in the least human activity that she never needed to do more than record her observations. In the best of her work—in "At the Bay", "The Doll's House", "Prelude", "The Daughters of the Late Colonel"—art and life are identified to a unique degree for the very reason that art as such is never allowed to obtrude.

II

There is more in Katherine Mansfield's stories than the "point," the extracting of "the truth of the idea." The moment of insight is always prepared for, the setting of the story is always adequate and convincing; the descriptive passages are often brilliantly done. A consideration of her technique in description will reveal some of her finest qualities as a writer. It is, after all, the description, the creation of atmosphere, that makes "At the Bay", "The Garden Party" and "Prelude" so memorable. One of the reasons for her success here is that the scenes described were real scenes, remembered with great vividness from her own early experience. Those aspects of New Zealand landscape especially, which occur so frequently in her work, are presented with a concreteness and a reality which are largely responsible for that quality of freshness that pervades her writing. The first section of "At the Bay" provides one of the finest examples of her descriptive technique. It starts quite simply with a statement of the time: "Very early morning." Then immediately the phrase is localised: "The sun was not yet risen, and the whole of Crescent Bay was hidden under a white sea-mist." There follows a selection of details, not sufficient to be tedious, just enough to give the reader an adequate visual picture and a sense of atmosphere. First the hills behind, covered with mist, and a suggestion of what the mist concealed; then a description of the big drops of dew hanging on the bushes. The first paragraph ends with a characteristic imaginative touch:

> It looked as though the sea had beaten up softly in the darkness, as though one immense wave had come rippling, rippling—how far? Perhaps if you had waked up in the middle of the night you might have seen a big fish flicking in at the window and gone again . . .

The descriptive details are informed with life by this impinging of the human mind on their objective passivity. And it is no fault here that Katherine Mansfield looked at the scene in terms of her *own* imagination, because she has not yet introduced the characters who are to take control. We see in this first paragraph the creation of atmosphere by the selection and arrangement of detail lit up by a touch of human imagination. Thus the emotional potentialities of the landscape are indicated. It is not enough for the story-teller to describe a scene for its own sake, leaving it as a passive background for the action. Some relation must be established between the setting and the action, human values must pervade *everything* in a story if it is to be really organic in structure. That is why the description in Hardy's novels is so much more integral to the story than that in Scott. Scott's description often takes the form of preliminary set pieces, which, however effective in themselves, are not sufficiently related to the human significance of the story to be really one with it. With Katherine Mansfield, as, in so different ways, with Hardy and Conrad, there is no such isolation of the descriptive element.

But to return to the opening of "At the Bay". After the first paragraph, with its selection of detail and enlivening imaginative element, there is a quick return to the sea, this time its audible (not its visual) qualities being noted:

> Ah-Aah! sounded the sleepy sea. And from the bush there came the sound of little streams flowing, quickly, lightly, slipping between the smooth stones, gushing into ferny basins and out again; and there was the splashing of big drops on large leaves, and something else—what was it?—a faint stirring and shaking, the snapping of a twig and then such silence that it seemed some one was listening.

One could write a whole essay on style from a consideration of the effect of the juxtaposition of this paragraph and the previous. We see how the scene is built up while at the same time the reader is gradually enwrapped in the appropriate atmosphere. Early morning—white mist—bungalows—heavy dew—mist merging beach and sea—sea rippling up in the darkness. *Then* our escape is finally cut off by our hearing the moaning of the sleepy sea in the background. We are caught in the atmosphere now; it is all round us. That little sentence, "Ah-Aah! sounded the sleepy sea," gains supreme effect by being in just the right place. It comes after a pause, after the misty bay has been presented to our sight and to our imagination. It is as though we were bidden to stand quite still and hear what had been going on all the time without our realising. Everything has become quite quiet and we can hear the sea. And, our ears now becoming sensitive to what is going on, the next moment we hear too the sound of the little streams and the splashing of big drops on large leaves. It is not only the selection of right detail that matters, but the *order* in which it is presented to the reader.

"The Daughters of the Late Colonel" shows Katherine Mansfield in another mood, but is equally typical of her method of creating atmosphere. Unlike most of her stories, it contains no sudden change at the end; it is more even in tone and the same mood remains all through. Here again the main feature is the quiet arrangement of detail, and purely by means of effective arrangement every ounce of meaning is squeezed out of slight and casual incidents. Nothing is superfluous, nothing is mere decoration or trimming, everything has its part to play in producing the required effect.

> But the strain told on them when they were back in the dining-room. They sat down, very shaky, and looked at each other.
> "I don't feel I can settle to anything," said Josephine, "until I've had something. Do you think we could ask Kate for two cups of hot water?"
> "I really don't see why we shouldn't" said Constantia carefully. She was quite normal again. "I won't ring. I'll go to the kitchen door and ask her."
> "Yes, do," said Josephine, sinking down into a chair. "Tell her, just two cups, Con, nothing else—on a tray." . . .
> Their cold lips quivered at the greenish brims. Josephine curved her small red hands round the cup; Constantia sat up and blew on the wavy steam, making it flutter from one side to the other.

Every detail here is relevant. The cups of hot water, Josephine curving her small red hands round the cup, the attitude to Kate ("just two cups, Con, nothing else" and "I'll go to the kitchen door and ask her"), Constantia blowing the steam—all this shows that quiet and pertinent observation utilised to create atmosphere. Everything has reference to the *mood* of the story, everything is organised so as to bring "the deepest truth out of the idea." It is largely a matter of selection and method of presentation. That so much should be achieved by such an economy of means is the greatest tribute to Katherine Mansfield's technique. "The Daughters of the Late Colonel" is a landmark in the history of the English short story.

To record objectively, with nevertheless complete understanding and complete knowledge of every aspect of the situation, was Katherine Mansfield's aim. This reconciling of complete objectivity with complete knowledge implies a constant state of unstable equilibrium on the part of the author. She could not impose her own consciousness too much on the situation, yet at the same time she had to employ her own imagination and sensibility in recording it. The older writers solved the problem by leaving themselves free to observe and comment in their own person. From Fielding through Thackeray right on to the present day this practice has continued, different authors making use of it in differing degrees. Joyce, in *Ulysses,* solves the problem in a completely different way: he presents everything through the consciousness of his characters, never appearing in his own person at all, never even *observing* in his own person.[1] Nothing is known absolutely, only in so far as it impinges on the consciousness of one or other of his characters. Katherine Mansfield's method lies somewhere between the traditional one and that of Joyce and other modern writers. She refuses to sacrifice her powers of independent observation, but at the same time she takes note of nothing which is not in the highest sense relevant to the situation she is presenting. She frees herself by a deliberate effort from any irrelevant emotion or pre-supposition. "One must learn, one must practise to *forget* oneself. I can't tell the truth about Aunt Anne until I am free to enter into her life without self-consciousness." To enter Aunt Anne's life—yes, but retaining her own powers of insight and imagination, her own interest in human emotion, her own curiosity and truthfulness. "Lord, make me crystal clear for thy light to shine through," she wrote in her journal, but the process could not be as simple as that—it might be compared rather to refraction.

This ability to put her own mind inside other people's sometimes led Katherine Mansfield to substitute her own sensitive reactions for those appropriate to the character. The unstable equilibrium could not be maintained over a long period without occasional wavering. We have seen how, in entering into the mind of a child, she lets herself on one occasion introduce a piece of imagination quite unchildlike in quality. It is a slight point, but interesting as indicative of the difficulty of her method. Now and again we find her more articulate about the emotions of her characters, more conscious of their real nature, than the characters themselves could be. The nameless heroine of "Psychology" lets her visitor go without having established the contact with him she intended:

> She was right. He did see nothing at all. Misery! He'd missed it. It was too late to do anything now. Was it too late? Yes, it was. A cold snatch of hateful wind blew into the garden. Curse life! He heard her cry "au revoir" and the door slammed.

There is no fault to find here. A mood of which the character was quite conscious has been adequately rendered into words. It does not matter if the character herself would not have used those actual words: they represent what she might have thought, her mood being potentially quite articulate. But the story continues:

> Running back into the studio she behaved so strangely. She ran up and down lifting her arms and crying: "Oh! Oh! How stupid! How imbecile! How stupid!" And then she flung herself down on the *sommier* thinking of nothing—just lying there in her rage. All was over. What was over? Oh—something was . . .

But would the character herself have been conscious of these things? Has not Katherine Mansfield here substituted her own sensitive and interested mind so that the character is portrayed as being articulate about what she could not consciously have had any knowledge of? "And then she flung herself down on the *sommier* thinking of nothing—just lying there in her rage." That is convincing, and seems to convey the truth of the situation. But to put into the mind of a girl who was enraged without knowing why, who is lying thinking of nothing, the conscious thought that "all was over. What was over? Oh—something was"—this is to allow the author's objective comment to masquerade as part of the consciousness of the character. Sometimes Katherine Mansfield succumbs to the temptation of substituting her own clear vision for the blindness of those whose reactions she is portraying. But she never does this sufficiently to interfere with the reality of the story or with that creation of atmosphere which is one of her greatest achievements.

III

Katherine Mansfield's development was the result of increased consciousness of what she wanted to achieve in her writing. She was not one of those writers who improve with practice automatically. She saw quite clearly the gap between her achievement and her aim—a bigger gap to her sight than it is to ours—and set herself to remove it. To read her journal alongside her stories is to realise how deliberately she disciplined herself in response to the high ideal that was always before her. It was not that she wanted her work to be impressive or important; she wanted only that it should correspond to her sense of truth. She had not to search for her themes; that power of observation and insight that was always with her provided her with more material than she was able to use. "There is so much to do, and I do so little," she wrote in her journal. "Look at the stories that wait and wait just at the threshold." She felt that life awaited her pen, and that her duty was to embody it *truly* in her art. And always it was through the single situation that she approached truth of reality.

The time has come when we can look back on Katherine Mansfield's work and place it in its true perspective. We can see it now as one of the greatest contributions to the development of the art of the short story ever made. Her work has shown new possibilities for the small-scale writer, and by the uniqueness of its achievement points the way to a new critical approach to that age-long problem, the relation of "art" to "life." No writer in either the creative or the critical field has yet shown himself of the calibre to profit to the full from this twofold contribution to literature.

New Literary Values: Studies in Modern Literature, Edinburgh, Oliver & Boyd, 1936, pp. 83-114.

---

1   This, too, is the method of the "epistolary" novel, as used e.g. by Richardson, but the technique here is clumsier.

Arthur Sewell, from *Katherine Mansfield - A Critical Essay*

In her best short stories, Katherine Mansfield holds a unique place in English literature. It is, I think, a two-fold achievement that gives her this place. First, she enlarged the potentialities of language, of the English language. She made something out of words quite new and unthought-of. She wrought a new texture in prose. Second, she explored a realm of emotional experience, she communicated a quality of emotional experience found nowhere else in literature. It is not merely that no one else has taken the New Zealand sea-side as subject-matter for story-telling. It is not merely that no one else has conveyed, for example, the salty, sandy, gritty memory of a summer day on the beach. What Katherine Mansfield wrote *about* only partly explains this quality in her stories. It has something to do with her way of taking "a long look at life", something to do with her people, too, her old maids and her children. It is a kind of tremulous quality, as when experience is a little uncertain in its lights and shadows and we don't know whether to laugh—no, to smile or cry.

I

It may be impossible to describe this quality in Katherine Mansfield's stories that makes them unique. Mr Middleton Murry, in his introduction to her journal, wrote

> Her secret died with her. And of the many critics who have tried to define the quality in her work which makes it so inimitable, every one has been compelled to give up the attempt in despair.

I hope the matter is not so desperate: or this paper had better not have been written. I think the secret did not die with her. It is there in her stories and many clues to it are in her journal and her letters, too.

Mr Murry makes an attempt to detect "one element of her nature" which "was essential to a peculiar quality of her work". This quality he describes as "purity"—"as though the glass through which she looked upon life were crystal-clear". This is true, so far as it goes. But it is not enough. It is the quality of all great literature—and, particularly, of all great poetry—to be "pure", to be the translucent image of the "idea". But the purity in Katherine Mansfield's work was of such a special kind that when we use the word we use it in a more exquisite, more absolute sense.

We may call her style "pure", but there are many purities in style different from hers. There is the cold clarity of French prose style, a kind of choice mosaic-like quality in words which makes for logical exactness and seeming precision in emotional analysis. Katherine Mansfield, however, found French prose deficient in clarity, even woolly in statement. In a letter to Mr Middleton Murry, February 27, 1918, she wrote:

> I do find the French language, style, attack, point of view, hard to stomach at present. It's all so tainted. It all seems to me to lead to dishonesty—Dishonesty Made Easy— made superbly easy. All these *half*-words which have never really been born and seen the light, like "me trouble", "vague", "tiède", "blottant", "inexprimable" (these are bad examples, but you know the kinds I mean) and the phrases and whole paragraphs that go with them—they won't at the moment do at all. Some of them are charming and one is loth to do without them, but they are like certain plants—once they are in your garden they spread and spread and spread, and make a showing perhaps but they are *weeds*.

We know the kind of words she means. They are words which leave an emotion half-expressed or vaguely waved at with an imperfect gesture. They indicate, perhaps, the direction in which the idea or the feeling may be found, but they never take you there. And prose may achieve a kind of over-simplified clarity through the use of such words. But it lacks detail: it is not positive.

Katherine Mansfield's purity of style is a quality of English words. And she aimed at a special *English* directness and truth.

> "It's the result of Shakespeare, I think," she wrote in the same letter. "The English language is damned difficult, but it's also damned rich, and so clear and bright that you can search out the darkest places with it. Also it's *heavenly* simple and true".

We find the same idea more fully expressed in a letter to Arnold Gibbons (June 24, 1922). She is criticizing a volume of his stories and she complains that too many of them are written "in the shadow" of Tchekov—almost as though they were translations from the Russian:

> We have less words (than the Russian) but they are more vital; we need less. So though one can accept this recapitulating process from Russian writers it sounds strange to me coming from your pen. For instance in *Going Home* you get in five lines: "enthusiasm, doubtful, mistrust, acute terror, anxious joy, sadness, pain, final dissolution, filth and degradation". *Or* (p.2) "the unhappiness, the misery and cruelty, all the squalor and abnormal spiritual anguish". Again, last page but one of *The Sister*; "futility, monotony, suffocated, pettiness, sordidness, vulgar minuteness". When one writes like that in English it's as though the *nerve* of the feeling were gone.

I think we approach here very near to the "nerve" of the feeling of purity in her own writing. These words—"futility", "sordidness", "vulgar minuteness" etc— describe the emotion, they do not make it. They do not accurately describe it either. It is as though none of these words will quite do: but if you take a little from each of them, you get pretty near to the feeling which the author wants to communicate. This is the method of *recapitulation* and the English language has a better way than that.

> "How are we", she goes on to ask, "to convey these overtones, half tones, quarter tones, these hesitations, doubts, beginnings, if we go at them *directly* ? It is most devilishly difficult, but I do believe that there is a way of doing it and that's by trying to get as near to the *exact truth* as possible."

And Katherine Mansfield could get to the exact truth in her writing. She does it in quite small things, in those trivial little items of experience which no one but a sensitive artist would notice or think worth noticing—and yet, once noticed, we say: How right! In "The Garden Party", she talks about that "absolute inward look that only comes from whipped cream". I do not know whether you feel there, as I do, the intense absorption that is partly the joy of eating whipped cream, partly too the fear of messing. Her similes can be exactly true, so that they are not similes at all but true metaphor. In one of her letters she talks about a "sea like quilted silk" and "a whole flock of little winds". In the fragmentary story, "Weak Heart", she describes a bed of hyacinths, "pink and white, the colour of cocoanut ice". All this is "purity", perhaps, on a lower level, but it is part of her quality.

This stylistic "purity" was never something that came to Katherine Mansfield's writing easily or luckily. She worked hard for it, one may be sure: and she knew what she was working for. In a letter to Richard Murry (January 17, 1921), she wrote:

> It's a very queer thing how craft comes into writing. I mean down to details. Par exemple. In "Miss Brill" I choose not only the length of every sentence, but even the sound of every sentence. I choose the rise and fall of every paragraph to fit her, and to fit her on that day at that very moment. After I'd written it I read it aloud—numbers of times—just as one would *play over* a musical composition—trying to get it nearer and nearer to the expression of Miss Brill—until it fitted her.

It is this kind of labouring to find a prose which will give the *absolute* form to the idea that makes Katherine Mansfield's work akin, as Mr Murry has suggested, to the English poets rather than to the English prose-writers. This absolute communication of the whole of an emotional experience is usually the work of poetry. Katherine Mansfield does it in prose. She herself had something of this same idea about her own work, when she wrote to Richard Murry:

> People have hardly begun to write yet. Put poetry out of it for a moment and leave out Shakespeare—now I mean prose. Take the very best of it. Aren't they still cutting up sections rather than tackling the whole of the mind?

Words only capture the "whole of the mind" when they are used poetically, when the "over-tones, the half-tones and quarter-tones" are given by the shadows that memory and association may cast over words—when words have a phantom-life as well as sound and meaning.

To deliver the "truth" directly, a writer must be very sparing in his use of words. If you compare "The Aloe" with "Prelude", you will see how rigorously Katherine Mansfield exercised economy in writing—how she would throw aside pages of writing around and about the experience just so soon as she had hit on the very words and the very details which *make* the experience. There are two shorter passages in her Journal in which a similar comparison may be made. She is describing the geraniums in her garden. Here are the first sentences:

> The red geraniums have bought the garden over my head. They are here, established, back in the old home, every leaf and flower unpacked and in its place—and quite determined that no power on earth will ever move them again.

This is the rewritten version:

> The red geraniums have bought the garden over my head and taken possession. They are settled in, every leaf and flower unpacked and in its place, and never do they mean to move again.

There is much more strength in the second version. "Settled in" is more direct than "here, established, back in the old home": and "never do they mean to move again" is far better than "quite determined that no power on earth will ever move them again".

All Katherine Mansfield's best stories are written with this economy. She does not *strip* her sentences: she compresses them.

"If a thing has really come off", she once wrote, "it seems to me there mustn't be one single word out of place, or one word that could be taken out".

That is a hard saying, but I believe it is true of stories such as "Miss Brill" or "The Daughters of the Late Colonel".

From "Katherine Mansfield, A Critical Essay", Auckland, New Zealand, 1936.

Katherine Anne Porter, "The Art of Katherine Mansfield"

This past fourteenth of October would have been Katherine Mansfield's forty-ninth birthday. This year is the fifteenth since her death. During her life she had a fabulous prestige among young writers in England and America. Her readers were not numerous but they were devoted. It must be a round dozen years since I have read any of her stories; reading them again in this recently collected edition, which contains some that are new to me, I am certain she deserved her fame, and I wonder why it was not greater.

Of late I find my interest diverted somewhat from her achievement as artist to the enigma of her personal history. Actually there is little in her work to justify this, since the work itself can stand alone without clues or notes as to its origins in her experience; a paper chase for autobiographical data in these stories may be interesting in itself, but it adds nothing to the value of the stories. They exist in their own right. Yet I find it impossible to make these few notes without a certain pre-occupation with her personal life of alternate flight and search; her beginnings in New Zealand, going to London to find the kind of place and the kind of people she wanted, her life there first as musician and then as writer; the many influences upon her mind and emotions of her friends and enemies—who in effect seem to have been interchangeable; her prolonged struggle with illness; her insoluble religious dilemma; her mysterious loss of faith in her own gifts and faculties; the disastrous failure of her forces at thirty-three, and the slowly engulfing despair that brought her finally to die at Fontainebleau.

These things are of first importance in a study which is yet to be done of the causes of Katherine Mansfield's own sense of failure in her work and in her life, but they do little to explain the work itself, which is superb. This misplaced emphasis of my attention I owe perhaps to her literary executor, who has edited and published her letters and journals with a kind of merciless insistence, a professional anxiety for her fame on what seems to be the wrong grounds, and from which in any case his personal relation to her might have excused him for a time. Katherine Mansfield's work is the important fact about her, and she is in danger of the worst fate that an artist can suffer—to be overwhelmed by her own legend, to have her work neglected for an interest in her "personality."

There are eighty-eight stories in this book, fifteen of which, her last, were left unfinished. The matter for regret is in these fifteen stories. Some of her best work is in them. She had been developing steadily, along a straight and fairly narrow path, working faithfully toward depth and concentration. Her handling of her material was firmer, her style had reached the flexibility of high tension and control, she had all her prime virtues and was shedding her faults, but her work had improved strictly in kind and not in difference. It is the same quick, ironic, perceptive mind, the same (very feminine) emotional nature, at work here from beginning to end.

In her the homely humility of the good craftsman toward his medium deepened slowly into a fatal self-distrust, and she set up for herself a standard of impossible perfection. It seems to have been on the grounds of the morality of art and not aesthetics that she began to desire a change in her own nature, who would have had quite literally to be born again to change. But the point is, she believed she could achieve a spiritual and mental rebirth by the practice of certain disciplines and the study of esoteric doctrines. She was innately religious, but she had no point of reference, theologically speaking; she was unable to accept her traditional religion, and she did finally, by what appears to have been an act of the will against all her grain, adopt means to make her fatal experiment in purification. As her health failed, her fears grew, her religious impulse wasted itself in an anxious straining toward some unknown infinite source of strength, of energy-renewing power, from which she might at the cost of single-hearted invocation find some fulfilment of true being beyond her flawed mortal nature. Now for her help and counsel in this weighty matter she had all about her, at difference periods, the advice and influence of John Middleton Murry, A.R. Orage, D.H. Lawrence, and, through Orage, Gurdjieff.

Katherine Mansfield has been called a mystic, and perhaps she was, but in the severe hierarchy of mysticism her rank cannot be very high. André Maurois only yesterday wrote of her "pure feminine mysticism." Such as it was, her mysticism was not particularly feminine, or any purer than the mysticism of D.H. Lawrence; and that was very impure matter indeed. The secret of her powers did not lie in this domain of her mind, and that is the puzzle: that such a good artist could so have misjudged herself, her own capacities and directions. In that rather loosely defined and changing "group" of variously gifted persons with whom Katherine Mansfield was associated through nearly all her working years, Lawrence was the prophet, and the idol of John Middleton Murry. They all were nervously irritable, self-conscious, and groping, each bent on painting his own portrait (The Young Man as Genius), and Katherine Mansfield's nerves suffered too from the teaching and the preaching and the quarreling and the strange vocabulary of ecstasy that threw a pall over any true joy of living.

She possessed, for it is in her work, a real gaiety and a natural sense of comedy; there were many sides to her that made her able to perceive and convey in her stories a sense of human beings living on many planes at once, with all the elements justly ordered and in right proportion. This is a great gift, and she was the only one among them who had it, or at least the only one able to express it. Lawrence, whose disciple she was not, was unjust to her as he was to no one else, and that is saying a good deal. He did his part to undermine her.

Mr. Murry's words in praise of her are too characteristic of the time and the special point of view to be ignored. Even today he can write that "her art was of a peculiarly instinctive kind." I confess I cannot understand the use of this word. That she was born with the potentialities of an artist, perhaps? I judge her work to have been to a great degree a matter of intelligent use of her faculties, a conscious practice of a hard-won craftsmanship, a triumph of discipline over the unruly circumstances and confusions of her personal life and over certain destructive elements in her own nature. She was deliberate in her choice of material and in her methods of using it, her technical resources grew continually, she cleared away all easy effects and tricky turns of phrase; and such mastership is not gained by letting the instincts have it all their own way.

Again Mr. Murry, in his preface: "She accepted life . . . she gave herself . . . to life, to love . . . she loved life, with all its beauty and pain . . . she responded to life more completely than any writer I have known except D.H. Lawrence. . . ."

Life, love, beauty, pain, acceptance, response, these are great words and they should mean something, and their meaning depends upon their exact application and reference. Whose life? What kind of love? What sort of beauty? And so on. It was this kind of explicitness that Katherine Mansfield possessed and was able to use, when she was at her best and strongest. She was magnificent in her objective view of things, her real sensitiveness to climate, mental or physical, her genuinely first-rate equipment in the matter of the five senses, and my guess, based on the evidence of her stories, is that she by no means accepted everything, either abstractly or in detail, and that whatever her vague love of something called Life may have been, there was as much to hate as to love in her individual living. Mistakenly she fought in herself those very elements that combined to form her virtue: a certain grim, quiet ruthlessness of judgment, an unsparing and sometimes cruel eye, a natural malicious wit, an intelligent humor; and beyond all she had a burning, indignant heart that was capable of great compassion. Read "The Woman at the Store," or "A Birthday," and "The Child-Who-Was-Tired," one of the most terrible of stories; read "The Fly,"and then read "Millie," or "The Life of Ma Parker." With fine objectivity she bares a moment of experience, real experience, in the life of some one human being; she states no belief, gives no motives, airs no theories, but simply presents to the reader a situation, a place, and a character, and there it is; and the emotional content is present as implicitly as the germ is in the grain of wheat.

Katherine Mansfield has a reputation for an almost finicking delicacy. She was delicate as a surgeon's scalpel is delicate. Her choice of words was sure, a matter of good judgment and a good ear. Delicate? Read, in "A Married Man's Story," the passage describing the prostitute who has been beaten, coming into the shop of the evil little chemist for his famous "pick-me-up." Or such a scene as the fat man spitting over the balcony in "Violet"; or the seduction of Miss Moss in "Pictures." "An Indiscreet Journey" is a story of a young pair of lovers, set with the delicacy of sober knowledge against the desolate and brutalized scene of, not war, but a small village where there has been fighting, and the soldiers in the place are young Frenchmen, and the inn is "really a barn, set out with dilapidated tables and chairs." There are a few stories which she fails to bring off, quite, and these because she falls dangerously near to triviality or a sentimental wistfulness, of which she had more than a streak in certain moments. But these are few, and far outweighed by her best stories, which are many. Her celebrated "Prelude" and "At the Bay," "The Doll's House," "The Daughters of the Late Colonel" keep their freshness and curious timelessness. Here is not her view of life but her many views of many kinds of lives, and there is no sign of even a tacit acquiescence in these sufferings, these conflicts, these evils deep-rooted in human nature. Mr Murry writes of her adjusting herself to life as a flower, etc.; there is an elegiac poesy in this thought, but—and remember I am judging by her pages here under my eye—I see no sign that she ever adjusted herself to anything or anybody, except at an angle where she could get exactly the slant and the light she needed for the spectacle.

She had, then, all her clues; she had won her knowledge honestly, and she turned away from what she knew to pursue some untenable theory of personal salvation under a most dubious teacher. "I fail in my personal life," she wrote in her journal, and this sense of failure infected her life as artist, which is also personal. Her decision to go to Fontainebleau was no whim, no accident. She had long been under the influence of Orage, her first publisher and her devoted friend, and he was the chief disciple of Gurdjieff in England. In her last finished story, "The Canary," a deep parable of her confusion and despair, occurs the hopeless phrase: "Perhaps it does not so much matter what one loves in this world. But love something one must." It seems to me that St. Augustine knew the real truth of the matter: "It doth make a difference whence cometh a man's joy."

"The Canary" was finished in July, 1922. In the October following she deliberately abandoned writing for a time and went into retirement at Fontainebleau, where she died suddenly and unexpectedly on the night of January 9, 1923. And so joined that ghostly company of unfulfilled, unhappy English artists who died and are buried in strange lands.

The Nation, October 23, 1937, vol. 145, p. 435.

Anonymous review of *Katherine Mansfield's Stories*

On January 9, 1923, Katherine Mansfield, in her thirty-fifth year, died at Fontainebleau. In the course of the following ten years there were published two posthumous collections of stories, her *Journal,* her letters, a collection of her reviews of novelists and a biography of her early life up till 1911. She had gained an assured position among English writers in her all too short lifetime, and the publication of her letters and *Journal* focused, at the time, a good deal of attention on this revelation of a remarkable personality. Now, for the first time, we have a complete collection of her stories, including *In a German Pension*— her first book (1911) which she refused to republish—without any comment except the original introductory notes to the two posthumously published volumes "The Doves' Nest" and "Something Childish," written by her husband, Mr. Middleton Murry. Her work as a whole is laid before today's public of voracious readers, to be enjoyed and judged, not only in the light of her contemporaries or of those who knew and remembered her, but in the light of circumstances and influences of which neither she nor they could have been prophetically aware.

A whole generation, racked by more pains and disasters than her own, has matured since she wrote, with a taste formed by other influences than those which moulded the minds of writers and readers in the nineteen-twenties. For instance, the adoration of Chekhov, to which Katherine Mansfield herself was prone, has resolved itself into a more reasonable attitude; the work, often brilliant, of both the "tough" and the "windy" schools of American fiction has had a profound effect; the gale of James Joyce has blown over the civilized world, while the inexorable waves of the poets' discontent, first a little petulant in "The Waste Land," grew to a powerful swell beating against the world's complacency. Above all, in the face of movements and events, the individual has seemed to recede into the mass, and the problems of people to transcend those of persons. The performance of every artist, if it is to survive, must stand the test of exposure to a world different from that in which he lived: so it is a good thing that Katherine Mansfield's should now stand alone in a comparatively alien world, to be judged by those to whom it comes fresh as well as by those who remember. Individual judgments will undoubtedly differ. To some her scope may seem narrow, to others her pity misdirected, to others again her very perfections insignificant, while the balance will be righted by quite contrary appreciations. A certain winnowing is bound to take place, but the finer grain, one may be sure, will survive.

In a recent radio discussion on reading aloud and what to read, one debater, a woman, decided for a story by Katherine Mansfield. It is no bad approach—though not conclusive—to the work of a short story-writer to consider which story to read aloud, presuming a congenial audience; for the short story, as a form, must possess many of the qualities necessary for effective "rendering." A definite pattern, a certain vivacity of colour, unity of emotion and singleness of purpose are some of these; and there will probably not be much disagreement with the view that, in Katherine Mansfield's stories which have the New Zealand background, these qualities are united in the highest degree. "Prelude," "At the Bay," "The Garden Party" and "The Doll's House," today no less than when they first appeared, present an immediacy of artistic achievement that she never surpassed. To say, as some might, that they are simply episodes which a great novelist—a Dickens or a Tolstoy—would have taken in his stride at the same artistic level is quite irrelevant. In their author's intention, of which she often confessed to falling short, they were complete in themselves, visions and memories of observed life painfully refined in the crucible of the reflective and creative brain until, purged of dross, they crystallized a gleam of that poetic truth by which alone art lives.

Although the ending of "The Doll's House" with its two out-cast waifs sitting by the dusty road and one comforting the other:

Presently our Else nudged up close to her sister. But now she had forgotten the cross lady. She put out a finger and stroked her sister's quill; she smiled her rare smile. "I seen the little lamp," she said softly. Then both were silent once more.

is a masterpiece, best of all is "At the Bay," simply a dawn to dusk of a pretty little bay between hills inhabited by quite ordinary mortals: business men who went to town after the morning dip, the grandmother who selflessly ran the house and looked after two tiny girls, the mother dreamy and withdrawn, her unmarried young sister all unsatisfied self, Alice the maid, her counterpart on a lower scale, a few neighbours, the sun, the wind and the moon. That is all. Day breaks as a frowsy old shepherd pilots his flock through the haze, the sun rises, people get up and do things and say things, are selfish or unselfish, wound or comfort, tempt or are tempted, all comparatively trivial as history but, to the artist's sense, composing a rhythm, almost palpable in the pre-creative reverie, elusive as Puck at the first creative grasp. One could compare "At the Bay" to music such as the first piece of Debussy's "La Mer" with which the effect of the first three pages, descriptive of that particular dawn, has something in common: but then comes a sharp transition from landscape to literature, when bustling Stanley Burnell plunges into the sea and finds there another human egoism against which to stub his own. Katherine Mansfield's poetry was not wholly compact of sensuous imagery or of pathos: it admitted satirical observation and a slightly astringent humour of very individual flavour, though she seems herself to have looked on these gifts, remarkably evident in the still delightfully fresh *German Pension* stories, with increasing suspicion as her artistic self matured and her striving for integrity became more agonized.

The fault of which Katherine Mansfield accused herself in one entry of her later Journal was triviality, a fault that she loathed. It would be an error on the part of anyone else lightly to accept and endorse this self-criticism in all its baldness, for, when she used the word "trivial" of her own published work, she did so to mark a failure to achieve a standard of "importance" so high that only the few attain it, and then only by the artistic equivalent of prayer and fasting. Nevertheless, a critic, understanding what she meant, may be allowed to use it in expressing the view that the part of her work least exposed to this reproach is that of the New Zealand stories. There are nearly twenty of these scattered about this volume, including one or two unfinished. They are not of equal merit, though some which she seems to have rejected, "The Woman at the Store," "Millie" and "Ole Underwood," especially the first, show a narrative power of high degree. When she desired to do so—and that was not often—Katherine Mansfield could make a story, as distinct from a sketch or a study or a prose lyric, with a sure and accomplished hand. By the standard of Maupassant, let us say, "Je ne parle pas français,"that brilliant little horror told by a pimp, "The Fly," in which a sadistic instinct sweeps away a sense of loss, "An Indiscreet Journey,"which is a tale of the first great war, and those tantalizingly unfinished tales, "The Married Man" and "The Dove's Nest," must surely gain high praise.

But there is present in the New Zealand tales something which is absent from the rest, considered as a whole: it is a definite background and environment, completely seized by the author's reflective memory, in which scenes and moods of childhood and young girlhood blend, and so rendered as to convey it clearly to the reader, with the result that every incident and touch of character make their effect, and the internal monologues, far from seeming trivial or haphazard, help to clinch the intended pattern. It was indeed a strange revenge on the part of that restricted life and society from which Katherine Mansfield almost savagely burst free that it became more and more a precious part of her inner, artistic self, and that, with a humility at times desperate, she continually wrestled to extract its essence. But so it was: and therefore Stanley Burnell, the "Pa" man, the brisk and selfless grandmother, dreamy Linda in love with her husband but not with her children, the vain, dissatisfied Beryl and the pathetic little child Kezia, have taken on the real unchangeable forms which, to use Pirandello's simile, the artist gives to the insubstantial characters that flock to him asking for life.

For various reasons, some of them connected with her own stormy temperament, Katherine Mansfield never again found an assured background for her creative imagination. During her year at Queen's College her mind had been opened, but not particularly well directed. There had not been enough to counteract the *fin de siècle* ideas, Oscar Wilde, Pater and so forth, then prevalent, so that when, after a protesting and uncomfortable return to her home, she finally insisted on coming to London to be a writer, both the geographical and the ideal goal were somewhat nebulous, nor did their outlines ever resolve themselves. This want of definition is patent as one reads through this collection, which it is, in a sense, unfair to do, since each story is, more or less, an achievement in itself. Even pictures, though hung together in galleries, have a frame; but the poor short story, in a book, has nothing to mark the necessary, intervening space for repose of the eye and contemplation. Yet, although its effect is exaggerated by juxtaposition, this impression of indefinite background and population is not to be gainsaid, as one passes from one slightly vague *milieu* to another—the Continental *pension*, the Riviera hotel, middle-class houses somewhere in western London and shadowy Bohemias with fluctuating standards of living.

"Bliss", for instance, is an episode in the life of the fairly well-to-do, on the borders of literary coteries, and the monologue of "The Lady's Maid" illustrates the under-side of an even more prosperous society; "Pictures" and "Life of Ma Parker" create for us tragic moments in the life of an ageing chorus-girl and an old charwoman, and the literary gentleman on whom the latter attends weekly lives in a state most squalid and insanitary. "Miss Brill," the spinster whose illusion is shattered by a chance word, "Mr. and Mrs. Dove," amorous and about to marry, and the dialogues of two egoists in "Psychology" and "A Dill Pickle" might be placed almost anywhere; and, while "The Daughters of the Late Colonel"—one of the very best in this kind—belongs somewhere near Harley Street, "The Young Girl," "Escape" and "The Man Without a Temperament" belong to that sad and beautiful coast where sick people went to get well and rich people to amuse themselves, both depending upon victims—husbands, daughters, companions—whose agonies of resignation and revolt our author so poignantly seizes. These fleeting registrations, then, beautifully as some of them are finished and deep as is their penetration into human emotions, suffer from want of a third dimension; without this, certain virtues of the short story, in particular, liveliness of movement and suggestion of impending drama, are impossible. One is presented, rather, with carefully chosen spectacles of life in the flat, the main vehicles being conversation and the reverie, which Katherine Mansfield, herself a self-confessed solitary who enjoyed the unobserved observation of her fellow-creatures at all their queer antics, handled supremely well, because she so deeply understood. Indeed, she sympathized, sometimes, to the verge of the sentimental. But the difficulty of progressing from the flat into the solid was not overcome. "Bliss" is an example. It opens dead on the note:

> Although Bertha Young was thirty she still had moments like this when she wanted to run instead of walk, to take dancing steps on and off the pavement, to bowl a hoop, to throw something up in the air and catch it again, or to stand still and laugh at— nothing—at nothing, simply. What can you do if you are thirty and, turning the corner of your own street, you are overcome, suddenly, by a feeling of bliss—absolute bliss!—as though you'd suddenly swallowed a bright piece of that late afternoon sun and it had burned in your bosom, sending out a little shower of sparks into every particle, into every finger and toe! . . .

And it goes on to represent Bertha's bliss for the rest of the afternoon and evening: feeding the baby, arranging the table for a dinner party and the arrival of the guests, the last a woman, seeming all the evening to share in her hostess's sense of magic to a pitch of intercommunication which culminates when Bertha draws aside the drawing-room curtains and shows her guest the pear tree flowering in the moonlight.

> How long did they stand there? Both, as it were, caught in the circle of unearthly light, understanding each other perfectly, creatures of another world, and wondering what they were to do in this one with all this blissful treasure that burned in their bosoms and dropped, in silver flowers, from their hair and hands?

It was an illusion. The intercommunication was due, not to a magic of mutual comprehension but to a common desire. Bertha, engaged in smart literary conversation with a young man, catches sight of her husband making love to Miss Fulton in the hall, and Miss Fulton departs, murmuring to her deluded hostess "Your lovely pear tree!" Whether this *coup de théâtre* comes off or not is beside the question. The ending is just this:

> Bertha simply ran over to the long windows. "Oh, what is going to happen now?" she cried. But the pear tree was as lovely as ever and as full of flower and as still.

As a "still" indeed it is quite successful: but what *was* going to happen? Not knowing Bertha or Harry her husband the reader cannot possibly guess, just as he could not guess what happened to the daughters of the late colonel when the first week of their freedom from the yoke, suggested with such infinite art, was over. But one ought to have a clue. A short story is not merely a picture; and even pictures by great artists give clues, by their handling of human feature and attitude. Moreover, the clue is there in Katherine Mansfield's New Zealand stories, because the space for drama and all its attributes accompanies the actual scene.

Many readers, no doubt, to whom her stories are new will wonder whether so sensitive an artist was aware, not only of her strength but of such defects as strike them as they read. They will then be led to read her Journal and her letters, and will find answered there some questions of that kind. They will learn, too, that in the last few months of her life she renounced writing altogether, for she was on the threshold, by her own confession, of some *vita nuova* infinitely richer both in wisdom and in inspiration. "If I had gone on with my old life," she wrote in a letter, "I never would have written again, for I was dying of poverty of life." In face of that renunciation, practically a disavowal of all her previous work, criticism, even the most appreciative, seems inept. Here is her work in truth, and how, finding much to praise, can we reject it? Yet Katherine Mansfield, as she passed out of sight, seems to have shed it like her mortal garment, leaving, for the last time, no clue.

The Times Literary Supplement, March 2, 1946, p. 102.

John Middleton Murry, "Katherine Mansfield"

Compiler's Note:
This study of Katherine Mansfield was delivered as a lecture in America in 1935 and re-cast in essay form. Although John Middleton Murry edited and published all Katherine Mansfield's works 'he very rarely wrote about her' (p.xiii) 'In fact, this study is his only full appreciation of her in existence.'

There are very few writers who have been put more fully into the possession of the public than Katherine Mansfield has been. Quite deliberately, as soon as possible after her death, I made it my duty to gather together and to publish her *Journal* and her *Letters*. It seemed to me a matter of cardinal importance that the world should know what manner of woman—or girl (for she wasn't much more when she died)—Katherine Mansfield was. If ever there were a writer whose life and work were one and inseparable, it was she. I can think only of Keats to compare with her in this respect, that her letters are essential to a real understanding of her work. They form a single whole with her stories: one naturally fulfils and completes the other. Indeed, there were moments when it seemed to me that her letters more completely expressed the nature of her genius than even the most remarkable of her stories. There have been moments when I have felt the same about the poetry and the letters of Keats.

When I set myself to publish the *Letters* and *Journal* of Katherine Mansfield, I was acting, not in a personal capacity, as a man eager to erect a memorial to one whom he had loved and lost, but as a conscious literary critic deeply convinced of the peculiar quality of Katherine's genius and determined to establish it before the world. I disregarded completely all the expostulations of those who—a little over-weeningly—professed to be more sensitive than I and tried to represent my action as the violation of an intimacy. Perhaps they were sincere; but I had made up my mind that Katherine Mansfield no longer belonged to me, but to the world. Above all, I believed it my duty to pass on what she herself had called her 'legacy of truth', and I believed that the world would find it as precious as I did.

> Honesty is the only thing one seems to prize beyond life, love, death, everything. It alone remaineth. O those that come after me, will you believe it? At the end, *Truth* is the only thing *worth having*; it's more thrilling than love, more joyful and more passionate.

And my confidence was justified, as I felt it would be. Today her *Journal* and her *Letters* are European classics.

I do not propose, therefore, to indulge in personal recollections of her. They are unnecessary; and if the reader should desire to know more about our ten years' life together, the full story is told in the first volume of my autobiography. For herself, in her habit as she lived, the *Journal* and *Letters* must suffice, together with the simple verdict of one of her most intimate friends: 'Katherine had a greater genius for being *simply a human being* than anyone I have ever known, or read of'.

It is a simple verdict, and a true one. It is implied in the fact that her *Letters* and *Journal* and her short stories are a single whole to an extent that can be paralleled only in the case of Keats. What does that really mean? It means that there was no difference in kind between her casual and her deliberate utterances; it means that her art was not really distinct from her life; it means that she was never what we understand by a professional writer; it means that she was distinguished by the peculiar gift of *spontaneity*.

I do not wish this word spontaneity to be misunderstood. It is not used to imply that Katherine Mansfield wrote as a bird sings, without effort. On the contrary, I hope to show that an effort—of a very arduous and particular kind—was involved in her writing. When I speak of the peculiar spontaneity of Katherine Mansfield's writing, I use the word in a critical sense precisely as I should apply it to Keats. Keats even in his short life passed through many periods of what he called *agonie ennuyeuse*, 'tedious agony', periods of creative sterility and inward despair. One such period intervened immediately before the writing of the great "Odes", which mark the topmost pinnacle of spontaneous utterance in our poetry since Shakespeare. Spontaneity in this critical sense, means an absence of any cleavage or separation between the living self and the writing self. The art corresponds to the human experience: every major advance in the art corresponds to a progression of some sort in the human being. When the human being is confused, at a standstill, bewildered in its own living experience, then the voice of the art is silent. Utterance comes only as the result of inward clarification. That, I think, makes clear what I mean: first, by claiming spontaneity as the distinguishing mark of Katherine Mansfield's genius, and second, by insisting so definitely that she was not a professional writer. She was not a person who constructed patterns of objective beauty; she was not a person who 'told stories'; she was essentially a person who responded—through the instrument of a 'more than ordinary organic sensibility'—to her experience of Life.

From the beginning Katherine Mansfield was marked by a curious eagerness for experience. Her youthful passion for the philosophy of Pater (who bade us 'burn with a hard gem-like flame') and Wilde, her early habit of keeping (and destroying) what she afterwards smilingly called those 'huge complaining diaries' —intimate records of her own experiences—of which only tiny fragments survive, her fierce determination not to be swallowed up again, after her English education, in the life of New Zealand; and, of course, earlier than all these, that intense and innocent childish awareness of life—of even the subtleties of adult psychology—which was afterwards to supply the substance of some of her most magical work: these were all symptoms of an intrinsic eagerness for experience which is in the last resort unanalysable. We have, as Walter Bagehot said, simply to accept the fact that the essential to a great artist is 'an experiencing nature'. Katherine Mansfield seems to have been born with one.

As is generally known, Katherine Mansfield went to London to 'finish' her education. There she became passionately enamoured of music and wanted to become a professional musician. Whether she would have realised her genius in that medium, I don't know. I am no judge of music. The fact that I used to think her playing and her singing marvellous means nothing—except that I am sure that had she so desired she could have achieved an extraordinary reputation as a *diseuse*. However,—instead of being allowed to stay on as a musician in London, she had to go back to New Zealand. She went, reluctantly and rebelliously.

Her development as a writer dates from her return to England in July 1908. It was by no means a triumphant return. Her family was bitterly opposed to her determination to go back to England; and she carried her way only after a fearful struggle. Her family had, naturally, not the faintest belief in her capacity to succeed as a writer. It was not a *possible* occupation for a New Zealand girl a generation ago; and they were resolved to give their rebellious daughter no more than the absolute minimum of help. And Katherine herself, in 1908, was undecided whether she would be a musician or a writer. Of the ensuing three years of her life—from 20 to 23—little is known: so far as might be, she deliberately destroyed all trace of it. Scarcely any of her journal entries remain— the one which does, and is printed at the beginning of the published *Journal*, bears witness to exhausting suffering, endured in isolation. The outcome of this period was the series of bitter and disillusioned sketches which were afterwards published as her first book—*In a German Pension* —in 1911. In after years it was only with the utmost reluctance that Katherine consented to have these sketches republished. She wanted to disown them completely. The same mood of embittered disillusion with life is expressed—I think more powerfully—in two stories of life in the New Zealand back-blocks which she wrote in the end of 1911. One of these—"The Woman at the Store"—she sent to me as editor of a small and unsuccessful literary review. I was deeply and durably impressed by it. And that is how we met. That I fell in love with her and she with me would be a matter of purely private significance: were it not that this happening—as was inevitable in one so constituted as she—had an effect upon her as a writer.

She was to write years afterwards, in a passage of her letters which will concern us later, that 'had she not known Love', the feeling of despair and hopelessness which had inspired her writing so far 'would have been her all'. But we hardly need her own plain statement to know that such a nature as hers would be deeply influenced by her love. Under the influence her work began to change. At first the readjustment was so confusing to her that she could not write at all. The bitterness and disillusion of her work so far were in conflict with her new experience: and only after many months emerged the story of "Something

Childish but very Natural", which is saturated with wistful and childlike idealism. This conflict between Love and Disillusion; Disillusion and Love which made its appearance at this time in Katherine Mansfield's life was to endure to the end. It is the ground pattern of her life and work.

I want to make clear the nature of this conflict. To understand it, is essential to an understanding of Katherine's genius; and an understanding of it enables us to grasp the singular likeness between the nature of Katherine and Keats to which I have already referred. What was the conflict? It was simply the conflict between the idealism of love and the bitterness of realising the cruelty of life—what Katherine called 'the snail under the leaf'. The conflict had begun before—there is not the faintest doubt. In those painful years concerning which she was so reticent, Katherine had stretched out eagerly to life: and she had been bitterly disappointed. The bitterness of which I have spoken—the savage and almost cynical realism of *In a German Pension* and "The Woman at the Store"—was the bitterness of a disappointed idealism. Now it had yielded before a new access of love: but after a year or two, partly through untoward circumstance, partly perhaps because of the character of her lover, but above all through the insidious encroachment of the war, the love again gradually gave way to disenchantment. In this particular realm we have a record of the process which was characteristic of Katherine, in a paragraph in her *Journal*.

> For a long time she said she did not want to change anything in him, and she meant it. Yet she hated things in him, and wished they were otherwise. Then she said she did not want to change anything in him, and she meant it. And the dark things that she had hated she now regarded with indifference. Then she said she did not want to change anything in him. But now she loved him so that even the dark things she loved, too. She wished them there; she was not indifferent. Still they were dark and strange, but she loved them. And it was for this that they had been waiting. They changed. They shed their darkness—the curse was lifted and they shone forth as Royal Princes once more, as creatures of light.

I quote that merely that we may have an authentic glimpse of the natural movement of Katherine Mansfield's soul. The reference is particular, but the movement itself is universal in her. In objective terms we may put it thus: she discovers and loves Beauty, then she discovers and hates the ugliness that seems to be inseparable from the Beauty—'the snail under the leaf'; then she becomes indifferent towards it; then, finally, she discovers and loves a new Beauty, in which the ugliness is included. This movement of the soul, which I have instanced in regard to her personal love, was exactly the same in the growth of her impersonal love—her love towards life itself. Love—disillusion—a new and more comprehensive love: that was the movement in the subject. Beauty—darkness—a new and more comprehensive Beauty: that was the reality in the object. She reveals essentially the same movement over and over again in her *Letters* and her *Journal*. Thus: 'Everything in life that we really accept *undergoes a change*. So suffering must become love. This is the mystery. This is what I must do. I must pass from personal to greater love.' And what was this impersonal love towards which she constantly strained? It was the power—to use the phrase of Keats—'of seeing Beauty *in all things*'. And to see the beauty of all things by the power of love was to see their truth. 'Why should one love?' she wrote. 'No reason; it's just a mystery. But it is like a light. I can see things truly, only in its rays.' Or again, 'Honesty (why?) is the only thing one seems to prize beyond life, love, death, everything. It alone remaineth. O those that come after me, will you believe it? At the end, *Truth* is the only thing *worth having*; it's more thrilling than love, more joyful and more passionate.' More thrilling (she means) than personal love, is the impersonal love that discovers the beauty of the total truth. It is hardly necessary to recall that this was precisely Keats's own final finding.

> Beauty is truth, truth beauty—that is all
> Ye know on earth, and all ye need to know.

§

Now, having laid as it were the groundwork of the pattern: before we consider in more detail how it was worked out in Katherine's live and writing, I will quote one simple example of the process at work, so to speak, in the very texture of her stories. I could choose any one of a dozen instances: but this one, for a good reason, is particularly dear to me:

'What are you looking at, my grandma? Why do you keep stopping and sort of staring at the wall?'

Kezia and her grandmother were taking their siesta together. The little girl, wearing only her short drawers and her under-bodice, her arms and legs bare, lay on one of the puffed-up pillows of her grandma's bed, and the old woman, in a white ruffled dressing-gown, sat in a rocker at the window, with a long piece of pink knitting in her lap. This room that they shared, like the other rooms of the bungalow, was of light varnished wood and the floor was bare. The furniture was of the shabbiest, the simplest. The dressing-table, for instance, was a packing-case in a sprigged muslin petticoat, and the mirror above was very strange; it was as though a little piece of forked lightning was imprisoned in it. On the table there stood a jar of sea-pinks, pressed so tightly together they looked more like a velvet pin-cushion, and a special shell which Kezia had given her grandma for a pin-tray, and another even more special which she had thought would make a very nice place for a watch to curl up in.

'Tell me, grandma,' said Kezia.

The old woman sighed, whipped the wool twice round her thumb and drew the bone needle through. She was casting on.

'I was thinking of your Uncle William, darling,' she said quietly.

'My Australian Uncle William?' said Kezia. She had another.

'Yes, of course.'

'The one I never saw?'

'That was the one.'

'Well, what happened to him?' Kezia knew perfectly well, but she wanted to be told again.

'He went to the mines, and he got a sunstroke there and died,' said old Mrs. Fairfield.

Kezia blinked and considered the picture again. . . . A little man fallen over like a tin soldier by the side of a big black hole.

'Does it make you sad to think about him, grandma?' she hated her grandma to be sad.

It was the old woman's turn to consider. Did it make her sad? To look back, back. To stare down the years, as Kezia had seen her doing. To look after *them* as a woman does, long after *they* were out of sight. Did it make her sad? No, life was like that.

'No, Kezia.'

'But why?' asked Kezia. She lifted one bare arm and began to draw things in the air. 'Why did Uncle William have to die? He wasn't old.'

Mrs Fairfield began counting the stitches in threes.

'It just happened,' she said in an absorbed voice.

'Does everybody have to die?' asked Kezia.

'Everybody!'

'*Me*?' Kezia sounded fearfully incredulous.

'Some day, my darling.'

'But, grandma.' Kezia waved her left leg and waggled the toes. They felt sandy. 'What if I just won't?'

The old woman sighed again and drew a long thread from the ball.

'We're not asked, Kezia,' she said sadly. 'It happens to all of us sooner or later.'

Kezia lay still thinking this over. She didn't want to die. It meant she would have to leave here, leave everywhere, for ever, leave—leave her grandma. She rolled over quickly.

'Grandma,' she said in a startled voice.

'What, my pet!'

'*You're* not to die.' Kezia was very decided.

'Ah, Kezia'—her grandma looked up and smiled and shook her head—'don't let's talk about it.'

'But you're not to. You couldn't leave me. You couldn't not be there.' This was awful. 'Promise me you won't ever do it, grandma,' pleaded Kezia.

The old woman went on knitting.

'Promise me! Say never!'

But still her grandma was silent.

Kezia rolled off the bed; she couldn't bear it any longer, and lightly she leapt on to her grandma's knees; clasped her hands round the old woman's throat and began kissing her, under the chin, behind the ear, and blowing down her neck.

'Say never . . . say never . . . say never—'

She gasped between the kisses. And then she began, very softly and lightly, to tickle her grandma.

'Kezia!' The old woman dropped her knitting. She swung back in the rocker. She began to tickle Kezia. 'Say never, say never, say never,' gurgled Kezia, while they lay there laughing in each other's arms. 'Come, that's enough, my squirrel! That's enough, my wild pony!' said old Mrs. Fairfield, setting her cap straight. 'Pick up my knitting.'

Both of them had forgotten what the 'never' was about.

The simplicity of that is very subtle. The grandmother who looks back on the death of her son, and finds that the sadness has departed—she represents, instinctively, the discovery of the Beauty of the whole Truth: the acceptance of suffering and death and its change by acceptance in Beauty, seen by the Love which is true wisdom. It is not peculiar to writers of genius. It is the wisdom of Life itself. But it takes genius to express it: to convey to us the simple and surpassing truth that *'life is like that .'* But Kezia, on the other hand, represents the Innocence which has not yet discovered 'the snail under the leaf'. For one startled, frightened moment a glimpse of the grim fact that life is not eternal nor love enduring breaks in upon her: and her world almost breaks into pieces. But Innocence, so complete, eludes the impact of Experience; just as in the grandmother experience has passed beyond itself and become Innocence once more. And so the exquisite counterpoint is resolved. Wisdom and Innocence become one. 'Say never, say never, say never. Both of them had forgotten what the "never" was about.' The consciousness of life is gathered back again into the soft instinctive flow of life itself. To my mind the effortless perfection of this simplicity, containing in its transparent depths the jewel of a serene life-wisdom, is a masterpiece of art. It is for this, and things like this, that H. G. Wells deliberately placed Katherine Mansfield's stories at their highest as belonging to a world beyond the ordinary 'world of effort and compromise', in which even writers of genius are condemned to struggle.

§

There is an inexplicable element in true literary genius; and I do not pretend wholly to explain the genius of Katherine Mansfield. But there are also elements in it which are, I think, explicable: elements, further, which have meaning for our common humanity. That astonishing simplicity of hers by which she renders some of the most complex and evanescent conditions of the human soul, responsive to the truth and beauty of life—that simplicity was not (as it has often been represented to be) in the main a technical achievement. It could not be. It was the consequence of a moral or spiritual victory won at the end of a long travail of soul: a sustained effort at self-purgation, of self-refinement into a condition of 'crystal clarity' for which Katherine Mansfield unconsciously struggled and towards the end of her life consciously prayed.

A peculiar, a unique circumstance in Katherine Mansfield's progress was that a crucial moment in the progress towards this condition of inward clarity was intimately connected with her attitude towards her own country, New Zealand, and her memories of it. She had suffered in New Zealand, unconsciously and silently as a little child, consciously and resentfully as an adolescent girl. For many years her resentment against New Zealand became as it were the symbol of her resentment against life itself; into her feeling against what seemed to her in youth the stupidity and cruelty of her own country towards her, she concentrated much of her bitterness against the general cruelty of life: what she called 'the snail under the leaf'; 'Pas de nougat pour le Noël'. A moment came when all this was changed.

This moment came when the cruelty of life had dealt her a deadly blow. In the spring of 1915 her only brother had come from New Zealand to serve in the war. He was six years younger than she, and she felt towards him all the affectionate and protective tenderness which a little child feels towards a baby; and since Katherine Mansfield had left New Zealand to be educated in England when she was fourteen and her brother seven, their common memories were childish memories. And how they used to talk about them! I remember only too well, because I was sensitive and very much in love and felt very much out of it. 'Do you remember? . . . Do you remember?'

In October 1915 the brother's training ended. He sailed gaily and confidently for France.

> 'It's so curious—my absolute confidence that I'll come back. I feel it's as certain as this pear.'
> 'I feel that, too.'
> 'I couldn't not come back. You know that feeling. It's awfully mysterious.'

Within ten days a Mills bomb had exploded in his hands.

The shock to Katherine Mansfield was tremendous; but it was a shock of a peculiar kind. It was scarcely a personal grief to her: it was the occasion of a complete upheaval. Suddenly, all her values went into the melting-pot: and one alone emerged—that was Love. She felt an imperious need to shed all the bitterness and cynicism which she thought were still part of her. And this love which suddenly became her supreme value was at once personal and impersonal. Without Love, she suddenly knew, there was no Truth.

> Why should one love? No reason; it's just a mystery. But it is like a light. I can see things truly only in its rays.

But that was written afterwards, when the victory was won, and she knew the nature of her own discovery. For the moment her experience was that her early life in New Zealand appeared extraordinarily precious to her. Why, she hardly knew. Sometimes she thought it was something which she had pre-eminently shared with her brother. But, in fact, it was because it was something which awakened Love in her. And the self which was utterly surrendered to this Love— this self which could live as it were only in the radiance of Love, was (she felt) a new Self. And so the act of writing "Prelude", which she began at this time in the South of France, and which she felt could only be written out of this new Self, was itself one continual effort towards a spiritual rebirth.

Hence the inward struggle (of which we have so precious a record in the *Journal*) with which the writing of the first draft of "Prelude" was accompanied. 'You know how unhappy I have been lately'; she wrote as though to her dead brother on February 14, 1916. 'I almost felt: Perhaps "the new man" will not live. Perhaps I am not yet risen. . . . But now I do not doubt.' At that moment her brother was to her the counterpart and companion of her new, unseen, unknown self, whom she was struggling to bring to birth; but it was only for that moment. In the exclusive personal way which these remarkable pages of her *Journal* might suggest to the unadvised reader, her brother was not so supremely important to Katherine Mansfield. He was a symbol and a part of that world of Innocence and Truth and Beauty which only Love could apprehend: and that world again was something far beyond the New Zealand which she was actually remembering. If she could overcome in herself her old resentment against her own country, if her bitterness against it could be dissolved 'in forgiveness of ancient injuries', if she could cease to feel that she personally had been wronged by New Zealand, then the truth and beauty of Life would emerge in it and through her.

It is not, perhaps, easy to explain; and perhaps I have failed in conveying the nature of a process which I believe I understand. Her brother's death was, at once, itself and more than itself. No doubt it was indeed his bitter ending, the mockery of his own triumphant confidence in his safe return from the war, which brought her up sharp and sudden against the bitterness of her own memory of New Zealand, the elusive purpose of her own life, and the necessity of hastening on towards the goal she felt she must reach. The death of her brother was indeed a decisive event in Katherine Mansfield's life and art; but as an occasion, not as a cause. It brought to her a moment of profound self-knowledge.

§

From this moment onward her life was consciously directed towards the achievement of inward clarity—crystal clarity. It was not an uninterrupted ascent: no human progress in this order can ever be. But the first great stage in the progress was indubitably the writing of the first draft of "Prelude". The purification of her memory of New Zealand, the purging of all resentment from her soul until that island could emerge, as from the waters of its own Pacific, with all the bloom and brightness of a new creation, was the outward and visible sign of the inward and spiritual grace. To be worthy of her new vision of New Zealand was to be worthy in an absolute sense; it was to have achieved a new condition of being—to have recaptured the vision of Innocence. She afterwards described what she had tried to do, in "Prelude", in these words:

> In the early morning there I always remember feeling that this little island has dipped back into the dark blue sea during the night, only to rise again at the gleam of day, all hung with bright spangles and glittering drops. I tried to catch that moment—with something of its sparkle and flavour. And just as on those mornings white silky mists arise and uncover some beauty, then smother it again and again disclose it, I tried to lift that mist from my people and let them be seen and then to hide them again. . . .
> It's so difficult to describe all this, and it sounds perhaps over-ambitious and vain. But I don't feel anything but an intense longing to serve my subject as well as I can.

It really *was* difficult to describe. Katherine Mansfield was striving to make firm her hold upon a new kind of vision of which she was now visited by glimpses. To the full possession of this vision—which we may call indifferently the vision of Imagination or of Love—one achievement was absolutely necessary. There must be a complete abeyance of the Self.

Naturally, Katherine Mansfield had to feel her way towards expression of the nature of this inward necessity. Sometimes, as we have seen, the emphasis is on a sort of rebirth; in the passage I have quoted, written in October 1917, it is to be completely occupied to the exclusion of all other feeling by 'an intense longing to serve my subject as well as I can'; or it is 'to be made crystal clear' for the divine light to shine through; or it is 'to be simple as one would be simple before God'. She expresses it in many different ways: some artistic, some unmistakably religious: but they all have essentially the same meaning. And they all belong to that rare province of human experience where art and religion are veritably one. It is the authentic discovery of the necessity of self-effacement—the compulsion whereby the artist (if he is faithful to his calling) becomes, according to the doctrine of William Blake, the priest of the Everlasting Gospel.

What that Everlasting Gospel is cannot be simply expressed in words; or if in words, the words are so simple that they are easily misunderstood in spite, or because, of the depth of meaning with which they are burdened. The most famous statement of it is the lines of Keats, already quoted:

> Beauty is truth, truth beauty.

This power to see and feel the beauty of the truth is a rare power, though I suspect there are moments when we all are visited by it. It is what has been called the Divine Love—the Love in whose light alone, as Katherine Mansfield said, she could see things truly. But this was not and could not be a steady and continuous power. It was achieved through a continual and recurrent resolution of the conflict between Love and Disillusion.

In February 1918 she was ill and alone in the South of France. She began to write a long, beautiful and strange story "Je ne parle pas Français". In sending it to me she wrote to explain its nature.

> I've two kick-offs in the writing game [she wrote in February 1918]. One is joy— real joy—the thing that made me write when we lived at Pauline, and that sort of writing I could only do in just that state of being in some perfectly blissful way at peace. Then something delicate and lovely seems to open before my eyes, like a flower without thought of a frost or a cold breath, knowing that all about it is warm and tender and 'ready'. And that I try, ever so humbly, to express.
> The other kick-off is my old original one, and *had I not known love* it would have been my all. Not hate or destruction (both are beneath contempt as real motives) but an extremely deep sense of hopelessness, of everything doomed to disaster. There! I got it exactly—a cry against corruption—that is absolutely the nail on the head. Not a protest—a cry.

A week later came the first severe hæmorrhage, as she bounded out of bed to greet the morning sun: the first grim warning of the reality of her disease.

That passage from her *Letters* is vital to any true understanding of Katherine Mansfield. First we need to remember that the months at the Villa Pauline when she could, and did, write out of a state of being in some perfectly blissful way at peace—was the time when she was writing "Prelude", and it was also the time when the unadvised reader of her *Journal* would imagine that she was sorrowing over the death of her brother. She was; nevertheless, in fact, it was a time of pure joy: of the self-effacement of love in writing and living.

But there was that other creative condition in Katherine Mansfield—what she calls an extremely deep sense of hopelessness: and this she says would have been her only creative condition, if she had not known love. The most astonishing examples of creation from this state are her stories "Je ne parle pas Français" and the unduly neglected "The Married Man's Story". There is nothing strained or forced in them: they spring naturally from a like attitude of self-effacement: only there is in them no joy.

These two conditions alternated incessantly in Katherine Mansfield. She goes out to the world in the self-abandonment of joy and love: or she withdraws into herself in despair and hopelessness. I do not think it is possible to choose between them, or to say that one more than the other is characteristic of Katherine Mansfield. It is the alternation itself which is characteristic of her: and above all characteristic of her letters.

But I think that as her work reached its final stage, before she gave up writing altogether, these two conditions became somehow blended together in her art. I have, myself, not much doubt that her two most perfect stories are two of her very last, written less than a year before her death: "The Doll's House" and "The Fly". They are both very short: and they have, to my sense, an absolute finality about them. I can define their quality only in a phrase of Keats: they have in them 'a sorrow more beautiful than beauty's self'.

How was this achieved? I have tried to outline the movement of her mind and heart. I think it can only be understood as following some such pattern as this: (1) a sort of bitter revulsion from life—which is characteristic of her work prior to "Prelude"; (2) a joyous and loving acceptance of life—which finds its first complete expression in "Prelude" (3) then a far more poignant disillusion with and revulsion from life—'nessum maggior dolore'—which found its first complete expression in "Bliss", and gradually deepened through experience into the very profound sense of hopelessness which finds expression in "Je ne parle pas"; and, finally, (4) an acceptance even of this hopelessness: and out of this acceptance comes the last perfection of her work. This final change is the most difficult of them all to understand: but we get a glimpse of the nature of the metamorphosis in a letter which she wrote to me in 1920.

> And then bodily suffering such as I've known for three years. It has changed for ever everything—even the *appearance* of the world is not the same—there is something added. *Everything has its shadow.* Is it right to resist such suffering? Do you know I feel it has been an immense privilege? Yes, in spite of all. How blind we little creatures are! It's only the fairy tales we *really* live by. If we set out upon a journey, the more wonderful the treasure, the greater the temptations and perils to be overcome. And if someone rebels and says, Life isn't good enough on those terms, one can only say 'It is!' Don't misunderstand me. I don't mean a 'thorn in the flesh'—it's a million times more mysterious. It has taken me three years to understand this—to come to see this. We resist, we are terribly frightened. The little boat enters the dark fearful gulf and our only cry is to escape—'put me on land again'. But it's useless. Nobody listens. The shadowy figure rows on. One ought to sit still and uncover one's eyes.
>
> I believe the greatest failing of all is to be *frightened.* Perfect Love casteth out Fear. When I look back on my life all my mistakes have been because I was afraid. . . . Was that why I had to look on death? Would nothing less cure me? You know, one can't help wondering sometimes. . . . No, not a personal God. Much more likely—the soul's desperate choice.

'The soul's desperate choice'—those final words seem to me profound indeed: the inmost secret of an ultimate religion is in them.

What did she mean? She meant this: that an experiencing nature which obeys the compulsion of experience, which accepts experience truly for what it is, which does not turn the head away or avert the eyes, becomes ultimately the vehicle of a final wisdom. By this submission of the self to Life, the chosen nature finally becomes an instrument for the utterance of Life's secret. In the last resort, if we are not content with superficial understanding, Katherine Mansfield can only be comprehended, or the comprehension of her expressed, in some such terms as William Blake used to express his experience. His effort towards self-annihilation—the sole condition, as he believed, of the true, the Divine Imagination—was renewed in her. By 1921 it had become the burden of all her thinking on her purpose and herself. She had struggled through the abyss of despair that had overtaken her when she realised, in her illness and isolation in France in February 1918, that her dream of happy love on earth was to be denied her (as it was denied to Keats, and as he also realised it, and as he also struggled out of his despair). Now, in 1921, a bare eighteen months before her death, she was troubled with these things no longer. Her one concern was to be the pure vehicle of experience. 'Marks of earthly degradation still pursue me,' she wrote on July 16. 'I am not crystal clear.' Then, suddenly in her effort to write "At the Bay" she achieves the condition.

> There's my Grandmother, back in her chair with her pink knitting, there stalks my Uncle over the grass; I feel as I write, 'You are not dead, my darlings. All is remembered, I bow down to you. I efface myself so that you may live again through me in your richness and beauty.' And one is *possessed*.

The grandmother with her pink knitting: and now we see out of what a condition of soul that perfect and profound simplicity was created. There is the doctrine, there is the experience, there is Art. That in the last resort is what the supreme achievement of art is—the utterance of Life through a completely submissive being.

In scope Katherine Mansfield was a tiny artist; but because she was a perfectly pure, and perfectly submissive, artist she was a great one. In this order of artistic achievement, the small is veritably great, and the great no greater. In this order, achievement is absolute or not at all. There is Art, and there is not-Art; and between them is precisely the absolute difference which the philosophers of the Christian religion sought so often to express, between the descent of the divine grace and the utmost effort of the conscious personal being to achieve it. As Blake said—the great artist who was isolated because he knew the ultimate identity of Christianity and Art—'We in *ourselves* are nothing'. And Katherine herself wrote to my brother:

> About religion. Did you mean 'the study of life' or Christ's religion 'Come unto me all ye that labour and are heavy laden and I will give you rest'? The queer thing is that one does not seem to contradict the other, to me. *If I lose myself in the study of life, and give up Self, then I am at rest.* But the more I study the religion of Christ the more I marvel at it. (29.3.22)

What may be the secret of this delicate and invincible integrity, no man dare say. It is perhaps enough that it should exist and that we should recognise and respond to it. But those who do recognise it see that it is manifest from the beginning in a strange compulsion to submit to experience. Between life and such natures the impact is not mitigated. It is naked all the while. Neither creed nor conception nor convention can interpose its comfortable medium. These natures are doomed, or privileged, to lead a life of 'sensations rather than of thoughts'. Such a life seemed, no doubt, good to Keats when he wrote those words, which after-generations have found it so easy to misunderstand; but he was to learn that as the joys of the immediate nature are incomparable, so are its sufferings; and that the time inevitably comes when the joy is suffering, and the suffering joy. For such natures, as though compelled by an inward law, return to the organic simplicity of the pre-conscious being; but in them that simplicity is enriched by all the subtleties of consciousness.

Of this simplicity in complexity—in life and art—Katherine Mansfield was a perfect example. She belonged, by birthright, to the 'experiencing natures'. They are sustained by some secret faith in life of which smaller souls are ignorant. They know what Blake meant when he proclaimed that 'the road of excess leads to the palace of wisdom'. They can take nothing in the matter of vital life-experience at second-hand. Always for them the truth must be proved as Keats said 'on their pulses'. And so, inevitably, in the eyes of the world they are not wise; for wisdom, in the world's eyes, consists precisely in refusing to expose ourselves to experience. The wise accept the report of others; of that great Other who is the worldly prudence of the race. They know that the Master of Life is a hard man, reaping where he did not sow, and they hide their talent in the earth. They take no risks with him.

And in this they *are* wise. But there is a greater wisdom than theirs. It is the wisdom which whispers 'Take the risk! If that is truly the urge of your secret soul, obey it. No matter what the cost, obey!' Or as D. H. Lawrence cried in his last and most lovely poem: 'Launch out, the fragile soul in the fragile ship of courage'. The same—identically the same image—that Katherine Mansfield used to express *her* final discovery, when she said 'The little boat enters the dark fearful gulf and our only cry is to escape—"put me on land again"'. But it's useless. Nobody listens. The shadowy figure rows on. One ought to sit still and uncover one's eyes'. Of what were these two friends speaking—in the same image? Of the same thing. Of the acceptance of Death and Suffering. Uncovering one's eyes before the final dark shadow of all existence—the supreme sadness— the type of all that pain and evil from which the soul seeks to avert its head. The death of the ideal, the death of love, the death that comes through the never-ending discovering of the snail under the leaf, the death of Bertha Young's happiness in "Bliss", the death of Laura's happiness in "The Garden Party"— these are all variations of the one unending theme.

But out of death always the birth of a new life: a new life doomed in turn to die, but destined always to be re-born, until the final acceptance of a complete self-surrender. Then, as Katherine said, 'Everything for ever is changed'. It is the final entry into what Blake called the world of true Imagination, which is Spiritual Sensation—a world of sensation because it is a world of immediate experience; a spiritual world, because it is not discerned by the five senses or their ratio which is the Intellect. It is beyond all these; yet it does not deny all these. The world—one is driven back to the phrase—of the 'beauty of the truth'.

> It seems to me [she wrote nine months before her death] that if Beauty were Absolute it would no longer be the kind of Beauty it is. Beauty triumphs over ugliness in life. That's what I feel. And that marvellous *triumph* is what I long to express. . . . I sit in a waiting-room where all is ugly, where it's dirty, dull, dreadful, where sick people waiting with me to see the doctor are all marked by suffering and sorrow. And a very poor workman comes in, takes off his cap humbly, beautifully, walks on tiptoe, has a look as though he were in church, has a look as though he believed that behind that doctor's door shone the miracle of healing. *And all is changed, all is marvellous.* It's only then that one sees for the first time what is happening. Life is, all at one and the same time, far more mysterious and far simpler than we know. It's like religion in that. *If we want to have faith, and without faith we die, we must learn to accept.* That's how it seems to me.

And so it is that if I had to choose one adjective to describe the essential quality of what she did and what she became, it would be the adjective 'serene'. And it seems to me that those who are responsive to her writing recognise this serenity—the serenity of a rainbow that shines through tears—and know that it comes from a heart at peace 'in spite of all'. Katherine could look back on her life, with all its miseries and all its brevity, and declare that 'in spite of all' it was good: that 'in spite of all' suffering was a privilege, pain the gateway to a deeper joy, sorrow the birth-pang of a new beauty. 'In spite of all'—the phrase, mysterious and simple as life, contains the secret of herself and her art. It is a phrase which more than any other echoes in my heart, with the sweetness of a long familiar pain, when I think back on what she was, and what she wrote from what she was. Beauty triumphs over Ugliness 'in spite of all'. In spite of all, the little lamp glows gently and eternally in "The Doll's House"; in spite of all the sleeping face of the dead man in "The Garden Party" murmurs that All is well; and though Ma Parker has nowhere to cry out her misery, she is beautiful for ever, in spite of all.

Katherine Mansfield and Other Literary Portraits, London, Peter Nevill Ltd., 1949, pp. 71-93.

Sam Hynes, "Katherine Mansfield: The Defeat of the Personal"

We are likely to be misled by Katherine Mansfield. We read her stories and see at once the surface of her writing—the impeccable style, the control, the exquisite sense of craft—and unconsciously we transfer that certainty to what she says; we confuse formal structure and moral structure. But in reality the moral structure of Miss Mansfield's work is as confused as her style is clear, as chaotic as her sense of form is precise. I should like to focus on that moral structure as a preliminary to an accurate evaluation of her worth as a writer.

We must start with definition. By moral structure I mean the terms to which the artist comes in his necessary compromise with reality, the view of the world which emerges from his work. The great artist develops toward some coherence and consistency in this structure (this is what we mean by artistic maturity); and this ultimate coherence is, or should be, an element in our final evaluation of the artist as artist. Literary value, then, is not equal to aesthetic value (it is here that we may err in evaluating Katherine Mansfield), but is the resultant of the aesthetic plus the moral. The Horatian dichotomy—pleasure and instruction— still defines in the simplest possible terms the way art works and the way we as critics must approach it.

This is not to assert any necessary correlation between ultimate value in art and a specific moral code: the Hound of Heaven has no predictable influence on literary merit. But it makes a difference whether or not the artist confronts the problem of man's relation to his world and resolves it. The resolution may be in Christian terms (as it is for T.S. Eliot, though this seems to me the most difficult position to reach in our time) or in non-Christian terms (those of Hardy and Conrad, for example). But whatever the conclusions, the artist will not turn away from the problem, he will not cease to struggle with it, and he will not be defeated by it. From the work of the greatest artists a moral certainty at last shines out.

Katherine Mansfield never achieved this quality of certainty in her stories, never came to terms with the world, never achieved maturity in this sense. She does not, in fact, seem to have developed at all except in the purely technical sense of increasing verbal felicity. Because of this lack of development in the writer as 'moral voice', the collected stories seem monotonous and repetitious and have the final effect of variations on a single immature theme. Monotony is most apparent in the point of view. We see the action of almost every story through the eyes of the child-heroine; this is true not only of the Kezia stories, but also of a great many in which the heroine is nominally an adult. Miss Mansfield's women are uniformly immature, horrified by the physical, repelled by sex and birth and the aggressiveness of men. "If only he wouldn't jump at her so"—Kezia's mother is thinking of her husband—"and bark so loudly, and watch her with such eager, loving eyes. He was too strong for her; she had always hated things that rush at her, from a child." Kezia and her mother share a common vision of the world, the vision of a sensitive, defenseless child, cowed by the grossness and gratuitous brutality of the outer, adult world. This vision provides the 'moral structure' of Miss Mansfield's work as a whole. There is little variation.

In the early story "A Wedding", the theme of the child-heroine versus the brutality of life is most overt; the women at the wedding feast see the bride as a sacrifice to male cruelty and violence. "Girls have a lot to learn," the central figure, Frau Brechenmacher, observes sadly; in typically Mansfield fashion she sees girlhood as a transitory period of perfect innocence, from which one is ravished by the world. While the music is playing she becomes "almost like a girl again," but her escape is brief. She goes home at last; her husband enters her bedroom. "Then even the memory of the wedding faded quite. She lay down on the bed and put her arm across her face like a child who expected to be hurt as Herr Brechenmacher lurched in." Few of the stories of children are free of this theme of adult brutality. It varies from the benevolent persecutions inflicted upon Kezia by her father to the grotesque sadism of "The Child Who Was Tired," a story which rivals "Way Down East" for gratuitous sentimentality. But regardless of the quality of the writing, the pattern is the same: authority, the world of adults, is viciously cruel to the child or the child-woman, who has no chance to escape, but must submit and be crushed.

It is not strange that Miss Mansfield chooses to state this theme most frequently in flowery imagery; flowers are beautiful, delicate, and transitory—like the innocence of childhood. Linda Burnell in "At the Bay" observes:

> If only one had time to look at these flowers long enough, time to get over the sense of novelty and strangeness, time to know them! But as soon as one paused to part the petals, to discover the under-side of the leaf, along came Life and one was swept away. . . . Along came Life like a wind and she was seized and shaken; she had to go. Oh dear, would it always be so? Was there no escape?

The answer, of course, is no. The child-heroine is sensitive and weak and flower-like; the adult world (which is masculine) is insensitive and strong. Willy-nilly, it will win out.

Katherine Mansfield never lost this frightened child's view of the world; she never found the terms by which she could accept the existence of evil, which is, perhaps, what the moral problem amounts to in the end. She chose instead the solution which is no solution, withdrawal. In her stories this is evidenced in escape fantasies like "How Pearl Button Was Kidnapped" and more elaborately in the retreat into her own childhood, which characterizes her work after 1915, the year in which her brother was killed in the war. Middleton Murry describes the development of this retreat in his Introduction to the *Collected Stories*:

> The war had come as a profound spiritual shock to her, as it did to many less gifted writers of her generation. For a long period the chaos into which her thoughts and ideals and purposes had been flung remained unresolved. Then slowly her mind began to turn back towards her early childhood as a life which had existed apart from, and uncontaminated by, the mechanical civilization which had produced the war.

Murry seems to regard this withdrawal as meritorious, and certainly the New Zealand stories which it produced are among Miss Mansfield's best. But they are escapist stories, the artist denying the reality of death by reversing time to the point at which death had not occurred. Time, unfortunately, is not reversible; the stories are weakened by the fact that they seek, not to assert the truth of the past, but to deny the truth of the present. "The present and the future," she wrote in her *Journal* at this time, "mean nothing to me. I am no longer 'curious' about people; I do not wish to go anywhere; and the only possible value that anything can have for me is that it should put me in mind of something that happened or was when he [her brother] was alive." Granted that this was written in an excess of grief, the attitude endured.

The *Journal* also records in considerable detail the development of escapism in Miss Mansfield's personal life, not the physical moves, which seem to have been dictated largely by the state of her health, but the development of an aestheticism which came to substitute, as it always does, art for life. Murry mentions Miss Mansfield's early admiration for Oscar Wilde and the English 'decadents'; the resemblances between her work and theirs is constantly apparent. Work became for her an ultimate value.

> Shall I be able to express one day my love of work—my desire to be a better writer—my longing to take greater pains. And the passion I feel. It takes the place of religion—it *is* my religion—of people—I create my people; of 'life'—it *is* Life. The temptation is to kneel before it, to adore, to prostrate myself, to stay too long in a state of ecstasy before the *idea* of it. I must be more busy about my master's business. (*Journal*, May 31, 1919).

To have worked each day was to exist in a state of grace; life was an interruption. But art is not life, as it is not religion; to attempt to substitute one for another is likely to make a failure of both.

The *Journal* of the last years shows a growing awareness of such failure. Trenchant criticisms of her work become more frequent; there is dissatisfaction with what she had done, despair over what she had not done. The failure is often stated as failure to capture truth artistically; but the problem is not, as she seemed to think, a purely aesthetic one. It is difficult to see how, given the framework, the 'moral structure' within which she worked, Miss Mansfield could have developed further. There is some evidence that, at the end, she was aware of the moral failure of her work. In a *Journal* entry for January 27, 1920, she wrote: "At the back of my mind I am so wretched. But all the while I am thinking over my philosophy—the defeat of the personal." "The defeat of the personal"—the phrase is tempting, ambiguous. Does she mean that the world destroys individuality, or that the individual must somehow achieve the defeat of himself, as a kind of exercise in purification? The evidence of the stories (in which the defeat of the sensitive soul by the world is an obsessive theme) supports the former interpretation. But the *Journal* suggests the latter, a new and radically different personal orientation.

This new 'moral structure,' which the *Journal* suggests in scattered entries rather than states, lay in a conscious suppression of the self, a facing outward which was the opposite of her entire attitude toward life. In literary terms, this would be a turn from romantic egocentricity, in which the external exists as stimulus for internal disturbances, toward the cold classicism that Eliot postulates when he says, "The progress of the artist is a continual self-sacrifice, a continual extinction of the personality." In individual, human terms 'the defeat of the personal' was a quest for salvation, aimless yet desperate, based on a sense (strong in the later entries of the *Journal),* that not only her art, but also her life had been a failure. This quest led at one point toward the Roman Catholic church, at another to Cosmic Anatomy; it ended in uncertainty. The *Journal* ends in October, 1922. The writer was near death then and knew it (she died three months later). She had written little in the last months; Murry records that "writing had become for her an almost impossible struggle, not only against disease, but against an inward conviction that some work of inward purification had to be accomplished before she could go forward. . . ." Yet her last words were: "I feel happy—deep down. *All is well.*"

And was it? For Katherine Mansfield as a writer we must conclude that it was not. 'The defeat of the personal' is not evident in the last stories, except in the earlier, immature sense of the phrase. There is still the sensitive victim, the child-heroine, still the brutal, incomprehensible world. The terms remain the terms of the earliest stories. Katherine Mansfield was aware at the end that she could not 'go forward.' To do so as an artist (and, we may add, as a person, though such considerations are beyond the scope of this essay) required that compromise with reality which is the mark of artistic maturity. It was a compromise she could not make; and so her work remains for us no more than an elaboration of its first terms, static in its perceptions, limited in its scope, and, at heart, sentimental and confused in its moral structure. It remains the lifelong expression of a wounded child's sensibilities, often brilliant, but in the end insufficient, because to the end immature.

South Atlantic Quarterly, vol. 52:4, October 1953, pp. 555-560.

Elizabeth Bowen, "A Living Writer"

If Katherine Mansfield were living, she would this year be sixty-eight. Is this fact out of accord with our idea of her? Sometimes it may be that an early death so fixes our image of a person that we cannot envisage them any older. Youth comes to seem an attribute of the personality—in the case of a beautiful woman or romantic artist, both of which Katherine Mansfield was, this happens particularly often. Yet in the case of Katherine Mansfield it seems particularly wrong. For one thing, we lose much and deny her something if we altogether banish her in imagination from the place she could have had in our own time. For another, she had no desire whatever to be 'spared' life or anything further it could bring. Useless as it is to lament her going, let us not forget she would have stayed if she could, and fought to do so with savage courage.

True, she could not have gone on as she was; she was far too ill. To restore health, at the stage her illness had reached, would have taken a miracle—she sought one. Could that have been granted, a fresh start, one can think of few people more fitted than Katherine Mansfield to have aged without decline, ignominy or fear. One can picture her at sunset, but not in twilight. Born with good nerve, she had learned comprehensive courage, and in a hard school. In spite of setback after setback, she was already on her own way towards equilibrium. Her spirit was of the kind which does not die down. Her beauty, even, was of the enduring kind, hardy and resolute in cast as it was mysterious in atmosphere—nor need one imagine her without the peculiar personal magic she emanated: a magic still so much part of her legend. Already she was 'old' in imagination—up to any age, would she not have been young in temperament?

She was drawn to old people, seeing them as victors. They stood to her for vision, and for the patience she so impatiently longed to have. (She was aware, of course, also of ancient monsters.) Is it too much to say that she envied old age, and the more so as her own hopes of attaining it grew slender? But one does not waste desire on the unlikely: her real need was pressing, and grew obsessive—she needed time, time in which to achieve 'a body of work'. By now, she would have had thirty-four years more. Enough? I suspect that in the extreme of her desperation she would have been content to compound for ten. There is never enough of the time a writer wants—but hers was cut so short, one is aghast. The more one sees the fulfilment in her work, the more one is awed by its stretching promise. The perfectedness of the major pieces sets up anguish that there could not be more of them. Equally, I may say that a fellow writer cannot but look on Katherine Mansfield's work as interrupted, hardly more than suspended, momentarily waiting to be gone on with. Page after page gives off the feeling of being still warm from the touch, fresh from the pen. Where is she—our missing contemporary?

2

'Katherine Mansfield's death, by coming so early, left her work still at the experimental stage.' This could be said—but would it be true? To me, such a verdict would be misleading, for two reasons. First, her writing already *had* touched perfection a recognisable number of times; second, she would have been bound to go on experimenting up to the end, however late that had come. One cannot imagine her settling down to any one fixed concept of the short story—her art was, by its very nature, tentative, responsive, exploratory. There are no signs that she was casting about to find a formula: a formula would, in fact, have been what she fled from. Her sense of the possibilities of the story was bounded by no hard-and-fast horizons: she grasped that it is imperative for the writer to expand his range, never contrast his method. Perception and language could not be kept too fresh, too alert, too fluid. Each story entailed a beginning right from the start, each brought unknown demands, new risks, unforeseeable developments. Often, she worked by trial-and-error.

So, ever on the move, she has left with us no 'typical' Katherine Mansfield story to anatomise. Concentrated afresh, each time, upon expression, she did not envisage 'technique' in the abstract. As it reached her, each idea for a story had inherent within it its own shape: there could be for it no other. That shape, it was for her to perceive, then outline—she thought (we learn from letters and journal) far more of perception than of construction. The story *is* there, but she has yet to come at it. One has the impression of a water-diviner, pacing, halting, awaiting the twitch of the hazel twig. Also, to judge from her writings about her writing, there were times when Katherine Mansfield believed a story to have a volition of its own—she seems to stand back, watching it take form. Yet this could not happen apart from her: the story drew on her steadily, into itself.

Yet all of her pieces, it seems clear, did not originate in the same order. Not in all cases was there the premonitory stirring of an idea: sometimes the external picture came to her first. She found herself seized upon by a scene, an isolated incident or a face which, something told her, must *have* meaning, though she had yet to divine what the meaning was. Appearances in themselves could touch alight her creative power. It is then that we see her moving into the story, from its visual periphery to its heart, recognising the 'why' as she penetrates. (It could seem that her great scenic New Zealand stories came into being by this process.) Her failures, as she uncompromisingly saw them, together with her host of abandoned fragments, give evidence of the state of mind she voices in anguished letters or journal entries—the sensation of having lost her way. She could finish a story by sheer craftsmanship; but only, later, to turn against the results.

Able and fine as was her intelligence, it was not upon that that she depended: intuitive knowing, vision, had to be the thing. She was a writer with whom there could be no secondary substitute for genius: genius was vision. One might speak of her as having a burning gaze. But she faced this trouble—vision at full intensity is not by nature able to be sustained; it is all but bound to be intermittent. And for Katherine Mansfield those intermittences set up an aesthetic disability, a bad, an antipathetic working condition. Under such a condition, her work abounded, and well she knew it, in perils peculiar to itself. She dreaded sagging of tension, slackening of grip, flaws in interior continuity, numbness, and, most of all, a sort of synthetic quality which could creep in. She speaks of one bad day's work as 'scrappy and dreamy'. Dreaminess meant for her, dilution.

Subjects, to be ideal for Katherine Mansfield, had first to attract, then hold, her power called vision. There occurred a false dawn, or false start, when a subject deceived her as to its possibilities—there were those which failed her, I feel, rather than she them. We must consider later which kind or what range of subject stood by her best, and why this may have been so. There was not a subject which did not tax her—raising, apart from anything else, exacting problems of treatment, focus and angle. Her work was a succession of attempts to do what was only just not impossible. There is danger that in speaking of 'attempts' one should call to mind those which have not succeeded: one forgets the no less attempt which is merged in victory. Katherine Mansfield's masterpiece stories cover their tracks; they have an air of serene inevitability, almost a touch of the miraculous. (But for the artist, remember, there are no miracles.) Her consummate achievements soar, like so many peaks, out of the foothills of her working life—spaced out, some nearer together in time than others. One asks oneself why the artist, requited thus, could not have been lastingly reassured, and how it could have happened that, after each trough of frustration, anxiety, dereliction should have awaited her once again?

The truth was, she implacably cut the cord between herself and any completed story. She admits, in the journal: 'It took me nearly a month to "recover" from "At the Bay". I made at least three false starts. But I could not get away from the sound of the sea, and Beryl fanning her hair at the window. These things would not *die* down.' She must not look back she must press forward. She had not time to form a consistent attitude to any one finished story: each stood to her as a milestone passed, not as a destination arrived at. Let us say, she reacted to success (if in Katherine Mansfield's eyes there were such a thing) as others react to failure—there seemed to be nothing left but to try again.

To be compelled to experiment is one thing, to be in love with experiment quite another. Of love for experiment for its own sake, Katherine Mansfield shows not a sign. Conscious artist, she carries none of the marks of the self-consciously 'experimentary' writer. Nothing in her approach to people or nature is revolutionary; her story-telling is, on its own plane, not much less straightforward than Jane Austen's. She uses no literary shock tactics. The singular beauty of her language consists, partly, in its hardly seeming to *be* language, so glass-transparent is it to her meaning. Words had but one appeal for her, that of speakingness. (In her journal we find, noted, 'The *panting* of a saw.') She was to evolve from noun, verb, adjective, a marvellous sensory notation hitherto undreamed of outside poetry; nonetheless she stayed subject to prose discipline. And her style, when the story-context requires, can be curt, decisive, factual, abrupt. It is a style generated by subject and tuned to mood—so flexible as to be hardly *a* style at all. One would recognise a passage from Katherine Mansfield not by the manner but by the content. There are no eccentricities.

Katherine Mansfield was not a rebel, she was an innovator. Born into the English traditions of prose narrative, she neither turned against these nor broke with them—simply, she passed beyond them. And now tradition, extending, has followed her. Had she not written, written as she did, one form of art might be still in infancy. One cannot attribute to Katherine Mansfield the entire growth, in our century, of the short story. Its developments have been speedy, inspired, various; it continues branching in a hundred directions, many of which show her influence not at all. What she did supply was an immense impetus—also, did she not first see in the short story the ideal reflector of modern day? We owe to her the prosperity of the 'free' story: she untrammelled it from conventions and, still more, gained for it a prestige till then unthought of. How much ground Katherine Mansfield broke for her successors may not be realised. Her imagination kindled unlikely matter; she was to alter for good and all our idea of what goes to make a story.

3

She could have been a writer of more than one kind. Alternations went on throughout her working life. In her letters appears a brusque, formidable, masculine streak, which we must not overlook in the stories. Her art has backbone. Her objectiveness, her quick sharp observations, her adept presentations—are these taken into account enough? Scenically, how keen is her eye for the telling detail! The street, quayside, café, shop interior, teatime terrace or public garden stand concretely forward into life. She is well documented. Her liking for activity, for the crowd at play, for people going about their work, her close interest in process and occupation, give an extra vitality to stories. Admire the evening Chinamen in "Ole Underwood", or Alice, the servant in "At the Bay", taking tea with Mrs. Stubbs of the local store.

She engraves a scene all the more deeply when it is (as few of her scenes are not) contributory to a mood or crisis. Here, at the opening of "The Voyage", are the awarenesses of a little girl going away with her grandmother after her mother's death:

> The Picton boat was due to leave at half-past eleven. It was a beautiful night, mild, starry, only when they got out of the cab and started to walk down the Old Wharf that jutted out into the harbour, a faint wind blowing off the water ruffled under Fenella's hat, and she had to put up a hand to keep it on. It was dark on the Old Wharf, very

dark; the wool sheds, the cattle trucks, the cranes standing up so high, the little squat railway engine, all seemed carved out of solid darkness. Here and there on a rounded woodpile, that was like the stalk of a huge black mushroom, there hung a lantern, but it seemed afraid to unfurl its timid quivering light in all that blackness; it burned softly, as if for itself.

Fancifulness, fantastic metaphor, play more part in her London (as opposed to New Zealand) scene-setting. Less seems taken for granted. "The Wrong House" furnishes one example. Here, in a residential backwater, an unloved old woman looks out of a window:

> It was a bitter autumn day; the wind ran in the street like a thin dog; the houses opposite looked as though they had been cut out with a pair of ugly steel scissors and pasted on to the grey paper sky. There was not a soul to be seen.

This factual firmness of Katherine Mansfield's provides a ballast, or antidote, to her other side—the high-strung susceptibility, the all but hallucinatory floatingness. Nothing is more isolated, more claustrophobic than the dream-fastness of a solitary person—no one knew the dangers better than she. Yet rooted among those dangers was her genius: totally disinfected, wholly adjusted, could she have written as she did? Perhaps there is no such thing as 'pure' imagination—all air must be breathed in, and some is tainting. Now and then the emotional level of her writing drops: a whimsical, petulant little-girlishness disfigures a few of the lesser pieces. And some others (how she disliked these) are febrile, or show a transferred self-pity. She could not always keep up the guard.

Katherine Mansfield was saved, it seems to me, by two things—her inveterate watchfulness as an artist, and a certain sturdiness in her nature which the English at their least friendly might call 'colonial.' She had much to stand out against. She was in danger of being driven, twice over, into herself—by exile to begin with, then by illness. In London she lived, as strangers are wont to do, in a largely self-fabricated world.

She lived, indeed, exactly the sort of life she had left New Zealand in hopes of finding. Writers and intellectuals surrounded her—some merely tempestuous, some destructive. She accustomed herself to love on a razor's edge. Other factors made for deep insecurity. She and her husband were agitatingly and endlessly short of money; for reasons even other than that they seemed doomed to uproot themselves from home after home. As intelligenzia, they were apt to be preyed upon by the intelligenzia-seeking sub-*beau monde*—types she was to stigmatise in "Bliss" and again in "Marriage à la Mode". Amid the etherealities of Bloomsbury she was more than half hostile, a dark-eyed tramp. For times together, there was difficulty as to the placing of her stories; individually, their reception was uncertain; no full recognition came till she published the volume *Bliss*. In England she moved, one gets the impression, among nothing but intimates or strangers—of family, familiar *old* friends, neighbours, girlhood contemporaries, there were none. Habits, associations were lacking also: here was a background without depth, thwarting to a woman's love of the normal. From this parched soil sprang the London stories.

To a degree it was better, or always began by being better, in the South of France. She felt a release among Mediterranean people; and the Midi light reminded her of New Zealand's. It was at Bandol, late in 1915, that she began "The Aloe", original version of "Prelude", and thereby crossed a threshold. At Bandol was suffered the agony out of which the story had to be born. She had retreated to Bandol to be alone with loss: her brother Chummie, over with the army from New Zealand, had been killed fighting in France. His last leave, before going to the front, had been spent with Katherine in London. That same month, late at night in her sea-facing French hotel room, she wrote in her journal:

> The present and future mean nothing to me. I am no longer 'curious' about people; I do not wish to go anywhere; and the only possible value that anything can have for me is that it should put me in mind of something that happened or was when we were alive.
> 'Do you remember, Katie?' I hear his voice in the trees and flowers, in scents and light and shadow. Have people, apart from these far-away people, ever existed for me? Or have they always failed me and faded because I denied them reality? Supposing I were to die as I sit at this table, playing with my Indian paper-knife, what would be the difference? No difference. Then why don't I commit suicide? Because I feel I have a duty to perform to the lovely time when we were both alive. I want to write about it, and he wanted me to. We talked it over in my little top room in London. I said: I will just put on the front page: To my brother, Leslie Heron Beauchamp. Very well, it shall be done.

That winter, though she had other maladies, tuberculosis had not declared itself. When it did, South of France winters became enforced. War continued, the wind whistled, *volets* clattered, the Mediterranean Sea turned to black iron. She burned, shivered, coughed, could not bear herself, wrote, wrote, wrote. 1919-20 brought the Italian nightmare, Ospedaletti. These weeks, months, in cut-price hotels, ramshackle villas, were exile twice over, exile with doubled force. One man's letters from London were the life-line, and letters did not invariably come. Who can measure the power of that insatiable longing we call homesickness? Home, now she was torn from it, became hers in London. She thought of the yellow table, the Dresden shepherdess, the kitten Wingley—growing up without her. Loneliness, burning its way into Katherine Mansfield, leaves its indelible mark upon her art.

She wrote the august, peaceful New Zealand stories. They would be miracles of memory if one considered them memories at all—more, they are what she foresaw them as: a re-living. And, spiritually as in art, they were her solution. Within them fuse the two Katherine Mansfields: the sturdy soul and the visionary are one. The day-to-day receives the full charge of poetry.

> And now one and now another of the windows leaped into light. Someone was walking through the empty rooms carrying a lamp. From a window downstairs the light of a fire flickered. A strange beautiful excitement seemed to stream from the house in quivering ripples.

This is the child Kezia's first, late-night sight of the Burnells' new home. Katherine Mansfield the artist is also home-coming.

Cornhill Magazine, No. 1010, Winter 1956-7, pp. 120-130.

III

New Approaches

Ian A. Gordon, "The Editing of Katherine Mansfield's *Journal* and *Scrapbook*"

The recent acquisition by the Government of New Zealand on behalf of the Alexander Turnbull Library in Wellington of a group of Katherine Mansfield's notebooks and papers (sold at auction for the estate of the late John Middleton Murry) offers for the first time the opportunity of studying her writing at the workshop pre-publication stage. The Library has also acquired, as a separate transaction, the originals of the letters she sent to her husband. These, at the time of writing, are on exhibition in London: but the group of some fifty items secured at auction has arrived in the Library and has been carefully examined. An analytical catalogue is in preparation.

Even the first cursory examinations suggested that in these papers lay much of the material of the *Journal*. Closer examination has revealed that the Turnbull Library now possesses the complete original 'manuscript' of the *Journal* (published in 1927), the *Scrapbook* (published in 1939) and the 'definitive edition' of the *Journal* (published in 1954). Of the entire text of the fifty items, approximately twenty-five per cent has never been published. The date of the earliest item is 1901, when the author was still at school; the date of the latest is 1922, a few weeks before her death.

The material is of various types. Firstly there is a set of diaries—the ordinary printed kind one can buy at any stationer. These are for the years 1914, 1915, 1920, and 1922. They are surprisingly empty. The 1914 diary has entries mainly for March and April. The others are like everybody else's diary—they begin with good intentions (sometimes expressed) and fill up January day by day. By mid-February the enthusiasm has cooled. From March onwards the pages are generally blank.

Next comes a group of about thirty notebooks. Some are dated by the author—usually with the precise date on which the note-book was started. Others are dated by Murry in a pencil note. The remainder can be dated fairly precisely from internal evidence. The contents of the notebooks are multifarious. There are drafts of stories and many dozens of brief conversations and scenes from stories—quite obviously Katherine Mansfield set down often on the spur of the moment short pieces of material that she was later to incorporate into a complete story. These pieces may come anywhere in the completed story—there are many more 'middle' pieces than beginnings. There are notes from her reading, with or without her comments, quotations copied from Shakespeare, Hardy, Tolstoy and many other authors; calculations of her finances; lists of household expenses in astonishing detail (dinner at 12.15 francs; a lemon at 40 centimes); comments on the people she liked and disliked; comments (sometimes years later) on what she had written previously in a notebook; occasionally a dated 'diary' type entry on what she was doing or thinking at the moment. She often wrote her letters in her working notebook, tearing out the pages for posting. Occasionally she has decided not to send a letter, and it remains in the book. In general the notebooks represent 'workshop' material. They contain the stuff from which her stories were worked up; fragmentary material that was later to appear in lesser stories like "The Wrong House" or major stories like "The Doll's House" and "The Garden Party".

The final group of material is even more miscellaneous; some hundred single sheets of paper of various sizes and rulings with poems (several dozen), a draft of a chapter of her abortive novel *Maata*, an unpublished and unfinished play entitled *Toots*, many pages of schoolgirl poems and 'vignettes' and stories, further complete later stories (some in a fair copy ready for the printer), a meticulously kept book of household accounts for 1914-1916, and a solidly bound volume into which she pasted her *Athenaeum* reviews (which includes apparently all her unsigned short notices to the same journal).

This heterogeneous mass is, in fact, the *Journal*. It is also the *Scrapbook*. It is also the final 1954 expanded edition of the *Journal*, which the title-page states is the 'definitive edition'. In the introduction to the original edition of 1927, the editor admitted that in addition to the 'Journal' there was 'material . . . of various kinds'. But in all his editing he invariably referred to *the* Journal, the implication being that there was such an entity. I can find little trace of it in the extant documents. The *Journal* is a brilliant piece of literary synthesis and editorial patchwork by Murry, based on pieces taken from some forty notebooks and diaries and a few hundred single scraps of paper. The existence of the four partially written-up diaries explains why the entries in the *Journal* come so thickly in a few months 1914, 1915, 1920, and 1922. Outside of these the editor made use of the occasional dated entries scattered through thirty notebooks. For the remainder he had recourse to the fragmentary story drafts in the notebooks and isolated paragraphs and even sentences which are everywhere—at the back of the diaries, throughout the notebooks, many on single sheets of writing paper and even on torn fragments of jotters and the proverbial backs of envelopes. These he assigned to what he considered were appropriate places in the *Journal*. The combination of the remains of a writer of the calibre of Katherine Mansfield and an editor of the calibre of Murry produced what he was later—justifiably—to describe as a minor classic, which ran through many printings. It is hardly too much to claim that it is as much Murry's work as Katherine Mansfield's, though his only acknowledged part in the 1927 edition was the introduction and the 'minimum necessary words of explanation'.

It is clear from the notes he made on the manuscripts that he returned to the material in 1938. 'Transcribe for Scrapbook' appears beside many passages that he had not previously used for the *Journal*. Katherine Mansfield's writing for the printer was precise, legible, fully and delicately punctuated. But her notebooks are filled with pages of almost illegible scribbling—her normal writing when she was composing rapidly. In the enforced leisure of an illness Murry tackled many of these difficult passages and did a superlative job in deciphering and transcribing. The result was the publication in 1939 of the *Scrapbook*. This has never had the appeal of the *Journal*, although some of the writing is every bit as good. Readers in 1939 had other things on their minds; and the very title implied something unfinished. But the *Scrapbook* was quarried from precisely the same bundle of notebooks and papers as the *Journal* had been a few years previously. Anything that was published in the one could with equal justification have been published in the other.

In 1954 appeared the last and definitive edition of the *Journal*. Murry, I think, found himself in something of a quandary. His own editorial work had led to the public acceptance of two books by his late wife, a *Journal* and a *Scrapbook*. He was aware, as an examination of his own notes on the manuscripts makes clear, that there was indeed only one batch of material, from which both were derived. But he wished to publish a much fuller *Journal*, firstly by printing those personal passages which he had (quite understandably and indeed quite properly) omitted from the 1927 edition, and secondly by printing as much as he wished of the original papers, irrespective of whether he had in the first instance called them 'Journal' or 'Scrapbook'. His explanation of his later editorial method is disingenuous:

> Other passages have been incorporated which, though actually published in the *Scrapbook* in 1939, really belong to the *Journal* and would have been included in it, if they had been discovered in time. (*Journal*, 1954, preface p. ix).

It is possible that in 1927 he had not 'discovered' all the material, in the restricted sense that certain of the notebooks he may not have wholly read—particularly the more illegible ones. But he had them all available. Moreover, a careful comparison of the originals with the printed texts reveals—to cite only one example—that this suggestion of a later 'discovery' of material cannot always be sustained. On pages 52-53 of the 1954 *Journal*, there are two passages, "A Dream" and "The Toothache Sunday" printed one after the other. "A Dream" was first printed in the 1927 *Journal*; "The Toothache Sunday" was first printed in the *Scrapbook*. The reader who (preface in mind), compares the two editions of the *Journal* is left with the presumption that this latter passage was not 'discovered in time' for the 1927 edition, and is therefore now put in its proper sequence in 1954. But both passages are derived from the same Katherine Mansfield notebook, (and that in a singularly clear script), which was begun on March 6th 1914. There "A Dream" (the title is editorial) occupies two pages, and the immediately following three pages are occupied by "The Toothache Sunday". To discover "The Toothache Sunday" in time for the 1927 *Journal*, one had only to turn over the page.

Indeed, Murry certainly turned the page—he marked the passage 'omit'. Later in 1938 he marked it 'transcribe for Scrapbook'. A close examination of Murry's considerable annotations and markings on the manuscripts leaves the careful reader with the certainty that he worked over all the pages very thoroughly for the 1927 edition. He marked with a 'tick' everything he wanted for the *Journal*; what (for a variety of reasons) he did not want he marked with square brackets, with a zero sign, or with the word 'omit'. In 1938 he clearly did a further garnering from fields he had already harvested.

The mild deception of his 1954 preface is, in one sense, unimportant. Murry did not deceive himself. His annotations on the manuscripts (once his very simple code has been worked out) are scrupulous and indicate precisely what he did with his material. Sometimes they even indicate his reasons: one passage in which Katherine Mansfield attacks a woman friend of Murry's has never been printed—and Murry has added a brief explanation of his reasons for the omission at the foot of the page of the notebook. What, after all, was Murry producing when he published the first edition of the *Journal*? Certainly not a biography of his dead wife, not even a narrative of their mutual relationships, though something of that was added by way of 'minimum necessary words of explanation'. He was producing partly a memorial, partly an edited collection of fragments by the best short-story writer of her time. Its success as a piece of literature was its own justification.

But in 1954 the situation was different. The successive studies by Sylvia Berkman and Antony Alpers (1953 in America, 1954 in London) had aroused considerable interest—and curiosity—about Katherine Mansfield's life. The publication by Murry in 1951 of her letters to him in their full text had supplanted a severely edited edition of 1928. The inclusion, in the full edition of the letters, of many passages in which the sick and terrified Katherine lashed out blindly— and often unfairly—at her husband leaves the reader convinced that Murry had courageously printed the entire letters, even when they seemed to do him discredit. This is certainly the implication of the 'definitive edition' which appears on the title page of the 1951 edition of the *Letters*. Then in 1954 came the parallel 'definitive edition' of the *Journal*. The Preface claimed that it restored passages 'which for various reasons were suppressed in the original edition of 1927'. *Scrapbook* material was now incorporated. Other material, which had appeared neither in the *Scrapbook* nor the earlier *Journal*, was added. The new *Journal* was almost twice as long as the earlier edition. Here, clearly, was not merely a new edition of a minor masterpiece but a solid piece of documentation for the life and writing of Katherine Mansfield. Is not that what is implied by the definitive edition of a writer's journal?

Unfortunately, whatever the literary value of the *Journal* the biographical value is severely limited by the editorial method. Certain passages are still omitted, sometimes for obviously personal reasons, sometimes through inadvertence. In spite of Murry's remarkable accuracy of transcription, a careful reader (admittedly with Murry's transcript before him; without it he'd be lost) can make corrections. Certain entries in Katherine Mansfield's diaries have been overlooked—usually short entries after a few blank pages. None of that is really important. What is important—and misleading to a biographer—is that many passages of apparently continuous writing are not really continuous at all. They have been assembled from different sources. Murry's instinct in joining them together may be right—he knew his wife better than anyone else could. But one can never depend on his text. One can never be sure when it is Katherine Mansfield speaking and when it is Murry blending and shuffling her material, and generally tidying her up.

Sometimes he is manifestly mistaken. On pages 53-4 of the *Journal* he prints the passage already referred to, "The Toothache Sunday" (Ida Baker has toothache and Katherine Mansfield is kind to her). Half-way down page 54 the final section is introduced by three dots . . . a favourite punctuation device of Katherine Mansfield's. In the manuscript the passage after the dots is separated by several pages from the previous passage, and has been grafted on by the editor. A reader with a sense of prose style can smell something wrong. "A Toothache Sunday" is a 'diary' entry, in which 'Katie' is Ida Baker's endearment for Katherine Mansfield. The tacked-on passage after the dots is a *story*: 'Katie' in this latter passage is the Cass-Katie-Kezia child of the Wellington stories. If it is to be linked to anything, it belongs to "A Dream" (which is about a child called K.T.) on page 52. This mistaken fusion in turn misled Mr Alpers who describes the 'toothache' incident and then the 'reverie' that followed it, though his labels of description and reverie for the respective sections indicate that instinctively he has sensed the difference between the tone of the two passages. But the biographer is here at the mercy of the editor.

Something like half of the printed *Journal* material consists of passages which were in no sense a 'journal'. The editor has interpolated them, often at precise dates, into the genuine journal material, even when his own annotations on the source manuscript indicate that he has doubts about its date. He regularly interpolates passages of poetry which Katherine copied out—sometimes on a single undateable sheet—and inserts them at 'appropriate' places. An outstanding example of this occurs on pages 191-8 of the *Journal*. This is a section of diary entries; the entries are approximately the same length, because they were written in the limited space of a printed diary for 1920. On January 15 she is shown as writing in her journal a verse of Thomas Hardy. She quotes him again at the end of January. Neither quotation appears in the 1920 diary. The editor has transferred them from another manuscript, and as he was in England and Katherine in Ospedaletti on these dates, it is impossible to see how he can interpolate them so precisely.

The patching together of material without indicating that it comes from separate sources sometimes produces a meaning that Katherine Mansfield certainly never intended. Two instances will suffice. On page 206 under August 8, 1920 she records that this was the day on which her mother died. She then quotes Hardy's little elegy

> How she would have loved
> A party today!

In the next line of the *Journal* she is shown as saying 'I hate this book. So awfully!!' What book? The reader can only assume it is the book that contains this pessimistic poem by Hardy. But the reference to her dead mother is in one notebook. 'I hate this book. So awfully!!' is written in another, and on a totally different theme. It was added to the top of the first page of a notebook begun in August 1920, in which she records a period in which she and Murry were at odds with each other. Some time later certainly—and perhaps as late as 1921 when she added other material to the book lamenting the temporary breakdown in their relationship—she added the regretful 'I hate this book' note. Murry's dating is at fault, but even more misleading is the blending of two entries that have nothing to do with each other. The result is a falsification of her character. She is given a pettish petulance (which she did not feel) and her real regrets over a more serious matter to her—a misunderstanding with Murry—simply drop from sight.

The second instance appears on page 54. She records, evidently in a mood of depression that she is sewing in a dispirited manner. 'In the middle of it' (her depression) she looks out of the window and sees a group of workmen eating their lunch. The passage concludes: 'I really have a faint idea that it might send one mad.' This portrait of a neurotic writer makes unpleasant reading. But in the original notebook this final sentence occurs several pages *earlier* than the rest of the passage. It stands in isolation at the head of an otherwise blank page—her regular indication of a 'story' idea which she would develop, if all went well, on the remainder of the sheet. Here a genuine 'journal' entry has been blended with 'story' material. If the relevant passage is read without the interpolation, the writer appears depressed—and then diverted, a very different conclusion.

The above are only samples of editorial method about which the general reader probably will not complain. I cannot see that detailed study of the source manuscripts and even publication of them is going to make much difference to the literary importance of the *Journals*. But any further critical or biographical work on Katherine Mansfield must be based on the original Notebooks and not on either of the present editions. The *Journals* present a complete and graceful *persona* of a writer, true in the essentials, but over-rarified. The Notebooks (were they ever published as they stand) would not be easy reading. They are scrappier, less tidy, full of false starts, loose ends, and material which is often apparently irrelevant for the job in hand. She may jot down the idea of a second story while she is engaged on a first. Real and fictional life get intermixed in her pages. She is capable of writing a factual diary entry and a story based on the experience simultaneously. The Katherine Mansfield of the Notebooks is a different creature from the Katherine Mansfield of the *Journals*. In the Notebooks she is not the intense writer of regular journal entries, but a perhaps truer and certainly more interesting figure, the writer in the workshop with her nose to the grindstone.

Landfall, No. XIII, Christchurch, New Zealand, March 1959, 1: pp. 62-69.

F. W. Bateson and B. Shahevitch, "Katherine Mansfield's 'The Fly': A Critical Exercise"

"The Fly" is probably the shortest *good* short story in modern English. Its two thousand words therefore permit, indeed encourage, the kind of close analysis that has been so successful in our time with lyric poetry but that is impossibly cumbrous or misleadingly incomplete when applied to the novel or the *conte*. The object of this exercise is to demonstrate that, granted the difference of *genres*, exactly the same critical procedure is in order for realistic fiction as for a poem. "The Fly" was written in February 1922 and was included later that year in *The Garden Party and Other Stories*.

"The Fly" assumes in its readers a readiness to accept and respond to two parallel series of symbolic conventions: (i) those constituting the English language as it was spoken and written in the first quarter of the twentieth century, (ii) those constituting the realistic narrative in prose of the same period. That this story is written in modern English is immediately apparent, and the initial display of irrelevant descriptive detail is an equally clear signal to the critical reader that the narrative *genre* to be employed here is realism. Why *Woodifield* (dozens of other surnames would have done just as well)? Why a *green* armchair (rather than light brown, purple, dark brown, etc.)? Why the cut back to the City on *Tuesdays* (rather than Mondays, Wednesdays, Thursdays or Fridays)?

That the critical reader does not in fact ask such questions is because of his familiarity already with the realistic formula. The particular suspension of disbelief that realism demands is an acquiescence in the author's limited omniscience provided his external setting 'looks' historically authentic. The reader must be able to say, 'On the evidence provided, which seems adequate, this series of events could have taken place in real life as I know it.'

It follows that to look for allegorical symbols in "The Fly" is to accuse Katherine Mansfield of a breach of her chosen convention. Specifically "The Fly" is not a beast-fable, like Blake's poem with the same title in "Songs of Experience". In this story the confrontation of the boss with the fly is only subjectively anthropomorphic. It is the boss who attributes human courage—and the human necessity to suffer pain under torture—to the fly. The boss's corrupt imagination has blown this up into the semblance of a human being, but objectively, as the reader knows, the fly is just an ordinary house-fly. Some earlier critics of "The Fly" have gone astray by ignoring the story's technical limitations, and various abstract 'themes' have been read into it, like 'time', 'cruelty' and 'life'[1]. Middleton Murry's own comment—'the profound and ineradicable impression made upon her by the War . . . found perfect utterance in the last year of her life in the story "The Fly"' [2]—may have encouraged such misinterpretations. It is certainly tempting to relate the story to Katherine Mansfield's tuberculosis and to her dislike of her father, who was a New Zealand banker. But such elements are of the nature of 'sources'. No doubt without them the story could not have been begun, but they are not *inside* the story. The realistic convention is resistant both to abstractions and to strict autobiography. The story must appear to tell itself; it must be the sort of concrete human situation that might have happened just so. And once the reader begins to detect the intrusion of abstract concepts or moral attitudes, such as the hatred of war, or alternatively of obviously autobiographical episodes, his confidence in the writer's omniscience will be weakened. An unnecessary strain is being put on the realistic suspension of disbelief.

The irrelevance of allegorical interpretations in this case can be clarified by contrasting the proverb, an even shorter narrative *genre*, with the realistic short story. The concrete details in a proverb are all functional. Nobody wants to know what kind of stone it is that gathers no moss, or that is thrown by the inhabitants of glasshouses. The exact size, colour, weight and shape of the respective stones are irrelevant, because a proverb demands immediate implicit conceptualisation ('Restlessness is unprofitable', 'Guilty parties should not accuse others of guilt'); it is in fact allegory in capsule form. But in a realistic short story the particularity is a large part of the meaning. Suppress Mr. Woodifield's name, the colour of the armchair, the day of the week allotted to his City visits, and the convention collapses. They are indispensable signals from author to reader; they also assume a common interest and confidence in the concrete detail of the phenomenal world. (We are on Dr. Johnson's side against Berkeley in the matter of the stone.)

But "The Fly" is something more than narrative imbedded in slice-of-life realism. Some sort of general statement about modern life is implicit in it. How has Katherine Mansfield managed to evade the limitations of the realistic convention? How can a value-judgement emerge at all from what appears to be a temporal sequence of particularities? These are the essential questions the critic must ask.

One answer, an important critical one, is that the medium of a narrative sequence is language, and that it is always possible to exploit the generality inherent in both vocabulary and grammar so that a value-judgement emerges. This is just what Katherine Mansfield does, but discreetly, tactfully. A simple linguistic device is to use descriptive epithets to hint at a generalisation. Thus at the beginning of "The Fly" the boss is 'stout' and 'rosy'. In combination with the 'snug' office to which Woodifield pays a tribute twice in the first two paragraphs, the epithets produce an impression of luxuriant good health, of self-indulgence perhaps, though at this stage in the story the indulgence is not apparently censured in any overt way. Later, in the mounting tension of the passage when the boss, having sent Woodifield on his way, returns to the office, he treads with 'firm heavy steps'. These, especially in contrast to Woodifield's 'shuffling footsteps', loom rather ominously. The boss who 'plumps' down in the spring-chair is no longer merely stout, he has become 'fat'. Still later, when he suddenly 'has an idea' and plunges his pen into the ink, before we quite know what he is up to we get a premonition of it as he leans his 'thick' wrist on the blotting paper. The harmless stout and rosy figure has turned out to be physically coarse, even brutal.

Similarly we get an inkling of the boss's character from the colouring of the verbs long before we are introduced to the decisive situation. When he is still 'stout and rosy', he 'rolls' in his chair. Soon he 'flips' his *Financial Times*—a slightly arrogant gesture. By this time he is 'planted' there, 'in full view of that frail old figure', and the adjective qualifying his satisfaction is 'solid'. Later on we suddenly see him 'swooping' across for two tumblers ('Coming down with the rush of a bird of prey . . . making a sudden attack', *Oxford Dictionary*).

The adjectives and verbs serve to 'place' Woodifield too, who never speaks but 'pipes' (three times) or 'quavers'. He does not look, he 'peers'. The wife and girls keep him 'boxed up' in his home. On Tuesdays, he did not dress but *was* 'dressed and brushed' and then 'allowed' to go to town—all images reinforcing the simile in which he is originally introduced, that of a baby in a pram.

But the crucial linguistic device in "The Fly" is the protagonist's anonymity. He is always referred to as 'the boss', twenty-five times to be precise, or approximately once every eighty words. The word is etymologically an Americanism (adopted from the Dutch *baas* =master in the beginning of the nineteenth century), which passed into British English about the middle of that century and had certainly lost all its foreignness by 1922. The dictionary meaning then as now is 'a master, a business manager, anyone who has a right to give orders'. The word has still an unpleasantly vulgar connotation, which is perhaps heightened by its use in U.S. political jargon, where 'boss' means the 'dictator of a party organisation'. Used with a capital it turns into a particular, not a general, word, in fact, from a common noun into a proper noun, thus making the connotation depend on what we know of the person so named. Thus 'Boss' may often have a kindly ring. But in "The Fly" Katherine Mansfield persists in spelling the word with a minuscule, that is, as a common noun, at the same time refusing to alternate it with any synonym or other appellation. She even refuses to let us know what the boss's actual name is. 'Mr. Woodifield', 'Gertrude', 'Woodifield', 'Macey', but the hero's names (and his son's) are resolutely excluded. Katherine Mansfield cannot, of course, altogether prevent the process by which a common noun becomes a proper noun, but she does her best to keep in the reader's mind the more general significance of the word. Each time we read it, the general somewhat repugnant idea of the term is again imprinted in our consciousness, even after it has almost become a proper name. The boss, clear-cut individual as he is in the realistic narrative, is *nominally* an allegorical figure simply by virtue of the word's insistent repetition.

The other linguistic device deserves notice. This is Katherine Mansfield's habit here of allowing direct description to merge into reported speech. Here are a few examples: 'His talk was over; it was time for him to be off. But he did not want to go. Since he had retired. . . .' Up to this point the description is in straightforward narrative prose, but in 'since his . . . stroke' the short break which the three dots denote—so expressive of the reluctance of a sick man to call his complaint by its frightening real name—turns author's statement into semi-direct speech. The reluctance is now Woodifield's, not the narrator's.

A few lines later an inversion occurs. 'Though what he did there, the wife and girls couldn't imagine' may still be taken as objective statement with emphasis causing the object-clause to be put first. But the following clause, 'Make a nuisance of himself they supposed' has the full effect of direct speech. Again the object-clause is given first, but the main clause does not seem to be the author speaking; it is as if between concealed quotation marks, a comment really spoken in the first person instead of the apparent third person.

A little later the boss's 'he explained, as he had explained for the past—how many?—weeks' seems to be another bit of direct speech that is masquerading as narrative statement. In a story within the realistic convention the author is supposed to know all about how often one of the characters did this or that. The slight uncertainty here, the momentary ignorance—perhaps only half genuine—belongs to everyday speech. The boss, not the author, is speaking.

Again in 'How on earth could he have slaved, denied himself, kept going all those years without the promise, for ever before him, of the boy's stepping into his shoes and carrying on where he left off?' the complete sentence in the form of a question is not introduced by any main clause, nor is it in quotation marks. But can it in fact be anything but a question asked by the boss himself?

This mixing of direct statement with indirect or concealed dialogue is used all through the story—by interpolating exclamation in otherwise regular narrative, by putting complete sentences in the form of questions not introduced by main clauses yet impossible to be taken otherwise than as questions asked by the characters, by breaks in the line, and by inversions of a colloquial nature. The result is that we have very little regular narrative. Instead, in a frame of thin lines of this quasi-narrative, which could almost be spoken by a chorus, we have the effect of drama. In this setting the repeated recurrence of the two words 'the boss' has the impersonality of a stage-direction, a datum, as it were, outside the narrative. It reiterates so as to become an alternative title to the story: "The Fly [Boss]: a Short Story".

The point at which a linguistic device, either of vocabulary ('the boss') or syntax (the indirect speech), becomes a rhetorical figure should not be detectable in realistic fiction. The reader has suspended his disbelief on condition that the naturalistic particularities are maintained, as they certainly are in "The Fly". What could be more reassuringly particular than the story's penultimate sentence? 'He took out his handkerchief and passed it inside his collar.' But in some of the devices here analysed language has unquestionably become rhetoric. The repetition of *any* phrase or construction will give it, if repeated often enough, a new semantic dimension. A similar process occurs if some parallelism establishes itself between the separate episodes in a narrative or drama. Gradually an unstated generality superimposes itself on the sequence of particulars. A narrative pattern emerges.

The most memorable episode in "The Fly" begins when the boss, having completed the rescue operations from the inkpot, conceives his 'idea'. This is the story's *peripeteia*, the point of dramatic reversal in the reader's attitude to the protagonist. We began with a distinct liking for him. Woodifield was expected by his family to make a nuisance of himself to his old friends on the Tuesday excursions into the City; and in general, from the specimen provided us of his conversational powers, their gloomy anticipations seem likely to be fulfilled. But the boss's reaction is different. The boss is genuinely delighted to see Woodifield, and he produces his best whisky to entertain him, 'feeling kindly', as the narrator (apparently it *is* the narrator) informs us. At this early point in "The Fly" the tone is light and almost comic: the bars in the electric heater are compared to sausages, and Woodifield couldn't have been more surprised, when the whisky bottle appears, 'if the boss had produced a rabbit'. This boss—in spite of his descriptive label—cannot be taken very tragically because of the disarming atmosphere of cordiality in which we make his acquaintance. Moreover his son has been killed in the war (of 1914-18), and we are naturally sorry for him. It is true some disturbing elements in the boss's character already contradict the generally good impression he creates. Some of the pleasure he takes in Woodifield's company seems to derive from the contrast he cannot help drawing between his own excellent health and the younger man's frail condition. And the ritual of immediately available tears in his son's memory, if pathetic, is also distasteful. But these reservations—the list could be extended—do not affect our general liking for him and sympathy with him until he turns his experimental attention on to the fly.

As the three blobs of ink fall the reader's attitude changes from considerable sympathy to total antipathy. The admiration the boss professes to feel for the fly's determination is no doubt real, but it does not prevent him from proceeding with his appalling 'idea'. The horrifying thing is that this admiration makes the experiment all the more entrancing for him. As flies to wanton boys are we to the gods, they kill us for their sport. If the victim did not show some spirit, the gods would lose half their sport. (A half-consciousness of Gloucester's dictum is no doubt expected in the reader.)

In the light we now possess of the boss's other nature we can see how ambiguous the boss's earlier words and actions were. From this moment therefore the story takes on a two-way pattern. It is read as mere 'story', so that we can discover what comes next, but with each step forward a mental step is also taken back into earlier more or less parallel episodes, and so we correct our first impressions in the light of the new information. A dual element reveals itself at this point in the boss's relations with both Woodifield and his son. The tenderness with the one or admiration for the other is not to be denied, but it is a sadistic tenderness, unconscious of course, but almost that of an executioner for his victim. Woodifield was not allowed whisky at home, and the boss must have known that drinking it might precipitate a second stroke. But the 'generous finger' is enthusiastically provided. The son was no doubt genuinely loved and mourned, but the son's death provided the boss with a splendid opportunity to demonstrate his superiority to other bereaved parents, like the Woodifields. *His* tears were Niobean; hence the shock of aggrieved disappointment when they finally dry up.

A second *peripeteia* presents itself, there, at the fly's death. The grinding and frightening feeling of wretchedness is not what either the boss or the reader had expected. This emotional reversal in the boss creates a new reversal in the reader's attitude to him. Had the boss perhaps glimpsed, briefly and startlingly, the abyss of moral nihilism into which he had unconsciously descended? Katherine Mansfield leaves the question unanswered, almost unasked, and the answer proposed by a recent American critic[3] does not convince ('he thought his grasp on his last pleasure was gone'—the pleasure of his office routine). But the framework of parallel episodes that has built itself up in the reader's mind forces us to half-formulate some ghost of a conceptual conclusion. What *had* the boss been thinking about before the fly entered his life? 'For the life of him he could not remember'. And so the reader dismisses him, finally, with some contempt. Early in the story we had quite liked the boss, then we had discovered that we detested him, and now we can merely despise him. The boss's final gesture with the handkerchief, which he passes inside his stiff collar to cool and dry the hot sticky skin, 'places' him with superb economy and precision. The intensity of the battle the mighty boss has waged with the minute fly has left him physically exhausted, mere weak brutal oblivious flesh.

In terms of plot, then, though there is dramatic progress (shifts in the reader's sympathies, a mounting intensity, a transition from the near-comic to the near-tragic), there is also dramatic repetition. The episodes combine similitude with dissimilitude in a kind of extended metaphor. If the Woodifield episode is called Act I, the re-enactment of the son's death Act II, and the murder of the fly Act III, then the parallelism works out as follows:

(i) in each of the three acts the boss holds the centre of the stage, and the three subsidiary characters' dramatic function is to throw light on him as the protagonist;

(ii) in Act I Woodifield's feebleness illumines the boss's image of himself as a man of affairs, in Act II it is the boss's image of himself as father that is illumined, in Act III the image is of the boss as animal-lover;

(iii) in each act the boss's image of his own altruism is found to be contradicted by his actions;

(iv) the cumulative effect of the parallelisms is to superimpose on the boss's image of himself in Act I the self-images of Acts II and III, but the image of the hospitable man of the world is blurred by that of the proud heart-broken father and the cheerer-on of flies in difficulties (the images do not cohere);

(v) contrasting with this blur is the clear-cut outline that emerges from the superimpositions of the essential boss as he really is all the time—an ordinary decent human being irretrievably demoralised by the power that corrupts.

A final critical corollary remains to be drawn. Katherine Mansfield's realism has begun with a tactful introduction of the story's setting. The reader, encouraged by the apparent authenticity of the details, tends unconsciously to identify himself with the *dramatis personae*, as though they were being presented by living actors in a West End theatre. They—that is, Katherine Mansfield's accounts of her characters—accept identification. Under the make-up and the costume a living heart is beating, but it is the actor's heart—in the case of a realistic short story, the reader's heart—not the *persona*'s. The authenticity is confirmed, re-created, guaranteed, by the reader. But the judgement that he passes on these impersonations of his, who are technically the characters of the story, is the author's contribution, not the reader's, because the reader is not aware that a moral attitude is gradually forming itself within his consciousness. The test of the good short story is therefore the degree of the reader's surprise when he discovers in himself the judgements that have been forced upon him. But the surprise has also to be followed by conviction. This is what the particular words and the particular word-orders *must* mean; this is what the significance of the dramatic episodes in their sequence of parallelisms *must* add up to.

It will be remembered that Dr. Johnson's discussion of poetic wit proposed a similar criterion: a good poem is 'at once natural and new', because what it is saying, 'though not obvious, . . . is acknowledged to be just'.

Essays in Criticism, January 1962, vol. 12., pp. 39-53.

---

[1] Brief critiques of "The Fly" have appeared in *The Explicator* (April 1945, Feb. 1947, May 1947, Feb. 1954, Nov. 1955, Oct. 1958).

2 Journal of Katherine Mansfield, 1954 ed., p. 107.
3 Thomas J. Assad, *The Explicator*, Nov. 1955.

Brigid Brophy, "Katherine Mansfield's Self-Depiction"

Once upon a time a sensitive soul was born in New Zealand, took the name Katherine Mansfield and came to Europe, where she wrote evocative fragments, loved delicately, and died young—technically of pulmonary tuberculosis but really because life was too gross for her.

Fortunately, this banal person never existed. Katherine Mansfield was in the habit of running up spare personalities for herself: one evening she would wear the decadent sophisticate, the next the unfathomable Russian. The fragile stray from elfland was the least pleasing of her creations but the longest-lasting—because it had the backing of her second husband, John Middleton Murry; and not only did Murry represent her after her death, but throughout their life together she was trying—to the point of falsifying her true personality—to capture his approval or even attention.

Her true personality, which includes the polymorphous poseuse, is at once more attractive, more cogent, and more bitingly tragic. This did not become wholly accessible to the public until the 'fifties, when Murry published the uncut text of her journal and of her letters to him and when the biography by Antony Alpers told the full facts of her picaresque life: the inconsequential, almost surrealistic first marriage; the two extramarital pregnancies, ending in a miscarriage and an abortion; the dash almost to the Front in 1915 for a few days' love affair with a literary French conscript. The life of the "free woman," which is now being imposed on us as a postwar phenomenon—post *our* war—was being lived by Katherine Mansfield, and with incomparably more style, before women were properly out of long skirts.

This pioneer did not shrink from life. (Neither did the girl who sang in the chorus of a touring light opera company because her lover played in the orchestra; or the young woman who picked up a casual income by attending posh parties and passing as a guest until called on to do a music-hall turn.) Yet Murry could afterwards record that he wanted to meet her in the first place because her stories expressed "a revulsion from the brutality of life akin to my own." It was true of Murry, author of a verse play about fairies. Of Katherine Mansfield—or so she feared—almost the opposite was true: if anything, she was too brutal for life. The crisis of her personality was how to govern a furious impulse of aggression.

Those early stories which Murry found so delicate were actually the grossly comic caricatures of German habits—especially eating habits—which had been collected in her first volume. Eating was Katherine Mansfield's most persistent metaphor for destruction; and it was probably through actual eating that she expressed her earliest, and crucial resentment, and first marked out her individuality. She, who became so thin as a tubercular adult, had been a fat little girl: the only one of the five children who was. Moreover, she knew that her mother did not love her. This she later made plain in a barely fictionalised portrait, which she shamelessly labelled with one of her mother's real names. Linda Burnell (real name:—Annie Burnell Beauchamp) has borne her children against her will and cannot even pretend to love them; exhausted, she has "no warmth left to give them." If the third child felt the chill more sharply than the others, it was probably because she was only a few weeks old when the mother sailed on a trip to Europe, leaving the baby in New Zealand in the care of the grandmother—whose lap, Antony Alpers comments, could perhaps "never have made up for the breasts of the mother." His surmise can be supported by another: that it was precisely in trying to make up that the fat little girl became fat. Later, one of her bitter descriptions of her relationship with Murry was "all this life drying up—like milk in an old breast."

There is an evident difficulty, almost a formal conundrum, about a daughter's identifying herself with a mother who did not want to have her in the first place. The difficulty in identification made for an uncertainty in identity. Katherine Mansfield attested this by her experiments in personality and even by playing on the formal components of the very mark of her identity, her name. The amateur cellist, Kathleen Beauchamp, did not change into the professional writer without trying a number of chrysalises, including the translation of Beauchamp into Shönfeld; she had already published several stories as Katherine Mansfield when she suddenly—and briefly—appeared as "Katherina" Mansfield. For personal use, she had almost as many names as friends. Quite apart from her innumerable love-names with Murry, she ran, between various relationships and the mirror of her journal, a Joycean gamut of pseudonyms: Kass, Kassie, Katie, K.T., Kath, Katya, Yékaterina.

Thus far an ingenious reader might reconstruct the author from her short stories. The obvious—indeed, dazzling—talent is for multiple impersonation, through sketches whose form must be derived partly from her music-hall turns. Her versatility is not pinned together by any single, fixed writing identity, except in the New Zealand stories. There she does depict a clutch of characters from a single viewpoint. She achieves it, however, not by asserting but by abnegating literary personality. She is a camera—of brilliantly accurate focus; but since the necessary biography—or even the information that they *are* biographical—is not given away with her fictions, the reader is left looking through an unusually professional family album from which the captions are missing. He cannot understand what point these sharp images are meant to impress on him, because he is left ignorant of what impelled the writer to make them. The impulse was, as a matter of fact, as in all her best writing, cruelty. To cast so dispassionate an eye on matter so personal was itself an un-charity. She wrote the New Zealand stories as a mixture of do-it-yourself psycho-analysis and do-it-yourself witchcraft. Her raking long-shots emphasized the distance she had put between herself and New Zealand, and avenged the mother's voyage to Europe when it was the baby who was left behind. Three years before her death Katherine Mansfield did, quite consciously, achieve identification with her mother, but she was also quite conscious of the cost. "I am become—Mother," she wrote in her journal, and followed it immediately with "I don't care a *rap* for people".

If there is no constant writing personality, Katherine Mansfield did leave, over most of her work, fingerprints which would identify her anywhere—sticky ones. With Murry's encouragement, she tried to domesticate her fierceness under suburban cosiness and tweeness.   One of the unseen presences at her Garden Party is undeniably a pottery gnome—with features very like Murry's. Murry, however, did not invent the stickiness she secreted under the stimulus of anything that might bear her own label of "Something Childish but Very Natural." At the unnatural age of fifteen, she was already cooing, "Are you very fond of small children? They always will captivate me." The difficulty of identification was redoubled when it was a question of the daughter's taking a motherly role herself. Her own mother's coldness probably left Katherine Mansfield psychologically incapable (Murry believed she eventually became physiologically incapable) of having a child: an incapacity she tried to overcome by swallowing a fantasy of motherhood—which could result only in children who ring false. Accurately as she observed or remembered her fictional children, there is a frightening mawkishness about them and their babytalk—and *her* babytalk:—her dear little this's and thats, the nursery friezes of toddlers in E.H. Shepard smocks, which decorate her letters, her whole tendency to curl up beneath toadstools. It goes beyond the pathetic into the pathological: beyond the merely uninformed fantasies of a woman who has never had children into the compensatory fantasies of a woman whose unconscious impulse is towards child-murder—of a woman who did, in fact, have an abortion rather than have a child. That her impulse towards the helpless and unprotected was not solely help and protection she revealed in "The Little Governess," a story which owes more to Hans Andersen than the form of the title and the fact that the governess is never given a name. The imagination that devised it was Neronic; and, because she for once did not slobber over the ambiguity of her own feelings, it is a masterpiece.

The ruthlessness which plays peep-bo behind her sentimentality is that of the unloved child towards its siblings. (Evidently she held herself unconsciously guilty of her brother's death in the war, since her reaction to it was to write in her journal a promise to join him.) If she could not bring herself to become a mother, it was because she could not forfeit the hope of belatedly becoming the loved child herself. Significantly, it was on hearing that her mother was coming to Europe that she decided to have the abortion. It is impossible not to wonder if the earlier miscarriage in Germany (which happened just after a meeting with her mother) was really or was wholly an accident. Immediately after it, she performed an act not merely surrealist but dissociated. If it was not dictated by compulsive remorse towards the child she at least unconsciously believed herself to have murdered, it was a moral monstrosity. She simply—she Neronically— sent to a friend in England demanding a child: any child. A small boy was found near Welbeck Street and despatched to her. He spent some weeks with her (knowing her by yet another pseudonym, Sally). She brought back to England the satires she had written on her fellow-guests in the German pension, and the boy was returned to Welbeck Street. Even Zeus gave Ganymede a permanent position at court. Katherine Mansfield, after satisfying a different but no less overweening lust, seems never to have given the boy another thought—except in the one way that is unforgivable: for, according to Alpers, the living little boy from Welbeck Street was the chief model for the dead little boy in "Life of Ma Parker," which of all Katherine Mansfield's stories teeters on the most perilous brink between the unbearably maudlin and the unbearably moving.

Her ambivalence was one legacy from her mother; another was Murry. It might seem the figure of Katherine Mansfield's father (brash, bearded, decisive, insensitive—everything that is called, to the slander of the male sex, typically masculine) which pointed to her choosing, for her only permanent lover, a man who was the opposite. Murry was eminently a man who had to be chosen. It was she who proposed herself for his mistress (he at first resisted); she who chose to stick to him despite their incompatibility and his supineness in the whole affair. He was too supine to leave her, as he was too supine to love her. He was ethereal, delicate in mind and body, and passive. With the terseness of literary genius, she summed him up in two syllables when she nicknamed him Betsy. But it was not, fundamentally, the contrast with her father that made Betsy attractive. Her crucial frustration had occurred before her father entered her emotional world at all, and he left no impression in his own right on her imagination. Her accusation that he grudged her money only echoed the deeper accusation that her mother grudged her love and nurture. In one of her stories (others sketch the same situation) a father tries to offer love to his children by giving them a present. (Characteristically, it is something to eat; symbolically, it is a fruit.) The gift is frustrated by the mother. It was Katherine Mansfield's mother who fore-doomed her to Murry: in relation to him she re-lived her infantile agony. She could no more wring love—or even hatred—from him than she could have wrung milk.

Yet Murry did publish her private writings, including her sardonic insights into him. (He was exhausted after a minor expedition: she noted down "He was dying, Egypt, dying.") He even gave himself away in his editorial comments, which read like one of those first-person stories—like her own "Je ne parle pas français" where the narrator exposes more than he knows of his own awfulness. It is the private writings that express both her genius and her personality at their most incisive, engaged not only with Murry's half-love but with the moving true-love extended to her by the woman who appears in them as L.M. Unlike the original mother, L.M. grudged nothing. She subjected her personality to Katherine Mansfield as generously as her name: 'L.M.' ("Lesley Moore") was itself a pseudonym foisted on her by Katherine Mansfield, and presently she even submitted to being called "Jones." (She was so often the companion of Katherine Mansfield's uncomfortable journeys to the continent in hope of health that I think this name must be a reference to Wordsworth's "Jones, as from Calais southward you and I . . . ") Katherine Mansfield made use of L.M. emotionally, financially, and for getting the chores done, admitted eventually that she had been a perfect friend but never stopped despatching at her sharpest and most Jane-Austenish ironies.

These are often couched in the favourite metaphor. The journal satirises L.M.'s way with bananas: "But she eats them so slowly, so terribly slowly. And they know it . . . I have seen bananas turn absolutely livid with terror on her plate." Discerning in L.M. a false delicacy at table, Katherine Mansfield was perhaps reminded of her own false delicacy over the cradle and her own indifference to adopted waifs (it was, of course, L.M. whom she had commissioned to obtain the child from Welbeck Street):

> 'Does anyone want that piece of bread and butter?' says L.M. You would really think from her tone that she was saving the poor little darling from the river or worse, willing to adopt it as her own child and bring it up so that it never should know it was once unwanted.

The metaphor became openly cannibalistic when L.M. fussed over Katherine Mansfield's health and was told it was "as though you took a piece of my flesh and gnawed it."

Katherine Mansfield had, indeed, a cannibalistic imagination. Her aperçus are of the world glimpsed by an assassin. A "darling baby" in a French café "is drowning her brioche in a cup of weak coffee." An English tourist cuts a Dundee cake "so tenderly that it almost seemed an act of cannibalism." The French maid is "throttling, strangling by the throat, a helpless, exhausted little black silk bag." Even when it had taken up every conceivable pretext in the outside world, her imagination still crackled with free aggression: her fantasy-life ran to inventing the receipt of unwanted or insulting gifts, so that she might flay the giver in imaginary thank-you letters in her journal.

She was, of course, far too intelligent to suppose that the murderousness of her world really resided in L.M. or French maids or anywhere other than in herself. For all her rage, she was wholly rational. She could no more submit to God than lose herself in elfland, though she tried briefly to do both. Even her final decision to put herself in the hands of Gurdjieff's quasi-mystical clinic merely expressed in the only terms available to her a truth nowadays known even to the medical profession, that in tuberculosis the mind counts as much as the body. ("Do I believe in medicine alone? No, never . . . It seems to me childish and ridiculous to suppose one can be cured like a cow *if one is not a cow.*") Her greatest literary gift was a beautifully illuminating and devastating intelligence, which led first to aggressive farce, then to wit, and finally to the more than Stendhalian self-comedy with which she recorded her own tragedy. She could turn against herself even her propensity for dear little this's and thats ("I must take some of my dear money out of the Bank"), and even her favourite metaphor: a marvellous mood-piece in her journal, which begins "What is the matter with today? It is thin, white, as lace curtains are white, full of ugly noises," enumerates nine of the day's gritty enormities and culminates in "10. The tea was not hot. I meant *not* to eat the bun but I ate it."

As everyone said, her illness exacerbated her anger. But her anger had been there first; it was probably one of the precipitators of her illness. (I think her inkling of its psychosomatic nature gave her a false feeling of being in control of her tuberculosis and that this may be why she was convinced she would not die of it. "I feel today"—three years before she did die of it—"that I shall die soon and suddenly: but not of my lungs.") At fifteen she had described how she "felt *ill* with anger." At thirty-one, she *was*, in a sense, ill with anger; but she knew herself with total honesty. On the subject of honesty, she said in her journal, she would like "to write a *long, long* story": and in honesty she added "And another on the subject of HATE."

Terrified by her passion of hatred, warned by not mere rages but cold-blooded day-dreams in which she wished L.M. dead, Katherine Mansfield resolved her crisis by diverting her aggression from the outside world to herself. Perhaps the logical conclusion of identifying herself with her mother and coming thereby to the knowledge that her mother would have preferred not to give her birth was to acquiesce in the mother's preference (she arranged, as it were, for her mother to have a postdated abortion—of herself). When Katherine Mansfield refused to undertake a proper cure for her illness, she was acting out what she had written years before as a healthy but wrought-up adolescent: "I shall end—of course—by killing myself." The disease through which she did kill herself was consumption (this was the name she regularly used for it)—the cannibal disease which *consumes* its victim. Seeing life as a choice between eating and being eaten, she came to the conclusion that the honest course was to be consumed. To eat the bun—or the friend—, when you have meant not to, was sham; honesty lay in starving. Three months before dying she wrote in her journal "I feel a bit of a sham. . . And so I am. One of the K.M.s is so sorry. But of course she is. She has to die. *Don't* feed her." (Her mother *hadn't* fed her.)

Katherine Mansfield died in 1923 at the age of thirty-four. She was buried at Fontainebleau, her epitaph the epigraph of "Bliss": ". . . but I tell you, my lord fool, out of this nettle danger, we pluck this flower, safety." In her journal she had left her "Last Words to Life"—the title of the long, long story she would have liked to write, whose theme would have been: "Honesty (why?) is the only thing one seems to prize beyond life, love, death, everything. It alone remaineth."

Michigan Quarterly Review, vol. 5, Spring 1966, pp. 89-93.

Christiane Mortelier, "The Genesis and Development of the Katherine Mansfield Legend in France"[1]

That a curiously distorted view of Katherine Mansfield is widespread and persistent in France is not usually suspected by her English readers. The fascination with her personality noticeable forty years ago has given place, in England and America, to a scrutiny of her techniques, but in France critics are still obsessed with a partial and unreal image of her derived from false associations between her life and her art. Sylvia Berkman in her critical study of K.M.[2] praised the cool literary judgment of the French, but it can be shown that their assessments were often mistaken. I propose to follow the legend's chronological development in France, then to try to account for it.

Pierre Citron in 1940 was the first French critic to use the word 'legend' of K.M. He however only used it tentatively, because the editions of her works and the biographies published up to 1939 offered him insufficient evidence on which to base a firmer rejection of the current notions of K.M.'s 'purity and perfection'.[3]

Citron's article was reconsidered in 1966-67 by J.O. Miller,[4] a Canadian critic writing in French; contrasting Anglo-American criticism with its French counterpart, he examined some elements of the legend though not its origins. Yet he too may not have realized how widespread the idealization had been and still was. It would be a mistake to dismiss *all* French critical assessments of K.M. I am concerned here solely with the distortions which have created a Mansfield legend in France, reserving for another occasion a review of the positive contributions which French critics have made to the understanding of her writings. In the considerable range of critical material, from books and articles to prefaces and reviews, most writers repeat the same basic information; often, through the years, the same contribution tours in a wide variety of printed forms.[5]

K.M. was first mentioned in France in 1924, one year after her death, and has attracted steady attention ever since. We can distinguish roughly five main phases of interest:

1.   *1924-1930: a pre-translation phase of enthusiastic discovery.* In this phase, critics proclaimed that a new talent had appeared on the English writing scene, which should be made accessible in French. Indeed, as early as 1922-23, Charles du Bos planned a translation for Plon, the publishers, as he reveals in his *Journal.*[6]   In 1924, Louis Gillet wrote the first outline of her life and the first French article of her stories;[7] in 1929, he discussed the *Journal.*[8]   In the same year, Gabriel Marcel concentrated on the *Letters* and the *Journal*, which had appeared in England in 1927 and 1928 respectively, but were not yet translated.[9]

2.   *1931-1939: the launching phase and the flourishing of the legend.* In 1931-32, the translation in rapid succession of several books of short stories,[10] of the *Letters* in July 1931 and the *Journal* in December 1931, had the effect of establishing Mansfield's reputation as a writer of the first magnitude. A personality cult is apparent in the numerous ecstatic articles.[11]   In 1933, the legend was further encouraged by the testimony of the only French writer with more than a nodding acquaintance with her. The pious tone of F. Carco's "Souvenirs sur Katherine Mansfield" might have seemed suspect to readers familiar with his novels,[12] but his account of his 'amitié pure' with K. Mansfield could not be seriously questioned, since her autobiographical short story "An Indiscreet Journey". had not been translated. For the French, "Je ne parle pas français" was the only evidence of her relationship with Carco in 1913, and this story might suggest indeed 'une amitié pure et désintéressée'. By 1915, however, this briefly developed into something more intimate; the proof lies in the entries of her *Journal* which appeared first in the definitive edition translated into French in 1955, in the story "An Indiscreet Journey" itself, and in John Middleton Murry's own admission.[13] By December 1933, Marcel Thiébaut[14] was showing some reluctance to endorse Carco's account; he had read Carco's novel, *Les Innocents,* published in 1916, in which Mansfield appears as 'Winnie', an amoral and predatory English authoress totally different from the Mansfield of the legend; but the *Journal* of 1931 and the other texts of the time were incomplete

and coy, and he eventually accepted Carco's explanations that the character of 'Winnie' resembled Mansfield's only in what it had retained of her purity. 'K. Mansfield n'a posé du personnage que ce qu'il présente de pur et d'intact'.[15] So Carco, the only person with accurate knowledge of Katherine's bohemian days, was accepted by the critics as reliable and helped to preserve the romantic legend.

In 1935, with the translation of the first biography: *La Jeunesse de Katherine Mansfield,*[16] the New Zealand childhood and rebellious adolescence of Mansfield were revealed for the first time. Extracts from the Diary of her journey to the Urewera country in the interior of the North Island of New Zealand emphasized the image of her native land as a kind of untamed, yet exotic, South Pacific Island. Excerpts from her adolescent novel *Juliet* illustrated her 'white gardenia' period—and reinforced the romantic elements in the legend. Future articles throve on them.

In 1935 also, André Maurois in his lectures on the leading contemporary English novelists,[17] placed her alongside such writers as Aldous Huxley and D.H. Lawrence, and gave her the fullest critical assessment in French to date. It was not altogether free from the idealization 'de bon ton' current at the time. From 1935-39, the legend flourished; year after year countless articles celebrated her art; eventually commemorative ceremonies gathered the faithful worshippers around her tomb at Fontainebleau, in a kind of Mansfieldian chapel, with Henri Bordeaux pronouncing the panegyric.[18] In Menton, 'Les Amitiés Méditerranéennes' followed suit by setting a plaque on the Villa Isola Bella where she had lived, thus creating a second shrine for yearly worshippers—which the Menton municipality has encouraged to this day. With the Second World War approaching, the collection of stories *In a German Pension* was translated, though she had refused permission to reprint at the beginning of the First World War. In the national emergency attention was directed elsewhere, but the work of translation went on. The *Poems* appeared in 1941 and John Middleton Murry's *Katherine Mansfield and I* was translated in 1942.

3.   *In a third post-war phase the legend was enriched by a Roman Catholic modification and by a melodramatic distortion.* In 1946, Odette Lenoël's *La Vocation Spirituelle de Katherine Mansfield* was published;[19] it had been mostly written in the pre-war cultist phase, and was indebted to preceding Catholic critics. She derived her evidence mainly from the *Journal* of 1931 and *Letters*. Daniel Rops wrote an introduction to this book which he entitled *Deux Mémoires*. Parallels were drawn between Odette Lenoël and Mansfield: illness, early untimely death at the same age, attachment to a young brother who died prematurely, and progression towards an ideal of Truth and Absolute Love. But a major difference between K.M. and Lenoël was underlined; while K.M. adored the false god of Art, Lenoël had found true religion in a conversion to the Roman Catholic faith, and used to pray, on the anniversary of K.M.'s birth, for the repose of her soul. Nevertheless, in the fifth section of his Introduction, Daniel Rops could confidently dismiss her negation of a personal God, and affirm that she had discovered the central truth of the Christian faith, for she had said: 'Je fais de l'amour toute ma religion.' Since God is Love, says Daniel Rops, K.M. is 'saved'.

So the Legend assumed another dimension for some French critics: together with the Legend of a suffering woman writer prematurely snatched away by Death, we were given a 'mystic' Mansfield.

This first French edition of the *Journal*, condensed and stripped of most of its non-spiritual entries, had offered substance for this view. Since little else but her personal problems and spiritual aspirations was seen in these jottings, she had been early taken over by Catholic writers. Religious elements were first noticed by Gabriel Marcel in 1929 and 1931;[20] in 1931 also the *Action Française*[21] deplored her death in a Theosophical Colony, blaming her Protestant education for her tragic end. In 1931-32 her spiritual attitude was analysed in *Etudes*,[22] in the *Cahiers du Sud*, and in *Figaro*. To the image of the sick woman writer was added that of a poet in prose and a mystic, almost an agnostic saint. Lenoël's book and Daniel Rops's Introduction encouraged G. Lamarche in French Canada in 1947 to view her philosophy of aestheticism in the wider context of 'La carence spirituelle imputable au Protestantisme et au Catholicisme d'avant-guerre'.[23]

The translation in 1950 of "An Indiscreet Journey" gave the legend a new melodramatic emphasis. Now greater attention was given to her emotional problems by Roland Merlin in his *Le drame secret de Katherine Mansfield*. Her flight to Carco in 1915 was read through her short story, but since the definitive edition of the *Journal* was not yet published, her 'amour impossible' was not fully comprehended. It was still possible to believe in the earlier Carco account. Mansfield's past being credited with 'a wealth of feelings but not of sexual experiences'.[24] Meanwhile, Murry became the villain of the story, and the 'Secret Drama' of Mansfield's life was shown to have been her love for an incompatible husband who did not really look after her welfare, remarried only 16 months after her death, and gave her mortal remains a most improper burial. The last chapter of Merlin's book reprints an earlier article of the widely read *France-Illustration*.[25] Its last note is one of necrological lyricism, which however reveals the extent of the idealisation of Mansfield. Merlin reports that when K.M.'s body was placed in its own tomb in 1929, the lid of the coffin opened to reveal an incorrupt Mansfield: 'death had preserved her in the state that it had carried her off six years earlier . . .', and the cemetery keeper's wife exclaimed: 'we must raise the lid so that Katherine may breathe!' Even death could not touch Mansfield's 'purity' and 'integrity'.

So the legend in its various forms prospered and assumed amazing proportions.

4. *In the fourth phase from 1954-65* the romantic elements of the legend were strengthened into melodrama as the result of the publication of personal and previously unpublished material, the *Letters to J.M.M.*[26] and the definitive edition of the *Journal*. These letters, relating her impossible search for a completely satisfying love-relationship with her husband, were now read as a tragic 'roman d'amour'.

This view includes the passage from *La Table Ronde* of May 1954: [27] 'This extraordinary collection of letters reads like a novel; we follow anxiously the inexorable unfolding of a tragedy in which fate plays the leading part. The lovers are continually threatened by three blind forces: poverty, illness and war . . .'

Another more sensational example was offered typically by *Paris-Presse l'Intransigeant*: [28] 'Un long cri d'amour haletant, déchirant, la correspondance de Katherine Mansfield révélée trente ans après!' Many more examples could be cited: [29] clearly, Mansfield had become the heroine of a romance which ended in tragedy. Only in 1959, five years after publication, was Anthony Alpers' *Life of Katherine Mansfield* translated. One would have expected it to clear the air, but it had almost no effect:[30] the legendary image persisted. Few critics acclaimed it. On the contrary it was severely condemned by one critic even as a 'profanation'.[31] Others disapproved of it for the very reasons for which it had been praised in the Anglo-American world. The *Bulletin des Lettres*[32] would have preferred a more sophisticated treatment of the biography better suited to the subject, something 'à la Maurois', and regretted this writer's 'don de la biographie vivante qui sait joindre l'anecdote bien conduite à l'analyse d'âme, son goût des vies romantiques, son style enfin. . . .'

One writer who did realize the implications of the facts was François Mauriac. His comments clearly show in what light Mansfield's writings had been viewed in France. On the front page of the weekly *Figaro Littéraire*, [33] Mauriac voiced a feeling of regret for the dispelling of the legend built around Mansfield's life, and his effort to reconcile the pre-war image with the revised one shows how hard it was to dislodge the idol of the legend. He wrote:

> La vie de K.M. par A. Alpers . . . m'a surpris. Je croyais bien la connaitre, cette Katherine . . . ses lettres, son journal ont été traduits. Je les ai lus et relus. J'ignorais tout pourtant de la vraie Katherine. Cette biographie m'a rappelé ce que je savais déjà . . . c'est qu'à son insu un écrivain flatte toujours l'image qu'il nous livre de lui . . .; à mesure que j'avance dans cette biographie, je retrouve la K.M. que j'avais imaginée d'après son oeuvre et alors que j'ignorais qu'elle avait mené cette triste vie. A partir de sa rencontre avec J.M.M., elle ressemble de plus en plus à l'image que je me faisais d'elle, et quand elle mourra, elle l'aura rejointe: elle aura retrouvé son âme.[34]

So even if K.M.'s life was not as pure as one assumed, her writings had nevertheless revealed a soul aiming at purity and purified by suffering; 'la petite fille perdue s'est trompée de route. Mais elle a cherché, elle a aspiré. C'est tout ce qui nous est demandé. Le reste relève de la grâce.'

But Mauriac was something of an exception, for Alpers' book did not affect most critics nor the majority of the public. Only 1,000 copies were sold and the rest was remaindered.[35] No wonder that one year after it appeared A.M. Monnet still enthused over her dramatised heroine in her *Katherine Mansfield*. Characteristically again, *Le Prix Fémina* was awarded to this book in which: 'La romancière anglaise revit sous nos yeux dans son destin où *le moderne* le dispute curieusement au *romantisme*'.[36] Such exciting ingredients should ensure ready sale to benighted members of the Second Sex.

5.   *The K.M. Exhibition in Paris, 1966.* A fifth phase in the development of the legend was reached in 1966 with the Katherine Mansfield Exhibition in Paris, the effect of which was to reinforce the pre-war cultist tendencies. After the exhibition, however, a few new voices were heard when the first complete edition

effect of which was to reinforce the pre-war cultist tendencies. After the exhibition, however, a few new voices were heard when the first complete edition of her short stories appeared as *Oeuvre romanesque de Katherine Mansfield*.[37] Almost free from cultist tendencies, they offer, though too briefly, a sober appreciation of K.M.'s literary achievements and an objective assessment of her personality. The novelty of her approach and her role as significant witness of a change of consciousness were underlined in *l'Express, Les Lettres Françaises* and *Le Nouveau Candide*.[38]

In spite of this in 1967 a fresh case of 'Mansfielditis Legendaria' was reported in the provinces: a thirteen-page *Ode to Katherine Mansfield*.[39] This testimony of passionate lyricism to a dead Mansfield merits quotation:

> C'est vous
> Je vous découvre au détour du chemin
> Je ne vous connais pas mais déjà sur vos mains
> Vous portez l'amitié de tous les anciens jours
> Votre nom ne m'est pas inconnu Familier
> Votre visage l'est depuis que poings liés
> Je vous suis à travers vos terrestres contours
>
> J'essaie au demeurant d'appuyer ma pensée
> Sur celle de vous voir un instant délaisser
> Ces tourments vains objets que mon âme édulcore
> Je vous suis du regard je vous touche et j'abreuve
> Ce grand désir de vous qu'en silence sans preuve
> Votre présence en moi doucement fait éclore. . . .

To turn to more serious work. When discussing her short stories, French critics (right up to the present day) cannot refrain from mixing her life and work, and from drawing significant parallels with the revelations contained in her *Journal* and *Letters*: the novelty of her talent, her devotion to her Art, her poetic prose, her almost mystical quality distorted by her aesthetic philosophy. For the French, used to the precision of Maupassant, Mansfield came as a revelation of a new way of expressing modern consciousness. 'Woman', 'Tuberculosis', 'English', 'Poet', 'Mystic'—these were highly charged words for the French mind of the thirties, for their overtones were related to intuition, an aspect of the cognitive process to which Bergson had drawn attention. If Mansfield took on so well in France, it is because her self-revelations were in key with the presuppositions of the French.

It is still astonishing that something so far divorced from fact could develop and persist despite the evidence of its inaccuracy. This state of affairs calls for some explanation. Pre-war French critics and publishers down to our own time have relied heavily on the editing of J.M. Murry.[40] The extent and nature of Murry's distortions of his raw material became clear, however, only after his death in 1957, when the Mansfield Manuscript Papers were bought by the Alexander Turnbull Library, Wellington, New Zealand. A preliminary examination of them by I.A. Gordon[41] revealed that the material for the *Journal* of 1927, the *Complete Journal* of 1954, the *Scrapbook* of 1939, the complete *Short Stories* of 1946, which includes many unfinished stories, all came from the record of personal events and inner life. Murry's selective editing has distorted both the form and emphasis of his wife's jottings.

The publications offered to the public as 'Journals' were, then, coloured by the attitudes of Murry himself, as editor and literary executor of the Mansfield Papers. This work came at a difficult time in Murry's life; a time of spiritual and intellectual crisis subsequent to a protracted period of varied domestic problems which was discussed by F.A. Lea.[42] The salient factors may be quickly summarized. Murry's life and thoughts down to 1929 were influenced by the 'presence' of his dead wife, Katherine Mansfield. Domestically she was 'present' even in the person of his second wife, who sought to become a duplicate Mansfield in order to secure his more complete devotion. She had adopted 'Katherine's dress, hair style, hand-writing and mannerisms . . .' She wrote short stories, and even contracted tuberculosis in 1927. She is reported to have told Murry with joy: 'I wanted you to love me as much as you loved K . . . and how could you, without this?'[43]

John Middleton Murry was at this time preoccupied with religion. He reports a mystical experience shortly after Katherine Mansfield's death, which changed his outlook on life. His writings of the time betray his spiritual preoccupations, for example *Keats and Shakespeare*, followed by *The Life of Jesus*, and his article "Towards a new synthesis" published in the *Criterion* in 1926. His letter to Charles du Bos in July, 1929, indicates an attraction to Catholicism:

> Two years ago I was trembling on the very verge of Catholicism. My sheer isolation had become unbearable. As you know, I had married again. Within two years of my marriage, my wife was struck down with pulmonary tuberculosis. The repetition of my destiny preyed upon me, and working together with my intellectual and spiritual isolation, produced in me a hunger for communion such as I had not known before. At that precise time I was reading Bossuet, very patiently. . . . Suddenly he, and Catholicism, became intimate and human. Why . . . should I not make the same effort . . .[44]

Lea considered 1927-8 'were the least productive years of his literary life'[45] partly because of the demands made by the illness of Violet, his second wife. Away from London and incapable of creative work, he had turned his hand (in these years) to the Mansfield papers and edited the *Journal* and *Letters*. The 1927 Journal, though made up of genuinely Mansfieldian excerpts, nevertheless reflected the editor's mystical leanings and attraction to Catholicism. It is not surprising that Catholic critics constantly reviewed it in France.

These facts also account for the distortions evident in J.M. Murry's editing. There is a strong confessional element in all Murry's writing. I feel myself that he was probably basically honest, though from Aldous Huxley[46] in the thirties to Leonard Woolf in the sixties, some writers have had reservations.[47]

But more generally his views have influenced generations of French critics and readers: Katherine Mansfield is still misread in France.[48]

With new editors free from personal involvement, the distance brought by the years, and the outlook of a new generation, the Katherine Mansfield legend will probably alter. However, until a new edition of the *Journal* and a really complete edition of her *Letters* are made, the Legend will survive and perhaps inspire more hallucinated poets to cultivate her unreal figure. For the present, a serious assessment of Katherine Mansfield's contribution to the world of letters must remain provisional, but what is needed is not the earlier romanticism, but some of the sharpened realism she brought to so high a pitch in her stories.

AUMLA, Vol. XXXIV, Christchurch, New Zealand, 1970, pp. 252-263. Also in French in *Etudes Anglaises,* Vol. XXIII, 1970, pp. 357-68.

---

[1] This article is based on a paper delivered at the 12th A.U.L.L.A. Congress in Perth, February 1969. The research material was obtained with the financial help of the University Grants Committee. I should like to thank the Reference Library, Victoria University of Wellington, and the Turnbull Library for their courteous assistance.

[2] Sylvia Berkman, *Katherine Mansfield: A Critical Study*, Yale University Press, 1951, p. 7.

[3] Pierre Citron, 'Katherine Mansfield et la France', *Revue de Littérature Comparée*, Paris, 1940, pp. 173-193.

[4] J.O. Miller, *Katherine Mansfield en France*, Thèse de Doctorat de l'Université de Strasbourg, 1966. After this study had been completed, Dr Miller's came to my attention; I was pleased to find that we had arrived independently at some of the same conclusions.

[5] *For example*: A Maurois's lecture on K.M. to the Société de Conférences in 1935, was published in his collection of essays on Modern English Literature, *Poets and Prophets*. Some thirty years later it was resurrected in extenso as the feature lecture given at the Sorbonne in conjunction with the *Katherine Mansfield Exhibition* of 1966, and a mini version was used as a Preface to the *Oeuvre Romanesque* of the same year. F. Carco's two illustrated articles: 'Souvenirs sur Katherine Mansfield' published in *Les Annales* (27 Jan., 3 Feb., 1933) were reprinted separately in November, 1934 by Le Divan. They form chapter X of his book *Montmartre à 20 ans,* Albin Michel, 1938, and are extended in his second book of recollections *Ma Bohème et mon coeur*, Albin Michel, 1940.

[6] C. Du Bos, *Journal 1921-1923* , Corrêa, Paris, 1945.

[7] L. Gillet, *La Revue des Deux Mondes* XXIV, 5 Dec., 1924, pp. 929-942.

[8] L. Gillet, *La Revue des Deux Mondes* LI, 1 May, 1929, pp. 213-227.

[9] G. Marcel, *Nouvelle Revue Francaise* XXXII, 1 Feb., 1929, pp. 258-273.

[10] Félicité' and 'La Garden-Party' were translated in 1931; the introduction to 'La Garden-Party' written by Edmond Jaloux analysed 'Prelude' and praised Mansfield's art. 'La Monde' was translated in April, 1933.

[11] For a complete list of articles on Katherine Mansfield in French, see P. Citron, op. cit. Berkman, op. cit., and E. Harrison's Bibliography, University of London, May, 1958.

[12] F. Carco, op. cit. in note No. 5.

[13] J.M. Murry in the notes to the definitive edition of the *Journal.*

[14] M. Thiébaut, "K.M.", *Revue de Paris*, Nov.-Dec., 1933.

[15] F. Carco, op. cit.

[16] A translation of R. E. Mantz & J.M. Murry, *The Life of Katherine Mansfield*, London, 1933.

[17] A. Maurois, *Poets and Prophets*, Paris, 1935. He analyses her 'feminine impressionism' in particular and stresses her qualities as a woman writer.

[18] H. Bordeaux, "Le Souvenir de Katherine Mansfield", *La Revue Hebdomadaire*, 17 June, 1939.

[19] Odette Lenoël, *La Vocation Spirituelle de Katherine Mansfield*, Albin Michel, Paris, 1946.

[20] G. Marcel, *Nouvelle Revue Française* XXXII, 1 Feb., 1929, pp. 268-273. Preface to *Lettres de Katherine Mansfield*, Stock, Paris, July, 1931.

[21] Anonymous article, *Action Française* "Lettres de Katherine Mansfield", Paris, 9 August, 1931, p.7.

[22] P. Defrennes, "L'Homme et sa plume; la correspondance de Katherine Mansfield" *Etudes* des Pères de la Cie de Jésus, vol. 209, Paris, Oct.-Dec., 1931, pp. 314-324.
G. B. Bertrand "L'Attitude de Spirituelle de Katherine Mansfield", *Figaro*, 14 Jan., 1932, p.5.
A. Blanchet, "Le Secret de Katherine Mansfield", *Etudes*, 20 Novembre and 5 Decembre, 1939.

[23] G. Lamarche, "L'Equipe Murry-Mansfield", *Carnets Viatoriens*, published by Le Scolasticat des Clercs de St Viateur, Joliette, P.Q., Canada, October, 1947, pp. 277-291.

[24] R. Merlin, *Le drame secret de Katherine Mansfield*, Seuil, Paris, 1950, p. 130.

[25] R. Merlin, "Le drame de Katherine Mansfield", *France-Illustration*, 19 Jan., 1946, pp. 59-62.

[26] *Letters to John Middleton Murry* published in England in 1951; they were translated into French in three volumes from November, 1954, to 1957.

[27] Signed J.T., *La Table Ronde*, Paris, May, 1954.

[28] By Anne Masson, 16 April, 1954.

[29] Some review titles are clearly indicative of the transmogrification of the writer as: "K.M. ou la passion torturée", Renée Willy, *Massilia*, 21 April, 1954; "Un coeur mis à nu", P.O. Walzer, *Curieux*, 17 Feb., 1955: "Un douloureux roman", *Tribune de Genève*, 18 May, 1957.

[30] Gabrielle Gras, *Europe*, Sept., 1959, was a notable exception.

[31] Renée Daumière, *Paris-Normandie*, 2 July, 1959.

[32] Lyons, 15 Oct., 1959.

[33] "De Katherine Mansfield aux tricheurs ou la petite fille qui retrouva son âme", 18 April, 1959.

[34] The last three lines of Mauriac's commentary support my conclusions in the second part of this article.

[35] A. Alpers, *Katherine Mansfield: l'Oeuvre et la Vie*, Seghers, Paris, 1959. Information provided by P. Seghers in a letter in my possession. This would explain why so many French critics preserved a legendary view on K.M.

[36] A.M. Monnet, *Katherine Mansfield*, Editions du Temps, Paris, 1960. These words are found on the jacket of the book. An interview with the author printed at the end of this book mentions that she had begun to write it in 1939 at the time of the Commemorative ceremonies held at Le Prieuré, Avon, for K.M.'s 50th Anniversary.

[37] Stock, Paris, 1956. A. Bay wrote the preface.

[38] Jacques Caban, *l'Express*, 15 August, 1966: Lia Lacombre *Les Lettres Françaises*, 7 July, 1966: Kléber Haedenx, *Le Nouveau Candide*, 1 August, 1966.

[39] P.A. Hauvette, *Ode à Katherine Mansfield*, L'Auvergne Littéraire, Clermont-Ferrand, 1967.

[40] André Bay, the General Secretary of Stock Publishers, Paris, met John Middleton Murry and acknowledged his help when drafting his Prefaces and Notes to the French Editions of K.M.'s works. See A. Bay, Carrefour, Paris, 8.2.1956 (on the definitive edition of the *Journal*.)

[41] I.A. Gordon, "The Editing of the Katherine Mansfield manuscript papers", *Landfall*, 1959.

[42] F.A. Lea, *The Life of John Middleton Murry*, Methuen, London, 1959, especially ch. IX to XIII.

[43] F..A. Lea, op. cit., p. 144.

[44] Charles Dédéyan, *Le Cosmopolitisme Littéraire* de C. Du Bos, S.E.D.E.S., Paris, 1966, vol. I, tome 3, p. 129-130. Du Bos and J.M. Murry were close friends and corresponded regularly. They were groping for a religious answer to the problems of modern intellectuals. Du Bos underwent a religious conversion on July 29, 1927. In his *Journal* (1921 to 1929) Du Bos repeatedly acknowledges that Murry's writings of the time, in particular *The Life of Jesus*, were instrumental in bringing about his own conversion and deplores that his friend could not finally take the same step. (*Journal* IV, 28 Oct., 1928, Corrêa, Paris, p. 213.)

[45] F.A. Lea, op. cit., p. 147.

[46] Aldous Huxley, *Point Counterpoint*, London, 1928, in which J.M.M. is portrayed as Denis Burlap.

[47] Leonard Woolf, *Downhill all the way 1919-1939*, Volume 4 of his autobiography, London, 1968, p. 49 and p. 203. Charges of 'Pecksniffianism' were laid against J.M.M. by L. Woolf.

[48] Generally speaking of course, for many valid articles and book reviews have been published over the years in *Etudes Anglaises*. They were written by academic critics who read Mansfield in English and were acquainted with Anglo-American criticism on the subject.

Eileen Baldeshwiler, "Katherine Mansfield's Theory of Fiction"

Critics of Katherine Mansfield—even such perceptive and positive ones as Elizabeth Bowen—have tended to write off this author as a more or less pure inspirationist, a careful craftsman it is true but one with no fundamental view of her art. Thus according to Miss Bowen, Miss Mansfield possessed intelligence but "it was not upon that she depended: intuitive knowing, vision, had to be the thing" (Introduction to *Stories by Katherine Mansfield*, 1956, x). It is true that many of Miss Mansfield's remarks about writing are cast in a tone of adolescent pique or enthusiasm that tends to throw doubt on her seriousness, that she never produced a full-length discussion of the story writer's art, that most of her comments on formal or aesthetic questions were dropped casually into letters, journals, or in the pot-boiling reviews she had to turn out. Yet if the critic, putting aside his irritation with tone, takes the trouble to cull these ephemeral writings for serious statements about narrative form and technique, he will be surprised at the depth and consistency of Miss Mansfield's view of her art.

One of Katherine Mansfield's most tenaciously held convictions about the art of the story, a point to which she returns again and again, is the notion that a coolly "objective" view of one's subject is not enough. Quite simply, she remarks of the sisters in "The Daughters of the Late Colonel" that while she at first found them merely amusing, looking deeper, she "bowed down to the beauty that was hidden in their lives." Finally, "to discover that was all my desire" (*The Letters of Katherine Mansfield*, J. Middleton Murry, ed., 1941, p. 389). Elsewhere she wrote to S. S. Koteliansky, "Do you, too, feel an infinite delight and value in *detail*—not for the sake of detail but for the life *in* the life of it?" (*Letters*, p. 27). What is essential is to penetrate one's subject, not to take a flat view of it; thus feelings, and objects as well, must be contemplated—or rather "submitted to"—until one is truly lost in them. Miss Mansfield's remarks on the genesis of stories illustrate this truth, as in her description of an afternoon's wait for her father—

> Life is so strange—so full of extraordinary things. . . . Today, this afternoon, waiting for my Father to come to tea—I felt I could have made—but only of that waiting—a whole book. I began thinking of all the time one has "waited" for so many and strange people and things—the special quality it has—the agony of it and the strange sense that there is a second you who is outside yourself and does nothing—nothing but just listen—the other complicated you goes on—and then there is this keen, unsleeping creature—waiting to leap—It is like a dark beast and he who comes is its prey—(*Letters*, p. 215).

Her account of the way "Kew Gardens" might have begun is well known:

> It happens so often—or so seldom—in life, as we move among the trees, up and down the known and unknown paths, across the lawns and into the shade and out again, that something—for no reason that we can discover—gives us pause. Why is it that, thinking back upon that July afternoon, we see so distinctly that flower-bed? We must have passed myriads of flowers that day; why do these particular ones return? It is true, we stopped in front of them, and talked a little and then moved on. But, though we weren't conscious of it at the time, something was happening—something. (Review of "Kew Gardens," June 13, 1919, reprinted in *Novels and Novelists*, J. Middleton Murry, ed., 1930, p. 40).

In a more playful mood, Miss Mansfield observed to Lady Brett in 1917, "When I write about ducks I swear that I am a white duck with a round eye," a condition she says Lawrence would probably call "this consummation with the duck" (*Letters,* p. 74). Elsewhere she records that when she wrote "The Voyage," she was on the boat, "going down those stairs, smelling the smell of the saloon." But emphatically this was *not* a memory of a real experience; it was instead "a kind of *possession*" (*Letters*, p. 453). Yet the first identification with the subject is only a "prelude"; there follows the moment "when you are *more* duck, *more* apple, or *more* Natasha than any of these objects could ever possibly be, and so you *create* them anew" (*Letters*, p. 47). Thus Katherine Mansfield calls her writing "a cry against corruption"; not a protest but a cry, a lament for "everything doomed to disaster, almost wilfully, stupidly, like the almond tree and 'pas de nougat pour l'noel'" (a reference to a 19th-century Provençal poem telling of the withering of the tree's blossoms in cold).

Above all, one does not sit and watch a spectacle: indeed, as she says, "one IS the spectacle for the time" (*Letters*, p. 347). Thus the true artist must both be free and must submit: "he must be controlled by none other than his deepest self, his truest self," and then "he must accept Life . . . give himself so utterly that no personal . . . self remains" (*Letters*, p. 365). The impulse to write, she feels intensely, is not the impulse to turn life into a case or a problem. While a novel or story ought to be scientifically correct, or capable of being proved so, "the impulse to write is a different impulse," for when the author really penetrates his subject, he in turn receives from it a kind of "subconscious . . . wisdom," a "divine flower to all his terrific hard gardening" (*Letters*, p. 330). The psychology of writing is subtle and difficult, and for herself, she finds the greatest travail is precisely "learning to submit"—"Not that one ought to be without resistance. . . . But when I am writing of 'another' I want so to lose myself in the soul of the other that I am not" (*Letters*, p. 365). The act of faith, of surrender, requires "pure risk," the absolute belief in "one's own essential freedom." It is hard to let go, "yet one's creative life depends on it and one *desires* to do nothing else." (*Letters*, p. 351)

Conversely , to remain in full possession, as some writers do, while infinitely less exhausting, produces tell-tale effects. Thus a novel such as *Esther Waters* is as dry as "the remainder biscuit after a voyage" because it has no emotion. "Here is a world of objects accurately recorded, here are states of mind set down, and here . . . is . . . good Esther . . . and who cares?" (*Novels and Novelists*, p. 245). Inquiring why so many characters of 1920 novels were "book-bound," Miss Mansfield suggests that, in contrast to the personages of the classic English novels, more recent ones are seen "in relation to an intellectual idea of life." In this second case "life is made to fit them; something is abstracted—something quite unessential—that they wouldn't in the least know what to do with . . . and they are set in motion." (*Novels and Novelists*, p. 131)

But there is a facility that is as deadly a fault as the failure to penetrate the subject and endow it with life. Of one of her own stories, Katherine Mansfield writes, "I feel again that this kind of knowledge is too easy for me; it's a kind of trickery" and the result "only looks and smells like a story." (*Journal of Katherine Mansfield*, J. Middleton Murry, ed., 1946, p. 187). One must draw nearer and nearer, never merely making use of material. Miss Mansfield's deepest dissatisfaction is reserved for work that she finds "once removed" (*Letters*, p. 114); her sustained endeavor in all writing is to be "*Dead* true. . . I mean like one takes a sounding—(yet gay withal)" (*Letters*, p. 319). To produce fiction that is "dead true" requires both thought and feeling, but it is precisely the relationship of these activities that is important:

what is the use, to your artist at any rate, of thought that is not the outcome of feeling? You must feel before you can think; you must think before you can express yourself. It is not enough to feel and write; or to think and write. True expression is the outcome of them both, yet a third thing, and separate" (*Novels and Novelists*, p.205).

What Katherine Mansfield means, then, by the "visionary consciousness," she describes in a letter to a kindred spirit, Richard Murry, the painter: "There is *this* world, and there is the world that the artist creates in this world, which is nevertheless *his* world, and subject to *his* laws—his 'vision'" (*Letters*, p. 387). But art makes its "*divine* spring into the bounding outline of things" not through sensitive perception alone. Pure vision "is not enough," as Miss Mansfield pointed out to her friends Sydney and Violet Schiff, for one must find "the exact way in which to convey the delicate perception" (*Letters*, p. 312). Vision must be articulated through form and by means of technique.

It is in her observations on form that Miss Mansfield perhaps best reveals the strength and subtlety of her thought about fiction. Occasionally she equates form loosely with "pattern," as when she remarks that too many women take a naive pleasure in writing for writing's sake, "forgetting all about the pattern they intended to follow or embroidering it so thickly that none but themselves can discover its original outline" (*Novels and Novelists*, p. 106). Pattern alone, at least in the sense of plot, will not guarantee a living form. Thus, remarking on a quality of inertness in Sheila Kaye-Smith's fiction, Katherine Mansfield notes that to this writer, the plot's the thing, and "having decided upon it she gets her team together and gives out the parts." Then there is nothing but to speak them. (*Novels and Novelists*, p. 80)

Again, Miss Mansfield sometimes refers to form merely as that which results from the author's discipline. At one time, explaining to her husband and editor that she was unable further to cut a piece she had written because every word in it had been carefully selected in the first place, she said: "I don't 'just ramble on' you know, but this thing happened to just fix six and a half pages . . . I'm a powerful stickler for form in this style of work. I hate the sort of license that English people give themselves . . . to spread over and flop and roll about. I feel as fastidious as though I wrote with acid" (*Letters*, p. 4). Another time, she described the form of "Prelude" simply as "my own invention" (*Letters*, p. 74)

In a more extended discussion of the formal requirements for novels, Miss Mansfield explains that there are two main categories of long fiction, each of which requires "story," because

> . . . having decided on the novel form, one cannot lightly throw one's story over the mill without replacing it with another story which is, in its way, obedient to the rules of that discarded one. There must be the same setting out upon a voyage of discovery (but through unknown seas instead of charted waters), the same difficulties and dangers must be encountered, and there must be an ever-increasing sense of the greatness of the adventure and an ever more passionate desire to possess and explore the mysterious country. There must be given the crisis when the great final attempt is made which succeeds—or does not succeed. Who shall say?
>
> The crisis, then, is the chief of our "central points of significance" and the endeavours and the emotions are stages on our journey towards or away from it. For without it, the form of the novel, as we see it, is lost. Without it, how are we to appreciate the importance of one "spiritual event" rather than another? What is to prevent each being unrelated—complete in itself—if the gradual unfolding in growing, gaining light is not to be followed by one blazing moment? (*Novels and Novelists*, p. 32)

Unless the demand for form in the novel requires at least the "setting out on a journey" through "central points of significance" culminating in a final success or failure to "possess and explore the mysterious country," what is to prevent everyone from becoming a writer? Without form, by which "one thing is to be related to another thing," why cannot any man, woman, or child write an autobiography "and so provide reading matter for the ages?" (*Novels and Novelists*, p. 44)

If form in one of its senses is to be taken as structural pattern, what about the relation of detail to form, a question of perhaps special importance for the realistic writer? In this respect, Miss Mansfield decries above all a lack of selectivity. "My particular difficulty," she confesses, "is a kind of fertility— which I suspect very much because it is not solid enough" (*Letters*, p. 387). Not long before her death she still is able to say "The trouble with writing is that one seethes with stories" (*Letters*, p. 449). In the great masters of narrative writing, however, details serve the function of linking the individual mind to the larger whole. In a discussion of the trivialization she observed in much modern fiction, Miss Mansfield asks,

> Can we of this age go on being content with stories and sketches and impressions and novels which are less than adventures of the soul? It is all so wearying, so wearying—this vision of the happy or unhappy pair or company, driving through the exhibition, meeting with adventures on the way and so safe home, or not safe home, at last. How can anything not trivial happen to them while the author still thinks it necessary to drive them at such a pace? Why will he not see that we would rather— far rather—they stayed at home, mysteriously themselves, with time to be conscious, in the deepest, richest sense, of what is happening to them. . . . Then, indeed, as in the stories of Tchehov, we should become aware of the rain pattering on the roof all night long, of the languid, feverish wind, of the moonlit orchard and the first snow, passionately realized, not indeed as analogous to a state of mind, but as linking that mind to the larger whole. (*Novels and Novelists*, p. 54)

A plethora of detail not responsible to a larger structure or a deeper significance will result only in a dissipation of total impression, with the result that the reader will be overcome by weariness and boredom. Or he may experience a kind of exhaustion at the abundance of sensation he is required to undergo. "Can one," Miss Mansfield inquires, "think for one moment of the mystery of life when one is at the mercy of surface impressions?"

> Can one *think* when one is not only taking part but being snatched at, pulled about flung here and there, cuffed and kissed, and played with? Is it not the abiding satisfaction of a work of art that the writer was master of the situation when he wrote it and at the mercy of nothing less mysterious than a greater work of art? (*Novels and Novelists*, pp. 44-45)

The inept handling of detail may also result in flatness, the sense, as Miss Mansfield remarks of Edith Wharton's *Age of Innocence,* that we are looking at portraits, human beings "arranged for exhibition purposes." What is required is that there be sufficient emotion and control of subject to animate particulars; one must ask that the feeling "be greater than the cause that excites it." One wishes also to share "the moment of exposition," for is it not to that moment that all writing leads? (*Novels and Novelists*, p. 320). In order not to lose perspective, it is, moreover, important for the writer occasionally to stand away from his work, to free himself, as it were from the fascination of his facts. Thus Miss Mansfield describes a lasting impression she derived from seeing two Van Gogh paintings—"They taught me something about writing, which was queer, a kind of freedom—or rather, a shaking free. When one has been working for a long stretch one begins to narrow one's vision a bit, to fine things down too much. And it's only when something else breaks through, a picture or something seen out of doors, that one realises it" (*Letters*, p. 423)

But if form can be described structurally, it can also be seen as "organic," and Miss Mansfield occasionally uses metaphors of natural process in describing the genesis and development of her own work as well as that of others. Commenting to a correspondent on "The Daughters of the Late Colonel," she says that like the earlier "Prelude," the story "just unfolds and opens" (*Letters*, p. 359). Referring to *The Gay Dombeys* by Sir Harry Johnston, Miss Mansfield points out that it would be difficult to summarize its story, for it is made up of several narratives "each as separate as flowers on a tree" but all contributing to the one effect (*Novels and Novelists*, p.18-19). Pursuing the image in a more general statement about the novel she holds that we may understand the central idea in a book as "a lusty growing stem from which the branches spring clothed with leaves, and the buds become flowers and fruits." We think of the author as choosing "with infinite deliberation the very air in which that tree shall be nourished." The writer will be deeply aware that the novel's coming to perfection depends upon the strength with which the central idea "supports its beautiful accumulations" (*Novels and Novelists*, p. 236).

Form will be known through its effects. In the presence of fully achieved form, one will experience the "feeling of inevitability that there is in a great work of art" (*Letters*, p. 459), pointing to a life beyond the life we know. Form is also in a special way illuminative, lending to the work a quality that is "immediately, perfectly recognizable." Such a work as "About Love" or "The Lady with the Dog" can say of its form, it belongs to me; it is of my essence. In fact, "I am often given away in the first sentence. I seem almost to stand or fall by it. It is to me what the first phrase of the song is to the singer. Those who know me feel: 'Yes, this is it.' And they are from the moment prepared for what is to follow" (*Novels and Novelists*, p. 220).

Without form there is not fiction but only reportage, autobiography, or the celebration of moments. It is her inability to do more than re-capture the momentary details of sensation that Miss Mansfield faults in Dorothy Richardson, who, she says, "has no memory." True, anything that goes into her mind can be summoned forth, complete in every detail, with nothing taken away from it and nothing added. This is a rare gift, yet while life can be swift and breathless if one is to be truly alive, he must sometimes "creep away into . . . caves of contemplation." Then in the silence, "Memory mounts his throne and judges all that is in our minds—appointing each his separate place, high or low, rejecting this, selecting that—putting this one to shine in the light and throwing that one into the darkness." Until, in other words, form has truly intervened into the world of sense through a judgment of experience, there can be no art. Until details have been given their place in the whole scheme, "they have no meaning in the world of art" (*Novels and Novelists*, p. 5-6). Form, at once, then, arranges, interprets, and expresses experience.

That form is the chief agent for giving unity to a work, Miss Mansfield demonstrates in several ways. She herself avers a passion for "technique," for "making the thing into a *whole*" (*Letters*, p. 364). In reading and thinking about the work of Chekhov, again and again she gives testimony to the mysterious life that is contained in his stories, a life that can only arise through the achievement or the discovery of perfect form. Her admiration of "The Steppe" is profound. "One says of things: they are immortal," but "One feels about this story not that it *becomes* immortal—it always was." Why is this so? The answer lies in the perfection of its vision of the true inner shape of experience, for the narrative "has no beginning or end. Tchekhov just touched one point with his pen (.------.) and then another point: *enclosed* something which had, as it were, been there for ever" (*Letters*, p. 215). For Katherine Mansfield, then, form is invented, it expresses itself in pattern, it unifies, bestows inevitability, and animates detail as it orders and illuminates what memory retains from its judgment of experience. Form will be actualized by means of technique.

Miss Mansfield herself can lay claim to being one of the most scrupulous craftsmen in the language, and here again is abundant evidence that she is no intuitionist. Technique she refers to as "extraordinarily difficult" (*Letters*, p. 387). But she acknowledges to her husband that "the older I grow, the more exquisite I want to be, *fine* down to every minutest particular, as a writer, as a talker, in my home, in my life, and in all my ways" (*Letters*, p. 225), while she points out elsewhere that a friend's easy talk about good art and bad art used to embarrass her "because I felt she wasn't *working* . . . wasn't really *getting down to it* . . . humbly" (*Letters* p. 353). For Katherine Mansfield there were no short cuts; on the contrary, the artist must make all his discoveries afresh. In the long run, she thought, writers must be their own teachers. To do this means putting everything to the test. The great ideal, for herself and for all artists, is "To be *thorough*—to be honest." Indeed, in her opinion, if artists really possessed integrity, they would "save the world." With her it is axiomatic that "Good work takes upon itself a Life—bad work has death in it" (*Letters*, p. 363)

Occasionally, though dissatisfied with the piece she is working on, she will continue with it for the practice, for "getting into my stride" (*Letters*, p. 216). When the work is satisfactory, she feels that it is "the real thing" and that she did not, as she remarks of "Je ne parle pas français," "shirk it" (*Letters*, p. 113). Looking back upon the process of composing some of her stories, she ruminates, "It's a very queer thing how *craft* comes into writing, even down to details. For example, in 'Miss Brill,' I choose not only the length of every sentence but even the sound of every sentence. I choose the rise and fall of every paragraph to fit her, and to fit her on that day at that very moment. After I'd written it I read it aloud—numbers of times—just as one would *play over* a musical composition— trying to get it nearer and nearer to the expression of Miss Brill—until it fitted her" (*Letters*, p. 360-361).

Discussing tone in her reviews and letters, Miss Mansfield is as likely to point out deficiencies and faults as note successes. Thus she writes of Stephen Hudson's *Richard Kurt* (1919) that its tone is that of an introduction, an effect created by the author's over-eagerness to make his protagonist vivid through adjectives alone (*Novels and Novelists*, p. 107). In another place she notes the "dreadful glaze of 'intellectuality' which is like a curse upon so many English writers" (*Letters*, p. 479). But an appropriate suppleness, warmth, and freshness is obtained indirectly. The real question is "how are we going to convey these overtones, half tones, quarter tones, these hesitations, doubts, beginnings, if we go at them *directly*? . . . I do believe there is a way of doing it and that's by trying to get as near to the *exact truth* as possible" (*Letters*, p. 476). Above all, one must never tell the reader what he is to feel. The characters of William Gerhardi for example, are being shown off, rather than seen (*Letters*, p. 417). Mulling over *The Oxford Book of English Verse* in 1915, she complains, too, of lapses in tone among the poets, likening their deficiencies to the lack of a good ear in musicians. Hardly any are exactly on pitch, she feels, and worse, hardly anyone seems to understand "what the middle of the note is. . . . It's not that they are even 'sharp' or 'flat'—It's something much more subtle—they are not playing on the very *note itself*" (*Letters*, p. 35). In her own work, she abhors what appears in retrospect to be its "triviality," the inability to create or capture the right atmosphere. Without that, she says, "nothing is worth doing" (*Letters*, p. 324). This delicate adjustment is the fruit of subtle taste, for "Better a half-truth, beautifully whispered, than a whole . . . solemnly shouted" (*Novels and Novelists*, p. 201).

If, however, after sufficient contemplation an object or experience has made its impression upon the writer, he will be seized by the specific emotion that alone can give "a close and intimate unity" to his materials (*Novels and Novelists* p. 246). This over-all emotional atmosphere Miss Mansfield sometimes likens to charm or tenderness in painting or the tone produced by a first-rate musician (*Letters,* p. 447). Above all, tone is capable of lending to fiction an essential continuity. Thus Tolstoy has only to touch the old Tartar waiter in *Anna Karenina* and "he gives out a note" that "persists, is a part of the whole book" Others "introduce their cooks, aunts, strange gentlemen, and so on, and once the pen is off them they are gone—*dropped* down a hole. Can one explain this by what you might call—a *covering* atmosphere?" (*Letters*, p. 324). It is important, Miss Mansfield writes in a critique of Virginia Woolf's *Night and Day*, that the author hold his characters within a circle of steady light, that he cause this light to shine not merely at but through them (*Novels and Novelists*, p. 114). The ideal is "to tackle the whole of the mind." Why is it, she asks, that the very best prose writers are still "cutting up sections"?

Once he has found his subject and absorbed its peculiar emotionality to the point where he can convey it fully to the reader, the writer still must address himself to the problem of structure. Difficulties arise when the writer creates too few or too many climaxes. Thus some stories flow along so gently and smoothly that the reader is put to sleep, while other books fail in the opposite way. Thus Mary Gaunt's method is "to think of an extraordinary background, double it, add one man, multiply by one terrible danger, keep on multiplying, subtract all possible means of escape, draw a line, add one absolutely unexpected means of escape," and so on (*Novels and Novelists*, p. 176). Compression and selection are of utmost importance, as she suggests to William Gerhardi (*Letters*, p. 418).

Miss Mansfield acknowledged her own difficulty with "curtains", and protested that Clement Shorter's request for a thirteen-segment story was well-nigh impossible for her to fulfill (*Letters*, p. 411). In a note on Joseph Hergesheimer's *Gold and Iron*, she describes this author's struggles with arrangement—

> In the long, slow approach to the "crisis", he writes well and freely; he takes his time, one has the impression that he feels, here, at this point he is safe, and can afford to let himself go. But when the heart of the story is reached, when there is nothing left to depend upon—to cling to—then he is like a young swimmer who can even swim very well, disport himself unafraid and at ease as long as he knows that the water is not out of his depth. When he discovers that it is—he disappears. (*Novels and Novelists*, p.158)

She voices strenuous objection to an editor's cutting of her work ("Shall I pluck the eyes out of a story for forty pounds?") (*Letters*, p. 307). What the problem of structure finally comes down to for Katherine Mansfield is determining how much can be omitted without robbing the characters of their "situation" (*Novels and Novelists*, p. 165).

Her hopes for prose are boundless; she believed it a medium hardly understood in her time. Deploring the fact that younger writers were still preoccupied with "the decomposing vapours of poor Jules Laforgue," she exclaims, "I *do* believe that the time has come for a 'new word' but I imagine the new word will not be spoken easily. People have never explored the lovely medium of prose. It is a hidden country still—I feel that so profoundly" (*Letters*, p. 210, 1919). Prose is still an almost undiscovered medium and that there are "extraordinary, thrilling possibilities" (*Novels and Novelists*, p. 96).

To her contemporaries Miss Mansfield suggests emphatically that they eliminate Russianisms and Gallicisms from their diction. Arnold Gibbons, for example, has learned much from Chekhov, but has also absorbed the Russian's manner of expression to a point where Gibbons' stories sound like translations (*Letters*, p. 475-476). Speaking of a new French story her husband had sent, Katherine Mansfield notes that the English writer should admit no Gallic "half-expressions," which like certain plants let into the garden, appear showy at first but soon spread like weeds (*Letters*, p. 122-123). It is true that the English language is extremely difficult, but it is also extraordinarily rich, "so clear and bright that one can search out the darkest places with it." It is likewise "heavenly simple and true" (*Letters*, p. 123). Quoting some of her favorite lines from Shakespeare (*The Winter's Tale*, V. iii, 132-135), she explains that it is her "passion for solidity and honesty in all things" that draws her to the Elizabethans, as well as to Keats, Wordsworth, Coleridge, Shelley, and DeQuincey (*Letters*, p. 126). In style she looks for precision: "You know how I *choose* my words; they can't be changed . . . if you don't like it or think it is wrong *just as it is* I'd rather you didn't print it," (*Letters*, p. 329), control: ("We are so accustomed to the horse without the rider, roaming very free, or the rider very desperate, looking for the horse," (*Novels and Novelists*, p. 10), and expressiveness: "Can we afford to leave it out of a page, of a paragraph—after Tchekhov?" (*Novels and Novelists*, p. 92). The most difficult problem of style for all writers, but especially for those of today, is simply "to find their true expression and to make it adequate to the new fields of experience" (*Novels and Novelists*, p. 272).

In all these ways, then, technique brings before the reader the shapings that art makes of memory. The writer must be at once free and submissive, but all liberty has its risks. Great artists are not "drunken men"; on the contrary, they know that the moon cannot be bought for sixpence and that liberty is "only a profound realization of the greatness of the dangers in their midst" (*Novels and Novelists*, p. 22). The writer's freedom will always carry him into new realms of emotion and expression; it is only when he passes beyond conveying knowledge, however fine, that we are literally enthralled (*Novels and Novelists*, p. 119). We ask of a book, "Is there a moment when . . . despite the artist's control he himself is borne away, as unconscious as we are of the stage and the setting?"(*Novels and Novelists*, p. 206). For the ultimate achievement of fictional art, writing with a purpose is not enough. Neither is it enough to set problems. What, Miss Mansfield asks, was Chaucer's or Shakespeare's? The fact is that the problem as fictional subject is the invention of the nineteenth century. (One remembers Chekhov's reiterated protest that he had no problem.) True art arises from a different impulse—the maker takes "a long look at life. He says softly, 'So this is what life is, is it?' And he proceeds to express that" (*Letters*, p. 416). Profound experience will leave common things intensified and illumined, but with a tragic, secret knowledge, always presented by indirection. "I might," she says, "write about a boy eating strawberries or a woman combing her hair on a windy morning. . . .", for that is the only way to mention "deserts." But "they *must* be there. Nothing less will do" (*Letters*, p. 225).

Studies in Short Fiction, 1970, vol. 7, pp. 421-432.

IV

Consolidation

Margaret Scott, "The Extant Manuscripts of Katherine Mansfield"

When Katherine Mansfield died her manuscripts consisted of 46 notebooks, several boxes of miscellaneous loose papers, and such of her letters as the recipients had chosen to preserve. There must also be, somewhere on American territory, the manuscripts of at least some of her stories for in a letter of 1948 to the Alexander Turnbull Library, Wellington, New Zealand, Middleton Murry wrote 'I sold the MSS of nearly all the stories to U.S.A. in 1938'. Attempts to trace these have so far failed. But Middleton Murry's exchange of letters with the Turnbull Library brought to his notice that New Zealand, although belatedly, had a warm and to some extent proprietorial interest in Katherine Mansfield. The country which had bred her and had become for her insufferably parochial and limiting by the time she was eighteen, was now, if not a little shame-faced, then at least regretful at the immaturity in itself which had driven her away. She had found no climate here for the kind of work she wanted to do, but later writers had stayed and had begun the slow task of creating such a climate. We were no longer as raw and slumbering as when she left us, and we were very awake to what we had lost.

Aware of New Zealand's interest, then, Middleton Murry made a will which stipulated that all the letters of Katherine Mansfield of which he died possessed (approximately 500) were to be offered to the British Museum for £1,000, and after that, if the British Museum did not buy them, to the Alexander Turnbull Library for the same price. The matter arose in 1957 and the British Museum, mentioning insufficient resources, turned the offer down. In those days the Turnbull Library was administered by the Department of Internal Affairs and, despite much good-will, there was pitifully little money for acquisitions. Certainly there was nothing like £1,000 for the letters of a writer to whom England, France, and the U.S.A. all laid some kind of specified or unspecified claim. But she *had* been born here, spent her childhood here, and derived most of her best material from this country.

New Zealand was stirred. A special Government grant was made and a public appeal was launched by the Friends of the Turnbull Library. The interest was such that it was decided to bid for the other manuscripts which were to be auctioned at Sotheby's in London at about the same time, and so it was that Katherine Mansfield's 500 or so letters to her husband, her 46 note-books and diaries, and a large number of her other manuscripts came to the Alexander Turnbull Library. Since then, the Turnbull has had a vigorous acquisition policy with regard to Mansfield material, both manuscript and published, and it is the primary purpose of this article to describe the Turnbull's Mansfield collection, within the framework of other, more widely-known repositories of Mansfield papers elsewhere in the world.

The nature of my own involvement needs to be explained. For some years, until recently, I have been a librarian in the Manuscripts Section of the Alexander Turnbull Library. I have also, for about the same time but in a quite different context, had a contract with Oxford University Press to collect and edit the letters of Katherine Mansfield. It has therefore been my concern to locate manuscripts in other parts of the world for my own private project, and, in my professional capacity, to strengthen the Turnbull's collection of Mansfield manuscripts.

Elsewhere in the world most Mansfield papers have by now come to rest in academic or special libraries, and only a small (but unfortunately not accurately assessable) proportion remains in private hands. In England, the letters to Middleton Murry's brother are still in the possession of Mr. Richard Murry, but most of the manuscripts which remain in England are in the British Museum. The Strachey Trust has four letters to Lytton Strachey, the University of Birmingham Library has one letter to John Galsworthy, the Library of the University of Sussex has typed transcripts of a group of letters to Virginia Woolf, the originals of which have vanished. But the British Museum has acquired a number of important groups of letters: to Ida Baker, to S.S. Koteliansky, to Elizabeth, Countess Russell (Elizabeth von Arnim), to Sydney and Violet Schiff, and one to Mark Gertler.

In Canada, McMaster University, Hamilton, holds the letters to Bertrand Russell; and at Assumption University, Windsor, Ontario, are letters to Garnet Trowell—also biographically important, presumably—but these are under an embargo and have been withheld from inclusion in the *Collected Letters*. The biggest collection of Mansfield manuscripts outside the Turnbull Library is in the United States: at the Academic Center Library, University of Texas. Among other material in the Texas holdings are about 80 letters to Lady Ottoline Morrell. Letters to Virginia Woolf are in the Berg Collection, New York Public Library, and in the Huntington Library are typed transcripts of letters to Elizabeth, Countess Russell, some of the originals of which are located while others are not. The manuscripts in the Stanford University Libraries, California, are varied and include ten letters to Lady Ottoline Morrell. Mr. William Targ of New York owns Katherine Mansfield's letters to her publisher, Constable.

With the exception of the Trowell letters in the library of Assumption University, all the letters of Katherine Mansfield which I have been able to locate have been made available for publication in the *Collected Letters*. More than that, most repositories and all private owners have given permission for the xerox copies of their letters to be incorporated in the Turnbull's collection. The two exceptions to this are the Berg Collection, and the Academic Center of the

University of Texas whose policies will not allow xerox copies of their manuscripts to be retained either by the purchaser or by any other person or institution. These—particularly the letters to Lady Ottoline Morrell and to Virginia Woolf—are regrettable lacunae in the Turnbull's collection in view of the fact that the Turnbull already holds 14 original letters from Lady Ottoline Morrell to the New Zealand poet D'Arcy Cresswell, and one from Virginia Woolf to Katherine Mansfield.

A good deal of material—I am reluctant to speculate how much—remains untraced. Over a hundred letters to the Hon. Dorothy Brett were sold in 1941 to a John W. Turner of New York and cannot be found. Some letters to members of the family were sold in the early forties to an American dealer and are lost. Letters to Katherine Mansfield's father, Sir Harold Beauchamp, of which he deposited typescript copies in the Turnbull during his lifetime, have apparently disappeared. The manuscripts of stories, referred to above, which Middleton Murry 'sold to U.S.A. in 1938', and some manuscripts in the possession of Miss Ida Baker which were sold to a London dealer in the fifties, are still not traced. Undoubtedly there will be other letters in private hands which wide advertising has so far failed to bring to light.

Having looked at the Northern Hemisphere we return now to Wellington. Alexander Turnbull, who collected primarily New Zealand and Pacific material and English literature, including manuscripts in both fields, died in 1918, bequeathing his library to the nation. In 1920 it opened to the public with a minimum of staff and finance, but from the beginning acquired the works of Katherine Mansfield. What first gave the Mansfield collection its special quality was Sir Harold Beauchamp's gift of specially designed Zaehnsdorf bindings for all the volumes of his daughter's works. Later he gave the typescript copies, mentioned above, of his letters from her—though it must be noted that without the originals there is no way of knowing to what extent these copies, which were made by Sir Harold's secretary under his instruction, are complete or accurate. The recent chance acquisition of one of them suggests that the transcriptions are poor. As time went on other material—some of it deposited by Antony Alpers after completion of his biography—began to accumulate until the Turnbull had the nucleus of several Mansfield collections: books and periodicals, manuscripts, photographs, association articles.

On to this scene, then, burst the news of the Mansfield manuscripts to be sold from the Murry estate. The letters were the primary consideration since they were specifically offered to the Turnbull Library, and they were secured first. They had been edited by Middleton Murry and published by Constable in 1951. A dozen of the published ones are missing from the originals for no apparent reason and, on the other hand, the originals include nine which were not published. A few from October 1919 were written in ink which has faded so badly that they gave Middleton Murry considerable trouble. They have faded further since then, but modern methods of colour reproduction have gone some way to restoring them. The 42 telegrams and ten of the 13 postcards among the originals are unpublished. As anyone who has read the published edition knows, these letters are a superb account of Katherine Mansfield's inner and outer life for the periods during which they were written. They are the product of a rare mind and a rare sensibility, and as such have a value quite beyond their specifically Mansfield interest. However, in editing them, Middleton Murry kept himself well in the background and did not, for instance, attempt to justify or defend himself when she attacked him. I have always thought it sad that he did not quote from his own letters the passages which from time to time provoked outbursts from her, so that we could make some kind of rough judgement for ourselves as to whether or not she was justified in reacting as she did. And I have often wondered about Murry's letters to Mansfield: whether they still existed (surely she would have kept them?), and if so, where they were. Then, suddenly, luck was on my side. I made enquiries and found that they did still exist and were, in fact, in England. Soon after that, in 1971, as the holder of the Winn-Manson Menton Fellowship which enables a New Zealand writer to live and work for some months in Menton in the South of France ('Menton seems to hold years of life' wrote KM to LM) I was fortunate in being able to go also to England, Canada and the U.S.A. in my search for manuscripts. In England I was permitted to examine the Murry letters (426, including telegrams and postcards) and to set in train the negotiations which resulted some months later in their being purchased by the Turnbull Library. Although they are closed to readers (except for purposes of editing the *Collected Letters*) during the lifetime of Mrs. Mary Middleton Murry, they are secured for the future, and there is no doubt that these two groups of letters (hers and his) constitute a correspondence which is unique in the history of English literature. What other literary couple—so much in love, so torn apart, so capable of self-expression—produced a voluminous correspondence which survives today in its original form? With these Murry letters the Turnbull also bought a group of 17 letters from Katherine Mansfield to various people such as Dr Victor Sorapure, Dr Manoukhine, Lady Ottoline Morrell, Arnold Gibbons, Anne Estelle Drey. And a further group of letters (also acquired) from others to Katherine Mansfield included 19 from Elizabeth, Countess Russell, and one or two each from Hugh Walpole, Constance Garnett, William Gerhardi, S.S. Koteliansky, Frieda Lawrence (with D.H.L's corrections and postscript), Frederick Goodyear, Edmund Blunden.

From the 1957 Sotheby's auction came the 46 notebooks and diaries, and several hundred loose sheets of paper. It was from these that Middleton Murry constructed the *Journal* (1927), the *Scrapbook* (1939), and the 'definitive edition' of the *Journal* (1954). A description by Professor Ian Gordon of this material and of Middleton Murry's editorial methods was published in the March 1959 issue of *Landfall* a New Zealand literary quarterly, and remains the only informed published analysis of the construction of the *Journal*. 'The *Journal* is a brilliant piece of literary synthesis and editorial patchwork by Murry' wrote Professor Gordon; and the implications of his article clearly are that the manuscripts offer scope for an approach and interpretation quite different from Murry's. And, indeed, a study of the 1954 edition of the *Journal* against the manuscripts from which it was constructed is enlightening. Middleton Murry worked with great sincerity and skill and was often aware of his inability to read the writing (in which cases he substituted '[illegible]' for the intractable word or passage), but often simply mis-read words. Thus 'the tram sends me half-crazy' (p. 21) should read 'the broom sends me half-crazy', and 'black as jet' (p. 31) should read 'black-ridged'. Many of the passages he found illegible have ceased to be so, and a great deal of correction and tidying up of his script is now possible. There is no doubt that he was hampered to some extent by his close emotional involvement with the person he was transcribing so that, for example, when she wrote 'Ah, I wish I had a lover to nurse me' he found the word 'nurse' illegible. But, in trying to establish that these manuscripts now would benefit from a more detached and professional approach, I by no means wish to detract from the sensitivity and painstaking hard work which Middleton Murry brought to bear on them: some parts of his achievement could not have been brought about by anyone else. Particularly is he to be praised for his honesty. When he made choices or decisions or selections which might later be open to question, he noted his reasons briefly in pencil on the manuscript. My own experience is that these notes are usually admirable and often moving. Thus, in deciding to omit a passage in which KM denigrates a woman friend (whom we shall designate here as 'T') for her repellent personal habits, and condemns JMM for his susceptibility to 'T's flattery and his need of her company in spite of her negative qualities, JMM does not remove the offending page (which would have been possible) but simply adds a signed note: 'Not used, because of 'T'—and JMM, a little.'

Professor Gordon estimated that approximately twenty-five per cent of the material had never been published. There seem, in my judgement, to have been two main reasons for Middleton Murry's exclusion of many pieces. Either, as juvenilia, they were of limited, or no literary value, or he was unable to read them. It must be said here that Katherine Mansfield's handwriting, when she was writing for her own eye alone (and sometimes also in her letters) is often desperately difficult to read, even for those with years of experience and something of a flair (one needs both). But in time much of the more intractable material has yielded, so that the *Turnbull Library Record* has, since 1970, been carrying a series under the general title of 'The Unpublished Manuscripts of Katherine Mansfield'. Since the *Record* does not have a wide circulation the series is largely unknown, but it may be possible eventually to publish the pieces as a collection. They are certainly not without interest, both biographical and stylistic. Of the five parts so far published, the first was *Juliet*—some ten or twelve thousand words towards a novel, which Katherine Mansfield began when she was seventeen and abandoned when she was eighteen. Miss R. Mantz, in her biography of 1933, had given publication to approximately a quarter of it but this version suffered from the fact that it was not possible, at that time, to give the handwriting the long, persevering study which it demands. The reproduction, in the *Record*, of two pages of the manuscript is sufficient illustration of the difficulties. The second part of the series consisted of some shorter pieces from the same thick black notebook in which *Juliet* was written, and therefore of the same vintage. The most important of these, "Summer Idylle", is dated 1906. The remaining pieces from this notebook were given in part three, together with the unfinished play *Toots* which is presented again in this journal by Mme Mortelier.

When Miss Baker sold her manuscripts to a dealer in London she took the precaution of retaining xerox copies. Xeroxing twenty years ago was an unreliable process, and these copies are poor. Since they were originally written for Katherine Mansfield's eye alone and are in her hasty, barely legible scrawl, the task of transcribing the xerox copies was formidable, and had not, in fact, been done when Miss Baker sent me the xeroxes in 1971. They took a long time and it was only gradually that I realised that one of the manuscripts was a complete short story, entitled "Brave Love". This story had not only never been published, it had never been transcribed, though there are one or two references to it in the published *Journal,* where Katherine Mansfield comments on having finished it, and being puzzled by it. Although a few words remained impossible to read (and will yield only when the original manuscript is found), the story was nevertheless given its first publication in the March 1972 issue of *Landfall.*

The other item of which Miss Baker sent the xerox copy to New Zealand was a notebook of some 28 small pages containing two large parts of an unfinished story. Of considerable biographical interest this story concerns a young woman with a small boy travelling in Germany. Their surname is "Bendall" which is the name KM travelled under when she was pregnant and travelling to Bavaria in 1909. Although it seems not to have been written until 1914 it vividly evokes the 1909 experience. This was published, also in 1972, as part four of the *Turnbull Library Record* series. The most recently published part of this series was another unfinished play, *The Laurels,* which has an added interest of context. On the 29th of December 1916, Aldous Huxley, writing to his brother Julian Huxley from Garsington where he was a guest of Lady Ottoline Morrell, wrote: "An amusing Xmas party here. Murry, Katherine Mansfield, Lytton Strachey, Brett and Carrington, Bertrand Russell and Maria Nys. We performed a superb play invented by Katherine, improvising as we went along. It was a huge success, with Murry as a Dostoïevsky character and Lytton as an incredibly wicked old grandfather." On the manuscript of *The Laurels* (which features an incredibly wicked old grandfather, and which is among the papers in the Turnbull Library) Katherine Mansfield has listed the names of the actors: Lytton, Carrington, Mansfield, Aldous, Maria, Murry. It is hoped that the next in the series will be the two parts in the Turnbull of another unfinished novel, *Maata.* The major portion of *Maata* was sold at auction at Sotheby's in the same sale in which the Turnbull bought the notebooks. *Maata* was auctioned in a separate lot, and the Turnbull was unsuccessful in bidding for it. Unfortunately, the dealer who procured it sold it then to a purchaser who instructed that his anonymity be preserved, and so the whereabouts of this manuscript is not known. However, the two parts of *Maata* which were among the papers bought by the Turnbull are substantial enough to justify publication in the *Record* series.

The heterogeneity of these manuscripts—the loose sheets as well as the diaries and notebooks—constitutes a major challenge to anyone who would impose some kind of order and shape on to them. They include poems, stories, diary entries, lists of clothes, shopping lists, vocabulary lists, comments on books, people and situations, drafts of letters, notes for stories, two unfinished plays, and a whole host of fragmentary reflections and communications with herself. Dating is often difficult, and the fragility of many of the pages requires the work to be done from xerox copies wherever possible. (The entire collection of Mansfield manuscripts exists on microfilm and in xerox copy form.)

Since 1957 the Turnbull has acquired, either by gift or by purchase, a number of small groups of Mansfield letters (some originals, some copies), correspondence of others concerning Katherine Mansfield or her work, letters to her from Elizabeth, Countess Russell, and one from Virginia Woolf, collections of newspaper clippings, reviews and obituary notices, Katherine Mansfield's Bible with some markings and notes by her, texts of talks and lectures, the manuscript of Miss Baker's book *Katherine Mansfield: The Memories of LM* and a giant-sized scrapbook compiled and given by Mrs. Vera Mackintosh Bell, Katherine Mansfield's older sister, containing a wide variety of relevant material collected by Mrs. Bell through half a century. These items (together with many smaller ones) come within the province of the Manuscripts Section of the Library. The Photograph Section has about 150 photographs of which about 50 feature KM herself, while the others are of people and places associated with her. The collection of published material includes KM's own works (all editions and translations), and all books and periodical articles about her or her work. And gradually some of her own possessions have come to rest in the Turnbull because there is no more appropriate place for them: KM's little Corona typewriter, on which she typed her stories, a chair which she once gave to S.S. Koteliansky, a miniature portrait of her which was commissioned by her father, a brooch, a shawl, a lock of hair, several dressing-table jars, a Chinese embroidered jacket, a fruit-knife, a fan. These articles are valued for their association with Katherine Mansfield but it is her manuscripts, above all, which have given rise to the Turnbull occasionally being referred to as "the Katherine Mansfield library".

Etudes Anglaises, vol. XXVI, 1973, pp. 413-19.

T. O. Beachcroft, "Katherine Mansfield's Encounter with Theocritus"

That Katherine Mansfield had at one time read a translation of the XVth Idyll of Theocritus and had given it considerable thought may not at first glance seem a very important piece of information. Yet it has a remarkable interest in the development of her own art and thus of the modern short story; and when Antony Alpers, author of *Katherine Mansfield* (1954), wrote to tell me that in the course of writing a new biography dealing with Katherine Mansfield and her circle he had discovered evidence of this encounter between Katherine Mansfield and Theocritus, it had the same effect as the discovery of an important piece that had been missing from the middle of a puzzle. It is the object of this article to explain why.

At the outset a brief definition is needed of the elusive phrase 'the modern short story'. Without making a lengthy analysis, may I say that by the modern short story I mean the story that has been developed especially since the work of Chekhov and that has often been thought of as the 'Chekhov kind' of story.

Many critics have adopted this as a standpoint—Austin McGiffert Wright, for instance, in *The American Short Story in the Twenties* (1961) asks why it is that the stories of Sherwood Anderson, published over forty years ago, still do not seem dated in the manner of Garland's *Main Travelled Roads*; and he refers especially to the kind of story that 'can be called modern', and is to be found in Hemingway, Katherine Mansfield, or Katherine Anne Porter. In the view of Austin Wright the explanation lies in the contrast of the modern or 'dramatic' technique with the older or 'narrative'. In the modern form the story is revealed rather than narrated. Comment is eliminated. The method has often been described as 'epiphanic'. Austin Wright among other critics holds the view that the difference is not merely one of technique, but is concerned fundamentally with the kind of story that can be told and the kind of truth that it reveals.

For centuries before the days of print, the short story was dominated by the presence of the story teller. This living narrator was essential: he could moralize, explain, cover years in a moment. He was not so much the author as the man who vouched for the authenticity of his story, sometimes saying it was all fact, and he had seen it happen.

Long after short stories were being printed, the idea of the 'I', the personal narrator, lingered on, with many of the tricks of his trade. Somerset Maugham, for instance, liked to portray himself as a skilled raconteur who could capture an audience in a ship's smoking-room. Often he appears as the 'I' who has seen the story happen.

However, throughout the long development of the short story there existed in the XVth Idyll of Theocritus an almost perfect model of the short realistic story that is intended for reading and reveals itself without a personal narrator. At the time of the Renaissance, translations from Greek Romances influenced the authors of longer Elizabethan fiction; Cassaubon's version of Theophrastus in 1592 inaugurated the whole movement of 'character-writing': yet the XVth Idyll of Theocritus remained more or less unnoticed.

Theocritus was, of course, not unknown, and there is a mention of him as early as 1523 in Skelton's *Garland of Laurell*. There were, however, only a few scattered translations, and he was not thought of as a writer of stories. His influence was felt in the moods of pastoral poetry, developing later into the formalized graces of the eighteenth century, the Dresden Shepherd and Shepherdess rather than the natural truths of the Idylls of Theocritus. A similar and sometimes increasingly sugary interpretation continued in the nineteenth century, and in *Macmillan's Magazine* in 1887 an anonymous reviewer complains that the 'simplicity' and 'wholesomeness' of Theocritus himself emerges all the more clearly through each 'renewed travesty' of imitation 'amid the din of Pastorals and Bucolics'. Evidently there was some reason for putting into the mouth of Bunthorne the words

> High diddle diddle
> Will rank as an idyll
> If I pronounce it chaste!

Let us by way of contrast look at the *Adoniazusae* or XVth Idyll itself. It simply tells—or rather presents to us in dramatic form, two young married women who leave their daily household chores to visit the crowded festival of Adonis. Praxinoa calls for Gorgo at her house. They discuss their husbands with gossip that is dateless yet wonderfully modern. They set off through the streets, talking volubly to each other and to people in the crowd.

Then the mood becomes more serious. The two young women reach the scene of the performance and listen to the incantation of a richly beautiful and allusive poem about the rites of Adonis. They are deeply moved yet their comments are foolish and remain on their own level of everyday banality. 'The woman's a marvel', they say of the actress. 'Fancy knowing all that. Still, it's time for home', and we leave them talking about their husbands' dinners and bad tempers. Throughout this brief episode the two young women are vividly alive; they are silly yet endearing and they are put before us in all their human frailty and their vaguely stirring insights with loving care.

The *Adoniazusae* reads almost as if it had been written by Katherine Mansfield two thousand and three hundred years ago, and it has been repeatedly praised by scholars and professors of Greek literature in exactly the same terms as many critics have used about modern short stories.

Professor Hadas (*A History of Greek Literature*, 1950) calls it 'a masterpiece in a humble style . . . so vivid a picture is given not only of the characters of the ladies but the gay turbulence of the streets, and the emotional excitement of the service that one is amazed on turning back to find that the whole thing is done in less than six pages'. The *Adoniazusae* is in its way unique. The other idylls of Theocritus do not approach the story form so nearly. Other mimes from the ancient world, those of Herodas for instance, lack the intensity and the poetry. They are closer to 'scripts', waiting to be brought to life by actors.

Some mimes were little more than farce and knockabout, and the whole form seems to have had its origin in gesture and dancing as much as in words. The mime was by origin a spectacle, a happening; and it is precisely in this form that suddenly in the hands of a poet it comes close to the modern idea of the short story. At one stroke the mime presentation disposes of the narrator; it gets rid of moralizing and explanation; it moves at once into dialogue; scenes from everyday life fall naturally within its scope, while large-scale events and long periods of time do not. Its brevity is that of a flash, not of a condensed narrative. The Greek word ~*êidúlliôn* does not carry the popular connotation of the modern English word Idyll, that is a story which is wonderfully happy. In literary terms it means simply a short descriptive poem: but as a diminutive of the word ~*êidoß* it conveys the notion of something seen, a small picture; ~*êdiôn* is in fact used as the aorist tense of the verb~ *Hôráw* I see.

Mention of Theocritus as a story writer is scarcely heard of in England before the twentieth century; and this gives the final point of interest in learning that the *Adoniazusae* of all ancient poems was known to Katherine Mansfield of all writers, became known to her at a particular point in her development, and continued for years as a creative influence in her mind.

In Antony Alpers's letter referring to my book *The Modest Art* (1968) he said:

> I delight to find you speaking of the *Adoniazusae* for an interesting reason. My old book (p.14) speaking of the Coronation in June 1911 asserts that Harold Beauchamp's "ungrateful daughter who probably had a route-side seat at his expense derided the whole occasion in a feebly satirical skit for the next *New Age.*"

Katherine in fact wrote for *The New Age* a conversation between two young women who wander about the streets of London on the day of the Coronation. This brief sketch, however, never appeared in a book. On referring back to it, Mr. Alpers has recalled the line of acknowledgement that he had not recorded in his 1954 book. Katherine Mansfield's skit is in fact called "The Festival of the Coronation—*With apologies to Theocritus*"

In replying to Antony Alpers, I said:

> I have been interested for many years in analysing the difference between the kind of things an artist of the short story can do with the personally narrated technique and the technique of lifting the curtain, and letting the scene act itself out. All of which makes your discovery of the Katherine Mansfield/Theocritus sketch extremely interesting. Had she seen her sketch of the "Festival of the Coronation" as one of her own flashes, one of these stories she simply had to write, she would have given it the poetic life it lacks.

"The Festival of the Coronation" is certainly not conceived on one of her deeper levels. It is no more than an amusing conversation between two bored young women, intended to give an unexpected view of the general jubilation. Unlike Praxinoa and Gorgo, Gwennie and Tilly never catch any sparks of fire and they merely linger at the back of the crowd, but the two young women who struggle and push their way into the Adonis Festival are animated, colourful and in the end swept into the community of feeling in which they participate very deeply; their response to what is natural, desirable, even sensual, becomes, thanks to Theocritus, numinous; sacred as well as profane. This is just what the mature stories of Katherine Mansfield also achieve at times.

Antony Alpers suggests in his letter 'She had absolutely no Classics in her education. My guess is that Orage (or possibly J.M. Kennedy) put Andrew Lang's translation (1892) into her hands and said, "Here, you could make something of this for next week" .' Alpers may well be right. The Loeb edition by J.M. Edmonds did not appear till the next year. By this time or soon after the editors of *The Masterpiece Library of Short Stories* were also probably already at work. Their aim was to collect 'The Thousand Best Complete Tales of all Times and all Countries', and the editorial panel included some of the best-known names among literary critics and Professors of English Literature. Andrew Lang, for instance, and Q, were among them, as well as the American Professor Brander Matthews and Carl Van Doren. The *Adoniazusae* is among their choices and is recognized as having 'the best qualities of the modern French conte'. Their twenty volumes were published in 1920.

Having made the link with Theocritus, we can consider more closely how it affected Katherine Mansfield's thoughts and then her work. To say that once she had seen the *Adoniazusae* her own art moved nearer to the mime form and to the especial character of Theocritus, would be a great over-simplification. The first use she made of it was a slight affair, yet she plainly pondered on it at length, because she returned to it with far greater effect a few years later. It was a question rather of absorbing an influence with which she was already sympathetic. Antony Alpers has pointed out that whatever influences helped Katherine Mansfield in forming her mature art, signs of it can be seen in flashes long before its full realization. He says, for instance, that in "The Tiredness of Rosabel", written in 1908, when she was only nineteen, she suddenly hits on something very like her fully developed technique. However, she takes years to recapture it, and in the meantime she tries various styles and methods.

Meanwhile the influence of Theocritus was at work. In February 1914 she was in Paris and wrote to Middleton Murry, 'I spent a great part of the day reading Theocritus and late last night happening upon our only Sainte-Beuve I found the first essay was all about him [i.e. Theocritus]' (Katherine Mansfield's Letters to John Middleton Murry, 1951).

Sainte-Beuve has a number of references to Theocritus, but Katherine is presumably referring to the full-scale appreciative article which she could have found in various collected editions.

Sainte-Beuve's article may well have given her an insight into sympathetic elements in Theocritus: his feeling for poetry in everyday scenes; his linking of complex feelings with simple expression and clear imagery: a sensation of sadness that comes with joy itself. However he says very little about the XVth Idyll and does not discuss it as a story.

Nevertheless her reading of Theocritus and particularly of the XVth Idyll continued to dwell in her mind and to influence her. Eighteen months later in November 1915 she contributed a second story in mime form, "Stay-Laces", to *The New Age*; and eighteen months later again, in May and June of 1917, a whole group of stories which are completely in dialogue or monologue appeared in *The New Age*.

On 3 May came "Two Tuppenny Ones, Please", and on the 17th "The Black Cap": both were collected later in *Something Childish but Very Natural*. In the intervening week, 10 May, "Late at Night" appeared, which was also printed in the same book. This, though not a dialogue, is in the form of dramatic monologue without any narrative. It can be compared with the far more telling "The Lady's Maid" which was printed in *The Garden Party*. Then next week, on 24 May, came "In Confidence"; this is a series of conversations at a house party which was probably based on impressions of Garsington and Lady Ottoline Morrell. This was never used in a book. On 31 May "The Common Round" appeared, and Katherine thought this good enough to reprint in *Bliss* with the changed title of "Pictures". It is interesting to see how this story was slightly altered by converting the theatrical form, complete with stage directions, in which it was originally printed, into a brief narrative, giving the page the normal appearance of fiction. This was followed by "A Pic-nic", which appeared in *The New Age* on 7 June, but was never collected. She was also about this time trying her hand at a play about her own family. Then strikingly on 14 June came the well-known "Mr. Reginald Peacock's Day", which was also included in *Bliss* and has a very close relation to dialogue form without keeping to it completely. Throughout these months, then, the influence of mime can be seen at work, and it was about this time also, Mr. Alpers tells me, that she drew up a list of the eight dialogue stories that she had by now contributed to *The New Age*. This certainly suggests a conscious realization of this particular form.

However, before looking at the technique of these stories more closely, it is worth recalling that in her Journal and letters Katherine Mansfield never says much that is consciously explicit about narrative method. She does refer to problems of time-levels and 'the need for a very subtle variation of tense from the present to the past, and back to the present' (*Journal*, 21 November 1921). But her main conscious consideration is given to the truth of her vision and the sincerity with which she can capture it. Incidentally, Katherine Mansfield was something of a mimic herself, and could do amusing dramatic monologues of a more or less professional standard; and while her Journal shows that she was apt to see her stories as pictures, she must in working them out have had a great faculty for imagining tones of voice.

"Stay-Laces" is not very noticeable except for its method. A chattering woman takes a bus and goes shopping in Oxford Street; she is talking to a friend whose voice is not heard. "Two Tuppenny Ones, Please", which is the first of the 1917 group, also does not go very deep. This time the voluble woman argues about the fare with the bus conductor, complains unpleasantly about maid-servants: this time the answering voices of her friend and of the bus conductor are heard. Neither of these two stories are very different from her original Coronation sketch. "The Black Cap" is far more dramatic, more far-fetched and in a way absurd; it has several very brief scenes and tells the story of a wife who left her husband; and then in great haste left her lover to rejoin her husband. Even if not very deeply conceived, its heroine is, or could become, a typical Katherine Mansfield character.

All through these years Katherine was not only writing stories quickly for immediate publication, but she was experimenting with form as she did so. An earlier story, "Spring Pictures", written in 1915, had been conceived almost entirely as visual description and bears some resemblance to the scenario of a brief silent film. She was seeking in various ways to combine the animation of the mime with a story intended for reading, and this, it may well be argued, is exactly what the *Adoniazusae* succeeds in doing. Theocritus must have traversed similar paths of artistic experience, and it can be argued that he faced the same problems quite consciously, as another French critic, P.E. Legrand, has shown.

M. Legrand makes a point of considering in detail the precise genre in which Theocritus was writing. In *Etude sur Théocrite* (1898), he points out that while the XVth Idyll is written as a dramatic mime, strictly speaking it diverges from the true mime form; it would be difficult to act it on a small stage. The two main figures wander about, jostle with crowds and several voices are given lines besides those of Gorgo and Praxinoa. M. Legrand feels that all this is beyond the scope of dramatic presentation on a small scale; on the other hand, it could hardly be given to a single actress, reciting all the parts in turn, which was also an accepted way of presenting a mime. He writes in his chapter 'Le caractère livresque du recueil—La Confusion des genres' that the *Adoniazusae* is in fact more suitable to be read silently and alone; and is not in the full sense a mime designed for acting:

> Impropre à la représentation, impropre au monologue, le texte des Syracusaines ne se prête qu'à la lecture silencieuse; un lecteur, à qui l'écriture manuscrite, comme aujourd'hui la typographie, signalait les changements de rôles, à qui, en cas de besoin, il était loisible de revenir en arrière, de revoir un détail d'abord inaperçu pour se faire une idée de décors imaginaires, est le seul qui, du temps de Théocrite comme

de notre temps, ait pu goûter pleinement dans la quinzième idylle la prestesse de l'action, l'exactitude des mœurs, les nuances fines des caractères; le seul, n'en doutons pas, pour qui le poète ait entendu écrire sa petite pièce. (pp. 417-18)

Perhaps M. Legrand takes this too far, and two skilled actresses could have given the impression of bustle and movement around them and of other voices breaking in, but he argues further that the brilliant characterization of Gorgo and Praxinoa is in itself the best way of conveying the entire scene to the mind's eye; and it is all done, he says, with such poetic skill that there is no need to put narrative remarks into the mouths of the actors describing the scene of which they are part, which would really come from the author and would spoil the effect— 'voile la vraisemblance' (p. 432).

M. Legrand's analysis is written without any conscious eye on the development of the modern short story, and we have no evidence that Katherine Mansfield ever saw it, but it comes remarkably close to many modern contrasts between 'author-narrative' and 'dramatic technique'. M. Legrand goes on to develop the thought that Theocritus is inventing a new poetic form, and this he maintains can be seen especially in the *Adoniazusae*. In fact he places far more emphasis on the *Adoniazusae* than Sainte-Beuve does.

It is interesting after reading M. Legrand's analysis to see again how the original typographical setting of one of Katherine Mansfield's stories, such as "Pictures", which was first of all presented in the form of a playlet, is turned by slight touches into the more normal appearance of narrative, when reprinted in a book. In "A Pic-nic", the movement and variety of scene is taken further than in "Pictures". It includes a boat trip, a picnic, rough weather as the ferry crosses the harbour mouth, touches of description, even thoughts in people's minds, all given in the form of stage directions, and yet plainly intended for reading. This story, however, was never altered for inclusion in a book.

Some time after 1917, when she was using the mime with increasing effect, Katherine Mansfield wrote two other stories, both reprinted in *Something Childish*, in which the form of the mime has been developed with touches of vivid description and begins to look far more like her finished art—the mime and the narrative truly combined.

These are "Carnation" and "See-Saw". "Carnation" is, again, a single scene. We see a number of adolescent girls at a French class. They whisper, pass remarks to each other, smile. One draws pictures on her own arm; another plays with a carnation. In the end the elderly Frenchman who is their teacher agrees that it is too hot for a lesson, and he will simply read them some poetry. And here the story enters a different level and the mime technique takes a new turn. While remaining vivid and picturesque, it becomes interior. It begins to turn into a mime of thoughts and feelings.

There is also in "Carnation" and several other stories more than a surface resemblance to the *Adoniazusae*. There is an underlying resemblance of theme and feeling, and in "Carnation" we find something of that inexplicable poetry that plays over the surface of Theocritus. We see emerging, also, the ecstatic, hysterical, vulnerable young woman, who knows joy and suffering in the same instant; who struggles to find and understand her sincere inward self amid the kaleidoscope of impressions and emotions. In some of her finest and best-known stories, with Bertha in "Bliss", for instance, or with Beryl Fairfield in "Prelude", this theme is pursued and concentrated from the attempts of her earlier days. It is significant that it was about this time that she was re-casting "The Aloe" into its later version as "Prelude". Of course there were other influences. The influence of Chekhov has been much discussed, and at times considerably overstated. It is well known that Katherine Mansfield collaborated with Koteliansky in translating Chekhov's letters, that she felt an admiration and personal regard for him, as she tells us in her Journal. It is plain, however, that there is much about her art, and especially about her technique, that she did not learn from Chekhov. In lightness of movement, in swiftly changing time-levels, in the art of revealing a human situation rather than telling us about it, she does not follow Chekhov, she develops her own method. In any case Katherine Mansfield's final and finished art is not an amalgam of influences. It is her own unique vision.

While Chekhov tells us a story with his own deep sympathy and compassion, Katherine Mansfield becomes the people, becomes the scene itself.

> 'I've *been* this man, been this woman', she writes to Murry on 3 November 1920. 'I've been out in the stream waiting to be berthed. I've been a seagull hovering at the stern . . . It is not as if one sits and watches the spectacle. That would be thrilling enough God knows. But one *is* the spectacle, for the time being.

One *is* the spectacle: one *is* the story; and one is not the narrator. And it is at this point that the mime form, if it is not seen as a mere technique, becomes a vital help.

We see increasingly in her Journal in later years, hopes and even prayers that she may be made 'crystal-clear', or simply that she may be made good. In her Journal from July to November 1921 phrase after phrase suggests that the creation of her stories was becoming almost a religious experience. She becomes acutely aware that the truth she seeks in her art is dependent on an inner realization and control of her wayward self. How can she *be* the scene if at the same time she clouds it? 'I have a sense of guilt . . . Marks of earthly degradation still pursue me . . . I try to pray and I think of something clever.' She fears her writing will still be 'full of sediment'. 'Lord, make me crystal clear for thy light to shine through.' As the years of the First World War dragged on, with the loss of her brother, with her long absences from Middleton Murry, and her increasing illness, her volatile personality is profoundly saddened and moved, yet still apprehends experience with an extraordinary brilliance and sensitivity.

This steady deepening of self-knowledge could be accounted for and described in terms of religious experience. Yet to Katherine herself it is a process of her art. She prays in order that she may *be* her stories with perfect truth. 'And the passion I feel,' she writes, 'it takes the place of religion. It is my religion of people.'

Middleton Murry, moved by his own loss and love for Katherine, thought that these religious moods would lead on to some finer achievement; but many people would agree with Katherine Anne Porter's comment that Middleton Murry was confusing religious longings with artistic performance. Katherine Anne Porter thinks that Katherine Mansfield was in danger of moving away from an art that she had already mastered; and that her aspirations and her association with Gurdjieff would have clouded her artistic achievement.

Whatever she might have done in the future, her true admirers will always be fascinated and moved by those few outstanding stories of her finest level. In them we see the poetic vision, the intensity of the prayer, and the mastery of the technique all fused together. Her genius gives the insight. Mime gives the diamond-pointed cutting edge, helps to transfer to the printed page the flash that moves as quickly as a glimpse of the eye and heart at life itself.

If I may be allowed to quote from my own book, *The Modest Art*, this was how I expressed it before I knew that Katherine Mansfield had ever seen the *Adoniazusae* of Theocritus:

> It is in this mood that she becomes the most intense practitioner of the technique by which the short story reveals itself—the mime form: but a mime in which the characters are suffused with light from within. All the information, the narrative flow is contained in the words spoken and the scene as it appears in the eyes of the characters. The use of interior vision is brilliantly externalised in imagery, so that when we enter into somebody's thoughts and feelings we do not leave the world of sensation. In this way she accomplished what Virginia Woolf accomplished later, but she does it in far less space.

She has, in fact, created not the interior monologue but the interior mime.

English, XXIII, Spring 1974, no. 115, pp. 13-19.

Ruth Elvish Mantz, "Katherine Mansfield: Tormentor and Tormented"

"Mr. John Middleton Murry!" announced the Warden of Crosby Hall on the Chelsea Embankment, and the man with the Anatole France smile, as Katherine Mansfield once described him, stepped forward and held out both hands.

"You—*you* are Ruth Mantz!"

Thus began my acquaintance with Jack Murry who, after seeing a copy of my *Critical Bibliography of Katherine Mansfield*, had persuaded Stanford University to send me to England on the Charlotte Ashely Felton Memorial Fellowship "to finish editing the papers of KM."

Murry was not a difficult man to work with. Right from the beginning we agreed on meeting regularly either at Crosby Hall over tea or on the steps of the British Museum. Sometimes he would stare at the hostile concrete and make such remarks as "I know I am a very good editor," or "KM took the wrong people into her holy of holies," or "No one *could* finish "The Married Man's Story" and *live*." When I once teased him over the frequently reprinted "first publication" of Katherine's poem, "Sunset", he commented: "I have a bad memory, you know. I always had a very bad memory." As to his personal life with Katherine, he admitted candidly: "We had some terrible times, the only happy time we had was at Bandol." Otherwise our conversations and working sessions were devoted only to the deciphering of KM's handwriting, to collating and assessing the facts then available, and of course to agreeing on the data I had assembled during my research in New Zealand.

JMM was quite surprised to hear how at first some Wellingtonians reacted to my irrepressible hunt for anything connected with KM. New Zealanders were astonished that anyone would come so far to talk of Kass Beauchamp, whom some saw simply as a photographer of people and places. "You think she is a writer; she simply described the things she knew here. Her own family, too! It caused a great stir, I can tell you," said amiable Mr. George Nathan, one of the "swarm" of little Samuel Josephs of "Prelude" and "The Aloe". "Maybe in America, so far away," wrote one female reporter, "Katherine Mansfield may seem a writer, but here in New Zealand she is a pain in the neck." Yet among KM's real friends, those who had joined in a combo with her, some of her school friends and teachers, and those who wrote with her, there was superior comprehension and appreciation for "the rebel", Kass. Sir Harold Beauchamp, though fear lay at the back of his small blue eyes, tried manfully to recall the childhood of his third daughter. "Her *Journal* hurt many people in New Zealand," he said; then he added, "But I don't think she meant it that way."

In London also, one met astonishment that KM had aroused international interest. Beatrice Campbell for instance, observed: "Katherine was the last person that anyone would have *expected* to become a successful writer." Most people believed in her only as a rare person. Sydney Schiff, friend of Proust, was still considering KM as a potential fictional character. Lady Ottoline Morrell was wondering: "*Was* Katherine really a *friend* ?"

Both Koteliansky, protective and "Jehovah-like", and the philosopher Orage found time for long reminiscences and discussions. And always there was the warm understanding of Ida Baker, "LM", who never tired of explaining almost all she knew about "Katie" as we walked in the New Forest, or during interminable journeys on top of London buses.

At the home of Anne Rice I discovered the unfinished portrait of KM which she had painted at Looe in May 1918. She "could not get the mouth right." I told Anne it was valuable and she eventually finished the painting with the aid of LM's well-known photograph of "Katie." The portrait is now at the New Zealand National Library.

Though Murry praised what he called "the rhythm of poetry" in KM's early writings, he always drew a dividing line between Katherine's earlier life and the period after their meeting. When he wrote *Between Two Worlds* (1936), he broke off at KM's first sign of illness in 1917. The first step towards establishing what one might call the "Mansfield Myth" was taken at the time when "The Dove's Nest" first appeared in June 1923, five months after Katherine's death. In his Introduction Murry developed the theme of "purity" at the expense of other qualities that had endeared Katherine to her few real friends. In Murry's editing of the *Journal*, KM the mimic, the cynic, the mystic, the flirt who had to try her charm on every man, was ignored; neglected also was the "masked" pretender, the entertainer in the merciless parody of LM, or her "campbelling"—"making sport of all her friends," as Koteliansky put it.

Within five years of KM's death, Murry had compiled sufficient additional notes to publish the *Journal* covering the years 1914-1922. The holograph material was by Katherine Mansfield, but she had never put into any sequence the random jottings made on the margins of stories or in the middle or at the end of her tales. Katherine had kept actual diaries some half a dozen times, but most of these were entered only for a few days or weeks. Taken separately, certain of the diary jottings no doubt give an insight into the mood and manner of the workings of KM's mind, but arranged as they are in the *Journal* the result is biographically inaccurate.

It is fair to say that in preserving, selecting, arranging and editing the scraps which Katherine left of stories, sketches, random notes, and a few consecutive journal entries, Murry actually served Katherine well. If he steeped KM's *Journal* in pathos and pain, he apparently thought that doing this would catch the sympathy and imagination of a wider readership and thus bring her public acclaim, years before she might otherwise have been discovered. For readers and critics of the *Journal* the pathos aroused a sympathetic and compassionate response. The "Mansfield Myth" as portrayed in the *Journal* attracted readers like a magnet.

When I once remarked inadvertently that any comprehensive work on Katherine would have to try to dispel the "Mansfield Myth", Murry's reaction was immediate and left no doubt that he knew what he was doing. He recoiled and said angrily, "There *is* no 'Myth'!" Just as KM idealized herself as the child "Kezia" in "Prelude", Murry idealized her in the *Journal* to protect her posthumously after he had been haunted by nightmares of her rising and smiling among the flowers in her coffin. Actually, the "pain on every page" that marks KM's later diary entries (1919-1922) was caused by Katherine's psychological and physical separation from her husband, John Middleton Murry. Yet Murry ends the published *Journal of KM* with a quotation from her letter to him, dated October 10, and he concludes "With those words ('All is well'), Katherine Mansfield's *Journal* comes to a fitting end".

Katherine Mansfield Exhibition Catalogue, Austin, Texas University Press, 1975, pp. 5-7.

Vincent O'Sullivan, "The Magnetic Chain: Notes and Approaches to K.M."

In June 1906, at the end of her final term at Queen's College, London, the young Katherine Mansfield was given a notebook as a keepsake from one of her school friends. At once she filled several pages with quotations which, one presumes, she thought of particular relevance to her own circumstances as a talented, rebellious, and misunderstood seventeen-year-old. Almost fifty years later, in editing the many notebooks for his 'definitive edition' of the *Journal of Katherine Mansfield*, Middleton Murry divided this list into two, omitted various passages, and so broke its true effect.[1] Here, after all, was what she had culled by way of sophistication in her three years away from home, and the panoply with which she would meet her small philistine city on the other side of the world.

The most frequent source of these extracts is Oscar Wilde, and her own imitations of his epigrammatic *mots* signed with the initials 'A.W.'—A Woman. In her recent memoirs Ida Baker recalls how Mansfield had been selected at Queen's College by one of her teachers, a man 'interested only in girls of original or remarkable intelligence', and under his direction began reading writers in English and French from the end of the nineteenth century. 'She was introduced both to Wilde's and Walter Pater's work . . . the influence on her opinions, her clothes and her writing was great.'[2]

Mansfield's notebook included extracts as well from George Eliot, John Stuart Mill, and others, but clearly it was Wilde to whom she was drawn. His works offered a witty compendium of views appropriated from writers as diverse as Matthew Arnold and Chuang Tzu, and he provided, only a decade after his trials, the most provocative colours to march under should one's intention be to pursue the high calling of art, or thoroughly to irritate a rich and ambitious father whose message, as in her early attempted novel *Juliet*, was 'You must learn to realise that the silken cords of parental authority are very tight ropes indeed. I want no erratic spasmodic daughter. I demand a sane healthy-minded girl.'[3] ('We are not sent into the world to air our moral prejudices', and 'I do not want to earn a living; I want to live', are two of the epigrams she included in her list.) Surely to claim kinship, as the early pages of the *Journal* frequently do, with the infamous Irish homosexual, and to attempt his insouciance in the Wellington of 1907 and 1908, was as extravagant a gesture for independence as a girl from Thorndon could command. And although she might copy from *The Picture of Dorian Gray* that 'All influence is immoral—immoral from the scientific point of view',[4] Wilde had given her a vocabulary and a preciosity that her notebooks and early sketches declare as pervasive. It was Wilde who directed her insistence on art, and what an artist might expect from life. It was he who furnished the diction for the *Journal*'s rather hysterical claims for one's own personality against the dual barbarisms of a colonial society, and her 'blatantly vulgar'[5] family. The case might be sustained that Wilde's domination of Mansfield for at least four years of her life contributed to the 'theatrical' in her personality, and to her astuteness in depicting it in her characters. And by the 'theatrical' I mean simply her ability to accept the mood of the moment as all important for that moment, the fact that ambivalent or even contradictory behaviour must be accepted as a valid human process. One may, from these years, point to those swings in mood in the *Journal*, or to the letters she wrote back from Wellington to a cousin in England, letters in which a happy young girl, and an irate frustrated one, alternate the gossip of dances and proposals with the conviction that 'This place—steals your Youth that is just what it does—I feel years and years older and sadder.'[6] Both the obvious influence of Wilde, and her own restlessness to return to Europe, meant that Mansfield did not value the consistency which was the very ground of her middle-class family. It was inimical to breadth of experience, it bound one to stale emotions. As well, it would prevent that deliberate attempt to shape one's life as one would shape, by craft and intuition, a work of art. And one might detect that intention in a letter she had written as early as December 1903: 'Don't think that I mean half I look and say to other people. I cannot think why I so seldom am myself. I think I rather keep myself to myself too much. Don't you? Not that it is beautiful or precious. It is a very shapeless, very undecorated thing just yet.'[7]

This belief that life would assume the features one decided on, and the call for intensity as the touchstone by which experience was to be assessed, are the strongest derivatives from Wilde. Mansfield would inscribe in her notebook such epigrams as 'Push everything as far as it will go', and 'Nothing should reveal the body but itself', and in her own prose in these early years use over and again those words which Wilde made peculiarly his own—*hideous, exquisite, curious, charming.* Frequently there is extended pastiche, most obviously in the bizarre dramatic fragment "Radiana and Guido".[8] The style is partly that of *Salome*—the biblical parallelism, the inversions, the repetitions, the oblique trance-like dialogue, the symbolism of moon and hair—and aspects of the plot, as the name of the hero, are lifted from Wilde's verse play *The Duchess of Padua*. Mansfield cancelled the manuscript, and Margaret Scott quite properly limits its appeal to 'interest for scholars . . . in being able to see the kind of turgid material which came to her in this period and which in critical mood she felt she must reject.'[9] Other fragments from this time tell how forcefully *Dorian Gray* had taken possession of the young Mansfield. It is quoted from at length in the *Journal*; it is mentioned as well as echoed, in *Juliet* and the end of Wilde's novel, when Dorian destroys the picture and falls to the floor, his corpse so transformed that 'It was not till they examined the rings that they recognized who it was', is closely imitated in a sketch called "The Man, the Monkey and the Mask", where a man wrenches a curtain from in front of a mask, and strikes it. 'But the mask crashed down upon the floor in a thousand pieces, and the man fell too, silently. He looked like a bundle of worn out rags.'[10]

Wilde's influence may be detected in numerous turns of phrase, in isolated images. These may be so obvious as to read like a parody, as does "Silhouettes", published in an Australian periodical in 1907, and a piece which, oddly perhaps, helped to convince Harold Beauchamp that his daughter's gifts might add up. This is the language of Wilde's prose-poems, or of the incriminating letters to Douglas. 'I want the night to come, and kiss me with her hot mouth, and lead me through an amethyst twilight to the place of the white gardenia.'[11] (And had not Dorian reminded the man he was about to kill, 'Though your sins be as scarlet, yet I will make them white as snow'?) Mansfield outgrew these imitations, the pilferings which betray greater or lesser degrees of adaptive skill. In the few years between the earliest published pieces and the stories she was to give to Orage's *The New Age* in 1910 and 1911—the stories which were the bulk of her first collection, *In a German Pension*—her own experiences would have brought it home that intensity can in fact stand in the way of life's being shaped as one might desire, and that pushing experience to its end may instruct rather than delight. Wilde's *presence* she left behind, but his traces will be in her work for the rest of her life. Her way of describing flowers, for instance; her precision in parodying the language of aesthetes; the brittleness of much of the conversation in her fiction; those inversions which are a mark of her style always, as in these sentences from "A Cup of Tea", published in the last year of her life: 'There was a cold bitter taste in the air, and the new-lighted lamps looked sad. Sad were the lights in the houses opposite.' I should be surprised if a painstaking search of the Mansfield canon did not turn up a couple of hundred instances (and by no means all of them from her apprentice work) of verbal links, echoes, or stylistic turns which could be followed through to her submission, during the years of adolescent enthusiasm, to Oscar Wilde.

After the appearance in 1910 of "A Fairy Story"[12] —in clear descent from "The Selfish Giant"—and after Murry rejected a similar piece for *Rhythm* the following year, Wilde's influence diminishes. Mansfield's stories deliberately moved towards what was declared in that magazine's manifesto, the call for an art that was contemporary, naturalistic, even brutal.[13] The mature writer would look back on that early influence with a good deal of amusement. In one of her most delightful letters, written to her husband in November 1920, Mansfield describes a dream:

> Oscar Wilde was very shabby. He wore a green overcoat. He kept tossing and tossing back his long greasy hair with the whitest hand. When he met me he said 'Oh *Katherine!*'—very affected.
>
> But I did find him a fascinating talker. So much so that I asked him to come to my home. He said would 12.30 tonight do? When I arrived home it seemed madness to have asked him. Father and Mother were in bed. What if Father came down and found that chap Wilde in one of the chintz armchairs? Too late now. I waited by the door. He came with Lady ——. I saw he was disgustingly pleased to have brought her. 'Dear Lady ——!' and M. in a red hat on her rust hair houynhyming along. He said 'Katherine's hand—the same gentle hand!' as he took mine. But again when we sat down—I couldn't help it. He *was* attractive—as a curiosity. He was fatuous *and* brilliant!
>
> 'You know, Katherine, when I was *in that dreadful place* I was haunted by the memory of a *cake*. It used to float in the air before me—a little delicate thing *stuffed* with cream and with the cream there was something *scarlet*. It was made of pastry and I used to call it my little Arabian Nights cake. But I couldn't remember the name. Oh, Katherine, it was *torture*. It used to *hang* in the air and *smile* at me. And every time I resolved that next time *they let someone* come and see me I would ask them to tell me what it was but every time, Katherine, I was *ashamed*. Even now. . .'
>
> I said 'Mille feuilles à la crême?'
>
> At that he turned round in the armchair and began to sob, and M. who carried a parasol, opened it, and put it over him. . . .[14]

That dream, and its witty retelling, draws together several threads—the parental opposition, experience longed for so avidly that its image becomes a *cake*, the extravagance of prose, the self-parody in the writing, the concession that her mentor was 'fatuous *and* brilliant.' Yet to read Mansfield completely and closely makes his role in her life far more than a casual one.

As early as 1908 she felt the first rifts in her discipleship. Over his shoulder, as it were, she saw more than he alone could offer.

> Eh bien—now where is my ideal and ideas of life? Does Oscar—and there is a gardenia yet alive beside my bed—does Oscar now keep so firm a stronghold in my soul? No; because I am growing capable of seeing a wider vision—a little Oscar, a little Symons, a little Dolf Wyllarde—Ibsen, Tolstoy, Elizabeth Robins, Shaw,

D'Annunzio, Meredith. To weave the intricate tapestry of one's own life, it is well to take a thread from many harmonious skeins—and to realise that there must be harmony.[15.]

II

Apart from matters of style, I suggested that the strongest indications of Mansfield's apprenticeship to Wilde were the supposition that one can give to life the shape one decides upon, and the demand that experience be intense. Both notions drive well past Wilde, and may be tracked primarily to two sources. One was the effect of science in breaking up concepts of permanence and enduring values, the emphasis which correspondingly was put on *choice* in human affairs. The other was that strong line of descent from Wordsworth's 'spots of time' at the beginning of one century, to Joyce's 'epiphanies' at the start of another. Both streams made it possible to view time not as a regular sequence, with each moment of comparable value to the next, but as an irregular series of significant occasions. Their importance was that they provided psychological bearings in a world which otherwise appeared impersonal and confusing. These occasions were to be grasped at, stored, restored, or celebrated in a number of possible ways, for various ends. (How various might be seen by setting Tennyson against Browning, Emerson against Whitman.)

When one considers these movements, and their most articulate availability in the later nineteenth century, one quickly passes through Wilde to the more austere and profound influence of Walter Pater, the discreetly pessimistic don who, one remembers, disliked the label of hedonist because of the unfortunate impression it may create on those who do not know Greek. Mansfield's conception of life was, I believe, close to Pater's own, before that scholar's views were touched by the temperament and performance of Wilde to become something rather more sensational than he should have cared to father. This is something I put forward without any elaborate claim of direct influence on Mansfield, or of her conscious adaptation. What I stake out by the similarities in imagery and tone, in the 'philosophy', if you will, that lies behind them, is that Mansfield was in an intellectual stream whose current was wide at the end of the last century, and strongest where it took its force from Pater. Implicitly this claims that her technique as a writer, no less than certain features of her personality, may better be understood once this is accepted.

Mansfield began reading Pater during her time at Queen's College. One of her notebooks has the jotting, probably from a lecture:

> *Walter Pater* an exquisite fineness. 'rêvé ce miracle d'une prose poetiqué musicale sans rhythme et sans rime' Philosophy is a systematic appreciation of a kind of music in the very nature of things. (Plato and Platonism.)[16]

Another note, elliptical but of considerable interest, is this:

> Wilde—as Symons so aptly says was the 'supreme artist in intellectual attitudes'.

To the Italian love 'comes from a root in Boccaccio—through the stem of Petrarch—to the flower of Dante'. And so he becomes the idealist of material things, instead of the materialist of ideal things—like Wilde—and like Beardsley, the spirit is known only through the body—the body is but clay in the shaping or destroying hands of the spirit. 'Soul & sense & senses & soul.'—here is the inmost spirit of Henry Wotton—here is the quintessence of Wilde's life— of Dowson and of Arthur Symons two most vitally interesting books of Poems [A long intricate line leads from the word 'two' in that sentence to the marginal note 'Good God! what a creature!']—W. Pater—this did not so exactly apply—yet there is a very real sensuousness in his earliest Portraits—a certain voluptuous pleasure in Garden scents—'Well, nature is immoral—Birth is a grossly sexual thing—Death is a grossly physical thing.'
The Renaissance cultivated personality as it cultivated orchids—[illegible] after a heightening of natural beauty which is but not nature—a perversity which may be poisonous. . . . 'KM says the *intensity* of an action is its truth—'[17]

At the end of 1908, in her first December back in England, it was Pater who offered the obvious model when Mansfield speculated on how she could draw upon the home which already was modified by distance.

I should like to write a life much in the style of Walter Pater's *Child in the House*. About a girl in Wellington; the singular charm and barrenness of that place—with climatic effects—wind, rain, spring, night—the sea, the cloud pageantry. And then to leave the place and go to Europe. To live there a dual existence—to go back and be utterly disillusioned, to find out the truth of all—to return to London—to live there an existence so full and strange that life itself seemed to greet her—and ill to the point of death return to W. and die there.[18]

No such story was written, although there were to be several pieces which took and expanded this or that aspect of her design. The Pater to which she refers is a short but superb story of an adult mind reflecting on a child's response to the sensible world, his awakening to the intricacies of atmosphere and event, of place and what emotion might lay upon it. A reader is not likely to turn from the *Journal* entry to Pater's tale without its early pages putting to one with surprising accuracy, not how Mansfield wrote, but the manner in which she *remembered* after the death of her brother, and after her resolve for 'getting down to the New Zealand atmosphere', [19] those houses where they had lived as children.

The true aspect of the place, especially of the house there in which he had lived as a child, the fashion of its doors, its hearths, its windows, the very scent upon the air of it, was with him in sleep for a season; only, with tints more musically blent on wall and floor, and some finer light and shadow running in and out along its curves and angles, and with all its little carvings daintier. . . . With the image of the place so clear and favourable upon him, he fell to thinking of himself therein, and how his thoughts had grown up to him. In that half-spiritualised house he could watch the better, over again, the gradual expansion of the soul which had come to be there—of which indeed, through the law which makes the material objects about them so large an element in children's lives, it had actually become a part; inward and outward being woven through and through each other into one inextricable texture—half, tint and trace and accident of homely colour and form, from the wood and the bricks; half, mere soul-stuff, floated thither from who knows how far.[20]

I have selected this extract to demonstrate, very simply, the congeniality of response to one important area of life. This may be extended, with more substantial effect, to that part of living which Pater diagnosed as inevitable and permanent to the modern mind, the feeling that one is only peripherally, as it were, in relation to other minds. In his 'Conclusion' to *The Renaissance*, which he dated in 1868, and which still, as Yeats's *Autobiographies* makes clear, was an authoritative voice at the end of the century, Pater's insistence was on what we might conclude from the scientific fact that 'Our physical life is a perpetual motion'.[21] Should we dwell on this fact, on a life which is formed 'but of impressions, unstable, flickering, inconsistent', we must face this realisation:

> Experience, already reduced to a group of impressions, is ringed round for each one of us by that thick wall of personality through which no real voice has ever pierced on its way to us, or from us to that which we can only conjecture to be without. Every one of those impressions is the impression of the individual in his isolation, each mind keeping as a solitary prisoner its own dream of a world.

It is now a commonplace in Mansfield criticism that loneliness is a keynote to her work—the loneliness of the child who considers itself rejected; the solitary mind of a sensitive adolescent; the isolation of the invalid, the bereaved, the hard-up, the woman without love. In *Juliet* Mansfield wrote 'Her childhood had been lonely, the dream-face her only confidante.' In the same piece, the girl, who like the author, felt herself imprisoned by Wellington, observes how Tinakori Hill 'spread like a great wall behind the little town.'[22] In a note which Murry dated December 1919, Mansfield felt that 'There's something like a great wall of sand between me and the whole of my "world".'[23] And yet closer to the tone of Pater's 'Conclusion', she wrote to Lady Ottoline Morrell in 1921:

> How strange talking is—what mists rise and fall—how one loses the other and then thinks to have found the other—then down comes another soft final curtain. . . . But it is incredible—don't you feel—how mysterious and isolated we each of us are—at the last. I suppose one ought to make this discovery once and for all, but I seem to be always making it again.[24]

A similar feeling could apply even to oneself. On May 21, 1918, she notes:

> I positively feel, in my hideous modern way, that I can't get into touch with my mind. I am standing gasping in one of those disgusting telephone boxes and I can't 'get through'.
>
> . . . .
>
> Then I suppose there is nobody in the building—nobody at all. Not even an old fool of a watchman. No, it's dark and empty and quiet . . . above all—empty.[25]

In "A Married Man's Story", that late, unfinished, but almost perfect piece of fiction, the narrator, at some midway point one feels between sanity and its loss, remembers his childhood, his loneliness, the way his family sealed him from external life. Particularly, he recalls that night in adolescence when he felt that 'the barriers were down', that he was to be free from the suffocation of his whoring father, the memory of his poisoned mother. That intimation of freedom is preceded by his playing with a burning candle, an image that catches nicely his own individuality set in the circumstances that ring it—'there was a small lake of liquid wax, surrounded by a white, smooth wall. I took a pin and made little holes in this wall and then sealed them up faster than the wax could escape.' Two paragraphs later, the narrator admits 'I did not consciously turn away from the world of human beings; I had never known it.' Earlier, he had remarked how we realise 'the hopelessness of trying to escape'. One notes this conjunction of inevitable isolation, and the wall of one kind or another which is its physical emblem. As she told her husband towards the end of 1919, 'Ah, how terrible life can be! I sometimes see an immense wall of black rock, shining, in a place—just after death perhaps—and *smiling*—the *adamant of desire*.'[26] A month later, she writes that perhaps she will adopt a child as she 'can't stick' her loneliness. 'You know I am going to Menton I hope for a few days when I am better—to *break the iron ring*.'[27]

Earlier in that story of the married man, in the small world dominated by his father, the narrator had seen a beaten woman enter the shop, who 'stared in front of her as if she could not believe what she saw.' Once she leaves, 'I crouched in my corner, and when I think back it's as though I felt my whole body vibrating— "So that's what it's like outside," I thought. "That's what it's like out there".'

To come 'out there' could hold its terrors no less for Mansfield. After her first spitting of blood at Bandol in February, 1918, she wrote to Middleton Murry: 'I feel so awfully like a tiny girl whom someone has locked up in the dark cupboard, even though it's daytime. I don't want to bang at the door or make a noise, but I want you to come with a key you've made yourself and let me out, and then we should tiptoe away together into a kinder place where everybody was more of our heart and size.'[28]

In the story, what the wall of isolation for the time being keeps out are two aspects of life which exercised Mansfield so much as a writer, and distressed her as a woman. One was what she called 'the corruption' of the world. The other was sex. And I think that is the implication in the letter from Bandol, in its hope for that 'kinder place' where her own illness would be cured, the pressures of normal life contained; and where the relationship between man and woman would be of a manageable kind.

III

At least one important study has invited comparison between Mansfield and Joyce.[29] With her near contemporary, she believed that a writer does not intrude into the fabric of his fiction, and does not use it for airing a point of view. 'We single out,' she wrote of true artistic purpose, 'we bring into the light—we put up higher.'[30] Near the end of 1921, writing to Dorothy Brett, she said more fully, of the writer whom she most highly regarded as her mentor:

> Tchekov *said* over and over again, he protested, he begged, that he had no problem ... It worried him, but he always said the same. No problem. And when you came to think of it, what was Chaucer's problem or Shakespeare's? The 'problem' is the invention of the 19th century. The artist takes a *long look* at life. He says softly, 'So this is what life is, is it?' And he proceeds to express that. All the rest he leaves.[31]

This is not dissimilar to Joyce, constantly obsessed with the material of his personal experience, yet insisting that the writer himself, like God, be invisible behind his creation. Mansfield's way of putting it was that the artist must 'accept Life, he must submit—give himself so utterly to Life that no personal *qua* personal self remains.'[32] Or when she wrote that 'all must be told with a sense of mystery, a radiance, an afterglow',[33] Joyce's Thomist demand for harmony and unity and radiance is not such a different thing. But Mansfield's conviction that it is for art to offer these moments of clarity, just as one may perceive them oneself, springs from a more simple root than Joyce's comparable but more intellectually fashioned theory. What Mansfield wanted her stories to do was to carry 'that marvellous triumph' when beauty holds the balance over the ugliness in life. (Joyce, in *A Portrait of the Artist as a Young Man*, puts it 'to press out again, from the gross earth or what it brings forth, from sound and shape and colour . . . an image of the beauty we have come to understand—that is art.')

One might say there are stories like "Prelude", like "The Garden Party" and "Taking the Veil" and "The Singing Lesson", which do fairly much what she claimed to aim at. There are other stories where 'epiphanies', to take that convenient term from Joyce, occur for characters within the stories, just as the story in its completeness is meant to preserve and offer the reader the author's perception of life, an 'image', as Joyce would say, which the writer 'could disentangle . . . from its mesh of defining circumstances most exactly.' One turns to a scene like that in "Her First Ball", the kind of brief experience of bliss which occurs in dozens of the stories.

> She clutched her fan, and gazing at the gleaming, golden floor, the azaleas, the lanterns, the stage at one end with its red carpet and gilt chairs and the band in a corner, she thought breathlessly, 'How heavenly; how simply heavenly!'

Or there are those rarer, more important moments, like that most famous of all, I suppose, when the child of a convict and a washerwoman sees the little lamp in "The Doll's House", a moment which, as a reviewer in *The Times Literary Supplement* remarked, may be taken as the 'emblem of ecstasy, paradise, the world's desire.'[34]

The act of writing, the creating and refinement of a piece of fiction, had often to provide for Mansfield herself those moments behind which the rest of life fell into some kind of order. In 1920, after at least six years of increasing illness, of grief and loneliness and much confusion, she told her brother-in-law:

> God forbid that another should ever live the life I have known here and yet there are *moments* you know, old Boy, when after a dark day there comes a sunset—such a glowing gorgeous marvellous sky that one forgets all in the beauty of it—these are the moments when I am *really writing*—Whatever happens I have had these blissful, perfect moments and they are worth living for.[35]

Whatever weight one gives these rare moments when life is experienced as harmonious and fulfilling, and whether they come, as do Wordsworth's 'spots of time' and Hopkins' perceptions of sustained pattern, from a God whom our minds may apprehend, or as Browning's 'infinite moment' and Pater's own discrimination of 'some tragic dividing of forces on their way', from a more naturally heightened junction of time and personality, there is one fact which is a corollary to them all. This is the certainty that there are intervals between points of illumination, and the intervals are likely to be marked by the mundane, by drabness, perhaps by distress of one kind or another.

In the years from the death of her brother, there is a clear-cut movement in her prose to see life in terms which relate to the vileness of existence on one level, the sudden and intense presence of beauty on another. The large correspondence provides numerous instances which might chart the oscillations. She wrote to her husband, in 1918, that 'my love and longing for the external world—I mean the world of *nature*—has suddenly increased a million times', with her avowal of her '*absolute faith* and *hope* and *love*'.[36] She informed Lady Ottoline Morrell three months later that she is

> quite overcome, for the *n*th time by the *horror of life*—the sense that something is almost hopelessly wrong. What might be so divine is out of tune—or the instruments are all silent and nobody is going to play again. There *is* no concert for us. Isn't there? Is it all over? Is our desire and longing and eagerness, quite all that's left? Shall we sit here forever in this immense wretched hall—waiting for the lights to go up—which will never go up?[37]

A few months later again, in the general festivities for the Armistice, she could see only 'the wretched little picture I have of my brother's grave', and against that, 'Ticklers, squirts, portraits eight times as large as life of Lloyd George and Beatty blazing against the sky—and drunkenness and brawling and destruction . . . What is the meaning of it all?'[38] Its meaning, partly, was that the external world presented a fairly recognisable mirror image of her own personality, the feline delicacy and charm and openness to beauty, and the rages which raked her at all stages of her life, and found whatever opposed her as unbearable—the villain father, the witchlike nurse, the cruel husband, as Harold Beauchamp and Ida Baker and Middleton Murry at different times were cast. One calls to witness such a letter as she wrote to Murry in November 1919:

> Christ! to *hate* like I do. It's upon me today. You don't know what hatred is because you have never hated anyone—not as you have loved—equally.   That's what I do . . . . Hate is the *other* passion. It has all the opposite effects of Love. It fills you with death and corruption, it makes you feel hideous, degraded and old, it makes you long to DESTROY.[39]

That perception of what she called the 'snail on the under-side of the leaf'[40] was not a balanced view, with concession made to the extremes of bliss and despondency. Mansfield's state of mind between the accidental killing of her brother and her own death seven years later, was, for a complex variety of emotional and physical reasons, *usually* at one of those extremes. There is so much that is heightened in these years that—with our hindsight of her impending death—they assume the movement of a dramatic action. The themes of her stories, their frequently intense pitch, her own switching of roles in her correspondence, the at times frenetic awareness that she was pitted against time—

'they are cutting down the cherry trees'[41]—trace the alternations of pain, work, despondency, exhilaration, and confusion which were Mansfield's life. She astutely examined the dependency of her writing upon this swing:

> I've two 'kick-offs' in the writing game. *One* is joy—real joy—the thing that made me write when we lived at Pauline, and that sort of writing I could only do in just that state of being in some perfectly blissful way *at peace*. Then something delicate and lovely seems to open before my eyes, like a flower without thought of a frost or a cold breath—knowing that all about it is warm and tender and 'ready'. And *that* I try, ever so humbly, to express.
>
> The other 'kick-off' is my old original one, and (had I not known love) it would have been my all. Not hate or destruction (both are beneath contempt as real motives) but an *extremely* deep sense of hopelessness, of everything doomed to disaster, almost wilfully, stupidly, like the almond tree and 'pas de nougat pour le noël.' [A reference, Murry notes, 'to a beautiful poem in Provençal by Henri Fabre, the naturalist, telling of the withering of the almond blossom by the cold.'] There! as I took out a cigarette paper I got it exactly—*a cry against corruption*—that is *absolutely* the nail on the head. Not a protest—a *cry,* and I mean corruption in the widest sense of the word, of course.[42]

One does not erect a theory, or a critical approach, solely upon such a quotation as that. Yet here Mansfield places herself, consciously and deliberately, in the tradition of the lyric, the utterance which proceeds not from formulae or set convictions on the purpose or the quality of life, but from the pressure of a time, and a place, upon a sensibility—the call, which lyric writing is, that the moment demands from one personality, one mind in its business with the world. So one is led again to that concept of epiphany.

If the solitary figure,[43] the character isolated by grief (Ma Parker) or happiness ("Our Else") or neurosis ("A Married Man's Story") or desire ("Bliss"), is one constant in Mansfield's fiction, another, surely, is impermanence, that flickering of mood and atmosphere which, in the majority of the stories, prevents any feeling or perspective from lasting more than a short time in the narrative, or more than a few paragraphs in the text. One may recall how Pater had selected for the epigraph to his "Conclusion" the famous dictum of Heraclitus, declaring that while nothing remains, all things change. In his own exposition, Pater had reverted, more than to any other image, to that which he also drew from his Greek philosopher. This was the image of the stream, the endless change under the appearance of continuity. Transposed to the individual mind, this meant that perpetual movement and alteration which is consciousness, the awareness of endless variety and subtle differentiation in even the most placid of our hours.

> To such a tremulous wisp constantly reforming itself on the stream, to a single sharp impression, with a sense in it, a relic more or less fleeting, of such moments gone by, what is real in our life fines itself down. It is with this movement, with the passage and dissolution of impressions, images, sensations that analysis leaves off—that continual vanishing away, that strange, perpetual weaving and unweaving of ourselves.

To catch that flicker, to suggest the texture of that web, rather than to lay down lines which are meant to define or depict life in any larger way, was what Mansfield primarily sought in her own prose. Her own indirections, shifts of perspective, overlapping of minds, modulations of time, careful imprecisions of mood, the painstaking randomness of her best writing—the techniques which make so much, for example, of "The Daughters of the Late Colonel"—these are her attempt to fix the 'single sharp impression' against a background which denies both singleness and sharpness. (How much of Woolf's *Mrs Dalloway*, one might wonder, reaches back to Pater, and towards him specifically *through* Mansfield?) Mansfield's place in literature takes one, perhaps primarily, to her evolving and perfecting such technique, to her realising its necessity for what she wished to do with prose. As she asked a young writer, 'how are we going to convey these overtones, half-tones, quarter-tones, these hesitancies, doubts, beginnings, if we go at them *directly?*'[44]

There are many times, in reading the stories, when one is brought up by some sentence which takes one not so much to a Paterian phrase, but to a cast of mind, a gesture towards perception, which makes his name the most appropriate in any literary context. I think, for example, of that sentence from "The Dove's Nest", written in the early months of 1922. (And an enthusiast for echoes might wish to throw in memories of *The Cherry Orchard*.)

> Nothing is known—nothing. Everybody just waits for things to happen as they were waiting there for the stranger who came walking towards them through the sun and shadow under the budding plane trees. . . . In that moment of hovering silence something timid, something beseeching seemed to lift, seemed to offer itself, as the flowers in the salon, uplifted, gave themselves to the light.

Or that sentence from "A Married Man's Story", with its use of the common image of water to suggest the drift of time, the crossing currents of memory and the present:

> While I am here, I am there, lifting my face to the dim sky, and it seems to me it must be raining all over the world—that the whole earth is drenched, its sounding with a soft, quick patter or hard, steady drumming, or gurgling and something that is like sobbing and laughing mingled together, and that light, playful splashing that is of water falling into still lakes and flowing rivers.

It is a natural extension for water to become the symbol for loss of control, for purpose swept away before the pressure of the stream. In that late story, "Revelations", a trivial woman sits at her hairdresser's on the point, one feels, of some neurotic crisis:

> The wind rattled the window frame; a piece of iron banged, and the young man went on changing the tongs, crouching over her. Oh, how terrifying Life was, thought Monica. How dreadful. It is the loneliness which is so appalling. We whirl along like leaves, and nobody knows—nobody cares where we fall, in what black river we float away.

This example too might tend to propose that Mansfield's use of the wind, so often accompanying states of excitement or irritation or rapid changes of mood, and the frequent episodes in her writing when falling is associated with some degree of fear, may relate to the implications of expansive or moving waters. Water is her most reiterated image for fear and isolation when control is lost, when one drops from a world of clarity and definition to the dark confused movement of time without coherence. Margaret Scott has noted how 'all through *Juliet* and many other of the unpublished pieces of this period, is the recurring crisis of falling.'[45] The last written section of that attempted novel, but the one planned for the opening chapter, ends with the conclusion to a dream, an anticipation of the death later in the plot. 'There was no sunlight, no sound, nothing. Only the fierce wind that beat upon her face she could hardly stand against—she stretched her arms to cling to something—and fell.'[46]

The sea is present in Mansfield's writing, as a natural feature, on hundreds of occasions. There are numerous times when its appearance does service as well for the clarification of some mood, the exposure of an apprehension which finds in the sea, or in waters of some kind, its most evocative emblem. The imaginative extensions of the sea, of course, had long been common property in literature. Among those writers who were close to her, Pater had spoken of a pattern being woven upon the stream, when he wished to denote the individual mind in control of its passage through time, and of a whirlpool, to suggest its confusions. Yeats, especially in his use of Cuchulain, the hero whom grief drove to fight with the waves, constantly took the sea as his symbol for the bitter uncontrollable flood of experience. His contemporary Dowson, to name but one lesser figure, used the sea to similar ends. It is the dominant image in his poetry, and the protagonist of his novel *Adrian Rome* drowns at the end of the book: 'The sea that he loved had given him death; the sea that he had so loved; and the woman.' Joyce's Stephen in *A Portrait*, when he had won the scholarship money, tried to bring some order to his life by painting his room, and taking his family to concerts. 'How foolish his aim had been. He had tried to build a breakwater of order and elegance against the sordid tide of life without him. . . . From without as from within the waters had flowed over his barriers.' And Yeats and Dowson and Joyce would each have known, as did Mansfield, that curious story of Pater's "Sebastian van Stork", in which a young man prefers the rising sea to the possibilities of life.

Their traditional advantage, one could say, is that seas, tides, rivers, may suggest intensity, its overwhelming wash of emotion, as well as the very reverse, the obliteration of a mood, a state of mind, a life. One of Mansfield's first published pieces is of a girl overtaken by the sea.[47] The young Juliet, fatigued and regretful, considers "I'm alone in the heart of London, working and living . . ." Then another thought came—she shook her head and frowned, but a great wave of bitter sweeping memories broke over her and drowned all else. Where was he now?'[48] This is one instance from scores which speak of drifting, floating, submerging. Ole Underwood, still insane with jealousy after twenty years in prison, and for whom the sea brings back his earlier life, runs above the harbour. 'Away below, the sea heaving against the stone walls, and the little town just out of its reach close packed together, the better to face the grey water.' That water goads the old man to a fresh act of insanity. In this story, (so underestimated, it seems to me, by her commentators), Mansfield writes with that deftness which prevents an image hardening into a 'definable' emblem, and yet brings to bear the full pertinence of the old man's craziness. 'The sea sucked against the wharf-poles as though it drank something from the land.' The huddled town, the omnivorous sea; the murdered woman, the insanely jealous man; the confused present, the vivid past—these are inseparably and delicately bound in the heaving of a kitten into an open sewer, in the madman's ambiguous stalling above a sleeping sailor in a moment which has stayed the same for twenty years. Or look to the sea in "Six Years After", among the last stories Mansfield wrote in which she counterpointed the memories of her parents with her own creative detail. The woman's thought, as she is wrapped in a deck-chair by her husband, moves from the ship to the flying gulls, and what the sea's pallid loneliness draws up from her mind, the implications of loss and futility. 'They looked cold and lonely. How lonely it will be when we have passed by, she thought. There will be nothing but the waves and those birds and rain falling.' And through the imagined voice of her dead son, crying across the waves, she recalls his childhood, 'the circle of lamplight' pitted briefly against all this.

> This is anguish! How is it to be borne? Still, it is not the idea of her suffering which is unbearable—it is his. Can one do nothing for the dead? And for a long time the answer had been—Nothing!

These few examples submit the range of what the sea, and its associations, may achieve in Mansfield's prose. There is no question of a generality which will apply to each, and no imperative to draw from them, and from others like them, any symbolic confine which holds them all. The presence of the sea is a disposition of her mind, part of her way—in the words she had applied to Chekov—of taking 'a *long look* at life. He [the writer] says softly, So this is what life is, is it? And he proceeds to express that.'

IV

Part of what I have been saying of Mansfield is that life very often seemed to her *almost* an unequal battle, but that in its confusion, there were moments when there might be enlightenment and intense awareness. In her own life, such times came through writing and nature and love. A great many of her stories are the turning of some incident to catch that light, to hold up a fragment which is significant for so much more than what passes before the eye, or reaches the ear. In one way or another all of her stories have that as their aim, to take from the intricacy of experience those occasions where pattern seems evident, where one event may offer us, in miniature, something which holds true of an entire life, or perhaps of life itself. Where we need to modify this—and the modification brings one to as important a fact about Mansfield as any—is by observing that while epiphanies occur, as often as not they emphasise the unattractive reality under which human feeling persists. Mansfield, in other words, coming to the inheritance of that long line of romantic illumination, and while perfecting her conception of the short story as lyric, virtually stops that tradition short.

"Bliss" may be the obvious story of the epiphany which distorts, or even tricks. There are dozens of others. There is the early "In a Café", published in 1907, whose 'pale, dark girl' has 'an expression at once of intense eagerness and anticipated disillusion'. After a young man asked her for the violets she is wearing, the girl sits alone in the cafe, 'conscious of never having felt so happy before.' Within minutes, she sees the flowers discarded on the pavement. 'Then, very delicately and deliberately, she kicked the flowers into the gutter'.[49] The antithesis in this early story is crude, but the paradigm of feeling, if one may call it that, is to stay essentially the same to its sophisticated appearance, for example, in "The Stranger" fourteen years later. The rare moment when one *feels* oneself closest to some kind of harmony in life, as the recipient of a special fulfilment, is the moment when one perhaps is most the victim of those chance factors, or the acts of other people, or one's own fantasies, which turn life to disappointment or distress or trivia. At random, such stories come to mind as "Miss Brill", "Something Childish but Very Natural", "Marriage à la Mode", "Honeymoon". What seems constantly to underlie these stories is a conviction about life, or something in the temperament of the writer. Its appearance in the structure and the effect of the stories is in the way sadness or deception of various and many kinds is *preceded* by expectation, by desperate hope, at times by ecstasy. And the disillusion too may come in various ways, by an aging woman seeing her fur wrap as the young see it, by a telegram, a party, a misplaced word. Each of Mansfield's important stories usually is a moment of intensity, or the expansion into some broader awareness. The life which is made more clear, and its feeling more articulate, is a life very often which is cruel and corrupt. In her hands, the epiphany becomes so often a beam of light sweeping over the gulf. And in about fifty stories, both the illumination, and what remains when it fades, have to do with the way in which their author regarded the complications of sex.

The young Mansfield had been struck by her own sexual drive. Part of her exultation in it—the *Journal* alone justifies that word—may have had to do with the defiance of her conventional family, but there is no calling into question its force. And from what she wrote on the matter, there emerges with singular clarity that as a young woman (and to some extent all her life) Mansfield was bisexual. Its early appearance comes often in that ornate language she took from Wilde. In an unpublished note on a broken liaison with a girlfriend, she writes of her distress:

> This is madness—I know—but it is too real for sanity—it is too swiftly incredible to be doubted—Once again I must bear this changing of the tide—my life is a Rosary of Fierce combats for Two—each bound together with the powerful—magnetic chain of sex—and at the end—does the emblem of the crucified—hang—surely—[50]

Nor can Murry's editing disguise the physical involvement with other women. In the *Journal* for June, 1907, she admits:

> ... I cannot lie in my bed and not feel the magic of her body: which means that sex seems as nothing to me. I feel more powerfully all those so-termed sexual impulses with her than I have with any man. She enthrals, enslaves me—and her personal self—her body absolute—is my worship.[51]

Then drawing upon that pervasive image discussed a few paragraphs ago, 'All my troubles, my wretched fears, are swept away.'

One of Mansfield's own dicta at the end of her school-days, included in her list of quotations, had read 'All musicians, no matter how insignificant, come to life emasculated of this power to take life seriously. It is not one man or woman but the complete octave of sex that they desire.' On the ship back to New Zealand in November 1906, under the eye of a father who 'wouldn't have me fooling around in dark corners with fellows', and with a touring cricketer as 'my latest', [52] she has rephrased her earlier apothegm to 'It is not one man or woman that is music and violins—it is the whole octave of the sex.'[53]

Any hesitancy on the extent of Mansfield's lesbianism is dispelled in another note which did not attract Murry's editorial favour. Writing between June and early August 1907, she remembers her involvement with Maata Mahupuku, a fellow pupil four years before at Miss Swainson's School in Fitzherbert Terrace. The two had met again in Europe when Maata went on to Paris to complete her own schooling.

> Do other people of my own age feel as I do I wonder so absolutely powerful *licentious*. So almost physically ill—I alone in this silent clock filled room have become powerfully—I want Maata I want her—and I have had her—terribly—this is unclean I know but true. What an extraordinary thing—I feel savagely crude—and almost powerfully enamoured of the child I had thought that a thing of the Past—Heigh Ho!!!!!!!!!! My mind is like a Russian novel—[54]

One of the important matters biographers have approached too cautiously, is the extent to which lesbianism touched Mansfield's adult life. Criticism also might find its presence more marked in her work than has yet been conceded. As a nineteen-year-old, and in rather cryptic phrase, Mansfield wondered how it might be an impediment to her love for Arnold Trowell, the young Wellington cellist who now lived in London. (The italics at the end of the extract are mine.)

> He must always be everything to me—the one man whom I can call Master and Lover too—and though I know I shall have many fascinating connections in my Life none will be like this—so lasting—so deep—so everything—because he poured into my virgin soul the Life essence of Music . . . Never an hour passes free from his influence. I live him—*but I wonder with all my soul. And here is the kernel of the matter—the Oscar-like thread.* [55]

If one turns now to *Juliet*, the first extensive piece of fiction to take up sexual intrigue, one is held by those filaments which run through so much of her mature work, which offer a web of associations that is more or less permanent in her writing—the loneliness, the brevity of experience, the demand for love, the rapture of some attachment, its final loss. (And all these, one might note, in a prose constantly taking up the imagery of drifting, floating, inundation.) So much of this early story is by way of moving towards a fictive statement of that apprehension already marked out as constant in her work, and which was put succinctly in a private note:

> Beside me burns the steady flame of the candle, golden and like a blossom; but if
> I sit here long enough it will shrink down and flicker and die. And so is life, and so,
> above all, is Love—a vague, transitory, fleeting thing.[56]

Sex was not merely a matter of attachment or affection between two people. Here that frequent order for intensity, for the sharpness of sensation in the rapid flow of consciousness, soon enough brings one to the perverse. There is some hint of this in *Juliet*, when the heroine and her friend are discussing her 'mood'.

> 'The truth is, my dear girl—well I hardly like to own it to myself even, you
> understand. Bernard Shaw would be gratified.' 'You feel sexual.' 'Horribly—and
> in need of a physical shock or violence. Perhaps a good smacking would be
> beneficial.'[57]

"Summer Idylle", an exotic piece written at the same time as the longer fiction, is explicit. Marina, a part-Maori girl, tells her friend a legend concerning fern trees. '"They are cruel even as I might wish to be to thee, little Hinemoa." She looked at Hinemoa with half-shut eyes, her upper lip drawn back, showing her teeth, but Hinemoa caught her hand. "Don't be the same," she pleaded.'[58]

This is a feature of Mansfield which any perspective must include. The clues as a rule may be discreet, but their total impact is surprising. In "A Birthday", a story of domesticity and male selfishness, the husband looks at his wife's photograph. 'In the half-light of the drawing-room the smile seemed to deepen in Anna's portrait, and to become secret, even cruel.' The characters in "A Blaze", the final story in *In a German Pension*, blatantly confess to their relationship being 'a spider-and-fly business from first to last', and the woman's 'little pink claws could tear out a man's heart.' (Arundel del Re, Pound's instructor in Italian, and among the first perceptive reviewers of the early *Cantos*, told me some years ago that Mansfield's own presence was 'feline'. When he met her at Rupert Brooke's she lay curled like a cat on a sofa, said nothing, and made them very aware of her watching them.) The preceding story, "The Swing of the Pendulum", carries the exhilaration a girl feels in hurting a man who tries crudely to seduce her, the 'sensation of glorious, intoxicating happiness' after she bites his hand. 'She saw with joy that his eyes were full of tears.' The girl's behaviour might be described, at kindest, as hysterical:

> She rolled her eyes at him. 'If you don't go away this moment I'll bite you again,'
> she said, and the absurd words started her laughing. Even when the door was closed,
> hearing him descending the stairs, she laughed, and danced about the room.

Frequently the stories contain an image, or a sentence, which places in the background the possibility of savagery, or a hint, it may be, of what civilised relationships are both based on, and may revert to. She writes of the characters in "Psychology", as their fabric of intimate politeness is on the point of being torn by a more passionate rapport than either cares to own to, 'there they were—two hunters, bending over their fire, but hearing suddenly from the jungle beyond a shake of wind and a loud, questioning cry.' In "A Dill Pickle", when two former lovers meet by chance, the woman 'felt the strange beast that had slumbered so long within her bosom stir, stretch itself, yawn, prick up its ears, and suddenly bound to its feet.' And discussion of the New Zealand stories usually overlooks how much they hold that is sexually ambiguous. In "At the Bay", most obviously, there is the lesbianism of Mrs Kember, who swims 'quickly, like a rat', and rises from the water 'like a horrible caricature of her husband.' When that husband, as stirred by Beryl as is his wife, comes in the night to ask the girl to walk with him, 'that weak thing within her seemed to uncoil, to grow suddenly tremendously strong; she longed to go!'

The predatory comes to the surface in many stories—one woman preying upon another as in "A Cup of Tea"; women upon men in pieces such as "The Man Without a Temperament", or the aptly-named "Poison"; men upon women in "Je ne parle pas français", with its narrator like a dog and the woman named 'Mouse', or "The Woman at the Store", the mother, who is 'like a hungry bird' and has a 'rat of a child'. (Brigid Brophy, in a fine but erratic piece of criticism, draws attention to the repeated imagery of feeding and eating in Mansfield's work, and relates this to 'The crisis of her personality [which] was how to govern a furious impulse of aggression.')[59] The sense that sexual awareness brings one to the edge of the uncontrollable, to levels of the mind and behaviour which normally are not exposed, is permanent in Mansfield's writing about men and women. Also is the sense of one partner inevitably exploiting the other. Sex is the most intense experience in Mansfield's fiction, yet so much about it is said through implication. What *is* presented constantly and openly is the disillusion it entails.

The earliest full statement that sex quite literally bears its own destruction appears in "At Lehmann's", a story which would probably be marked out as assuming its cynicism to gratify the editors of *The New Age*, did it not articulate a theme which Mansfield returned to in so many later stories. This theme was the totally ambivalent and unresolvable fact that sex works compulsively through beauty and charm and fulfilment, and inexorably appals by its physical grossness and fear and impersonal mechanism. (One remembers that schoolgirl note 'Well, nature is immoral—Birth is a grossly sexual thing—Death is a grossly physical thing.') The contraries are nowhere so apparent as in this story. It may read as too obvious, unless one sees behind it the twenty-one-year-old Mansfield bearing an illegitimate child, and suffering its miscarriage, among a foreign people she detested. That scene where the young girl's being embraced by a man, and 'her breathing like a little frightened animal', is set against the 'frightful, tearing shriek' of a woman upstairs giving birth, has the starkness of a medieval tableau, with pleasure on one side, suffering the other. The moment of initiation to even mild sexuality is here the very moment of pain and fruition; the moment of personal bliss bound once and for all with impersonal process.

Whatever the simplifications of this story—and it is simplified for Mansfield only, I suspect, in the coincidence of events, but nothing else—this is one of her clearest delineations of the contraries present in sexual attraction. These are seen later and more subtly, in the fluctuations in mood and in the cleverly refined alternations, of narratives like "The Singing Lesson", or the much darker and neglected story, "The Escape", where sex is so related to physical illness that the tie between men and women is seen in terms of death. As a man watches his wife with her 'little bag, with its shiny silvery jaws', he thinks 'In Egypt she would be buried with those things.' The dust from the countryside falls on them 'like the finest ash', the woman speaks of 'the disgusting, revolting dust', while the man 'felt himself, lying there, a hollow man, a parched, withered man, as it were, of ashes.' Similarly 'Rot', that last word spoken in "The Man Without a Temperament", demands that we see the movement of a married relationship towards putrescence, the imminent physical death of the wife already matched by the emotional demise of her husband. Both these stories were written in the early months of 1920, shortly after Mansfield recovered from the depression in which 'To tell you the truth, I think I have been *mad*, but really, medically mad . . . I felt as though I'd been through some awful deathly strain, and just survived—been rescued from drowning or something like that.'[60] These stories preserve that depression, distance it, 'bring into the light', as she would say, the bitterness against her husband as it is taken into the pattern of fiction, and balanced with a cold appraisal of the invalid wife.

In other stories 'normality' is the reason for distress. In "Frau Brechenmacher Attends a Wedding", another story from *In a German Pension*, the jokes and coarseness of the wedding breakfast lead, not to the bridal chamber, but to the bedroom of a mother of five (like Mansfield's own mother). The woman is revolted by her drunken husband now as she had been by his advances when she herself was a bride. The end of that story sees the woman weary of what is 'Always the same . . . all over the world the same; but, God in heaven—but *stupid*.' ('Absurd' would be the word of the more refined Linda, as she thought of sex.) She is carried back to before her reluctance as a bride, to the time before maturity. It is one of those fine and typical effects in Mansfield when levels of time coalesce to one instant of feeling: 'She lay down on the bed and put her arm across her face like a child who expected to be hurt as Herr Brechenmacher lurched in.'

One may go forward eight years to the mature writer, and mark the line of descent from the German Frau waiting for her husband to Linda Burnell in "Prelude", lying in bed after her more agreeable but also physically demanding husband has left for work. She had woken that morning from a dream of her father, of her own childhood before her marriage. In "The Aloe", that long first version of "Prelude", this was at sixteen. (In fact Mansfield's mother had married at twenty.) That dream had moved on a level she cannot consciously admit to as a mother and wife, and once awake she cannot fully recall it. But what that dream said was very simple: her happiness with her father, that warm relationship with a kindly male, was transmuted in dream-language to the fondling of a small bird. This is replaced by the stronger, unwelcome image of tumescence and its consequences, the demands of children. Maleness had become quite something else when her father, in consenting to her marriage to the suitor whom, "The Aloe" had revealed, was nicknamed 'the whale' by her family, actually permitted the ravishing of the child-bride.

> 'How loud the birds are,' said Linda in her dream. She was walking with her father through a green paddock sprinkled with daisies. Suddenly he bent down and parted the grasses and showed her a tiny ball of fluff just at her feet. 'Oh, papa, the darling.' She made a cup of her hands and caught the tiny bird and stroked its head with her

finger. It was quite tame. But a funny thing happened. As she stroked it began to swell, it ruffled and pouched, it grew bigger and bigger and its round eyes seemed to smile knowingly at her. Now her arms were hardly wide enough to hold it and she dropped it into her apron. It had become a baby with a big naked head and a gaping bird-mouth, opening and shutting. Her father broke into a loud clattering laugh and she woke to see Burnell standing by the windows rattling the Venetian blind up to the very top.

One does not need to invoke Freud as witness to Mansfield's gifts as a story-teller. That dream rings true because its surreal distortion adds to what we know about Linda, and adds it in terms which are consistent with several features in "Prelude"—feeding children, the fear shared with Kezia of swelling, Linda's association with moonlight and her husband now breaking upon her rest with his clattering of blinds on a brilliant morning.

It is curious that discussion of this story has touched so lightly upon its important sexual implications. Perhaps the emphases upon its clarity, on the depiction of the children, or on Mansfield's own comments that this was her attempt to make the past live again, have prevented critics from perceiving how sex is at its very centre. The four ages of women which are caught in a fragment of family life cannot but include this aspect of experience. To prevent the charge that this is a reading of the story which is too insistent, or that it places centrally what is incidental, I would direct attention first to "Bliss".[61]

I mentioned Mansfield's manner of writing about flowers as among those things in which she always bore the impress of Wilde. In her notebooks, stories, letters, the references and detailed descriptions are numerous. Her response was intense to these most vivid of natural objects, the strongest and most colourful assertions of life. In 1920 she told her husband that even 'flower pictures affect me so much that I feel an instant tremendous excitement and delight. I mean as strong as if a great band played suddenly.'[62] This is the kind of *frisson* (like Wilde's own descriptions of flowers in the fairy stories, in *Dorian Gray*) one encounters time and again, as in "The Garden Party's" canna lilies, 'big pink flowers, wide open, radiant, almost frighteningly alive on bright crimson stems.' That earlier story, "The Swing of the Pendulum", with its hysteria and sadism, furnishes an example of how flowers may reflect and embody emotions in an emblematic way, as though they were a barometer of feeling. When the girl is irritated and restless, a jar of hyacinths 'stood on the table exuding a sickly perfume from its plump petals; there were even rich buds unfolding, and the leaves shone like oil.' But when a strange man appears, he provokes fantasies of wealth and pleasure, she asks him in, the flowers lose their unpleasantness. 'Her room was quite changed—it was full of sweet light and the scent of hyacinth flowers.' With the swing in her mood, she embraces the jar. '"Beautiful! Beautiful!" she cried—burying her head in the flowers—and sniffing greedily at the scent. Over the leaves she looked at the man and laughed.'

There is no ambiguity in that story, nor in the flowers as the emblems of sensuality and anticipation. The step is a short one which takes the reader on seven years to Bertha's pear tree in "Bliss". She looks down on her garden, to where 'At the far end, against the wall, there was a tall, slender pear tree in fullest, richest bloom; it stood perfect, as though becalmed against the jade-green sky.' Even with her eyes closed, 'she seemed to see on her eyelids the lovely pear-tree with its rich open blossoms of her own life.' The tree remains the firm reality behind the chatter and silliness of the dinner party. And Bertha knows its beauty is somehow related to a feeling she shares with the exotic Pearl Fulton. They stand near the window 'side by side looking at the slender, flowering tree. Although it was so still it seemed, like the flame of a candle, to stretch up, to point, to quiver in the bright air, to grow taller and taller as they gazed—almost to touch the rim of the round, silver moon.' Bertha's feeling for Pearl Fulton is a lesbian one. This may not be explicit, but it would be an obtuse reading of the story which overlooked it. There are those sentences, just after Bertha thinks 'She's wonderful, wonderful', and determines to convey this to her husband:

> '. . .I shall try to tell you when we are in bed tonight what has been happening, what she and I have shared.'
> At those last words something strange and almost terrifying darted into Bertha's mind. And this something blind and smiling whispered to her: 'Soon these people will go. The house will be quiet—quiet. The lights will be out. And you and he will be alone in the dark room—the warm bed. . . .'
> She jumped up from her chair and ran over to the piano. 'What a pity someone does not play!' she cried. 'What a pity someone does not play.'
> For the first time in her life Bertha Young desired her husband.

It is difficult to see what that 'strange and terrifying' thought could be, if not *partly* the realisation that she was sexually excited by her feelings towards Miss Fulton, and focuses this excitement upon a husband who has never before aroused her passion. This reading is backed a few lines later as Bertha suspects what is taking place. She thinks of her former coldness for her husband, 'But now— ardently! ardently! The word ached in her ardent body! Was this what that feeling of bliss had been leading up to? But then, then—'. What might that sentence, in mid-air, require to complete it, if not some admission that if the feeling related to the pear tree had led up to this, then it was Miss Fulton and not her husband who had called it forth? At the end of the party, when Bertha chances on her husband and her friend embracing, it is *his* 'hideous grin' she sees; Miss Fulton is untarnished. When the departing guest, who excited wife and husband equally, takes Bertha's hand,

> "Your lovely pear tree!" she murmured, and the wife runs to the window.
> "Oh, what is going to happen now?" she cried.
> But the pear tree was as lovely as ever and as full of flower and as still.

The conclusion seems inescapable. It may be read as proposing that the external world, the details of nature, remain the same however they are included in our emotional patterns. But it may not be read, I think, only as that. One must admit the tree's symbolic role, and the conclusion's proposing as well that sex in itself, *irrespective of partner or gender*, still holds its force. Or one may cast back to that stretching flame which grew 'taller and taller as they gazed—almost to touch the rim of the round silver moon' as the two women watched it, and then see the shared male near the end as Miss Fulton 'laid her moonbeam fingers on his cheeks.' For infidelity or distress does not have the final word. That word is still with bliss, with the pear-tree which variously was associated with both female and male—'the full octave', to take Mansfield's phrase from 1906—and which remains perfect on this evening of sexual titillation. (On the broader canvas of literary history, the extraordinary implication here is again what Mansfield brought to the stream which included Browning's 'infinite moment', Pater's experience of the gem-like flame, Joyce's of illumination and harmony. Through a succession of major writers, the emphasis on intensity was the mind's rescuing itself from impersonality, and from a mechanistic physical world, through the truth of one's own experience. Mansfield turned what she gave to this tradition, the moment of bliss, into the very moment of deception and the impersonal mechanism of sex.)

What I wish to put forward about "Prelude" may now be the clearer for my discussion of "Bliss", written a year after the famous New Zealand story was reworked from the longer narrative of "The Aloe" The controlling image of the story is the aloe tree itself, whose stem so startles Kezia. Linda, as much the creature of moonlight as Miss Fulton, already has had her dream as the harsh daylight woke her. She also had lain in bed and traced the pattern on the wall-paper, the phallic poppy that 'seemed to come alive' under her hand. When she looked at the aloe the description is quite different to when her daughter saw it. What struck the child was that the plant grew above generations, from both living and dead leaves. But her mother 'looked up at the fat swelling plant with its cruel leaves and fleshy stem. . . . The curving leaves seemed to be hiding something; the blind stem cut into the air as if no wind could ever shake it.'

In Section XI, Linda views the aloe again, this time with her mother. The plant which so clearly was male by daylight is now something else. But one does not forget its day-time significance, why she half closed her eyes and smiled as she imagines it flowering only once every hundred years. (The half-closing of a woman's eyes, together with her smiling, seems to have struck Mansfield as an indication of sensuality. Pearl Fulton has 'heavy eyelids' and a 'strange half smile' as Bertha responds to her. In "Summer Idylle" in 1906, the Maori girl looks at her friend 'with half shut eyes' as she says she would to be cruel to her, while a little later 'a strange half-smile' comes to her face. Photographs of Annie Beauchamp make it clear that this was Mansfield's mother's own expression.) The aloe can now be contemplated without fear, even with admiration. It has been transmuted as it were, by the feminine attributes of night and silence and moonlight, although it is still quite definitely sex, and Linda's looking at it leads her to thinking how she hates Stanley when he is sexually aggressive. The plant has become femininity protecting itself from the male threat. While seen as a boat with dripping oars, it also suggests escape.

> Looking at it from below she could see the long sharp thorns that edged the aloe leaves, and at the sight of them her heart grew hard . . . She particularly liked the long sharp thorns . . . Nobody would dare to come near her ship or to follow after.
>
> 'Not even my Newfoundland dog,' she thought, 'that I'm so fond of in the daytime.'

The plant which in sunlight—in Stanley's hours—looks so arrogantly male is transfigured by the moon. Seen with her daughter, it naturally suggests sexual fulfilment; seen with her mother, it brings to mind the peace which may come when the hours of the husband are over. The emphasis is now on dew, cold water, remoteness, on the plant as the boat which is its own freedom—'They rowed far away over the top of the garden trees'. 'Far away', one recalls, was also Kezia's intention when she wandered off alone. Like Pearl Fulton and Bertha before the pear tree, Linda and her mother face a plant which can be both male and female, and which this moment is sexual repose—'Don't you feel that it is coming toward us?' And then Linda laughs at the absurdity of life—she shall go on having children, Stanley will make more money, there will be 'whole fleets of aloes for me to choose from.'

V

Mansfield's feeling that she was a child rejected after the birth of another baby is one that criticism and biography now takes for granted. The importance of her grandmother in her childhood, and in the stories, is that there, in the old lady, is a fund of affection when that of her parents no longer is available. Most of her stories which touch on childhood make much of the distance between parents and their children, and the adult absorption in self or work which keeps the sensitive child on the edges of affection. As a rule it is with the grandmother, or with the servant, that there is any certainty of love and safety, only rarely with the ideal of a protective father. One thinks of the end of "The Little Girl", with the child carried from a nightmare in her own room to her father's bed. ' "Oh", said the little girl, "my head's on your heart; I can hear it going. What a big heart you've got, father dear."' This is the happiness the child yearns for.

More often, what she experiences is in line with the unfinished "Susannah"— 'All her little body bent forward. She looked as though she was going to bow down, to bow down to the ground, before her kind generous Father and beg for his forgiveness.' . . . The usual view of the father in the stories (and it is one, surely, which is not a separate matter from the mother's sexual recoil) is that, as "The Little Girl" also reveals, 'He was so big—his hands and his neck, especially his mouth when he yawned. Thinking about him alone in the nursery was like thinking about a giant.' No wonder, one is tempted to say, that it was so easy for Father and God to become the same thing, as in the poem she wrote in 1911:

> Oh God, I want to sit on your knees
> On the all-too-big throne of Heaven,
> And fall asleep with my hands tangled in your grey beard.[63]

Or in a very different mood, in 1922, the father in "The Fly" takes on the attributes of God the Boss, playing with life and death, stifling, by implication, the efforts of his children. As she had written to Murry after one of her father's visits to Europe:

> He was cheerful and poetic; a trifle puffed up, but very loving. I feel towards my Pa man like a little girl. I want to jump and stamp on his chest and cry 'You've *got* to love me.' When he says he does, I feel quite confident God is on my side.[64]

My point now is that as soon as the father rejects, or withdraws his affection, things lose their definition. The solid, certain love between father and child must be appropriated by other kinds of feeling. In a world which is uncertain, roles slip and alter, all human relations and physical conditions are in flux. And sex, the most intense of these, must do service for other relationships as well. It should provide stability and tenderness, while its very nature, the stories would imply, prevents it ever doing so.

How much, I think, the opening paragraph tells us in Part II of "All Serene!", that late, unfinished story. It is a narrative that follows the familiar pattern of closeness and trust between a man and a woman, with the deception in this case as certain as if the piece had been completed. Our clue to the husband, apart from the letter which arrives at breakfast, is in his very handsomeness—'How fantastic he looked, like a pierrot, like a mask'. One then picks up how close that wife comes to Mansfield herself, to the tone of her own love letters, to the flexibility of roles which is at the centre of her personality. She thinks (and one may cast back, for very similar wording, to Mansfield's writing as a teenager of her young lover 'Caesar') 'This is not only my lover and my husband but my brother, my dearest friend, my playmate, even at times a kind of very perfect father too.' *That*, we are meant to take, is how happy their marriage is. And of course she is wrong.

In reading the correspondence between Mansfield and Murry, one is checked time and again by how much make-believe there is in that relationship, and how much there was the need for it. A note in 1919 bears out that constant play-house atmosphere—'being "children" together gave us a practically unlimited chance to play at life, not to live. It was child love.'[65] And when that child love was found wanting, what else could there be so often but the dark web at the end of "Something Childish but Very Natural", the telegrams, the changes of plan, the gingerbread house lost once again? The letters put forward a cast of pets and dolls, birds and insects, endless diminutives, numerous nicknames, until the exclusion, finally, of almost anyone else from the game. One remembers how many games were played, and how many evasions elaborated, in the short stories. One loses count, over Mansfield's lifetime, of the number of names she uses for herself, and how many for Murry. He takes over the pet name for her brother, he is her playmate, they shelter each other from a cruel adult world. She can say, speaking of her friend Ida Baker, 'I don't deserve such a wife',[66] and she will write of Murry 'I had been the man and he had been the woman',[67] just as years before, as a nineteen-year-old, she had written 'I am child, woman, and more than half-man.'[68] Any relationship may slip into another in the hope of finding something better, or as her admission that customary borders have shifted ground.

Many of the stories, apart from their status as independent literary works, are clever impersonations, playing at mother, father, the entire family. They are the presentation of a world with that solid family structure behind the flicker of time and the cross-currents of feeling. I put it forward—and I know very well how speculative I am being—that a great deal in Katherine Mansfield goes back to those rare, intense occasions when childhood was happy, when her father was hers and not her mother's, and when, unlike Kezia at the end of "Prelude", she felt no guilt. Those were the rare moments—like writing for the adult woman, like the sharp fineness of nature and the brief periods of confident love—when it seemed that the world held order, and harmony was felt along the pulses. There was the certainty of those moments. Then the stream moves on, the little girl falls from favour, emotional categories are blurred, relationships revert to the sequence of instability and loneliness. There is not much in Mansfield which cannot be seen as the flow towards, or the ebb from, a pattern similar to that.

A final word. To isolate examples quite so starkly as I have done is naturally something for which one must ask indulgence. The crudity of cutting a sentence from here, lifting a paragraph from there, in the body of these stories and private papers, is not the most subtle of literary procedures. For justification, I would point to those many aspects of her work, such as the large question of her reading, and her assumptions about life, which have not yet brought forward much debate. Against that neglect, any gesture towards her complex maturity, towards the specific movement of our one uniquely modern mind, may take its place.

Landfall, Christchurch, New Zealand, June 1975, vol. 29, no. 2, 114:95-131.

---

[1] *Journal of Katherine Mansfield*, Definitive Edition, Constable, 1954, pp. 2-5 and pp. 10-17. The original is in the Mansfield collection in the Alexander Turnbull Library, Mansfield Notebook 39, Acc. 97273.

[2] *Katherine Mansfield: The Memoirs of LM*, Michael Joseph, 1971, p. 27, p. 25.

[3] The first in a series 'The Unpublished Manuscripts of Katherine Mansfield', edited by Margaret Scott, *The Turnbull Library Record*, Volume 3 (n.s.), number 1, March 1970, pp. 4-28. The quotation is from p. 25.

[4] *Journal*, p. 12.

[5] Ibid., pp. 6-7.

[6] Letter to Sylvia Payne, 8.1.07, Alexander Turnbull Library MS Papers 119/15.

[7] Letter to Sylvia Payne, 23.12.03, Alexander Turnbull Library MS Papers 119/15.

[8] "The Unpublished Manscripts of Katherine Mansfield", Part III, *The Turnbull Library Record*, Volume 4 (n.s.), number 1, May 1971, pp. 6-8.

[9] Ibid., p. 4.

[10] Ibid., p. 11.

[11] *The Native Companion*, Volume 2 (n.s.), number 4, November 1907, p. 229.

[12] This uncollected story appeared in *The Open Window*, Volume 1, October-March 1910-1911, pp. 164-176.

[13] See Antony Alpers *Katherine Mansfield*, Jonathan Cape, 1954, pp. 147-153.

[14] *Katherine Mansfield's Letters to John Middleton Murry*, edited by John Middleton Murry, Constable, 1951, pp. 582-583.

[15] *Journal*, p. 37.

[16] Mansfield Notebook 2, Alexander Turnbull Library, Acc. 97306.

[17] Ibid.

[18] *Journal*, pp. 37-38.

[19] Ibid., p. 96.

[20] *Walter Pater, Selected Works*, edited by Richard Aldington, Heinemann, 1948, p. 33.

[21] All quotations are from *The Renaissance, Studies in Art and Poetry*, with an Introduction by Kenneth Clarke, Fontana, 1961.

[22] *Juliet*, p. 7, p. 10.

[23] Mansfield Notebook 7, Alexander Turnbull Library, Acc. 97293.

[24] *The Letters of Katherine Mansfield*, edited by J. Middleton Murry, Constable, 1928, Volume II, p. 122.

[25] *Journal*, p. 133.

[26] *Letters to John Middleton Murry*, p. 377.

[27] Ibid., p. 425.

[28] Ibid., p. 175.

[29] Magalaner, Marvin, *The Fiction of Katherine Mansfield*, Southern Illinois University Press, 1971, pp. 17-20.

[30] *Journal*, p. 273.

[31] *The Letters of Katherine Mansfield*, Volume II, p. 152.

[32] Ibid., Volume II, p. 94.

[33] *Journal*, p. 94.

[34] *The Times Literary Supplement*, January 29, 1925, p. 61.

[35] *The Letters of Katherine Mansfield*, Volume II, p. 2.

[36] *Letters to John Middleton Murry*, p. 175.

[37] *The Letters of Katherine Mansfield*, Volume I, p. 176.

[38] Ibid., Volume I, pp. 219-220.

[39] *Letters to John Middleton Murry*, p. 399.

[40] Ibid., p. 342.

[41] Ibid., p. 544.

[42] Ibid., p. 149.

[43] A recent discussion is Russel S. King's "Katherine Mansfield as an Expatriate Writer", *The Journal of Commonwealth Literature*, Volume VIII, number 1, June 1973, pp. 97-109.

[44] *The Letters of Katherine Mansfield*, p. 221.

[45] *Juliet*, p. 5.

[46] Ibid., pp. 27-28.

[47] "Die Einsame", *Queen's College Magazine*, XXII, March 1904, pp. 129-131.

[48] *Juliet*, p. 13.

[49] *The Native Companion*, Volume 2, number 6, December 1907, pp. 265-269.

[50] Mansfield Notebook 39.

[51] *Journal*, p. 12.

[52] Ibid., p. 5, 6.

[53] Ibid., p. 5, emended from Mansfield Notebok 1, Alexander Turnbull Library Acc. 97266.

[54] Mansfield Notebook 39.

[55] *Journal*, p. 16, supplemented by Mansfield Notebook 39.

[56] Ibid., p. 13.

[57] *Juliet*, p. 16.

[58] "The Unpublished Manuscripts of Katherine Mansfield", Part II, *The Turnbull Library Record*, Volume 3 (n.s.), number 3, November 1970, p. 135. There is an editorial note that 'same' in the last sentence is an uncertain reading.

59 "Katherine Mansfield's Self-Depiction", *Michigan Quarterly Review*, 5, Winter 1966, p. 89.

60 *Letters to John Middleton Murry*, p. 657.

61 To some extent my views coincide with those of Helen B. Nebeker, 'The Pear Tree: Sexual Implications in Katherine Mansfield's "Bliss",' *Modern Fiction Studies*, Volume 18, number 4, Winter 1972-73.

62 *Letters to John Middleton Murry*, p. 501.

63 "To God the Father", *Poems*, Constable, 1923, p. 31.

64 *Letters to John Middleton Murry*, p. 3.

65 *Journal*, p. 184.

66 *The Letters of Katherine Mansfield*, Volume II, p. 212.

67 *Journal*, p. 183.

68 Ibid., p. 13, emended from Mansfield Notebook 1.

C.K. Stead, "Katherine Mansfield and the Art of Fiction"

Katherine Mansfield became famous only after her death, and it was as much for the extraordinary talent and personality revealed in her letters and journals as for the qualities of her stories. I think the fame was deserved; but it rested on style rather than substance, and for that reason it has survived better in France than in England. In England art is seldom valued for its own sake; it is a vehicle, like a coal truck; and from Dr. Johnson to Dr. Leavis the English critics have almost without exception seen their primary task as being to check the quantity and quality of the coal.

In Katherine Mansfield's letters and journals are displayed qualities of mind, imagination, sensibility, intelligence, wit—all finding verbal expression, coming to life on the page, running irresistibly day by day off the tip of the pen. This is not the same as saying that she is always controlled, or fair minded, or strong, or sensible. She is afraid, defeated, hysterical, waspish as often as she is affirmative, joyful, witty or wise. But whatever the state of her mind or soul, there is always distinction in the writing, distinction of intellect and of personality transmitted through all the rare and lovely skills of the natural writer. She has more than talent. She has genius—and only a part of that genius gets into the stories. Fiction writers usually do their best work after the age of forty. Katherine Mansfield died at 34, leaving about ninety stories, some of them unfinished—a total of perhaps 250-300 thousand words. It is clear that she needed a longer life to produce the best work she was capable of. Nevertheless she has a distinct place as one who made certain discoveries about the form of fiction. It is the nature of these discoveries that still call for critical definition; and at the same time, if they are to be usefully discussed, it becomes necessary to disengage the Mansfield image from some of the mythology that has surrounded it since her death in 1923.

To speak of Katherine Mansfield's discoveries in fiction is not to speak of something achieved in full consciousness, or critically articulated. In her conscious intentions she was often very conventional. She was always setting out to write a novel. What became "Prelude" began as a novel with the title *The Aloe.* As she wrote "Je ne parle pas français" she called its sections chapters, apparently expecting it to grow into a book. She planned a novel called *Maata,* and another called *Karori.* All these came either to nothing or to smaller items which, not being novels, we call stories, but which would be better described as fictions. It was not lack of stamina which brought this about. She had ample energy and fluency and determination as a writer. It was her instinct as an artist that gave her fictions their modern shape. She taught us the fiction as distinct from the narrative, and it is in that sense that she is an innovator.

It is usually agreed by critics that Katherine Mansfield's New Zealand stories are her best. But her identity as a New Zealander is revealed more interestingly in other ways, ways more indirect, than in the material of her stories. She is of largely Anglo-Saxon stock. But she comes from a physical environment in which there are empty spaces, distances, a great deal of sky (and usually water), and in which, whatever the season, there is ample light. Her visual sense is developed to a degree unusual in English writers; and this is just as apparent in her European stories as anywhere else:

> Four of the clock one July afternoon she appeared at the Pension Müller. I was sitting in the arbour and watched her bustling up the path followed by the red-bearded porter with her dress-basket in his arms and a sunflower between his teeth. The widow and her five innocent daughters stood tastefully grouped upon the steps in appropriate attitudes of welcome.[1]

Secondly, and more importantly, in the European context she has the detachment of someone who comes from a great way off, and on whom in terms of established convention very little has been decisively stamped. Her social sense is superficial. She adopts roles easily, without any real conviction about which of them properly belongs to her. She can take nothing for granted. She has both freedom, and uncertainty about how it should be used. She has very little custom—only intelligence and instinct to guide her. Virginia Woolf, who was both fascinated by Katherine Mansfield and intensely jealous of her, set out to be a writer and in due course produced a first novel because that was what writers wrote. Katherine Mansfield had it for review and was surprised. She expected something more original of Virginia. She could not say what it ought to have been, only that this conventional item was a disappointment.

Her own first book had emerged very differently, under the pressure of painful experience which made its stories all of a piece. This was the collection called *In a German Pension,* published in 1911 when she was 23. The received standard view of Katherine Mansfield, which is essentially that established by her husband, John Middleton Murry, invites us to excuse the book on the grounds of youth; yet what Murry calls its 'youthful bitterness and crude cynicism'[2] speak very directly to the 1970s. It is not, as it once seemed, an anti-German book so much as an anti-male book—but not quite simply anti-male either. It is full of that subtle humour, that dead-pan presentation of absurdities, which characterised

Katherine Mansfield's talk and letters and made her seem to Leonard Woolf the most amusing conversationalist he had known. But the humour of *In a German Pension* skates on very thin ice. It is laughter right at the brink of hysteria, tears, revulsion and hatred. The gross, insensitive German males dominate and enslave their fraus and turn them into domestic animals, while natural appetite is seen to be drawing the young girls towards sexual involvement and the same destruction. In one story a young man putting his hands over the breasts of a girl is interrupted by a 'frightful, tearing shriek' upstairs where a baby is being born. In another a young woman, disillusioned with her lover and determined to leave him, viciously bites the hand of a man who tries to kiss her, and immediately feels compliant once again towards the lover. There is violence just below the surface of these stories; and these two qualities, the violence and the humour, are held together by a third—a delicate precision in the portrayal of scene and atmosphere, so that in the best of the stories everything happens at a slight remove, it floats somewhere in the middle distance, as if on a stage with misty lighting or behind a gauze curtain:

> 'Are you American?' said the Vegetable lady, turning to me.
> 'No.'
> 'Then you are an Englishwoman?'
> 'Well, hardly—'
> 'You must be one of the two. You cannot help it. I have seen you walking alone several times. You wear your—'
> I got up and climbed on to the swing. The air was sweet and cool, rushing past my body. Above, white clouds trailed delicately through the blue sky. From the pine forest streamed a wild perfume, the branches swayed together, rhythmically, sonorously.

The chapter of biography that lies behind the writing of *In a German Pension* has yet to be fully written. Katherine Mansfield had come to London at the age of 20 to be a writer. She had had lovers. She had married a singing teacher, George Bowden, and had left him next day. She had possibly experimented with drugs. She had become pregnant by someone who was not her husband and gone to Bavaria to have the child, but the pregnancy miscarried. All this in 1909 or '10. As Brigid Brophy puts it: 'The life of the "free woman" which is now being imposed on us as a postwar phenomenon—post *our* war—was being lived by Katherine Mansfield, and with incomparably more style, before women were properly out of long skirts.'[3] With more style, no doubt; but also without antibiotics and without the pill, and it was very nearly too much for her. She survived the crisis, however, and under the pressure of so much experience wrote her first book very rapidly, not at all in the confessional manner most young gentlewomen in like circumstances would have chosen, but converting it all into black comedy. In the story called "The Modern Soul" there is a German professor who likes to eat cherries because he says they free saliva for his playing on the trombone. He is also very skilled at spitting the cherry stones great distances across the garden. He explains to a young woman that all cherries contain worms, but if you like cherries you must put up with that. ' . . . it amounts to this', he says; 'if one wants to satisfy the desires of nature one must be strong enough to ignore the facts of nature.' That is really the dilemma Katherine Mansfield is wrestling with in these stories. Only a rare talent would have allowed it to emerge in such a bizarre and oblique way.

The book was a success. It went through three printings before the publisher vanished abroad, pursued by a charge of bigamy.[4] But it left Katherine Mansfield uncertain what direction her writing should take. She experimented a great deal and did not publish another collection of stories for nine years. One brief experiment consists of three stories which are interesting because they indicate a whole line of development she denied herself by becoming a European writer. "Millie", "Ole Underwood", and "The Woman at the Store" are New Zealand stories quite different from the evocations of a middle-class childhood for which she is best known. They are stories of raw colonial life, conventionally shaped towards a denouement. They anticipate a whole genre of New Zealand fiction; and they lead Elizabeth Bowen to ask whether Katherine Mansfield might not, in different circumstances, have become a regional writer.[5] The denouement of "The Woman at the Store" is a very professional exercise in surprising us with what on reflection we have to concede was apparent all along. The revelation comes when the strangely malevolent child does for the visitors the drawing her mother has forbidden her to do. Subtly the story had led us to expect something pornographic. Instead, the drawing reveals that the woman, who is portrayed as having been ruined by neglect, maltreatment, and the strain of outback life, has murdered her husband. Thus elements of the thriller and the social documentary are combined; and at the same time the story can be seen to contain another version of Katherine Mansfield's central preoccupation—female sexual involvement and the destruction she seems to feel goes inevitably with it.

The experiment of those three stories was not continued. Linear narrative was not going to be Katherine Mansfield's fictional mode. She could manage it very skilfully; but so could many writers of much more limited talents. What she worked for continually was texture, density, a feeling of richness, of reality; and it is one of the dilemmas of fiction that the more totally the reader is engaged in an on-rushing narrative, the less he is left afterwards with a sense of having experienced a piece of real life. We can move so fast through a landscape that we experience, not the landscape, but only a sense of momentum.

There is a phenomenon I think characteristic of a great many respectable novels. It goes something like this. For the first 20 or 30, or even 50 pages, we are absorbed and enchanted by the articulation of a scene, a situation, a set of characters. The development is not a straight line but a movement in slow circles over the same ground. Then all at once the novelist feels obliged to set his characters moving along a narrative path towards a climax and a conclusion. What felt real and life-like both to reader and writer now turns conventional. The imagination gives up and the magic vanishes. I think Katherine Mansfield's artistic instinct was too strong ever to let this happen. Again and again she disappointed herself by not being able to force herself onward by sheer acts of will. But the instinct was right and the effort misplaced. The cut-off point often leaves an unconventional but artistically complete work.

Quite a number of her shorter fictions do have something of the character of a 'story', though few rely primarily on narrative for their effect. They develop around a single image or scene or situation, and they move towards the recognition, or realisation (in the French sense of making real) of something latent there. These pieces of five or ten pages are taken, and often written, at a single sitting. They are tightly unified, so that the mind holds them as a single item. With intermediate length fictions, however, there is the problem for the writer of how to add on if the addition is not to be linear, and here I think Katherine Mansfield developed two methods: one might be called 'accretion', the second 'circumlocution'. Accretion is the method of "Prelude" and "At the Bay"; circumlocution is the method of "Je ne parle pas français" and "The Daughters of the Late Colonel".

"Prelude" and "Je ne parle pas français" are crucial because each represents something of a technical break-through; and this means a break-through not merely for Katherine Mansfield but in the history of fiction. Frank O'Connor, by no means her kindest or fairest critic (he calls her 'the brassy little shopgirl of literature who made herself into a great writer'[6]) says of "Prelude" and "At the Bay": 'These extraordinary stories are Katherine Mansfield's masterpieces and in their own way comparable with Proust's breakthrough into the unconscious world.'[7] And Elizabeth Bowen, another practitioner: 'Had [Katherine Mansfield] not written . . . as she did, one form of art might still be in its infancy . . . We owe to her the prosperity of the "free" story: she untrammelled it from convention . . . How much ground [she] broke for her successors may not be realised . . . she was to alter for good and all our idea of what goes to make a story.'[8]

Can we characterise this breakthrough? If we are to try we must first disengage these stories from a certain amount of Mansfield mythology, emanating from John Middleton Murry's commentaries on his late wife's work, and abetted in certain particulars by what might be called New Zealand critical nationalism. Murry's account of his wife's fiction shows little comprehension of technical matters. He comprehends only the substance of the stories; and he divides them accordingly into two simple categories—positive and negative. At the centre of his interpretation he places a passage from a letter she wrote him on 3 February 1918. He quotes a passage in both of the full-length articles he published in her work[9] and he refers to it again and again in introductions to, and commentaries on, her letters, journals and stories. The passage, he insists, 'is vital to any true understanding of Katherine Mansfield'.[10] It was written while she was engaged on "Je ne parle pas français", and it goes as follows:

I've two 'Kick-offs' in the writing game. *One* is joy—real joy—the thing that made me write wh.en we lived at Pauline, and that sort of writing I could only do in just that state of being in some perfectly blissful way *at peace*. Then something delicate and lovely seems to open before my eyes, like a flower without thought of a frost or a cold breath—knowing that all about it is warm and tender and 'ready'. And *that* I try, ever so humbly, to express.

The other 'kick-off' is my old original one, and (had I not known love) it would have been my all. Not hate or destruction (both are beneath contempt as real motives) but an *extremely* deep sense of hopelessness, of everything domed to disaster, almost willfully, stupidly . . . there! as I took out a cigarette paper I got it exactly—*a cry against corruption*—that is *absolutely* the nail on the head. Not a protest—a *cry* .[11]

'Into those two categories', Murry comments, 'all Katherine Mansfield's best writing falls with remarkable precision'[12] and he proceeds to write the history of her development in these terms. *In a German Pension* represents her negative 'kick-off'—the 'cry against corruption'. "Prelude" represents the first flowering of her positive mode—'a new range of utterance, a new comprehension of experience, new complex harmonies'—and this occurs under the influence of 'two distinct and definite strands of experience . . . woven together. . . Her overwhelming grief at the death of her young and only brother, killed in France; and the almost simultaneous unfolding of a new love for her husband.'[13]

The 'husband' referred to here is of course Murry himself. He thus writes himself into her artistic development, and in all his commentaries he is assiduous in keeping himself there. "Prelude" represents the happiness she found with him in Bandol in the early months of 1916. "Je ne parle pas français" represents a return to her negative vein while she was away from him, in Bandol again, ill and disillusioned in February 1918. "A Married Man's Story" is a continuation of that negative phase. "At the Bay", like "Prelude", springs from love—another period when the Murrys lived and worked at peace together, this time at the Chalet des Sapins in Switzerland in 1921.

Thus the swing from positive to negative in the material of her fiction is made to correspond with the ups and downs of her marriage; and while the downs—"Je ne parle pas français" and "A Married Man's Story"—are interesting failures or partial successes, it is the ups, "Prelude" and "At the Bay", which represent the true fulfilment of the Mansfield talent.

Added on to this is the idea that with the death of her brother she returned to the material of her childhood—the New Zealand memories she and her brother had evoked together during his last leave before he went to the war in France. Under the double influence of love and grief any bitterness towards her own country and family was purged, and the New Zealand material became available to her for use in fiction. In support of this part of the mythology there are those passages in her journal in which she resolves to write for her dead brother and of New Zealand:

> Now—now I want to write recollections of my own country. Yes, I want to write about my own country till I simply exhaust my store. Not only because it is 'a sacred debt' . . . because my brother and I were born there, but also because in my thoughts I range with him over all the remembered places. I am never far away from them. I long to renew them in writing . . . Oh I want for one moment to make our undiscovered country leap into the eyes of the Old World.[14]

This then is Murry's picture of his wife's development. A new phase opens with the death of her brother and the full discovery of her love for her husband. The advance is not technical but spiritual, and it is marked by the writing of the first draft of "Prelude" (under the title "The Aloe") in the period of happiness husband and wife shared in Bandol in the early months of 1916. No doubt in retrospect Murry believed this simple account, which now pervades almost every critical and biographical commentary. But a look at the evidence of letters and journals shows it to be false. Here, briefly, is the real story.

In February 1915 Katherine Mansfield left Murry and went, on what she later called 'an indiscreet journey', all the way to the war zone in France to be with the French writer Francis Carco whom she had met in Paris and with whom she had been corresponding. After a brief affair with Carco she returned to England— 'disillusioned', Murry says,[15] but there is no evidence of that. In March she left Murry again and went to live alone in Carco's flat in Paris. On March 24 her journal entry reads 'kick-off'. Next day she is saying in a letter that she has written 'a huge chunk' of her 'first novel'.[16] Murry's footnote tells us that this 'almost certainly' refers, not to "The Aloe" which became "Prelude", but to something called "Brave Love". Murry is quite certainly wrong about "Brave Love" a story mentioned in her journal as having been completed on January 12, 1915[17] and I think the entry of March 24 must in fact record the beginning of "The Aloe".

She returned to London during April and was back in Paris again on May 5. On May 8 she writes in a letter to Murry 'I am writing my book. Ça marche, ça va, ça se dessine—it's good'.[18] Murry's 1951 note on this letter (a note written after his most influential commentaries on her work had had their effect) acknowledges that this refers to "The Aloe". Hitherto, he says, he had thought the work was begun at a later date; but he has recently found a letter of his dated May 11 which refers to "The Aloe" as a matter of familiar knowledge between them.[19]

On May 12 she writes that the work continues well: 'I could write it anywhere—it goes so easily and I know it so well'—which fits the material of "The Aloe". And on May 14 she says it is 'finished'[20]—it has only to be polished. A day later she writes to Murry 'Is your *book* worrying you? No, I can't send any of *mine* because I'm too dependent on it *as a whole* under my hand' (italics mine).[21]

It is clear that even at the speed Katherine Mansfield was capable of when she was in the vein she could not have completed a draft of something she conceived of as a 'book' between May 6 and May 14. It must have begun earlier—almost certainly on that earlier visit to Paris in March—and might have been continued in London during April. But in any case the crucial point is that the work was first conceived and largely executed in a period of separation from Murry and while her brother was still alive. Long before she wrote those passages about making her undiscovered country leap into the eyes of the Old World she was well launched on what was to become "Prelude".

For some months after her return to London in the latter half of May 1915 there is no reference in journals or letters to anything that might be "The Aloe". In October 1915 her brother is killed. In November she and Murry go to Bandol in the South of France, but he returns to England after 3 weeks, leaving her behind. On December 10 and 11 there are references in letters to some writing— references which Murry thinks are to a second attempt at "The Aloe".[22] I think this unlikely; but in any case whatever the letters refer to came to nothing. For the remainder of December, though she writes every day and in detail about her activities, there is no suggestion of anything being written except a sketch for a periodical called *The Signature*.

On 1 January 1916 Murry arrived back in Bandol and their three-month idyll at the Villa Pauline began. On January 22 she confides to her journal her determination to write for her brother and of New Zealand—but she is clearly not doing it.[23] On February 13 she admits she has written 'practically nothing yet . . . There is nothing done. I am no nearer my achievement than I was two months ago'[24]—so nothing had been achieved during December and January. On February 14 she acknowledges how difficult it is, but once again promises her dead brother that she will do it. On February 15 she seems to record a start on something—'I have broken silence'—but next day comes the crucial entry: 'I *found* "The Aloe" this morning' (italics hers).[25] She had evidently come upon the manuscript, which had probably been laid aside entirely since the previous May—for a period, that is, of nine months. Now she can see that what she had written the previous day was a false start. It 'was not quite "right". No . . . "The Aloe" is right. "The Aloe" is lovely. It simply fascinates me, and I know it is what you would wish me to write' (the 'you' being her dead brother). 'And now I know what the last chapter is. It is your birth . . . That chapter will end the book.'

What happened at Bandol then was not the simple flowering into fiction of love and memory but quite the reverse, a complete block—a total lack of anything but the wish to write—until she rediscovered and reread a work begun and extensively written in quite different circumstances. Further, if we accept Antony Alpers's statement that the manuscript of "The Aloe" shows it was completed on March 2 then she spent only two weeks on it in Bandol.[26]

Thus almost every statement Murry makes about the genesis of the work is misleading. It derives neither from her love for him nor from the death of her brother. It represents a technical development possibly dependent more than anything else on situations of isolation and estrangement. In such situations she learned to re-enter the characters of her childhood, to live their lives and imaginatively to reinterpret them in terms of an adult consciousness. In this way Linda and Stanley Burnell come to life, and through them she develops once again her theme of the female identity fully realising itself only in a sexual relationship which at the same time is seen as the source of pain, fear, and ultimate destruction.

Even at Bandol the work was not completed. The 30,000-word draft apparently brought to a conclusion there was revised, cut by a third, and renamed "Prelude" during the spring and summer of 1917—again a period when the Murrys were living apart. From start to finish it had taken two and a half years. It was published as a little book by Leonard and Virginia Woolf in 1918; and it became the principal story in her second collection, *Bliss and Other Stories*, published in 1920.

What had that prolonged exercise taught Katherine Mansfield? First I think it had taught her that fiction did not have to be shaped towards a conclusion, a climax, a denouement; or, as I have suggested already, that a fiction is not quite the same thing as a story. A fiction survives, not by leading us anywhere, but by being at every point authentic, a recreation of life, so that we experience it and remember it as we experience and remember actual life. It has a multiple texture, like the texture of life itself. Immediacy is of the utmost importance. The writer must imagine, not invent. She must efface herself. She must see and become the characters or the objects she wishes to represent. There is a letter to Dorothy Brett in which she talks of contemplating a duck or an apple or a character until 'you are *more* duck, *more* apple, *more* Natasha than any of these objects could be'. It is what she calls (in the same letter) 'that divine *spring* into the bounding outline of things'.[27]

An example of the kind of authenticity achieved is Stanley Burnell's dash for the water in "At the Bay". The scene is early morning:

> A few moments later the back door of one of the bungalows opened, and a figure in a broad-striped bathing suit flung down the paddock, cleared the stile, rushed through the tussock grass into the hollow, staggered up the sandy hillock, and raced for dear life over the big porous stones, over the cold, wet pebbles, on to the hard sand that gleamed like oil. Splish-splosh! Splish-splosh! The water bubbled round his legs as Stanley Burnell waded out exulting.

There is an extremely subtle mixture of precision and involvement there. In one sense the imaginative involvement is total. She has run every step in imagination—and the word that makes you feel it most clearly is 'staggered'— 'staggered up the sandy hillock'. It slows up the momentum of the sentence, not because Burnell is exhausted—in a moment he will be 'racing' again—but because despite his efforts to keep up the pace, his feet are sinking, the harder his strong legs drive them, into the soft dry sand. But there is at the same time a cool eye looking from outside on this figure 'racing' (and the conventional phrase seems to belong to him) 'for dear life' in his 'broad-striped bathing suit'.

Here style is of immense importance, not for its own sake, but because through it we receive a direct transmission of the author's sense of life. As the passage continues the character of Stanley Burnell is conveyed to us directly in every word she uses to represent his actions and the thoughts and feelings racing through his head. He wades out 'exulting'. He 'swoops' to 'souse' his head and neck, delighted with himself for being first in the water again. Then he hears Jonathan's voice and realises that he is not first in after all, and we get a succession of small explosions occurring inside his head. 'Great Scott! Damnation take it! . . . Why the Dickens didn't the fellow stick to his part of the sea? Why should he come barging over to this exact spot?' Stanley gives 'a kick, a lunge'. To escape from Jonathan's conversation, which he thinks of as 'piffle' and 'rot', he turns over on his back and kicks with his legs till he is 'a living waterspout'. Coming direct through the language is the characterisation— Burnell's energy, his confidence, his childlike delights and disappointments, his conventionality, the limits of his understanding. This is the same Stanley who will punish his wife by going off in the morning without saying goodbye, suffer all day for it, and arrive home full of remorse to find that the omission has gone unnoticed. We can describe him in abstract terms, which is what the lesser fiction writers would do, inviting us to do their imagining for them. Katherine Mansfield doesn't describe in abstract—she presents; and this can be seen even in the grammar. Its tense is almost exclusively past historic which, because it makes each action finite and exclusive, is hardly different in effect from present tense narration. There are no summaries, no imperfect tense, which is the characteristic

tense of a great deal of narrative. If any action is representative the grammar
doesn't tell us so. We make that only as our own assumption. To put it another
way, the author is not present in the grammar. Compare the Mansfield passage
with one from R.L. Stevenson's *Weir of Hermiston* (also about a family holiday):

> Thus, at least, when the family were at Hermiston, not only my lord, but Mrs. Weir
> too, enjoyed a holiday. Free from the dreadful looking-for of the miscarried dinner,
> she would mind her seam, read her piety book, and take her walk (which was my
> lord's orders), sometimes by herself, sometimes with Archie, the only child of that
> scarce natural union. The child was her next bond to life. Her frosted sentiment
> bloomed again, she breathed deep of life, she let loose her heart, in that society.[28]

Stevenson is a great story-teller and that is the story-teller giving the life of his
characters in summary before he narrows his focus on to a particular scene. We
hear it as a voice. Someone is telling us all this. Someone has made this
summary and may at any moment step in during the action and direct our
judgment. In the Mansfield, by contrast, rather than being related the events
occur. Immediacy is achieved by a combination of imaginative involvement and
intellectual detachment, a combination which Frank O'Connor, for example,
admires and yet is shocked by—precisely because explicit judgment is
eliminated, the author will not intervene directly. Of the scene in which the duck
is beheaded in "Prelude", O'Connor says: 'For me it is one of the most
remarkable scenes in modern literature.' But he is shocked by it because it seems
to him to be 'written in a complete hypnotic suspension of the critical faculties'.[29]

I described the method of "Prelude" and of "At the Bay" as accretion because
they both follow a sequential time line but that line is not in itself significant. In
terms of plot nothing is added on. "Prelude" is organised around the departure
from one house and the settling in at another. "At the Bay" follows the doings of
the family during a single day of their summer holiday. Both are divided into
twelve sections, and each section is itself a small fiction offering a view of one
character or relationship. In both it is the female characters who hold the centre
of the stage, and the two pieces together might be called "The Four Ages of
Woman'—Kezia the little girl, Beryl the young woman on the brink of
experience, Linda Burnell the young mother sinking under the oppression of
repeated child-bearing, and the Grandmother, the survivor. Stanley Burnell is the
characteristic Mansfield male, the 'pa-man'—bluff, successful in his work,
vigorous, simple, warm-hearted, generous, loving, but also demanding,
uncomprehending, insensitive, slightly ridiculous, above all less subtle than the
women who surround him and who suffer his benevolent despotism because
convention and circumstances require it. Put together, "Prelude" and "At the
Bay" make up a portrait of a marriage as subtle and complete as you are likely to
find in fiction. There is about the relationship a feeling of pathos and
inevitability. It is unsatisfactory though by no means a disaster. No one is to
blame, there is nothing to be done. Linda loves her husband despite her clear-
sighted recognition of his limitations; but her love has been complicated by fear
of child-bearing, and fear sours the marriage for her and makes her want to
escape from it. In her consciousness of the proximity of death she is joined in
"At the Bay" by Jonathan Trout, a male figure very different from the Mansfield

'pa-man', sensitive, artistic, a man who is wasting his talents and his life in clerical work for which he has no appetite and no aptitude. How much subtle female psychology there is folded away in Linda's final dismissal of Jonathan from her mind ('he is like a weed') is a subject one would not presume, or dare, to embark on.

These are the central relationships and themes of the two stories. But they come into clearer focus in "At the Bay" than they do in "Prelude". "Prelude" has been sharpened in the process of being cut down from the longer version, "The Aloe". But there is still, I think, especially in the early sections, an impression that the writer is feeling her way, that she is not quite sure where the centre of her interest lies. In "At the Bay" the writing is surer and the focus narrower—and it is significant that whereas the writing of "Prelude" was spread over two and a half years, "At the Bay" was completed in a matter of a few weeks. When she returned to that material a second time she demonstrated that she had learned how to handle it.

"Prelude" is the first story in the 1920 collection, *Bliss and Other Stories.* The second is "Je ne parle pas français", and it is here she discovered the method I called circumlocution for producing an extended fiction. At least in its potential I think this is an advance on "Prelude", though the technique is not something that could be applied simply by an act of will. It depends both on fullness and on singleness of imaginative identification. Whereas in "Prelude" and "At the Bay" Katherine Mansfield is entering into the lives of characters who existed in her childhood and discovering what might have been the truth of their feelings and relationships, in "Je ne parle pas français" she is creating a character, discovering him as she writes herself into him, extending her consciousness of him day by day: and it is in this articulation of the character of the Frenchman, Raoul Duquette, that the interest lies.

Once again, however, we need to disengage the story from the Mansfield mythology. Following Murry's lead again the commentaries have tended to see it as a piece of thinly veiled autobiography, with Mouse as Mansfield, Duquette as Carco, and Dick Harmon as Murry. The fate of the 'Mouse', Murry writes, 'caught in the toils of the world's evil, abandoned by her lover, is Katherine's fate'.[30] No approach is more likely to kill our interest. If Mouse is the centre of attention, and Mouse is Mansfield, the story must inevitably seem tedious and self-indulgent.

First let's consider Mansfield's own description of it as 'a cry against corruption'. This influences the commentaries and leads to some very heavy moralising about the character of Duquette, whose 'peculiar depravity', Sylvia Berkman says, the story 'is shaped to illuminate'.[31] But internal evidence suggests that not more than a third of the story was complete when Katherine Mansfield wrote the letter which Murry treats as her final word on the subject. In fact she continued to write to him day by day as the story progressed, and it is clear that her attitude changed. On February 3 the story was 'a cry against corruption'. Exactly a week later she is describing it as 'a tribute to love',[32] which does not at all suit Murry's simple distinction mentioned already, in which "Je ne parle pas français" represents the negative pole of her fiction. She had in fact swung from a negative to a positive state of feeling in the course of writing it; and I think one can feel that in the story itself. Her letters show a growing excitement in the technical aspects of the story; and that excitement in turn invades the whole conception, including the characterisation, so that Duquette ceases to be simply corrupt and becomes something subtler and more complicated. Sexually equivocal, a gigolo, self-absorbed and full of falseness and posturing, he is nevertheless gradually invested with Katherine Mansfield's own sense of comedy, her capacity for euphoria, her eye for the absurd, and this extra dimension, not present in the initial conception, in turn affects the view we have of the English couple, Dick Harmon and Mouse. Of course their suffering is real; but they are also absurd; and it is Duquette's mixture of mannered detachment and equivocal involvement that permits both the comedy and the tragedy of their situation to receive simultaneous expression. But the chief interest remains all the time in the character of Duquette himself. The story opens from that centre—Duquette and the café whose atmosphere is used to express his feeling about life in general—and it returns there.

Why did Katherine write after finishing "Je ne parle pas français" 'I feel I have found an *approach* to a story now which I must apply to everything'[33]? What was the technical advance she had made? In "Prelude" she had achieved immediacy, she had made 'that divine *spring* into the bounding outline of things', and she had broken the dominance of narrative in fiction; but the events were still arranged in a linear sequence. The real achievement of "Je ne parle pas français" (and it is something she repeated brilliantly in "The Daughters of the Late Colonel") is that it establishes a central point of reference and then moves in circles about it, going back and forward in time. The result is a further thickening of texture. Duquette's consciousness is real to us because it is a shifting thing, quite distinct yet difficult to pin down as it ranges about. We begin at the café at a certain point in time which I will call the 'present'. We go back to an earlier moment which is nevertheless later than the time of the principal events of the story. We come forward to the 'present'. We go back to Duquette's childhood. We move forward to his becoming tenant of a bachelor flat, which is before the principal events of the story. We come forward to the 'present'. He orders whisky and this reminds him of Dick Harmon. One third of the fiction has been written before Harmon is mentioned. From that point on there is something pretty close to a narrative sequence. But the sense of richness, of a texture, has been established. And into the narrative sequence are slotted elements which are in no sense at all part of the 'story', but are simply further extensions of the portrayal of Duquette's character. His confrontation with the concierge, his escape to the metro, his encounter with the lady who has flowers on her 'balcony'—none of these advances the narrative at all. They are not in any way significant to the outcome; but they add considerably to our sense of Duquette.

There is more 'story' to "Je ne parle pas français" than to "Prelude", but it is only an excuse on which to hang the fiction, or a way of winding it up, and if we pay too much attention to it it may leave us confused. There is a very fine, subjectively drawn line between richness and confusion. "Je ne parle pas français" begins as a cry against Duquette's corruption and becomes something like a celebration of it. The fiction is as equivocal as the character; and we may decide that this is a good or a bad thing according to mood and appetite. But the brilliance of detail, and the gusto, are beyond dispute; so, I believe, is the fact that technically the story represents a step forward into greater complexity.

The work most closely related to "Je ne parle pas français" in content and method is "A Married Man's Story" published as an unfinished piece in the posthumous collection *The Dove's Nest and Other Stories* (1923). Both these stories have a first person male narrator, a man who is in some degree cynical and at odds with the world. Both move in circles from a central point, going back and forward in time. But "A Married Man's Story" is darker, less ebullient, steadier in tone and purpose; it is probably the most sombre of all Katherine Mansfield's fictions; and it suggests a further range of feeling she might have been expected to explore and develop. Murry puts the two stories together, but once again it is according to the positive-negative classification already described, which he relates to the progress of their marriage. "Je ne parle pas français" and "A Married Man's Story" belonging to periods of estrangement and doubt, "Prelude" and "At the Bay" to periods of peace and love.[34] For this reason the exercise of attempting to date "A Married Man's Story" and to plot exactly where it comes in Katherine Mansfield's writing is particularly interesting.

During May 1918 she wrote regularly from Looe in Cornwall to Murry who was then in London. Once again they were friends apart. On the 28th she mentions a new story she is writing; and in his 1951 edition of her letters Murry footnotes this remark saying he believes the work referred to is "A Married Man's Story". [35] So far as I know there is no evidence other than this footnote for dating the story from that time; but every critic and commentator who gives it a date gives May 1918.[36] Murry had, however, 28 years before he published that footnote, dated the story differently. In his introductory note to *The Dove's Nest* (1923) he listed it among stories written 'Between October 1921 . . . and the end of January 1922'; and since this note went on reappearing in the *Collected Stories*, two contradictory pieces of information continued to be available after 1951, though it was a contradiction no one appeared to notice.

In fact, as might be expected, Murry's earlier dating, not the later, was nearer to being correct; but even it was significantly inaccurate, suggesting the story was not written until after *The Garden Party* stories were complete, whereas in fact it belongs among them. Among papers deposited in the British Museum by Violet Schiff on the death of her husband Sydney there are letters from Murry. On 23 August 1921 Murry writes from the Chalet des Sapins in Switzerland:

> K. is in the middle of the longest and last of her stories for her new book which is to be called (I believe, though this is confidential) "A Married Man" and other stories. It's the married man she's in the middle of now. I think it's an amazing piece of work.[37]

Thus "A Married Man's Story", the darkest of all her fictions, belongs not to a period of estrangement but to the second period of sustained marital harmony. More surprising, it belongs to the same month in which "At the Bay" was being written, and seems even to have interrupted the writing of "At the Bay". The sequence of that extraordinarily productive period seems to have been as follows: She is writing "At the Bay" on August 8.[38] By August 14 she has set it aside and completed "The Voyage". [39] On August 23 she is well into "A Married Man's

Story".[40] She becomes ill and lays it aside.[41] After the illness she returns to "At the Bay" and finishes it somewhere between September 5 and 22.[42] She makes several false starts on new stories, and then early in October writes "The Garden Party"[43] which becomes the title story for the new collection. "A Married Man's Story", being incomplete, remains unpublished until after her death, when Murry locates it first (1923) as coming after *The Garden Party* stories were complete, then (1951) as coming before they were begun.

"A Married Man's Story" is the strangest and most impenetrable of her fictions, and one of the most compelling. It has a remorselessly sinister quality. Its central character is negative in a way that throws up, when the comparison is made, all that is positive and life-affirming in Raoul Duquette. What the central idea was to be is not fully revealed. Something has happened 'last Autumn' which has turned the marriage sour and brought out the dark side of the narrator, causing him to revive the horror that hangs over him from childhood. The horror springs (I am now re-sorting the elements into something like a narrative) from the memory that his mother, who had been bed-ridden throughout his childhood, came to his bed-side the night she died (he was 13) and told him his father had poisoned her. Whether this really happened or not he doesn't know. The father was a chemist who sold a five-penny pick-me-up to young women whose 'gaudy looks' and 'free ways' fascinated the child. There is something sinister about this pick-me-up and the women who take it. The father's manner in selling it is 'discreet, sly, faintly amused and tinged with impudence'. After the mother's death the father consorts with some of these painted young women. He is an alien and frightening figure and the child thinks of him as Deadly Poison, or old D.P.

Some time after the mother's death the child, or young man, has had an experience which makes him feel that everything has changed, 'the barriers [are] down', he has 'come into [his] own world', he is no longer alien. He has turned, however, not towards human kind, but towards his 'silent brothers'; and this, the last phrase in the story as it stands, seems to refer back to the wolves, described earlier as his 'fleet grey brothers'. So as a young man he has discovered his identity, not in human brotherhood, but in a sense of absolute alienation from human kind. This separation has been concealed, and for a time he has lived a normal life, has married and earned the love and affection of his wife. What is it then which 'last Autumn' has changed it all, brought his subtle, submerged cruelty to the surface, and made his wife feel his coldness and the gap that exists between them? It must be, I think, the birth of the child. This must be the central idea, which remains incompletely expounded. He has become a father and now must act out the role of the father as he conceives it from his own experience. Symbolically, he has begun to poison his wife.

It is not a pretty story and it is easy to see why Katherine Mansfield laid it aside and never returned to it. But it is a gripping and impressive fictional exercise, and one whose symbolism takes hold of the imagination. It is also fascinating because it is once again an eruption of her central preoccupation—the male seen as the destroyer of the female in a sexual relationship.

I made the point early on that Katherine Mansfield worked largely by instinct. If I ask myself what it was an instinct *for*, I can only answer that it was for the real fiction, which comes from the exercise of imagination, rather than for the imitation which the constructing intellect can so obligingly produce when the imagination refuses to do its job. And it is this which places her among the moderns and makes her contemporary, in a meaningful sense, with Pound and Eliot.

If there is one discovery at the heart of the Modernist revolution of fifty years ago it is that there is something which is 'poetry' as distinct from anything else, and that this is not a form but a quality. Further, the fragments which exhibit this quality, if they come from the same person at the same period and out of related preoccupations, will naturally cohere, without structural linking. In fact the structural elements are almost always non-poetic, and are better dispensed with. This is the lesson of Pound's editorial exercise on the manuscripts of *The Waste Land*. This is the lesson which I believe Eliot showed he had not taken to heart when he wrote *Four Quartets*.

The earliest influence on Katherine Mansfield, when she was still at school, were the aesthetes; and her first regular place of publication was A.R. Orage's *The New Age*, where she must have read some of the theorising that lies behind the revolution that was going on at this time in all the arts.[44] In music, in painting, in poetry and fiction, every accepted structural principle was being questioned; and although Katherine Mansfield was only intermittently of a revolutionary disposition, she was aware of what was going on, and influenced in her practice by the feeling that the artist's job at that time was to 'make it new'. Her work considered not as a number of discrete pieces of finished writing but rather as a movement towards something, demonstrates that fiction, too, is a quality, not a form. The items of "Prelude" and "At the Bay" cohere without narrative linking. And individually they are most successful when they are not forced to make a point. When she pushed herself, when she tried to write virtuously, when she worked too deliberately to shape the fictional fragment, of whatever length, to make a point or to come to a conclusion, she produced her weakest work. In her later writing she is still learning to be content to be fragmentary, learning that it is part of the writer's job to engage the reader's imagination by leaving gaps as often as by filling them, learning not to interfere with the creative process once it has completed itself. Murry describes "A Married Man's Story" as 'unfinished yet somehow complete',[45] and in that he is right.

Where did it come from? With many of her stories the identification between life and fiction is so close that her chief problem is that of shaping family and personal history into art. But for "A Married Man's Story" I can see no source in her life except a few physical details suggesting her Wellington childhood. The story is like a dream, a nightmare, a necessary eruption from the unconscious.

In "At the Bay" Linda Burnell comes to accept the negative elements in the relations of the sexes and to affirm the whole process, even by implication the early death she seems to feel threatening her as a consequence of repeated child-bearing. Section VI, where she discovers the love for the new baby she thought she was incapable of; and the magnificent passage in section X when the beams of the sunset remind her, not of death, as they usually do, but of 'something infinitely joyful and loving'—these constitute something which feels very close to a resolving of that dilemma observed right from the earliest of Katherine Mansfield's stories. It is a fascinating thought that in order to achieve it she had to lay aside "At the Bay" and pour out the old horrors in the form of "A Married Man's Story". The result was a fragment as genuine and compelling as anything in her collected work.

The New Review, No. 4, September 1977, pp. 27-36; reprinted in *In the Glass Case: Essays on New Zealand Literature*, 1981, pp. 29-46.

---

[1] "Frau Fischer", *In a German Pension*, London, 1911.

[2] *In a German Pension*, Penguin reprint, London, 1964, Introductory Note, p.7.

[3] *Don't Never Forget*, London, 1966, p. 255.

[4] Mansfield biographers have never offered any explanation for Stephen Swift's disappearance, which left Mansfield and Murry in debt for their periodical *Rhythm* which Swift had undertaken to publish. The anecdote about a bigamy charge occurs among verbal reminiscences of Martin Secker, recounted by Mervyn Horder in the *TLS*, December 10, 1976, p.1565.

[5] Their flavour and vigour raise a question—could she have made a regional writer. Did she, by leaving her own country, deprive herself of a range of associations, of inborn knowledge, of vocabulary. *34 Short Stories, Katherine Mansfield,* selected by Elizabeth Bowen, London, 1957.

[6] *The Lonely Voice*, London, 1963, p.136.

[7] p.140.

[8] *34 Short Stories* , p.15.

[9] One in *Katherine Mansfield and other Literary Portraits*, (hereafter referred to as *Portraits*) London, undated (1949), the other in *Katherine Mansfield and other Literary Studies* (a completely different book despite the similar title), London, 1959, (hereafter referred to as *...Studies*).

[10] *Studies*, p.86.

[11] *The Letters of Katherine Mansfield to John Middleton Murry*. London, 1951, p.149 (hereafter referred to as *Letters* 1951).

[12] *Portraits*, p. 14.

[13] *Portraits*, p. 12.

[14] *The Journal of Katherine Mansfield*, London, 1954, pp. 93-4 (hereafter referred to as *Journal* 1954).

[15] *Journal* 1954, p.79. Carco was later, however, to be the chief model for Raoul Duquette in "Je ne parle pas français", though Duquette was also drawn in part from the painter Mark Gertler.

[16] *Letters* 1951, p.26.

[17] *Journal* 1954, p.68. "Brave Love" survived in manuscript and was recently transcribed by Margaret Scott and published in *Landfall*, 101, Christchurch, March 1972, pp. 3-29.

[18] *Letters* 1951, p.33.

[19] *Letters* 1951, p.14.

[20] *Letters* 1951, p.40.

[21] *Letters* 1951, p.42.

[22] *Letters* 1951, pp.47-8.

[23] *Journal* 1954, pp.93-4.

[24] *Journal* 1954, pp.94-5.

[25] *Journal* 1954, pp.97-8.

[26] *Katherine Mansfield*, Antony Alpers, London, 1954, p.219. Compare this fact with the following examples of statements by Murry: 'Now let us remember that the months at the Villa Pauline were the days when she was writing "Prelude" '—introduction to *The Life of Katherine Mansfield* by R. E. Mantz and J.M. Murry, London, 1933, pp. 5-6; and 'Katherine and I now entered on a period of simple happiness together, when every day was pure delight . . . There was Katherine, there was the book I was writing: both engrossed me. . .We sat on each side of a tiny table. And on her side of the table Katherine was writing the first draft of "Prelude".' *Between Two Worlds*, London, 1935, p. 393. Both Alpers and Sylvia Berkman in their books on Mansfield (1954 and 1951) appear to have the evidence in front of them but to be confused by Murry's account which conflicts with it. Both consequently, make statements about the writing of the first version of "Prelude" which are partly correct, partly inaccurate or misleading.

[27] *The Letters of Katherine Mansfield*, edited by John Middleton Murry, London, 1928 (hereafter referred to as *Letters* 1928), Vol. 1, pp.82-3.

[28] *Weir of Hermiston*, The Works of Robert Louis Stevenson, Colinton Edition, Vol. XII, London, undated, pp.9-10.

[29] *The Lonely Voice*, p.140 and p.139.

[30] *Between Two Worlds*, p.463.

[31] *Katherine Mansfield:A Critical Study*, London, 1951, p.154.

[32] *Letters* 1951, p.160.

[33] *Letters* 1951, p.166 (letter dated 14 February 1918).

[34] *Portraits*, p. 12. Compare 'at first Katherine was very happy at the Chalet des Sapins. She was once more "in some perfectly blissful way at peace"—the mood in which she could return to the vein of "Prelude". She wrote "At the Bay", its companion piece, *Letters*,1951, p.641. Here Murry's commentary links "Prelude" and "At the Bay", Bandol 1916 and Chalet des Sapins 1921, and once again invokes (in the phrase 'in some perfectly blissful way at peace') the letter of 3 February 1918.

[35] *Letters* 1951, p.268.

[36] These include Ian A. Gordon, Saralyn R. Daly, Max A. Schwendiman, L.M.(Ida Baker) (in a footnote, provided by her editor, to her memoirs of Katherine Mansfield) and Antony Alpers.

[37] British Museum MS.52921. In his new biography of Mansfield (1980, and the best to date) Antony Alpers refers to my conclusion that this story was written in Switzerland, and insists that it must be the story referred to in letters as having been written in Looe. He offers no new evidence for this. It appears to me he has not read Murry's letter to Schiff but only my transcription of a part of it; and I believe his footnote must be a late addition to his book, attempting to cope briefly with an article that does not confirm his own account. In the letter from Looe (28 May 1918) in which the story is referred to which is held to be "A Married Man's Story", K.M. says 'This new story has taken possession, and now, of course, I can't go out without my notebook and I lean against rocks and stones taking notes.' 'Taking notes' suggests observation, and outdoors Cornwall would hardly have helped her write "A Married Man's Story". Another point in my favour I think is that the story "Poison", written in Menton late in 1920, has the same theme—the lover who

'poisons' (metaphorically) his/her beloved. K.M. had thought it good but Murry persuaded her not to include it in *The Garden Party*. (He later acknowledged that he had been wrong and that it was a little masterpiece'.) It would be logical for her, having rejected "Poison" from the collection, to try to use the idea again. I concede that Alpers knows much more about Mansfield than I do, and that therefore he may yet be proved right. To date, however, I have more solid evidence on my side—chiefly in the form of Murry's letter to Schiff.

[38] *Letters* 1928, Vol. 2, p.126.

[39] *Journal* 1954, p. 259.

[40] British Museum MS letter from Murry to Schiff (see note 37 above).

[41] British Museum MS letter from Murry to Schiff. See also *Letters* 1928, Vol. 2, p.129.

[42] *Letters* 1928, Vol. 2, p.134.

[43] *Letters* 1928, Vol. 2, p.143, and *Journal* 1954, p.266. The letter to Violet Schiff on p. 137 of Vol. 2, *Letters* 1928, which also refers to *The Garden Party* as the title of the new book, is dated there as belonging to September which conflicts with the sequence I have outlined. But the MS of this letter in the British Museum is marked 'Received October 26 '21', so the dating of the published text is incorrect.

[44] They sought to renew English poetry. . . .Several of them, including Hulme and Flint, were aware of the relevance of modern French poetry to such an enterprise. As far back as 11 July 1908 Flint had written in *The New Age* of a similarity between Mallarmé and Japanese poetry and of the possibility of a poetry composed of suggestions rather than complete pictures; and he had declared: "To the poet who can catch and render, like these Japanese, the brief fragments of his soul's music, the future lies open." *The Life of Ezra Pound*, Noel Stock, London (Penguin edition), 1974, p.81.
. . . the art of attending to radioactive moments, "simply", in Pater's phrase, "for those moments' sake", had preoccupied two English generations. A central tradition of nineteenth-century decadence, a hyperaesthesia prizing and feeding on ecstatic instants, fragments of psychic continuum. . . .endorsed the kind of attention fragments exact if we are to make anything of them at all.' *The Pound Era*, Hugh Kenner, London, 1975 edition, p.60.

[45] *The Dove's Nest & Other Stories*. Introductory note, p.xii.

Jean E. Stone, from *Publications in Australia 1907-09*

Biographers, bibliographers and antiquarian booksellers are frequently at variance in their claims that Katherine Mansfield's earliest professional writing was first published in certain English periodicals. One result of the confusion has been that collectors have paid high prices for these publications, having been led to believe that included amongst the contributions to one or other of them was the first professional work of this world-acclaimed writer, for which she was paid.

As late as December 1976 in a prominent American antiquarian bookseller's catalogue it is stated that "A Fairy Story" by Katherina [sic] Mansfield in the short-lived English periodical the *Open Window* (III, December 1910, pp.162-76) was "the author's first publication". This statement is based on the perpetuation of error by previous bibliographers including Ruth Elvish Mantz, whose *Critical Bibliography of Katherine Mansfield* has an Introductory Note by John Middleton Murry. The only recorded use of the name "Katherina" Mansfield is in the publication of "The Fairy Story" in the *Open Window*. It is a fairy tale for adults with an ironic twist. The issues of this literary magazine from October 1910 to March 1911 were later brought out in one volume.

There is indisputable proof that Katherine Mansfield's earliest professional writing apppeared in an Australian periodical, the *Native Companion*, of which eleven issues (Vols. 1-2) were published between January and December 1907 in Melbourne, no copy being published in July. Six issues, January to June, were edited by Bertram Stevens and those for August to December by Edwin James Brady. Under the latter's editorship a total of four prose contributions by Katherine Mansfield appeared in the last three issues. The *Native Companion* was professionally edited and well produced and attracted to its pages the work of some of Australia's and New Zealand's best known authors, whose writing was already, or became, familiar to English publishers and booksellers.

Twenty-three years later E.J. Brady, indexing a file of his correspondence, now in the Mitchell Library, Sydney, made this note about Katherine Mansfield against the name of H.D. Beauchamp, her father: "I have always regarded her as *the* literary find of my editorial career".

In the serialized sections of his autobiography, *Life's Highway* (*Southerly*, vol.16 no.2 1955) Brady wrote:

> Her covering letter . . . informed me she was a girl of seventeen [In the letter Katherine wrote that she was "eighteen years of age"]. When her contributions began to flow in I grew suspicious—the matter and treatment seemed too sophisticated for a girl of seventeen. I thought perhaps that Frank Morton, then in New Zealand, who was also writing for me, might be 'putting one over'. I knew no writer at the time with a more finished literary style than Morton and somehow connected up with him on that line of doubt. So I wrote to Miss Beauchamp and queried her identity. Her father replied assuring me I need have no fear of being imposed on . . . She wrote for me under two or three *noms*; 'Julian Mark' was one. I had several stories and sketches of hers in hand and type when the magazine went out of publication. I regretfully returned accepted manuscripts to contributors. I parted with Katherine Mansfield's and Katharine Prichard's stories—some of which were in type—with pain. . . . I have consoled myself since by reflecting that if the *Native Companion* did no more than open the door of publication to Katherine Mansfield it was worth while
> . . .

Some time after her death E.J. Brady wrote some verses in memory of Katherine Mansfield which are quoted in full in *More Wellington Days* by Pat Lawler (1962).

The four pieces of Katherine Mansfield's early professional writing which appeared in the *Native Companion* in 1907, now brought together for the first time are: "Vignettes" (October), "Silhouettes" (November), "In a Café" (December) and "In the Botanical Gardens" (December). The first three were signed 'K. Mansfield', the last 'Julian Mark'. "In a Café" was illustrated by Alex Sass [Aleck MacWilliam].

From a literary point of view "In a Café" is the most interesting as it foreshadows later short stories whilst the other three are sketches. In this story

Katherine Mansfield breaks through the barrier between descriptive writing and both characterisation and impersonation. The young couple in the cafe tell their story through dialogue. The plot is slight—almost an impression. The girl thinks the young man wants to marry her—not so—she accidentally discovers this. She "laughed, and continued laughing all the way down the street". The story could have ended there and would have in later work but here there is a neat, conventional epilogue: "Thus is the High Torch of Tragedy kindled at the little spark of Sentiment, and the good God pity the bearer".

"Vignettes" is set in London and has lines typical of entries in Katherine's *Journal* at that time, expressing her desire to go back to that city: "In my streets there is the answer to all your achings and cryings. Prove yourself, permeate your senses with the heavy sweetness of the night. Let nothing remain hidden". Mood is evoked by descriptive lines like: "I have drawn the curtains . . . to shut out the weeping face of the world".

The influence of Oscar Wilde is most evident in "Silhouettes": "I want the night to come, and kiss me with her hot mouth, and lead me through an amethyst twilight to the place of the white gardenia". It is set in New Zealand.

"In the Botanical Gardens" contrasts vividly the orderly flower beds and lawns with the wild bush lying at the garden's end.

In these three pieces the style is lyrical with frequent references to music and colour to sustain the mood of waiting and expectation. Some of this material has been reprinted but has not been included in the collected work.

E.J. Brady was already a well known Australian author and editor and his acceptance of Katherine Mansfield's work strengthened her determination to leave her parents' home in Wellington and return to London, where she had been at school, to make a career as a writer. Her juvenile stories and sketches in the *Queen's College Magazine,* Harley Street, London, had inspired her to become an author but on arriving home in December 1906 she was disappointed at not finding a market for her work.

Tom L. Mills, a journalist on the New Zealand *Evening Post*, agreed at her father's request, to read some verses and sketches of Katherine's. He was most impressed with her talent and said he had read her work "with astonished delight, for I had discovered a genius right there in Wellington". However, when Katherine met him in a tearoom on Lambton Quay to talk about her writing, he was unable to suggest a local paper which would accept the vignettes she had sent him as he said they were "of the sex-problem type". Katherine, or Kathleen as she was then, answered sharply, "That's my business". His, she said, was to judge the quality of the writing. Tom Mills remained friendly and helpful. At his suggestion the poems were sent to *Harpers Magazine* in America, which rejected them. Three "Vignettes" and a short story went to the *Native Companion* which Mills suggested was a monthly magazine that "takes the sex story". All were accepted by E.J. Brady. Tom L. Mills as well as Brady could therefore claim Katherine Mansfield as a "literary find" but first publication belongs to the latter.

When E.J. Brady wrote to Katherine for information, she replied from 47 Fitzherbert Terrace, Wellington, on 23 September 1907:

Dear Sir -
    Thank you for your letter —I liked the perempatory [sic] tone-
    With regard to the "Vignettes" I am sorry that [they] resemble their illustrious relatives to so marked an extent—and assure you—they feel very much my own— This style of work absorbs me, at present, but well, it *cannot* be said that anything you have of mine is 'cribbed'—Frankly, I hate plagiarism.
    I send you some more work—practically there is nothing local, except the 'Botanical Garden' Vignette. The reason is that for the last few years London has held me very tightly indeed—and I've not yet escaped. You ask for some details as to myself. I am poor, obscure, just eighteen years of age—with rapacious appetite for everything and principles as light as my purse.
    If this pleases you—this MSS—please think that there is a great deal more where this comes from -
    I am very grateful to you and very interested in your Magazine.
                            Sincerely, K.M. Beauchamp

    The 'illustrious relatives' of the "Vignettes" referred to Brady's comment on Oscar Wilde's influence on her writing at that time. The statement that she was 'poor' was typical of a young girl in a well-to-do home with no income of her own. 'A rapacious appetite for everything and principles as light as my purse' also has Wildean overtones. Life had begun.
    It was natural that E.J. Brady should think of the *Triad*; on receiving a contribution from New Zealand of the type Katherine Mansfield sent. He assured her in a later letter that it was a compliment to be mistaken for Frank Morton. Brady was not to know, as Tom L. Mills undoubtedly did, and Antony Alpers confirms, that in the social milieu of the Beauchamp family the *Triad* was then considered too *avant garde*. It was a successful monthly magazine claiming to cover, as did the *Native Companion* the arts, music and literature and was paying its way at that time although New Zealand had a small population. Its illustrations were considered daring, whilst the music reviews by the editor, Charles Nalder Baeyertz, were said to be the equal of the best London notices. Music was one of Katherine's interests and she seriously thought of making a career as a 'cellist but her father considered she had insufficient talent, and she gave up the idea. Before leaving for London Katherine did send a contribution to the *Triad*, "Study—The Death of a Rose"; which appeared in July 1908, the month that she sailed.
    She replied to E.J. Brady's letter accepting and paying for her work, on 11 October 1907:

Dear Mr Brady,
    Thank you for your note—and cheque—too.
    Encouragement has studiously passed me by for so long, that I am very appreciative.
    I like the name "Silhouette"—If you do print more than the "Vignette" in the November issue, please do not use the name K.M. Beauchamp. I am anxious to be read only as K. Mansfield or K.M.
    Mr Brady—I am afraid that so much kindness on your part may result in an inundation of MSS from me—but the kindness is very pleasant.
                            Sincerely, Kathleen Beauchamp

This letter pinpoints the beginning of her use of the pseudonym 'Katherine Mansfield'. She had been baptized Kathleen Mansfield Beauchamp; Mansfield for her maternal grandmother, Margaret Isabella Dyer (née Mansfield). . . . Mrs Dyer, a widow, lived with the Beauchamp family when Katherine was a child and there was a close attachment between them.

> My daughter, Kathleen, has shown me the letters you have written in respect to her literary contributions and I desire to thank you sincerely for the practical encouragement you have given her. At the same time, I should like to assure you that you need never have any hesitation in accepting anything from her upon the assumption that it may not be original matter. She herself is, I think, a very original character, and writing—whether it be good or bad—comes to her quite naturally. In fact, since she was eight years of age, she has been producing poetry and prose. It may be that she inherits the literary talents of some members of our family, amongst them being my cousin, the authoress of 'Elizabeth and her German Garden' and other well known books.
>
> As to Kathleen's statement regarding her age, this, I notice, you politely question, but I can assure you she spoke quite correctly when she told you she was only eighteen years old.
>
> Until the close of 1906, she was a student at a college in London, and left that institution to return to New Zealand with me and the other members of my family, in October of that year. I may add that she has always been an omnivorous reader, and possesses a most retentive memory.
>
> Pardon me for troubling you with these details, but I wished to deal with the two points raised in your kind letters, viz., 'originality' and 'age'.
>
> In concluding, may I ask you to be good enough to treat this as a private letter and not to mention to Kathleen that I have written you concerning her.
>
> I am, Yours very truly, Harold Beauchamp.

The fifth item in this collection of Katherine Mansfield's early work published in Australia, is a poem, "A Day in Bed" in the *Lone Hand* (Sydney. Oct.1909) signed 'K.M. Beauchamp'.

Harold Beauchamp had prospered in New Zealand and Katherine's background resembled that of the Burnell family in "The Garden Party" (Constable & Co. Ltd., London, 1922), comfortably off and prominent in the social life of Wellington. Her mother was Annie Burnell Beauchamp (née Dyer).

Both Katherine's parents were born in Australia; her father on the gold-fields at Ararat, Victoria, and her mother in Sydney. The Beauchamp family originally went to New Zealand when Katherine's grandfather, Arthur Beauchamp, inherited shares in Edward Wakefield's colonial land scheme from his aunt, Jane Beauchamp. Joseph Dyer, her maternal grandfather, went to Sydney from England as a young man. There he married Margaret Isabella Mansfield, a Sydney girl of whose family nothing is known. They moved to New Zealand with their young family when Joseph's employer, the Australian Mutual Provident Society, gave him the chance of opening, at Wellington, its first New Zealand branch.

Harold Beauchamp's decision to let Katherine make her own life in London, supported by an allowance of £100 a year—an amount which was increased several times—was not made as smoothly as his *Reminiscences and Recollections* (New Plymouth, N.Z. 1937) suggests:

> After living in New Zealand for eighteen months, she begged to be allowed to go to London, confident that she could make good in the real world of letters. Work she had already done showed undoubted promise. There could be no question of standing in her light. Accordingly, in July 1908, she sailed from Lyttelton by the *Papanui* (6,582 tons) for London.

Ida Baker, known as Katherine's unselfish friend from Queen's College days, remembered a letter she had from her, which she burnt at Katherine's request in 1918. In *Katherine Mansfield: The Memories of LM,* (published at New York, 1972) Ida Baker writes:

> At Christmas [1907] an unfortunate incident occurred which caused the Beauchamps to reconsider their decision about her departure. They were disturbed by a description, which Katherine had written of something that had happened at a ball when she had sat out one of the dances with her partner, and which her mother discovered. In her usual fashion, Katherine had embellished the facts when writing them down, and her parents, taking them seriously, not unnaturally thought twice about letting her go to London.

Katherine's unhappy, agitated state of mind at this delay is indicated by her *Journal* entry on 17 May 1908, two months before she finally left New Zealand:

> 9 p.m. Sunday night. Full Moon.
> Now to plan it.
> O, Kathleen, do not weave any more of these fearful meshes—for you have been loathsomely unwise. Do take wisdom from all that you have and still must suffer. I really know that you *can't* stay as you are now. Be good—for the love of God—be good—and brave, and do tell the truth more, and live a better life—I am tired of all this deceit—and the moon still shines-and the stars are still there . . . Go anywhere. Don't stay here—accept work—fight against people. As it is, with a rapidity unimaginable, you are going to the Devil. PULL UP NOW YOURSELF.

Whilst in a letter to her relative Sylvia Payne, who had been at Queen's College with the Beauchamp girls, Katherine had expressed only loneliness and longing for London, she had now become rebellious, full of self-accusation and obsessed by the fear of failure. She had written to Sylvia Payne shortly after returning home from London, in January 1907:

> The New Year has come. I cannot really allow myself to think of it yet. I fell absolutely ill with grief and sadness here—it is a nightmare . . . I can't see how long it can drag on—I have not one friend . . . There is nothing on earth to do . . . my heart keeps flying off to Oxford Circus—Westminster Bridge at the Whistler hour—London by hansom—my old room—and a corner in the Library—it haunts me all so much—and I feel it must come back soon . . . If you knew how I hunger for it all . . .

The Memories of LM [Ida Baker] mention that in the English autumn of 1906 "The three years at Queen's College were drawing to a close. Katherine . . .

longed to stay on in England, but when her parents came to collect the three girls, she failed to persuade them to leave her behind. She was unhappy and rather desolate".

On returning home she was so lethargic in her self-centred unhappiness that she was unable to enter into her old life in any meaningful way. Her resentment at not being allowed to go back to London sooner led to strained relations with her father and she never did fully appreciate his part in launching her as a writer. Without his initiative in approaching Tom L. Mills it is unlikely she would have found an opening for her work in the *Native Companion*— a factor in her father's decision to let her go abroad. He believed she had talent but insisted that he had no knowledge of creative writing and was influenced by her success.

He had also arranged for her to have a reader's ticket at the Parliamentary Library in Wellington, where she borrowed books by Shaw, Henry James, European novelists, poetry and biography.

He sent her on a caravan trip with friends through the volcanic region of the North Island, when she filled a number of notebooks and gained an insight into a different part of her country. She made use of it in future writing but if Beauchamp hoped the change would make her more contented, he was disappointed.

At home she spent her time reading and writing in her room, was sometimes rude to visitors, and when she reluctantly joined the family in Wellington's social life, was contemptuous of its provincialism.

Katherine Mansfield was nineteen when she left New Zealand in July 1908. She was never to return. Biographical and critical accounts of the unhappy story of her life, personal and literary, have been, and will be, the subject of many monographs as further details emerge from the papers and diaries of her contemporaries. If recognition of her place in the world literature of the twentieth century seemed to come slowly, particularly in her native New Zealand, it was perhaps because she died at a comparatively early age. She had a lonely death at the Gurdjieff Institute at Fontainebleau in the evening of 9 January 1923 at the age of thirty-four. She had gone there in the hope of arresting the tuberculosis which had forced her in 1917 to leave her husband, John Middleton Murry, in England and live alone on the Continent. Characteristically, she continued to write until her death.

Publications in Australia 1907-1909, edited with introduction, Sydney: Wentworth Books, 1977.

Jeffrey Meyers, "Katherine Mansfield's 'To Stanislaw Wyspianski' "

Katherine Mansfield's elegy on the Polish painter and playwright, "To Stanislaw Wyspianski," was not included in the collection of her *Poems* which Middleton Murry rushed into print ten months after her death in November 1923. Fifteen years later, in 1938, the poem was privately printed by the London bookseller, Bertram Rota, in a limited edition of one hundred copies. Though all scholars have accepted this eight-page, grey-covered pamphlet as the first publication of Mansfield's longest poem, it was, in fact, translated by Floryan Sobieniowski and first published on December 26, 1910 in the Literary Supplement of the Warsaw Weekly *Gazety Poniedzialkowej* (Monday Newspaper). This hitherto unidentified Polish version, Mansfield's third published poem,[1] was accompanied by Floryan's introduction, the first critical essay on her work. An understanding of Mansfield's relations with Floryan will place her poem and his introduction in a clearer perspective.

Mansfield met Floryan and wrote this poem while living in Wörishofen—a cheap and conveniently obscure spa, fifty miles west of Munich and 2000 feet high in the Bavarian Alps—from June 1909 until January 1910. In the summer of 1909, she gave birth to a premature and stillborn infant, the illegitimate child of the New Zealand musician, Garnet Trowell. She struggled against the tempting oblivion of barbiturates and in the wretched circumstances of her convalescence wrote the bitter and satiric stories, *In a German Pension* (1911).

Mansfield, using the German she had learned at Queen's College, became acquainted with a group of literary *émigrés* (who had planned journals which would publish translations of her stories) and had an affair with the charming but untrustworthy Floryan. I have recently discovered some illuminating information about this shadowy and sinister figure in her life.

Floryan Sobieniowski was born in 1881 in southeastern Poland, then under Russian domination, belonged to the impoverished landed gentry, was educated at Cracow University, and studied aesthetics and art history in Munich and Paris from 1909 until 1911. He had a wonderful voice, a fine repertoire of Slavic songs, and a profound interest in the dramatic poet, Stanislaw Wyspianski (1869-1907), who had recently died of syphilis in Poland. Floryan, who was a drama critic in Cracow during 1911-1912, met Bernard Shaw in late 1912, obtained the Polish rights to *Pygmalion*, and eventually translated forty-two of Shaw's plays. He was always in financial difficulty and frequently pressed Shaw for money; but these demands merely irritated the playwright who constantly chided him for his lack of responsibility. Floryan ignored these admonitions and characteristically sold the letters from Shaw that portrayed him unfavorably. He lived in London from 1913 to 1929 and died in Cracow in 1964.

When Floryan had to leave Wörishofen, he arranged to meet Mansfield in Munich and travel with her to Poland and Russia. Though she looked forward to seeing him and wrote him enthusiastic and loving letters, they quarrelled in Munich, and she returned alone to England in January 1910. But their separation was not final, and her friendship with Floryan later led to unpleasant and ugly incidents.

Two and a half years later, when Mansfield was living with Murry in a country cottage at Runcton, near Chichester, the penniless Floryan suddenly reappeared with two big black trunks filled with books and manuscripts and moved in with them—against their will—from August to November 1912. He became the "Polish Correspondent" of their little magazine, *Rhythm*, which reproduced a drawing that portrays Floryan as an attractive and pensive man with dark wavy hair, a high forehead, broad nose, and thick moustache. Floryan also contributed an essay on his compatriot, Stanislaw Wyspianski: :"Poet and dramatist, painter and sculptor, architect and creator of new values for the Polish consciousness . . . his literary creation had two 'Leitmotiven'—one, the necessity for close connection with national tradition; the second, the awakening of independence."[2]

Floryan, who seemed to regard himself as their dependent for life, turned up again in November 1912 after Mansfield and Murry had moved from Runcton to the *Rhythm* office-flat in London; and his financial extortions anticipate his less successful attempts with Shaw. He "borrowed" more than £40 from them at a time when they were £400 in debt to the printers and had just had their furniture repossessed; and when they refused to support him any longer, had to "lend" him another £15 before he would leave. Floryan remained the "Polish Correspondent" until the last issue of *Rhythm* in March 1913, when Katherine's poem "Floryan Nachdenklich" appeared in the *Dominion*, published in Wellington. His power over them was based on his past sexual relations with Mansfield. Since Floryan threatened Mansfield, and Murry (who never suspected she had been Floryan's mistress) was passive by nature, they were forced to tolerate him until they could pay what he demanded.

After her final break with Floryan in the summer of 1913, Mansfield called him "a rather dangerous fraud." In September 1920, just before the publication of *Bliss* (her first book in nine years), she wrote to Murry from Menton about Floryan's threats of blackmail and confirmed that he had damaging letters (written when they were lovers) which she would pay anything to recover. She borrowed £40 from her friend, Ida Baker, and instructed Murry to buy the letters and burn them in a great fire:

> *It is true* that he does possess letters written during my acquaintance with him which I would give any money to recover. And it is true that especially if he is married [and needs money] he will never cease threatening. What I propose is this. I talked it over with Ida. She agreed to give me £40. I want you to go with F. to a solicitor, receive the letters, get his sworn statement [to leave me alone] and hand him my cheque for the amount. It's *not* a waste of £40. . . . I haven't worried an atom bit about F. except in so far as it worried you and affects US. I won't have that Pole outside our door. Burn all he gives you—won't you. A bon fire.[3]

In January 1910, however, Mansfield and Floryan were lovers, and he inspired her to write the poem about Wyspianski, who had composed several plays about the abortive Insurrection of 1830. His "voice tore at the conscience of the nation which was slowly becoming accustomed to slavery. . . . The word 'Poland' was heard on the stage with a power that had seldom been known, and reminded those who heard it of the nation's tragic lack of historical life, its terrible helplessness."[4]   Though a biographical note at the end of the elegy states "the lines suggest that the poem was conceived during her residence in New Zealand—probably at the time of Wyspianski's death in 1907," there is no evidence that Mansfield had heard of him before she came to Wörishofen.

"To Stanislaw Wyspianski" is a youthful poem written in long rhythmic lines comprising eight sentences, which shows the powerful influence of Walt Whitman, whom she had read in Wellington in 1907. The poem is more about Katherine Mansfield and New Zealand than about the Polish playwright, of whom we learn very little; and it seems clear that Mansfield took most of her enthusiasm and ideas from Floryan. Unlike Wordsworth, in his analogous poem about the dead Haitian revolutionary, "To Toussaint L'Ouverture," Mansfield does not share her subject's heroic idealism and nationalistic favor. Her elegy on her brother who was killed in the Great War, "To L.H.B." (*Poems*, p. 55), is far more moving and effective.

The poem is structured by the contrast between New Zealand and tragic Poland, both struggling (in very different ways) to create their historical destiny. Mansfield, who experienced Wyspianski's lawless and self-destructive energy (which led to her unhappy sexual adventures), sympathizes with his brave fight against death and introduces the political theme of salvation and resurrection by comparing Wyspianski with Christ. The elegy concludes as the individual "I" turns into the choric "we" and echoes the closing lines of Floryan's essay: "As an unconquered ever-watchful champion of this [patriotic] consciousness he met his death; and his figure will soon become a legend in harmony with his own words."

Floryan's brief introduction is, in many ways, more interesting than Mansfield's poem and is translated here for the first time:

> The young English poetess who writes under the pseudonym of K. Mansfield, of Irish origin—and French name—considered New Zealand her fatherland, "a little island cradled in the giant sea bosom," where she was born, spent her childhood, and where she temporarily resides after a lengthy stay in America and Europe.
>
> A gifted author has an artistic nature that wonderfully combines all the riches of European culture with the exotic elements that she acquired from the luxuriant and untouched nature of New Zealand—she absorbed all these traits from lengthy stays with wild aboriginal Maoris—and by a curious fate, she became acquainted with Polish history and literature. She gained a superficial knowledge of our history from a book of the late professor at Oxford University, William R. Morfill (*Stories of the Nations*),[5] knowledge of masterpieces of our literature from a few French, English and German translations, which were evoked in her "The Old Mother," and a profound enthusiasm for works that opened a completely new world of thought and feeling; and she decided to learn the Polish language.
>
> The greatest impression on her was made by Norwid[6] and Wyspianski. From Wyspianski's works she studied and learned *The Judges* and *The Curse*, translated into German by K. Rozycki.[7]
>
> From her knowledge of Wyspianski's entire creative work (from summaries done by myself), based on Polish history of the eighteenth and nineteenth centuries and the changes in Polish social thought, she was able to empathize with the tragic life of the author of *The Wedding*, which was clearly reflected in the sensitive soul of the author

of "The Wonder of Maoriland." The mirror of this impression is her poem, which could not, for a simple reason, be published in the pages of an English journal.

And this poem expresses only the voice of a single person who is not yet well known. But because of her profound enthusiasm and good will—because she may in the future be a great help to Polish literature—I would like to acquaint Polish readers with her poem.

In considering the poem itself, besides her sincere enthusiasm, her full critical awareness of the subtle difference of two worlds, we are also struck by the content of her thought: that there is only one common language for all human beings, understood in every geographical longitude and latitude—the language of action.

Floryan's essay about Mansfield contains many biographical errors and distortions which portray her as more cosmopolitan and knowledgeable than she actually was at that time. Though Mansfield's real name (Beauchamp) was French, her origin was English, not Irish; she had never been to America and did not return to New Zealand after her second departure for England in July 1908. Though she did travel in Maoriland for a month in November-December 1907, this was her only direct contact with the aborigines. Mansfield's works, referred to as "The Old Mother" and "The Wonder of Maoriland", have not been published, unless the latter was an earlier version of "In the Rangitaki Valley" (*Poems*, p.3).

In this essay, published eight years before Poland became independent, Floryan attributes his own feelings to Mansfield in order to pass Russian censorship and indirectly communicate them to the nationalistic admirers of Wyspianski. Floryan makes an ironic concession to his country's "liberalism" and suggests that in 1910, five years after the first Russian Revolution and three years after the Slavic anarchists were condemned in Conrad's *The Secret Agent*, Mansfield's poem could not be published in *England* for the "simple reason" that it was inflammatory and subversive. Floryan's conclusion: "there is only one common language . . . the language of action," uses "action" as a euphemism for "revolution."

In addition to their unusual bibliographical history, Mansfield's poem and Floryan's political critique shed new light on her intellectual interests and emotional relations with Floryan during an important but obscure period of her life. They reveal that Mansfield, who translated part of *The Judges*, seriously studied the language and history of Poland, became familiar with the major works of Wyspianski, and was strongly influenced by Floryan's artistic and political ideas. Her involvement with the unscrupulous Floryan was brief but profound and enabled the Pole to maintain his malign influence on her life for ten more years—when he forced her to capitulate to his blackmail.[8]

Modern Fiction Studies, XXIV, 1978, pp. 337-341.

---

[1] Her first two poems were "A Day in Bed," *Lone Hand* (Sydney), 5 (October 1909), reprinted in *Poems* (London, 1923), p. 95 and "November," *Daily News* (London), 3 November 1909.

2 *Rhythm*, 2 (December 1912), pp.311, 316. This essay includes a reproduction of the *Self Portrait* of Wyspianski, who became Professor at the Cracow Academy of Fine Arts in 1905.

3 Katherine Mansfield, *Letters to John Middleton Murry, 1913-1922* (London: Constable, 1951), pp. 536, 541. These letters do not identify Floryan and merely refer to him as "F".

4 Manfred Kridl, *A Survey of Polish Literature and Culture* (New York: Columbia University Press, 1956), pp. 463-464. For other criticism on Wyspianski see Roman Dyboski, *Modern Polish Literature* (London: Oxford University Press, 1924); Czeslaw Milosz, *The History of Polish Literature* (New York: Macmillan, 1969); and Claude Backvis, *Le Dramaturge de Stanislaw Wyspianski* (Paris: 1952).

5 *The Story of the Nations* (London: 1885). Morfill, Professor of Russian from about 1900 until his death in 1909, also wrote histories of Russia and Poland, grammars of Russian, Polish, Czech, Bulgarian, and Serbian, and a biography of Jan Huss.

6 Cyprian Norwid (1821-83), a poet who died in poverty and obscurity, was rediscovered and admired in the twentieth century.

7 *Klatwa (Der Fluch)* and *Sedziowie (Gericht)* were translated by K. Rozycki and published in Munich in 1909. I am grateful to Eugene Petriwsky for the translation of this essay.

8 For a thorough discussion of her life see my *Katherine Mansfield: A Biography* (London: Hamish Hamilton, 1978).

Cherry Hankin, "Fantasy and the Sense of an Ending in the Work of Katherine Mansfield"

As a genre, the short story has suffered from a certain critical neglect: it is the poor relation of poetry, on the one hand, and the novel, on the other. Indeed, the drawback as well as the strength of the short story form is that it partakes at once of the qualities of poetry and the novel. With lyric poetry it shares a limitation of length and a precision of expression which demands that every word count; it tends to strive for a single effect which is dramatic in its impact. Like the novel, the short story deals with characters and their social relationships; it presents us with one or more events which bring about a change in the awareness—and the expectations—of the reader, if not the central character. But to a far greater extent than the novel, the effectiveness of the modern short story hinges on that moment of change, on the reversal of expectations which brings the story to its conclusion. While the novel, with its expansive treatment of character, can afford to imitate the open-endedness of life in its conclusion, the linguistic economy of the short story imposes a more rigorous pattern. The closure or ending of the narrative is integral, not only to our sense of the work's completeness but to our perception of the design as a whole.

Because Katherine Mansfield's influence on the development of the modern short story in English was a formative one, an examination of the means she used to bring her stories to the point of closure is instructive; it furthers our understanding of the short story form itself, as well as of her own artistic practice.

Now one of the most striking features which emerges from a close study of Katherine Mansfield's stories is the frequency with which some pattern involving fantasy informs her "sense of an ending." This is interesting in the light of Nadine Gordimer's suggestion that the successful handling of fantasy distinguishes short story writers from novelists. "Fantasy in the hands of short story writers is so much more successful than when in the hands of novelists because it is necessary for it to hold good only for the brief illumination of the situation it develops," she writes. "In the series of developing situations of the novel the sustainment of the tone of fantasy becomes a high-pitched ringing in the reader's ears."[1] Herbert Gold likewise sees fantasy as an essential part of the short story writing process, one which has its origins deep in the author's psyche: "Those who love the art of storytelling cannot help dreaming out and trying to control their fantasies. The impulse to make stories is an essential part of all the dreaming about alternatives which makes men human."[2]

It is this "dreaming about alternatives" and a concomitant sharp contrast between fantasy and reality which sets in motion the change, if not the reversal of expectations, that characterizes the conclusions of a great many of Katherine Mansfield's stories. Indeed, in terms of their endings, her stories may be grouped roughly into four different categories: the central character may experience a reversal of expectations and disillusionment; an impending disillusionment or change in expectations may be deflected by the central character's transmutation of the experience into something positive; a reversal or surprise occurs—but at the expense of the reader rather than the character; or the ending may involve a surprise which is merely clever and effects no change in the attitude of either the central character or the reader. What is significant is that the stories acknowledged to be among Katherine Mansfield's best fall into the first two categories. In these stories, which almost invariably involve a reversal of expectations, fantasy plays a prominent role in the denouement. On the other hand, there is markedly less employment of fantasy in the endings of the generally weaker stories which fall into the last two categories.

Clearly, it is not just the element of fantasy in a central character's thought processes which sets apart such often-discussed works as "Miss Brill," "The Little Governess," "Bliss," "Daughters of the Late Colonel," "Prelude," "At the Bay," "Something Childish But Very Natural," and "Her First Ball" from Katherine Mansfield's less popular stories. But what does occur in the denouement of these stories, although not in ones even as competent as "The Woman at the Store," "Psychology," "A Dill Pickle," and "A Birthday," is a dreaming about alternatives and a reversal of expectations which emotionally engages the reader as well as the central character. Katherine Mansfield's gift, in her finest writing, is an ability to focus upon a situation in which the illusions and fantasies of her fictional characters echo those of ordinary human beings. Her appeal is not merely to the reader's sympathies; it is to his instinctive recognition of the similarly competing hopes and fears in his own inner life.

What I would argue, then, is that one of Katherine Mansfield's greatest strengths as a short story writer is her ability to depict with almost uncanny psychological insight the workings of fantasy in the minds of her fictional characters. Remarkably, she set out to do precisely this even in her childhood writing. In Herbert Gold's terms, she was a born storyteller, intent from the outset on using fiction to dream out and try to control her fantasies. Some of Katherine Mansfield's adolescent attempts at fiction are pure fantasy; but they cast considerable light on her artistic development: they reveal her in the act of instinctively discovering her subject-matter and at the same time groping for a form suitable to its expression. Obviously she learned at a young age that the eventual outcome of most fantasizing is disappointment. This awareness seems to have helped shape the form of her earliest narratives. For if the endings of some of her major works involve the contrasting forces of fantasy and reality as they meet in a moment of conflict, the most compelling of her juvenile stories end, too, in a crisis for the central character which entails some kind of confrontation between fantasy and reality. When resolution of this conflict is unattainable, the outcome is death. Death, as Frank Kermode notes, is the most final of endings: the conclusions of even Katherine Mansfield's immature stories demonstrate her inherent sense of the dramatic, her concern to ring down the curtain convincingly, and so complete the design.

The earliest of these extant works is "His Ideal,"[3] written in 1903 when Katherine Mansfield was aged fifteen. Here the author treats as real the fantasy which operates within the mind of the central (and only) character. Nameless, the hero has cherished from childhood onwards the vision of a beautiful lady who first appeared to him during illness. His longing to go with the magical lady, to be one with her, causes his gradual alienation from ordinary people. When he is a young man, she appears to him once more; her third and final visitation occurs when he is a lonely old man, walking by a river. He is on the verge of throwing himself into the river so that he may "see her again, for always and for ever," when the lady suddenly appears and, clasping him in her arms, grants his wish: "her name was Death." The conclusion of this story about a character to whom, by implication, fantasy is more valid than reality, is thus a very simple and final one. An interesting feature of the piece is that the young author was not satisfied with the ending; a year later she revised it in the attempt to introduce an element of conflict. In the second version, the claims of reality (and life) intervene as the old man walks by the river. Now he struggles against the death which is also the realization of his dreams: "He felt he was going to die. . . . He could not bear it. He must struggle, he must live." But the attractions of fantasy are stronger than those of reality; he welcomes the appearance of the beautiful lady, and the story ends as before: "Her name was Death."

Conflict between fantasy and reality is far more evident in "Die Einsame,"[4] a story Katherine published in the school magazine in 1904. Here a nameless lady is depicted living "all alone with her soul . . . on the top of a solitary hill." By day she wanders happily in the forest, by night she walks by the ocean, bewailing her loneliness and praying "Take me, Father, I cannot stay." The falling motion begins when, as if unable to endure the mental struggle incurred by this double life, she feels "that all [is] coming to an end." Drawn fascinated towards the sea, she sees on the horizon, "a white, wonderful boat fashioned of moonshine. . . . Then—ah, then!—she saw the Figure waiting for her, with his arms outstretched, and his lips smiling, and a wonderful light flooding him." The ending of this story involves a clear reversal of the central character's expectations; for after she has waded far out to sea to meet the fantastical boat and the welcoming Figure, they vanish. In vain she calls for help and tries to reach the land: "Then came a great wave, and there was silence." In both this story and "His Ideal," the central character acts as if there were no distinction between fantasy and reality; only the endings of the narratives convey the author's implicit recognition that the competing claims of fantasy and reality are unreconcilable. Death, in both stories, affords a solution to the impasse as well as an artistically conclusive finale. It also assumes a thematic function. In "His Ideal," death is the price paid for the fulfillment of fantasy; in "Die Einsame," disillusionment and death are the cost exacted for treating fantasy as if it were indistinguishable from reality.

Fantasy is again central to "My Potplants,"[5] another piece written in 1904; but a new self-consciousness and a greater degree of artistic control is now in evidence. Replacing the alter-ego central characters of the previous stories is a first-person narrator who is closely identified with the author. The story is firmly grounded in the real world as the narrator describes her present, external surroundings before allowing herself to be carried back in time by some childhood memories. Only when she launches into an account of what is, in effect, a childhood vision, does fantasy enter the narrative. In the vision, the lonely child (she is without family) meets in the woods a beautiful lady with whom she enters into an idyllic relationship: "All through the summer days we lived together. . . . I told her all my stories of my flowers and my trees, and she sang to me and read to me and talked to me. All my life seemed to begin anew in a wonderful way." The inevitable movement towards reality and disillusion begins at the end of the summer when the lady disappears. The next spring she does not return, as she has promised; instead a messenger leads the narrator to a house where "in a great white room she lay, my fairy of the woods." Reality is now clearly impinging on fantasy in the consciousness of the narrator, for she asks: "Are you the Queen of the snow . . . or one of my white lilies?" Unable either to sustain the fantasy or bring it to some satisfying conclusion, she breaks off with: "Stop! Why do I sit here and dream of all that is past . . . Life is before me. I must step into the ranks and fight with the rest of the world." But this sudden jerking back to reality leaves the story in mid-air. Faced with the problem of a suitable ending, Katherine Mansfield tries to reconcile the two conflicting forces: the narrator determines to fight on in the real world "until death shall come and hold [her] close"; in death she will at last be reunited with the lady of the woods. As if even this conclusion were not sufficiently satisfying—or final—however, there is a coda: the narrator, who has returned in thought to the present time and her immediate surroundings, observes that the primroses in her room "have withered and died!"

"My Potplants" surely reveals the young author in the act of acknowledging a dividing line between fantasy and reality and firmly opting for life in the real world. Nevertheless, it shows her still clinging to the idea of death as a fitting conclusion to her story. The fragmented sections of *Juliet*,[6] an autobiographical novel that Katherine Mansfield began writing in 1906 when she was seventeen and left off a year later, indicate her continuing interest in depicting a character whose indulgence in fantasy contributes to disappointment in real life. The incomplete, indeed jumbled episodes, are interesting, for they represent a transitional stage in Katherine Mansfield's artistic development. Three short, dream-like segments describe the unhappy Juliet overcome by feelings of weakness and falling to the ground in what appears to be a loss of consciousness. The closing word, "fell," in each of these segments has all the finality of "death" in the author's earlier writing. Clearly, Katherine Mansfield had reached the point where she could no longer use death as a means of either fulfilling a character's fantasy or enabling him to escape the disappointments of reality. The melodramatic ending, however, of one episode which depicts the disastrous consequences of Juliet's seduction by the friend of her former lover, shows that Katherine Mansfield was still attracted by the finality of death. There is an echo of the revised ending of "His Ideal" in the heroine's final struggle against her fate: " 'Oh—O—I want to live' she screamed. But Death put his hand over her mouth."

The difference between this adolescent writing and "The Education of Audrey,"[7] a story published in a New Zealand newspaper in January 1909, is remarkable. A new maturity is evident, both in the distance the author places between herself and the central character—and in her termination of the story. Audrey is a young London concert singer who decides to accept an invitation to visit Max, the lover who once rejected her, because she feels "that wonderful sense of power, of complete confidence in herself . . . which always followed her successful concerts." During their meeting, she asserts her emotional independence, telling Max that love is something she has "conquered and walked over." As in Katherine Mansfield's previous writing, the denouement involves a reversal at the expense of the central character which is based on an implied discrepancy between imagination and reality. For Max reasserts his power over the young woman by loftily pointing out that her splendid philosophy derives from fantasy—from "literature and a good deal of morbid imaginings"—rather than from experience. Her illusions about herself shattered, Audrey is reduced from being a self-confident career woman to one who is "still walking along the little white road of childhood." It is significant that the ending of this story is a movement towards life rather than towards death; nevertheless, the price of the heroine's final request, "Teach me, Max," is her regression from womanhood to childhood, from independence to dependence. What Katherine Mansfield seems to have stumbled upon, in her attempt to treat fantasy objectively, is a conclusion that is manifestly ironic. Underlining the irony of Audrey's recapitulation to Max is our sense that the heroine is renouncing one set of illusions only to seek the fulfillment of yet another fantasy—that of being loved by Max.

Katherine Mansfield continued to write about the conflict between fantasy and reality until the end of her life; and I would venture to suggest that it was because this subject sprang directly from her own earliest and deepest imaginative experiences that she was able to portray it with such emotional conviction. To survey some of her best-known stories is to observe not only her increasingly sophisticated treatment of the theme, but also the extent to which the contrast between illusion and disillusion shaped the endings of her mature narratives and, indeed, their form. When one considers the preoccupations of her adolescent writing, it is perhaps not surprising that the stories which engage the reader's emotions most immediately conclude with the disillusionment or defeat which is concomitant with a movement from fantasy to reality. A variation of this characteristic ending occurs when a character averts disillusionment by reversing the movement and recovering, or gaining sudden access to, the world of dream. In both types of narrative the outcome is aesthetically satisfying: there is a sense in which the artistic pattern is rounded off and the laws of life, like the laws of fiction, are felt to be obeyed.

Katherine Mansfield's most explicit adult handling of the theme of fantasy is the flawed, but regularly anthologized story, "Something Childish But Very Natural." The narrative centers on the emotional dilemma of two young people, Edna and Henry, who are drawn towards each other but are not ready for marriage. Their attempt to solve the problem by pretending to remain as children in a world of unspoiled innocence is echoed in the lines of a poem Henry likes:

> I'm always with you in my sleep
> The world is all one's own,
> But then one wakes and where am I?
> All, all alone.

The denouement occurs when fantasy can no longer be kept separate from reality, when the world of sleep gives way to the world of waking. Edna's agreement to join Henry in a rented cottage that might almost be a doll's house heralds the end of their game; as if realizing the implications of her decision, she fails to arrive. Henry's disappointment brings the story full circle: when he wakes from the world of fantasy, or make-believe, he finds himself in the real world, "all alone."

On the surface, "The Little Governess" is a very different kind of story; but it too portrays a central character who chooses to shut out some unpleasant aspects of reality by fantasizing as true her own deepest wishes. In the little governess's mind, the well-mannered man she meets during her train journey from England to Germany is not an aging roué but a "charming old grandfather." In the course of the day they spend together in Munich, her expectations seem to be fulfilled as he showers her with food and the promise of a gift. When the old man sheds his disguise, as it were, and approaches her sexually, the young woman is jerked harshly back from the comfortable world of fantasy. Like Henry in "Something Childish," she is left all alone—and stranded in a foreign city.

Yet another story which involves the self-deception of an immature central character is "Bliss". Bertha Young's daydreams culminate in the fantasy that she and her dinner guest, Pearl Fulton, share a special and very rare rapport which Miss Fulton will confirm with "a sign." As her guest moves towards the window and gazes with her at the "slender, flowering" pear tree in the garden, Bertha believes that the sign has indeed been given. What destroys her fantasy that they two are "creatures of another world" is the sight, at the end of the evening, of Pearl arranging an assignation with Bertha's husband.

A movement from fantasy to reality, and an accompanying destruction of illusion, likewise shapes the form of "Miss Brill." An aging, lonely spinster, Miss Brill compensates for the lack of interest in her life by listening to the conversations of others in the park and imagining their relationships. What gives her a vicarious sense of companionship with the people she listens to is the fantasy that she and they are all on stage, acting parts: "No doubt somebody would have noticed if she hadn't been there; she was part of the performance after all." Miss Brill's new-found delight in imagining herself, not only an actress but a necessary part of the company in the park, is shattered when she hears a young couple wishing that she'd "keep her silly old mug at home." The pattern of the work is complete when she returns to the sordid reality of her "little dark room."

Even such complex and lengthy stories as "Prelude" and "At the Bay" conclude with the movement of a central character from a wish-fulfilling dream to a more mundane reality. Unmarried and dissatisfied with life in her sister's household, Beryl Fairfield in "Prelude" fantasizes herself as beautiful and sought-after, the center of admiring attention. If Katherine Mansfield chose to focus the final episode of her long narrative on Beryl, who is less important than Kezia and Linda, it is probably because Beryl, in the closing pages, is depicted as "playing the same old game," as putting on an act for herself just as she habitually does for others. The reversal with which this story ends is comparatively gentle: Beryl's reverie is interrupted by Kezia bursting into her room with a summons to lunch—which is also a summons back to reality. In the closing episode of "At the Bay", too, Beryl is the central character. But here Katherine Mansfield underlines the contrast between fantasy and reality. Dreaming as she prepares for bed of the lover who will take her to a new life, Beryl is startled to see outside her window a married man, Harry Kember. Still under the spell of her fantasy, and urged on by the man's taunts, she joins him on the dark lawn. Even the remnants of her dream are dispelled, however, by the reality of his "bright, blind, terrifying smile" and her hasty dash for safety.

In some of the stories written towards the end of her life, Katherine Mansfield modified this pattern. Instead of the ending hinging on a character's return from pleasant fantasy to unpleasant reality, fantasy or the imagination intervenes to ameliorate a distressing situation in the real world. Perhaps the best-known example of this kind of reversal is found in "The Doll's House." Here the washerwoman's two children are shut out from the companionship of their middle-class schoolfellows and forbidden to see the Burnell girls' new doll's house. When Kezia defies her mother's orders and allows the pariah children a hurried glimpse, the reversal of their expectations occurs. What makes the ending so satisfying, however, is less this moment of justice than the manner in which the imagination of the two underprivileged but dreamy children is transfixed by the "little lamp." It is as if the lamp, with its symbolic associations of vision and beauty, has given them a kind of imaginative protection against the harsh, outside world. The colouring her imagination gives to reality protects Leila, too, in "Her First Ball." The young girl's enchantment with the fairy tale atmosphere of the ball gives way to distress and disillusionment when a fat, elderly dancing partner tells her that one day she will just be one of "the poor old dears" watching from the stage. This intrusion of reality into her fantasy of continuing youth and happiness is only momentary, however; the "melting, ravishing" music of the band casts its spell over her again, and the dream reasserts itself.

As the ending of "Daughters of the Late Colonel" shows, a final movement of the central character away from reality towards fantasy—no matter how regressive the fantasy—is always less painful than the reverse movement from fantasy to reality. The two middle-aged daughters of the late colonel have spent their lives immersed in the claustrophobic worlds of their father's house and their own confused imaginings. Then Father's death gives them the chance to emerge from their shell, to exchange the misty realm of dream for life in the real world. There is a tinge of regret in their final unspoken choice of a continuing half-life; yet we, as well as they, know that they have opted for the comparative safety afforded by fantasy, rather than the potential dangers of reality.

Bernard Bergonzi's contention that "the form of the short story tends to filter down experience to the prime elements of alienation and defeat"[8] is difficult to disprove in the writing here discussed. What Katherine Mansfield's handling of the theme of fantasy in conflict with reality does show is that she was in the vanguard of twentieth-century short story writers. "In a time of increasing isolation from conventional authority," Herbert Gold writes, "energy flows into fantasy; and the great fantasies seem more authentic and less unreal than the frights of everyday life."[9] Intuitively understanding this, Katherine Mansfield brought to her subject an acute psychological perceptiveness and an instinctive sense of form. There is a conclusiveness and a finality about the endings of her best stories which make us accept the aesthetic as well as the emotional rightness of the experience we have just sustained.

Modern Fiction Studies, XXIV, 1978, pp. 465-474.

---

[1] Nadine Gordimer, in "International Symposium on the Short Story," *Kenyon Review*, 30 (1968), p. 460.

[2] Herbert Gold, in "International Symposium on the Short Story," *Kenyon Review*, 30 (1968), p. 450.

[3] Alexander Turnbull Library MS Papers, 119.

[4] *The Queen's College Magazine*, 22 (March 1904).

[5] MS Papers, 119.

[6] *The Turnbull Library Record*, 111 (March 1970).

[7] *The Evening Post* (Wellington), January 30, 1909.

[8] Bernard Bergonzi, *The Situation of the Novel* (London: Macmillan, 1970), p. 215.

[9] Gold, p. 451-452.

V

One Hundred Years On

Antony Alpers, from *The Life of Katherine Mansfield*

"At the Bay" depicts the passage of a single summer's day, from sunrise to night, and from necessity to dream, in the lives of all the Burnell family at their summer cottage in "Crescent Bay." Aunt Beryl and the grandmother are with them, and Alice the maid, while Uncle Jonathan has taken a cottage there as well, so that we meet again the extended family which was Harold Beauchamp's richest gift to his daughter's art. The baby boy that Linda was expecting in the time of "Prelude" has been born; down at the beach we encounter the tribe of the Samuel Josephs, dragooned by the whistle of their "lady-help"; and the "fast" Mrs. Harry Kember, who smokes and is vulgar, and plays bridge on a summer afternoon. She and her equally hasty husband, whose crude advances will horrify Beryl after nightfall, stand for such evil as obtrudes upon the after-Christmas pastoral. To remind us of town and of necessity there is Stanley Burnell, blustering and practical and bossy, who must dash off to the office in a stiff collar, leaving the women and children—their relief is immense—to enjoy what he provides.

The story is given outward shape by the ancient universals, sun and moon and tide, and by the "sleepy sea," which is heard before sunrise and in the moonlit, Debussyan close. The cycle of the day affects the lives at first of sheep and sheepdog and the shepherd with his pipe (it is one that smokes), but in due course of every living thing that is present in the story, not least the flowers, nearly all of which are little insignificant invaders, like the human colonists—who, as in "Prelude", are colonists come out from a Colonial town. Their sense of isolation in time and place is implied by numerous local details, wonderfully remembered, and made explicit by Alice's thoughts as she walks along the empty road.

Though outwardly shaped by the ancient rhythms, more profoundly the story is structured within by something else. As "Prelude" shows the family's move to a new home and their thoughts as they go to sleep, "At the Bay" contrives for most of them to reflect, in their different ways, on the mysteries of birth and love and death, and in the process we notice that some are capable of dream or of deep reflection, and some are not. The story opens in the freshness of a dewy sunrise, its prose all alert and free of symbol. It ends, with a little envoi of a mere five lines, in the poetry of night and sea and moon. By then the littoral is symbolic.

The events of the day provide contrasting glimpses of the characters' thoughts on love and death. For some, this is done through their daydreams. Some wear masks, which are removed for us; others, like Stanley Burnell, wear none. Death makes at first a comic entry to the story, when the lewd Mrs. Kember (whose husband will surely have to murder her someday) is imagined by the other women, "stretched as she lay on the beach: but cold, bloody, and still with a cigarette stuck in the corner of her mouth." It tinges with sadness the siesta taken by Kezia with her grandmother, who has been drowsily thinking of the past and of her son who died; it returns in comic mode with Alice's visit to the widow Stubbs; it is a passing shadow over Jonathan's little talk with Linda in the garden about his wasted life, and over Linda's thoughts of her romantic youth. For the children, at their card game in the wash-house, it is reduced to the fear of spiders or Uncle Jonathan's sudden appearance at the darkening window. For Beryl, nightfall means the transformation of her romantic daydream into Harry Kember's cat-like snatching by the garden gate; after all of which come these few lines to enclose the whole:

> A cloud, small, serene, floated across the moon. In that moment of darkness the sea sounded deep, troubled. Then the cloud sailed away, and the sound of the sea was a vague murmur, as though it waked out of a dark dream. All was still.

The little envoi, impeccably shaped, with its three-word close, returns the story to the tonality of its lovely opening, and restores its dominant symbol, the sleepy sea.

Let us turn back to that opening, to its effects and purposes. This story with a three-word title and a three-word close has also a three-word beginning—in effect a stage direction:

> Very early morning. The sun was not yet risen, and the whole of Crescent Bay was hidden under a white sea-mist. The big bush-covered hills at the back were smothered. You could not see where they ended and the paddocks and bungalows began. The sandy road was gone and the paddocks and bungalows the other side of it; there were no white dunes covered with reddish grass beyond them; there was nothing to mark which was beach and where was the sea. A heavy dew had fallen. The grass was blue. Big drops hung on the bushes and just did not fall; the silvery, fluffy toi-toi was limp on its long stalks, and all the marigolds and the pinks in the bungalow gardens were bowed to the earth with wetness. Drenched were the cold fuchsias, round pearls of dew lay on the flat nasturtium leaves. It looked as though the sea had beaten up softly in the darkness, as though one immense wave had come rippling, rippling—how far? Perhaps if you had waked up in the middle of the night you might have seen a big fish flicking in at the window and gone again . . .
>
> Ah-Aah! sounded the sleepy sea. And from the bush there came the sound of little streams flowing, quickly, lightly, slipping between the smooth stones, gushing into ferny basins and out again; and there was the splashing of big drops on large leaves, and something else—what was it—a faint stirring and shaking, the snapping of a twig and then such silence that it seemed some one was listening.
>
> Round the corner of Crescent Bay, between the piled-up masses of broken rock, a flock of sheep came pattering. They were huddled together, a small, tossing, woolly mass, and their thin, stick-like legs trotted along quickly as if the cold and the quiet had frightened them. Behind them an old sheep-dog, his soaking paws covered with

sand, ran along with his nose to the ground, but carelessly, as if thinking of something else. And then in the rocky gateway the shepherd himself appeared. . . .

That is fresh and enticing for many reasons—perhaps chiefly because of its underlying assumption that the scene is already part of our experience. There is no narrator telling us of things we do not know. The sudden raising of the curtain has made us feel that we are the sole observer and it governs all that follows, making one bright wakeful instant of the whole first paragraph: an enchanting pop-up, sharp and specific, yet full of mystery to a child, in which adjectives are few and of the simplest sort. The Master, here, might be Theocritus.

There is at first no sound. The author, refined almost out of existence, only sees. But then when sounds take over, deep in the bush we only hear a clear cold stream, not a *writer*. When something disturbs the quiet, it is not the predictable bird that twenty other authors would produce, but the "snapping of a twig," and then, "such silence." Let us now put beside the opening of "At the Bay" this other sea-dawn opening:

> The sun had not yet risen. The sea was indistinguishable from the sky, except that the sea was slightly creased as if a cloth had wrinkles in it. Gradually as the sky whitened a dark line lay on the horizon dividing the sea from the sky and the grey cloth became barred with thick strokes moving, one after another, beneath the surface, following each other, pursuing each other, perpetually.
>
> As they neared the shore each bar rose, heaped itself, broke and swept a thin veil of white water across the sand. The wave paused, and then drew out again, sighing like a sleeper whose breath comes and goes unconsciously. Gradually the dark bar on the horizon became clear as if the sediment in an old wine-bottle had sunk and left the glass green. Behind it, too, the sky cleared as if the white sediment there had sunk, or as if the arm of a woman couched beneath the horizon had raised a lamp and flat bars of white, green and yellow spread across the sky like the blades of a fan. Then she raised her lamp higher and the air seemed to become fibrous and to tear away from the green surface flickering and flaming in red and yellow fibres like the smoky fire that roars from a bonfire. Gradually the fibres of the burning bonfire were fused into one haze, one incandescence which lifted the weight of the woollen grey sky on top of it and turned it to a million atoms of soft blue. The surface of the sea slowly became transparent and lay rippling and sparkling until the dark stripes were almost rubbed out. Slowly the arm that held the lamp raised it higher and then higher until a broad flame became visible; an arc of fire burnt on the rim of the horizon, and all round it the sea blazed gold.
>
> The light struck upon the trees in the garden, making one leaf transparent and then another. One bird chirped high up; there was a pause; another chirped lower down. The sun sharpened the walls of the house, and rested like the tip of a fan upon a white blind and made a blue finger-print of shadow under the leaf by the bedroom window. The blind stirred slightly, but all within was dim and unsubstantial. The birds sang their blank melody outside.[1]

Since the author of *The Waves* is looking out to sea and thinking much of time, the aim is not identical, but comparison can fairly be made, and the first thing we notice is that our own experience is not assumed. Not trusting us with "sea" or "sky", the writer first fetches a cloth, with wrinkles in it, then endows it with strokes, which turn to bars. The bars being found to be waves, each one gives a sigh, "like a sleeper whose breath comes and goes unconsciously"—laboured words and laboured breathing; no match for the natural poetry of its equivalent in the other place: "Ah-Aah! sounded the sleepy sea."

Rather confusingly, there is then a different bar, and alas, a wine-bottle too, in which dark sediment has sunk, to leave the wine "green". There is next white sediment, and on a couch, a Thurber-like woman with an arm which levitates a lamp. When the sun's rays have spread like the blades of a fan, hardware images have taken us far from sea and sky—though only "gradually," with all those nudging adverbs and over-numerous "as ifs." The ensuing description of the bonfire-dawn becomes at moments almost absurd, as the writer wrestles with the language and seems not to *like* the things of which she writes, or to know their names. At length the birds, one up, one down, leave us unsatisfied, and the passage closes flatly with "blank melody." On the showing of this comparison, Virginia's envy of Katherine Mansfield is understandable. True images came naturally to her.

"At the Bay" has indeed its weak moments, and it does not improve on "Prelude" at every point. The scene in the water between Stanley and Jonathan is flawed, and portrayal of Jonathan being worthy of the young James Joyce, but that of Stanley more like something out of Galsworthy. A more serious defect occurs in the portrayal of Alice: the dislike of her which Beryl feels becomes the author's too, and distracts attention from her important role.

It is Alice who gives overt expression to the sense of isolation of the little summer colony, the sense of there being no "others" in the background—an element of which V. S. Pritchett once actually complained when discussing Katherine Mansfield's work. He declared that the sense of a country, the sense of the "unseen characters," was as weak in her writing as it was strong in Chekhov's, where we are conscious all the time of "Mother Russia." Of "At the Bay" he asked, "Who *are* these people, who are their neighbours, what is the world they belong to? We can scarcely guess. . . . There is no silent character in the background."[2]

Of course there isn't, and that was the point, and it was Katherine Mansfield who made it. The "silent character" was the stillness of the bush, which had not known man or even mammals in the time of Christ. Even Beauchamp understood this, in his own rough way. He had known, as a boy, the emptiness which Alice feels, and wanted something different for his children. There being no Mother Russia, nor anything remotely like her, he gave them the extended family as their defence, and "Jonathan Trout" conjoined him in his wisdom. After their fashion, these two admitted history to the unhistoric scene. Thus, another of the things that Katherine Mansfield wished to do, and did do in "At the Bay", with art that conceals if not with intellect that obtrudes, was to give expression in symbolic form to a Colonial experience, now passed and not to be known again, which might perplex an old-world mind, but which still holds good as material for literature. Yet this is one of the least of its aims. Much more than for that, I believe that she meant it for Lawrence.

The Life of Katherine Mansfield, New York: Viking Press, 1980, pp. 342-347.

1 Virginia Woolf, *The Waves* (1931).
2 *New Statesman and Nation*, 2 February 1946.

Susan Gubar, from "The Birth of the Artist as Heroine: (Re)production, the *Künstlerroman* Tradition, and the Fiction of Katherine Mansfield"

The startling centrality of childbearing in the *Künstlerromane* of women represents a response to the hegemonic texts and contexts of our culture that either appropriate the birth metaphor to legitimize the "brain children" of men or, even more destructively, inscribe female creativity in the womb to insult women whose productions then smack of the mere *re*petition of *re*production, its involuntary physicality.[1] For the woman writer who seeks to uncover not only the fiction of male motherhood, but also the factious biological metaphor, the *Künstlerroman* conventions fashioned by male writers are insufficient.[2] Although it may seem audacious to focus here on the stories of Katherine Mansfield, a writer who never wrote a novel about a professional artist, such a choice highlights the reason why women's unique contributions to this tradition may be considered a critique of the genre constituting an anti-tradition of their own. If "women writers do not imagine women characters with even the autonomy they themselves have achieved," as Carolyn Heilbrun persuasively argues,[3] they cannot write in a genre that plots the continuous process by which a male artist progresses towards the transcendence necessary to create art. Certainly nineteenth-century women novelists exploit the artist-character to explain why women cannot sculpt or paint or write. Yet, in the modernist period women did produce recognizable *Künstlerromane*. To understand how they shaped the conventions of this genre to their own purposes, we need to analyze the shift in perspective that salvaged uniquely female images of creativity. As Mary Burgan has already demonstrated, the stories of Katherine Mansfield reveal how one woman artist overcomes her revulsion against generativity.[4] By coming to terms with the centrality of birth without mystifying it, by reconciling her writing with her rearing, Mansfield calls into question the identification of artistry with autonomy.

Precisely because her stories redefine creativity, they provide a model for understanding how feminist modernists accommodated their own freedom to the immanence and discontinuity that traditionally have characterized female culture, without portraying themselves as tokens or aberrations, alone of all their sex. Specifically, Mansfield claimed to write out of two "kick-offs": what she calls a *"cry against corruption,"* or a deep sense of hopelessness, and "real joy," a blissful state when everything seems to open before her eyes "like a flower."[5] Her early stories, cries against corruption, reiterate the painful contradictions of production and reproduction in late nineteenth-century fiction by writers like Rebecca Harding Davis, Olive Schreiner, and Elizabeth Stuart Phelps Ward. It is in "Prelude", the story published by Woolf's Hogarth Press, that Mansfield redefines women's unique creativity inside the gap that separates life and art. Finally Mansfield's later stories, written out of joy, typify the redefinition of women as paradigmatic creators in the artist novels of feminist-modernists like Dorothy Richardson, Willa Cather, and Virginia Woolf herself.

In the earliest of her New Zealand stories, Mansfield creates one of her most revealing portraits of the artist as a young girl. "The Woman at the Store" (1911) is narrated by one of three travelers who arrive, on a hot and dusty day, at a remote country store kept by a woman who is far different from the pretty bride she used to be:

> She was a figure of fun. Looking at her, you felt there was nothing but sticks and wires under that pinafore—her front teeth were knocked out, she had red pulpy hands, and she wore on her feet a pair of dirty Bluchers.[6]

Living in a room where the walls are plastered with old pages of English periodicals, alone except for her daughter, for whom she "adn't any milk till a month after she was born and she sickened like a cow," she explains that her husband is "away shearin'," but the travelers do not quite believe her because she seems to their eyes "mad." Still, one of them decides that "she'll look better by night light—at any rate, my buck, she's female flesh," so he spends the night with her, while his two companions are lodged with the little girl in the store, amid strings of onions, half hams, and ads for camp coffee. To get back at her mother for this confinement, the child draws the one picture she is forbidden to represent, "of the woman shooting at a man with a rook rifle and then digging a hole to bury him in."

This first child artist in Mansfield's work expresses her sense of vulnerability and her rage. The daughter's pictures, which are described as "repulsively vulgar" with a "lunatic's cleverness," are a revenge against the mother which simultaneously marks the daughter as "the dead spit" of the mother, for the daughter's "mad excitement" while drawing is a repetition of the mother's violence, a cycle that begins with the man who has situated the woman at the store in the wilderness, or so the woman claims:

> "it's six years since I was married, and four miscarriages. I says to 'im, I says, what do you think I'm doing up 'ere? If you was back at the Coast, I'd 'ave you lynched for child murder. Over and over I tells 'im—you've broken my spirit and spoiled my looks, and wot for!" (p. 131)

Even as it exposes marriage as miscarriage, the story of the woman at the store, who has been driven mad by "bein' shut up . . . like a broody 'en" (p. 132), explains what happens to a woman who is used as a store and deprived of any story but this one. In spite of her retribution, her daughter's picture implies that she is left minding the store, still handing out her self and her provisions to the men on the road, who may very well meet the same fate as her husband.

Heilbrun, Carolyn G., Margaret R. Higonnet (eds.) *The Representation of Women in Fiction: Selected Papers from the English Institute, 1981,* The Johns Hopkins University Press, Baltimore/London, 1983, pp. 26-29.

1 Mary Ellmann, *Thinking About Women* (New York: Harcourt Brace Jovanovich, 1968), p. 63; and Nina Auerbach, "Artists and Mothers: A False Alliance," *Women and Literature* 9 (Spring 1978): 3-5. Also, Terry Castle, "Lab'ring Bards," *Journal of English and Germanic Philology* 78, no. 2 (April 1979): 201; and Elizabeth Sacks, *Shakespeare's Images of Pregnancy* (New York: St. Martins Press, 1980).
2 Grace Stewart has written extensively about the disjunction between women's experience of their own creativity and the male *Künstlerroman* conventions in *A New Mythos: The Novel of the Artist as Heroine, 1877-1977* (St. Albans, Vt.: Eden Press, 1979). Specifically, she calls into question the categories of analysis employed by Maurice Beebe in *Ivory Towers and Sacred Founts: The Artist as Hero in Fiction from Goethe to Joyce* (New York: New York University Press, 1964).
3 Carolyn Heilbrun, *Reinventing Womanhood* (New York: Norton, 1979), p. 71.
4 Mary Burgan, "Childbirth Trauma in Katherine Mansfield's Early Stories," *Modern Fiction Studies* 24 (Autumn 1978): 395-412.
5 Katherine Mansfield to J. Middleton Murry, 3 February 1918, *The Letters of Katherine Mansfield,* ed. J. Middleton Murry (New York: Alfred A. Knopf, 1932), p. 106.
6 Katherine Mansfield, "The Woman at the Store," in *The Short Stories of Katherine Mansfield* (New York: Alfred A. Knopf, 1976), p. 126. Subsequent citations from stories refer to this edition and appear parenthetically in the text.

Andrew Gurr, "Katherine Mansfield: The Question of Perspectives in Commonwealth Literature"

Writing literary criticism as a collaborative act is a complex operation. It requires similar interests, similar styles of writing and above all a similarity of critical perspective which must be neither so narrow as to inhibit original thinking nor so broad as to allow real differences to show. Even parallel lines of thought can follow tracks different enough to be embarrassing when the aim is to present a coherent and unified view of the subject. When the writer is a regional figure with a metropolitan publishing history the strain of diversity can be acute.

I was asked some years ago to write a small book about Katherine Mansfield's prose fiction, an offer I was quick to accept. Perhaps there was a touch of atavistic loyalism in the speed of my response, and there was certainly an undertow of self-assurance which ought to have set off a few alarm signals. I felt that I knew her work well enough. Reading her at home in New Zealand as a New Zealand writer had given me that sense of inwardness which, translated to a foreign soil, unthinkingly turns into a feeling of possessiveness. By geographical accident I knew her better than any foreigner, metropolitan or whatever, I thought, and so should have no difficulty imposing my authority, like the archetypal one-eyed man in the country of the blind.

That was a mistake of simple ignorance, and this paper is not intended as an apology for my stupidity. I found soon enough how small were the helps that geography gives to criticism, and even knowledge of the pattern which a regional writer follows going into freedom and exile in the metropolis became dangerous, because the identified pattern too easily becomes a shaping mould.[1] At such times of crisis one of the sensible things to do is scream for help, and this I did. The answer to my scream was the act of collaboration on the book about Mansfield which gave me the materials for this paper, and the lessons which are its real subject.[2]

Clare Hanson, with whom I came to collaborate on the book, was an Oxford graduate who had recently completed an M.A. at Reading University where I was teaching. The M.A. course was on the interaction between literature and the visual arts in the nineteenth and twentieth centuries in England. Clare's dissertation for the course was on Middleton Murry's two 'little magazines', *Rhythm* and *The Blue Review* which he edited in 1911-1913, with Mansfield's help. Clare became interested in the magazines partly because of their place in the development of English Symbolism in art and literature at the beginning of the century, and substantially from her interest in Mansfield as a feminist writer. Those two lines of interest developed logically into a Ph.D. on Mansfield's involvement with Symbolism and her activities with Beatrice Hastings and the *New Age* group up to the evolution of her own distinctive art form with "Prelude" in 1916.

"Prelude", of course, was Mansfield's first masterpiece and was about her New Zealand childhood, which was where I, like any narrowly regional reader, thought I came in. I had read Ian Gordon's ingenious rearrangement of all Mansfield's New Zealand writing, in *Undiscovered Country*,[3] and had swallowed all its not particularly hidden assumptions about their autobiographical nature. *Undiscovered Country* presents the stories in sections and in a chronological sequence fitting every piece of fiction to the equivalent stage in Mansfield's real life. All the Burnell stories about young Kezia are in the first section, 'Spring', all the adolescent Sheridan stories in 'Summer' and so on. Taken in that sequence it makes a fascinating record of a writer's memories. What it does not supply with any of the needful precision is much indication of the fictitious nature of the constructs. It leaves us to assume that Mansfield was a faithful recorder of fact thinly veneered with fictitious names and dipped in an elegiac nostalgia, an evocative realist. The Burnell stories, one of which she put at the beginning of each of the three books of stories she issued after "Prelude",[4] can be read precisely as an evocation of childhood and its awakenings and no more than that. Sophisticated nostalgia, superbly composed in a realist mode of composition. The regional approach to Mansfield, fostered by the layout in *Undiscovered Country*, encouraged that kind of placing.

You can, if you try, accommodate the sections of "Prelude" and "At the Bay" which feature the adults into the prevailing perspective of Kezia, even though Kezia features in a minority of the sections in both stories. By doing so, however, you narrow the focus in ways that deny the fundamental principles of poetic symbolism by which Mansfield composed all her greatest stories. The narrower the perspective, the more of this kind of writing is lost to the reader.

That is one of the evident dangers of reading Mansfield just as a New Zealand writer.

English readers, who have on the whole known her as a Bloomsbury writer either in the shape of Lawrence's malign Gudrun or as Middleton Murry's sentimentalist, have tended to suffer from different versions of the biographical overload,[5] and have looked from an equally narrow perspective. Clare, who is English but who came to Mansfield through the Modernists who were not of the Bloomsbury group, was freed from the biographical burden partly by the demolition of Murry's view started by Ian Gordon in 1959[6] and completed by C.K. Stead in 1977,[7] but more substantially by her approach through the aesthetics of the Symbolists and the Modernist movement. She was also free of the preconceptions about realism inherent in what Stead has called 'the New Zealand critical nationalism'.[8] From my initially narrow standpoint she had more value as a corrector than as a collaborator.

The small book that did emerge as the product of collaborative criticism took relatively little time to write. But the process of collaboration was more than three years in preparation and involved much more than just modifications to the separate realist and modernist approaches. We exchanged views, articles and critiques of individual stories until we could be sure of knowing not just our differences but all the other avenues of approach too, before we actually started writing the book. The end product still contains submerged differences, apparent to anyone with the right kind of critical sonar, but it was not difficult to write and it was, I think, a much better book because it came from a collaboration than it might have been had either of us written it individually. Without it we should not have had the benefit of that Leavisite form of critical exchange so vital for the Modernists—'This is so, is it not? Yes, but . . . , and more substantially we should have lacked individually the breadth of perspective which is only now beginning to tackle the scale of Mansfield's literary achievement.

Mansfield's biographers are from New Zealand. Her principal exegetes have been American and French. British criticism has been patchy, and has generally selected an individual story for comment rather than the whole *oeuvre*, like Eliot on "Bliss" or Daiches on "The Daughters of the Late Colonel". She is as much a many-faceted writer as she was a many-faceted person, and few critics have tried with much success to comprehend all the facets. I find it a rather endearing irony, and also slightly worrying, that the two critics who have written best on her should have trodden the same approaches as our collaboration did. C.K. Stead began his critical work as a student of early twentieth-century poetic theory. Vincent O'Sullivan began as a student of the Symbolist poets of the 1890s. Both are New Zealanders.

The worry of course is that they may seem the best critics precisely because they share the same perspectives as we developed. Solipsism is a problem for critics as well as for writers. How can we be sure that our approach has a better load-bearing capacity than any of the others? One of the benefits that emerged from the collaboration was the confidence that we have an answer to that challenge. Out of that confidence I will try first to explain something of the nature of that benefit, and to offer a small lesson about the criticism of regional (meaning principally Commonwealth) literatures, and secondly to provide one rather elaborate illustration of it.

Much has been made in recent years, particularly over African writers who use English, about the disparity between the local, indigenous or regional view of them and the foreign, metropolitan or Eurocentric perspective. The same can be said about assessments of writers who publish in a metropolis but who write substantially about their home territories, like Naipaul, Patrick White and Nadine Gordimer. Alien critics who commit acts of what has not inappropriately been called 'Larsony'[9] are shot at by barrages from the walls of Stead's 'critical nationalism'. Alien critics, it is argued, lack the inwardness which local critics have for the writer's own cultural heritage and the materials the writer utilises. There is indeed much truth in that view. But it runs the risk of narrowness by assuming that the writer's experience and vision must be coextensive with the critic's. If the writer is not a contemporary of the critic, or has made international contacts alien to the critic, the assumption can be positively dangerous. Katherine Mansfield's New Zealand is not the same country as the land and culture which New Zealanders now encounter. She had formulated a Symbolist aesthetic of sorts before she finally left the country in 1908, and yet another eight years of intense experience and experimentation in the metropolis went by before she began to write the great New Zealand stories.

I am necessarily oversimplifying my picture, making a simple mould instead of tracing an intricate pattern, and it is true that Stead and O'Sullivan do not fit the mould. Nor have I any wish to advertise my own breadth of perspective by cataloguing the narrowness of others. It is better to make a symbolic exemplary picture than to put together a photo album of the multiple misrepresentations. Just one small example as a trailer to the symbolic picture. Ian Gordon writes in his introduction to *Undiscovered Country* that Mansfield wrote a kind of prose 'which draws on the stratagems of poetry, notably an unobtrusive—but powerful—use of symbolism'.[10] The assumption here is that Mansfield's prose is composed in Jakobson's metonymic mode, using symbolism as a pointer for the discursive narrative structure.[11] The Symbolist mode, in which she composed all her major work, is essentially metaphoric and poetic. She said that "Prufrock" is 'after all a short story',[12] and there is a close affinity between her compositions and Eliot's poems. To say that the stories *use* symbolism is to assume that their mode is primarily realistic, a misconception which hampers recognition of what the major stories are doing. The same assumption leads the critic to rearrange the stories in the chronological order of their author's life on the grounds that she would have done so herself had she lived to complete the book she called *Karori* and which was to have included all the Burnell stories.[13] That assumption ignores her own statement that the sequence of discrete, self-sufficient events which would compose *Karori* would conclude with the birth of the boy child, an event which in "At the Bay" is already some time in the past. And more generally it ignores the characteristically non-sequential "Prelude" technique of developing the narrative by discrete patterns of parallel and conflict.

So to my example, which is the central symbol in "Prelude". A symbol it has to be, because in botanical terms it is distinctly unreal. Viewed literally, Katherine Mansfield's famous aloe must have been largely an agave. Viewed literarily, on the other hand, it is a symbol of such potency that its botanical origin seems incidental. Viewed either way the nature of the plant which gave a name to the first version of her most famous story provides a basic test of the reader's perspective on all her major New Zealand stories.[14]

As the first of the major stories "Prelude" was in all sorts of ways an innovation. Its form, twelve episodes or scenes, each one linked obliquely by theme and implication rather than by incident to its predecessor, was original in fiction, its closest kin perhaps being the associative form Eliot developed at the same time for *The Waste Land*. The material, a highly contrived reshaping of childhood memories, was both Proustian and Symbolist. In the form of a search for the past the artist creates a present self out of the personal store of memory, a *recherche* for the timeless *temps perdu* which is timeless because of the memory which holds it and ultimately because art will capture it as a timeless moment, frozen for eternity. The influence of symbolism is not so aggressive as it became in poetry, but it is apparent in Mansfield's short fiction in several ways, notably the delicately etched minutiae which only become symbolic through their recurrence and their juxtapositions in the patterns of parallel and contrast through the discontinuities of the narrative. In "Prelude" two particularly powerful episodes, the scene in which Kezia watches the handyman Pat chop the duck's head off, and the scene in which Kezia and her mother look at the aloe, are particularly potent images. But because each image is offered in isolation, with no obviously recurrent symbolism, exactly what they signify has been much debated. It is for this reason that the botanical nature of the aloe is worth scrutinising.

"Prelude" was first drafted, under the title "The Aloe", in the winter of 1915-1916 which Mansfield spent at Bandol in the South of France after the death of her brother Leslie.[15] In part she wrote it as therapy for his death, a reconstruction of the childhood which they had spent so much time recalling lovingly through the summer of 1915. During 1916 and 1917 she worked on "The Aloe", revising it, and trimming it drastically into the discontinuous, tightly organised pattern of parallels and contrasts which is "Prelude". She cut out all explicit authorial analysis, explanation, and commentary so as to leave only the stark account. Explication is rejected, and implication becomes the only means of access. Implication has to be drawn from the patterns of parallel and contrast and from the recurrent images—birds, the sun and moon, the adults who turn the tables and chairs upside down at the beginning of the story, and Kezia who knocks the calico cat over at the end. Where in the original version the aloe was the only enigmatic image, because of its centrality, in "Prelude" the aloe is just the foremost of a complex of images all of whose significance is indicated only indirectly.

Nonetheless the aloe is more isolated than the other images. Pat and the duck are surrounded by references to birds, not least the dream which Linda, Kezia's mother, has on waking, of a monstrous baby bird which turns into a demanding bird-baby. The aloe likewise has links with the other images of flowers, such as the bouquet which Aunt Beryl's imaginary young man offers her at bedtime, but because it is the central image in the story, its linkages are less specific and more broadly suggestive than the sequence of bird images. It stands alone in the garden of the new house, seen by Kezia as a wholly strange and menacing phenomenon, and explained to her by Linda in a way which locates it as the pivot of the story's counterpointing of childhood awakening against adult experience.

Kezia finds the aloe at the end of the sixth of the story's twelve sections, exactly halfway. She has been exploring the wild garden of the new house. On one side of the drive are tall, dark trees and muddy paths, 'with tree roots spanned across them like the marks of big fowls' feet'. This is 'the frightening side'. In total contrast the other side is orderly, with low box borders and a delightful collection of roses, pansies and other flowering plants in dazzling variety. And in between, in the middle of the drive, where it branches around an island of grass, grows the aloe.

> . . . on her way back to the house she came to that island that lay in the middle of the drive, dividing the drive into two arms that met in front of the house. The island was made of grass banked up high. Nothing grew on the top except one huge plant with thick, grey-green, thorny leaves, and out of the middle there sprang up a tall stout stem. Some of the leaves of the plant were so old that they curled up in the air no longer; they turned back, they were split and broken; some of them lay flat and withered on the ground.
>
> Whatever could it be? She had never seen anything like it before. She stood and stared. And then she saw her mother coming down the path.
>
> 'Mother, what is it?' asked Kezia.
>
> Linda looked up at the fat swelling plant with its cruel leaves and fleshy stem. High above them, as though becalmed in the air, and yet holding so fast to the earth it grew from, it might have had claws instead of roots. The curving leaves seemed to be hiding something; the blind stem cut into the air as if no wind could ever shake it.
>
> 'That is an aloe, Kezia,' said her mother.
>
> 'Does it ever have any flowers?'
>
> 'Yes, Kezia,' and Linda smiled down at her, and half shut her eyes. 'Once every hundred years.'[16]

The context of the whole story, which dwells on Linda's timidity over sex and children (she is only in the garden because her mother, Kezia's beloved grandmother, sent her on a reluctant search for her children), and the adult world of Linda's escapism, her sister Beryl's moody preoccupation with young men and her husband Stanley Burnell's complacent masculinity, makes it hardly surprising that the aloe should be seen as a symbol of sexuality. It has however been variously interpreted in this role, as an image of male sexuality—'a phallic tree of knowledge', as one commentator has called it[17]—or as an image for the flowering of female sexuality, Kezia's first point of real contact with the adult world of her mother. It is because of this variety of interpretation that I feel it is worth drawing attention to the botanical curiosity which the plant in the story seems to be.

Strictly speaking, it is an aloe with one distinctive attribute peculiar to agaves. Agaves and aloes occupy roughly the same ecological niche. They are both large flowering succulents native to an arid climate. But the agave evolved in central America while the aloe evolved in West Africa, and so although they have an outwardly similar appearance, they differ in a number of significant ways. The true aloes vary widely in size and shape, but generally have a rosette or spray of broad, tapering, fleshy leaves with prickly edges, and a central spike on which a set of colourful flowers blooms for most of the year. Some of the larger varieties of aloe have grey-green, thorny leaves similar to the main varieties of agave, with the result that for many years agaves were thought to be a type of aloe.

Agaves differ from aloes in that their growing tip is the centre of the rosette of leaves. Only at the end of the plant's lifetime does this growing tip throw up the central spike which aloes have throughout their lives. The agave's spike is thrown up in a single season, growing perhaps as much as fifteen or twenty feet high. It flowers, and then the whole plant dies. The *agave americana*, which is still to be found in the Botanical Gardens in Tinakori Road, Wellington, where Katherine Mansfield lived as a child, and which grows wild in several parts of the city, exactly fits the description in "Prelude" in every detail except for the central stem, which should appear only immediately before the plant flowers and dies. The stem which Mansfield described in "Prelude" is either that of an agave about to burst into its unique flowering, or the spike of an aloe, which stands for year after year between flowerings, somehow transplanted by Mansfield's peculiar botany into the rosette of an agave.

Linda Burnell says that her 'aloe' flowers only once in a hundred years. In the nineteenth century when agaves were first propagated widely and were thought to be a variety of aloe they were commonly known as the 'century plant,' on the assumption that they flowered only once a century. The actual period between the leaves reaching the point of maximum growth, which might give it a spread of as much as six feet, and the throwing up of the stem on which the flowers appear is usually between twenty and thirty years, depending on climatic conditions. The abnormally dry summer of 1979-80 in New Zealand produced an exceptional display of flowering agaves, including the first in Wellington for nearly forty years.

The 'aloe' of "Prelude", then, is a variety of aloe similar to the *agave americanus* with the stem of an aloe grafted on but with the rare flowering characteristic of an agave. It is not a real plant at all. If it was a true aloe it would flower annually. If it was a true agave it would lack the 'tall stout stem', the blind phallos which 'cut into the air as if no wind could ever shake it'. The question which this botanical hybrid raises is whether Mansfield was simply ignorant of the plants which grew in the various gardens of her childhood, or whether she deliberately created a symbolic monstrosity, a unique image at the centre of her story possessing the features appropriate to her symbolism rather than to botany.

Since the aloe is the central image in "Prelude", and since "Prelude" was the first of the major New Zealand stories, the genesis for the *Karori* sequence and the first story to use the new Symbolist method of narration, our conclusions about it have implications for any critical approach to her *oeuvre* and any evaluation of her achievement. Most obviously an unreal aloe challenges the assumptions made about the function of memory in the construction of the New Zealand stories, and the general acceptance of the realistic basis for the literary method used in them.

It is not easy from her writings, whether fiction or otherwise, to locate the precise principles on which her art was based. In all the volumes of her personal writings, which Middleton Murry was so assiduous to publish, there is strikingly little about her artistic principles, and little enough about her practice. She developed as a Symbolist early on under the influence of Wilde and Symons, she wrote poetry and made several unsuccessful attempts at a novel, but she never obviously strayed far from the familiar conventions of realistic prose fiction. Our own expectations about the short story as a form can all too easily disguise the radical nature of the transformations she introduced into it in the wake of that great heyday it enjoyed from about 1890 to 1920. The 'poem in prose', the form which combines the subjective and imagist principles of post-romantic poetry with the realistic outlines of prose fiction, was her main vehicle. Two of her finest and most difficult stories, "Je ne parle pas français" and "A Married Man's Story", show her art at its most complex, and both are first-person narratives spoken by a persona who is a mixture of artist, liar and poseur. Mansfield was always ruled by her awareness of the inescapable subjectivity of human consciousness, and the vision of the great stories never professes to be an objective depiction of reality. She was always more a symbolist than a realist. So however readily we may identify the Tyrrell Street where the Sheridans live with Tinakori Road in Wellington, or the Karori house of "Prelude" with 'Chesney Wold' where Mansfield lived from the age of four till she was ten, we must acknowledge the essentially fictional nature of the world presented in the New Zealand stories. Memory was the secure basis for a wholly fictional set of constructions. The stories are not memories but artifacts.

If we recognise this feature of Katherine Mansfield's major work, then it becomes possible to look at "Prelude's" aloe with a more urgent concern for its artificiality as the central symbol in the story. The different interpretations of course reflect the different approaches to the story. Critics who see the method as realist have claimed that an aloe is an aloe is an aloe, like the pansies and the red hot pokers on the flowery side of the drive. Alternatively, its 'cruel' leaves and 'fleshy' stem are seen to symbolise the aggressive and frightening sexuality of Stanley Burnell. Stanley is the only male in the household's three generations—a female pyramid of grandmother, two sisters Linda and Beryl, and three daughters Lottie, Isabel and Kezia—and both of the older generations express their relief when Stanley leaves the house to go to work. His sexuality is evident not only in his complacent aggressiveness but in the bed-time image of him as a large turkey, and the picture of him doing his exercises in the exact centre of the square of morning sunlight on the bedroom floor. The turkey image has been linked with the episode in which Pat chops off the duck's head, an image of castration (or rather total mutilation) which most commentators relate to Linda's rejection of her husband's sexuality.

Linda is the queen of the household. She plays at the work which her mother and sister do as a routine. She loves her children but dreams of them as huge and voracious babies with gaping bird-mouths. She rests while others work, and only ventures into the wild garden when Grandmother Fairfield dismisses her from the kitchen and sends her to find her children. For Kezia the true mother-figure is her grandmother. Linda is too absorbed in the adult world and its sexual tensions to afford Kezia the single-minded routine love which she needs. Kezia plans to make gifts for her grandmother. Her only contact with Linda is the enquiry about the aloe, with its fat and fleshy stem which flowers only once in a hundred years.

Evidently the 'aloe' is a complex symbol. Its stem, cruel and fleshy, must relate to Stanley and by extension to Linda's timidity over sex and rejection of the children who came as a result of it. But Stanley's fleshy stem is obviously not the kind of object which flowers only once a century. The bird images confirm that aspect of the husband/wife relationship. So, it is argued, the rare flowering is Linda's, a single opening of herself which either has happened once only or perhaps will happen at some future time. On either of these interpretations, the hybrid Mansfield made by linking the aloe's perennial stem with the agave's unique flowering seems to imply above all else that the sex life of the adult Burnells was a distinctly unsatisfactory experience for them both.

There is undoubtedly a strong undercurrent of concern with sex throughout the story. Grandmother Fairfield is at ease because it does not concern her. Linda, married, is put under pressure by it both through her husband and through its products, her children. Her unmarried sister Beryl is tormented by it because she fears and wants fulfillment at the same time, and cannot really know what it is she wants. Linda and Beryl alternate through the story in a delicate pattern of contrast. They represent the Scylla and Charybdis between which Kezia will have to steer her way. The complex strains, the fear and the flowering, are essentially what the aloe represents for Kezia's future, standing as it does between the two aspects of life, the fearful and the delightful, on either side of the driveway in the strange garden of this new phase of Kezia's life.

A phallic tree of knowledge, then, the aloe certainly is. But its rare flowering is not at all the once-in-a-lifetime act of sexual joy for Linda which the more literal-minded commentators have called it. The flowering is Mansfield's necessary fiction; it is told to Kezia out of Linda's understanding—the recurrent contrast with Beryl's angry ignorance—and it is the promise that the future holds for Kezia. The promise of flowering is Kezia's not Linda's. What it symbolises is not simply sexual knowledge or even sexual fruition, but the flowering of life itself. The leaves are cruel, the stem hard and unpromising. But the semi-invalid Linda knows that life can flower, though she has been bruised and has retreated. She describes for Kezia the moment in her future when out of the menacing enigma of the aloe will come the momentary brilliant flowering, not just of sex but of life.

All the major New Zealand stories have a central symbol, and all the symbols represent something fragile and transient, which may be no more than a momentary gleam but which is a central reason for existence. In "The Doll's House" it is the little lamp, the essence of art. In "At the Bay" it is the baby boy, who appears in exactly the same place in the story as does the aloe in "Prelude", at the end of the sixth of the twelve sections. All of these symbols had a complex personal significance for Mansfield. And the first of all these central symbols, the aloe, signifies the daunting fears and pains of a lifetime, lived for a brief moment of flowering, that timeless moment which both illuminates and justifies all the rest of the pained and miserable time of learning.

Much of the best writing in English this century has been prose fiction by writers born outside the great metropolitan centres. Many writers followed

Mansfield in leaving their Commonwealth home for a form of exile in the metropolis. Consequently much of their finest fiction has been constructed about the distant homeland from the standpoint of exile. Away from the homeland the writer of realistic fiction necessarily relies on memory and the kind of mental reconstruction which, if it was content to reproduce only what memory had to offer, would be no more than an exercise in at best autobiography and at worst sentimental nostalgia (no homeland). What art adds to memory is complex and crucial. Memory is inescapably subjective, and the stronger and clearer the artistic vision, the more potently will the work of art simultaneously *seem* realistic and *be* imaginary. Whether Mansfield's aloe was a botanical monstrosity or an artistic hybrid does not matter. As a symbol it is the supreme exemplification of her subjective vision of life's threats and promises. We should value it above all for that.

Critical readers are as subjective as writers. The perspectives of a particular geographical or cultural orientation are inherently narrowing, more than is good for our appreciation of the kind of modern art which Mansfield's aloe represents. One of the ways to repay the debts we owe our great writers is not to approach their work either too lightly or too narrowly.

Kunapipi, vol. 6, 1984, 2: pp. 67-80.

---

[1] This is the subject of my *Writers in Exile* (Brighton: Harvester Press, 1981).

[2] The book is *Katherine Mansfield*, by Clare Hanson and Andrew Gurr (London: Macmillan, 1981).

[3] London: Longman, 1974.

[4] "Prelude" is the first story in *Bliss and other Stories*, 1920. Its sequel, "At the Bay", is the opening story in *The Garden Party, and other Stories*, 1922. "The Doll's House" opens *The Doves' Nest*, the volume published posthumously in 1923.

[5] A summary of these stereotypes is in Hanson and Gurr, *Katherine Mansfield*, p. 2-4.

[6] "The Editing of Katherine Mansfield's *Journal* and *Scrapbook*", *Landfall* 13 (1959), pp. 62-9.

[7] "Katherine Mansfield and the Art of Fiction", *The New Review* 4, No. 42, September 1977, pp.27-36.

[8] Ibid., p. 29.

[9] The term was used by Ayi Kwei Armah to describe Charles R. Larsons's *The Emergence of African Fiction* (Bloomington: University of Indiana, 1972) in his review 'Larsony or Fiction as Criticism of Fiction', *Asemka* 4 (1976), pp. 1-14.

[10] *Undiscovered Country*, p. xxi.

[11] Roman Jakobson, 'Two Aspects of Language and Two Types of Aphasic Disturbances', in *Fundamentals of Language*, eds. Jakobson and Halle (The Hague: Mouton, 1956).

[12] Letter to Virginia Woolf, undated, *Adam* 370 (1972), p. 19.

[13] *Op. cit.*, p. xiii.

[14] Clare Hanson's analysis of the Symbolist structure of "Prelude" is in the *Journal of Commonwealth Literature* XVI (1981).

[15] "The Aloe" was published separately by Murry in 1930.

16 *Collected Stories*, Constable, p. 34.
17 Peter Alcock, " 'An Aloe in the Garden': Something Essentially New Zealand in Miss Mansfield", *Journal of Commonwealth Literature* XI (1977), p. 61.

Claire Tomalin, "What is going to happen to us all?" from *Katherine Mansfield: A Secret Life*

Murry sent a telegram to Ida at once, and she arrived on the following day. Both she and Murry said they felt Katherine had benefited from her time at the Institute, bizarre as it was, and despite her death. Both must have known in their hearts that her death was, in any case, inevitable and close; perhaps it had been as well for her to spend her last weeks engaged in something she felt enthusiastic about rather than simply waiting for the end. It's a view one can share, whatever reservations may be entertained about Gurdjieff and his entourage.

The funeral took place in the Protestant Church in Fontainebleau, and was attended by Murry, Ida, Orage, Brett, and Katherine's sisters Chaddie and Jeanne: Koteliansky, refused permission to travel, mourned at home in Acacia Road. Ida threw marigolds on to the coffin, and travelled back to England with a distraught Murry.

In Wellington, Harold Beauchamp had just been honoured for his services to the Bank of New Zealand with a knighthood in the New Year's honours list, a fact that figured prominently in Katherine's obituary notice in *The Times* (which also placed her marriage to Murry in 1912). Beauchamp took as his motto *Verité sans peur*. With the growth of Katherine's fame he began to change his view of her, exactly as she had predicted. All the same, when Sir Harold came to write his memoirs, he was cautious enough to call in a 'literary expert' to write the chapter devoted to her, as though he did not trust himself to speak of her.

At Garsington, Ottoline sat down to write a memoir of her dead friend, which she read out to an invited group one evening by candlelight. It has not survived, and her friendship with Murry lapsed. Brett began a grieving diary addressed to Katherine (or 'Dearest Tig'); soon it became the repository of the details of her affair with Murry, who had no compunction about either seducing or dropping this forty-year-old virgin. Fortunately, the blood of the Eshers ran strongly in her veins, she showed great fortitude and found a new idol in Lawrence shortly afterwards.

Ida became, for a time, companion and housekeeper to Katherine's cousin Elizabeth; but she could not be handed on like a useful piece of furniture, and soon she settled alone in a cottage in the New Forest, a tiny, remote place where she lived out her long life with few disturbances beyond the occasional literary sleuth struggling up the overgrown path. When she came to write her book about Katherine, fifty years later, her memory was dim, but the power of Katherine's personality was not. She gave her the uncritical devotion of a perfect widow: in its pages, Katherine is always either a victim—of family, of lovers, of illness—or an idol, brilliant and irresistible in all her whims.

It took the news of Katherine's death to mend the quarrel between Murry and Lawrence, who wrote grieving from New Mexico,

> Yes, I always knew a bond in my heart. Feel a fear where the bond is broken now. Feel as if old moorings were breaking all. What is going to happen to us all? Perhaps it is good for Katherine not to have to see the next phase. We will unite up again when I come to England. It has been a savage enough pilgrimage these last four years. Perhaps K. has taken the only way for her.[1]

After this, Lawrence wrote regularly to Murry again, even inviting him to look for a country house where they might settle near one another, and offering to contribute to the new magazine Murry was setting up, the *Adelphi*, with a reconciled Koteliansky as business manager; this was not out of any need for money, for Lawrence's financial position was at last secure, thanks to sales of his books in America. An uneasy peace was reached, and when Frieda travelled to England alone in the summer, Lawrence asked Murry to look after her.

Murry sent Lawrence a copy of *The Dove's Nest*, a volume consisting of a few finished stories of Katherine's ("The Dolls House", "The Fly", "Honeymoon", "A Cup of Tea") but mostly fragments. At this, Lawrence scolded Murry for making excessive claims for her work:'Poor Katherine, she is delicate and touching—But not Great! Why say great?'[2] He complained to another correspondent, in his most acerbic tone, of Murry's cheek in asking the public to buy Katherine's 'waste-paper basket'.[3] He did not know about her request to Murry in her will; nor did Murry ever give him one of Katherine's books, as she had requested, or apparently even bother to tell him of the bequest. Lawrence was irritated by the puffing. He was not an attentive or generous reader of his contemporaries, but he was ready to admire certain strengths in Katherine's work; only not at Murry's bidding. 'She was a good writer they made out to be a genius,' he said in 1925. 'Katherine knew better herself but her husband, J.M. Murry, made capital out of her death.'[4]

Still, the links between the old foursome of 1913 remained tenacious. It appears that Frieda tried to seduce Murry in the summer of 1923 and, although she did not succeed, Lawrence was angry and jealous enough to write a series of stories in the 1920s in which he systematically humiliated and sometimes killed off a figure modelled on Murry. In one, the faun-like hero is visiting the dead body of his beautiful young wife in a foreign convent (shades of Le Prieuré); he finds himself, through his display of grief, magically and irresistibly forced to smile. Presently, the attendant nuns notice that the corpse too has broken out into a smile: a cynical, Katherine-like one.

In another story, as the hero wanders Murry-like from one woman to another in Hampstead, he is struck dead by the god Pan; and, in the oddest of all, another Murry-figure becomes the second husband of a widow whose first (a self-portrait by Lawrence) returns to haunt the guilty couple. The story culminates in the mysterious death of the second husband and the first husband's triumphant, ghostly, sexual repossession of his wife. For good measure, she is given the name of 'Katharine'. It does not take a Dr Eder to read the significance of these works.

Murry struck back in his own way after Lawrence's death, both by writing *Son of Woman*, which purports to praise but, in fact, denigrates him, often in crudely sexual terms; and by becoming Frieda's lover, briefly. No ghost appeared to strike him down. By the 1950s he and Frieda were corresponding warmly and nostalgically about the golden past.

Lawrence was not the only one who thought Murry's zeal on Katherine's behalf excessive. Although T.S. Eliot sent a letter of condolence in January, saying he would be writing a critical article on her work, in June he wrote to his assistant on the *Criterion*, Richard Aldington, asking him to get 'a copy of Katherine Mansfield's book for me when it comes out. I think her inflated reputation ought to be dealt with.'[5] The article was not apparently written. Another friend of the Murry's, Sylvia Lynd, also spoke of Murry 'boiling Katherine's bones to make soup'.[6]

It is true that Murry did boil the bones, puffing and promoting Katherine's work through his own magazine, and running with Constable a well-organized and enormously successful publishing campaign in which segments of her work, fragments of stories, reissues, scraps of letters and pieces of journal (followed by 'definitive' versions of the same) were issued to the public all through the 1920s, and indeed into the 1950s. The pathos of her early death undoubtedly gave her work an extra appeal—people love to dwell on the words of the dying—but that alone would not account for its popularity, in England and America, France, Germany and in most countries touched by English culture.

What did make her so popular? It was not only the delicacy, charm and pathos attributed to her by Lawrence. The sharp impersonality, the clarity and concision of the best stories made them genuinely startling. Her voice was the voice of modernity, bright, short-winded, sometimes whimsical, often ambiguous, with no claim to wisdom and no time for the scene-setting of the classical novelists. Her territory was that of the fragile emotions, half-understood feelings, the fine edge between the ridiculous and the pathetic; she could render the vulnerability of the young, the sad stirrings of the sick, the jealous, the powerless, those who make animals or inanimate objects the focus of their feelings. Other writers studied her approvingly for 'her economy, the boldness of her comic gift, her speed, her dramatic changes of the point of interest, her power to dissolve and reassemble a character and situation by a few lines.'[7] The decades may have taken some of the shine off the originality of her method, but they have not robbed the stories of their vigour. Even those who dislike them acknowledge that there is something pungently alive in them.

Katherine's assessment of her own work was modest. Like all writers, she was pleased when she was praised and hurt by unkind criticism or dismissal; but she reproached Murry with overpraising her: 'I don't want dismissing as a masterpiece'. Her success meant a great deal to her, and she was businesslike in her letters to the Pinker agency. She saw herself as a professional, writing for money, always trying to learn from the work of other writers, aware of her own limitations and dissatisfied with her own best efforts. She noted in her journal, for instance, that "The Garden Party", one of her most admired stories, 'is a moderately successful story, that's all'.[8] She accepted modestly enough Gerhardie telling her he did not like "The Fly", though he was younger than her, and unpublished himself. Murry's claim that she was a genius would have seemed bizarre to her, accompanied as it was by his publication of negligible and discarded scraps and obviously private letters. She would not have been pleased either by his denigration of the meticulous professionalism she took so seriously, when he wrote that 'there was no difference between her casual and her deliberate utterances; . . . her art was not really distinct from her life; . . . she was never what we understand by a professional writer'.[9] Unable to control her while she lived, Murry could not resist manipulating her after her death to fit the pattern he preferred.

Although Katherine and Murry often presented their relationship as the most important element in both their lives—and it did absorb a huge amount of their energy—there is a sense in which neither sought true understanding of the other. For each of them, the other became a symbolic figure very early on: she the good, suffering, spontaneous genius, he the ideally beautiful scholar-lover without whom neither life nor death could be properly contemplated. Each settled to a dream-version of the other. Murry, being the more self-absorbed of the two, was entirely content to live with a woman whose history he ignored and whose inner life he denied; and she, with her desperate desire for secrecy, was in some degree satisfied by this, even though, in the long run, it left her isolated and frightened in her perfectly protected privacy.

Katherine was outstandingly gifted, original and ambitious to develop her gifts. She needed time, freedom and tolerable living conditions in which to work; the pity was that she never found all at once. Had she done so, it is not unreasonable to think she could have grown into a major writer. As it was, she spent the best part of her energy battling against her family and its expectations of her; against her ruined health; against her resentment of Murry's inadequacies and still more, perhaps, against his vision of her and her role as an artist in his romantic pantheon; against her fears and hugely exaggerated feelings of guilt.

The iconized, sanitized, flawless Katherine insisted on by Murry must have increased the panic anxiety she felt at any threat to expose the secrets of her youth. Today, ironically, we have ceased to want our artists to be virtuous, and rather favour a history of dubious deeds as a basis for the creative life. Katherine, alive to irony, might laugh at the change in attitude; but she would probably hate to have our sympathy. Yet she deserves it, for it was largely through her adventurous spirit, her eagerness to grasp at experience and to succeed in her work, that she became ensnared in disaster. Her short life, so modern and busy, has the shape of a classic tragedy.

At her least likeable, she adopted sentimental postures, and used them as a shield for treacherous malice. Yet how much there is that is admirable about her. She was always more interested in the external world than in her own suffering. She was a worker to her bones, and prized the effort required by craft. She fought, bravely, stubbornly, tenaciously, against two terrifying and incurable diseases that finally destroyed her. If she was never a saint, she was certainly a martyr, and a heroine in her recklessness, her dedication and her courage.

Katherine Mansfield: A Secret Life, London: Viking Penguin, 1987, repr. 1988, pp. 238-243.

---

1 D.H. Lawrence to J.M.M., 2 February 1923, *The Letters of D.H. Lawrence*, Boulton, vol. IV, p. 375.

2 Ibid., 25 October 1923, p. 520.

3 D.H. Lawrence to Adele Seltzer, 24 September 1923, *The Letters of D.H. Lawrence*, Boulton, vol. IV, p. 503.

4 Testimony of K.S. Crichton in Edward Nehls, *D.H. Lawrence: A Composite Biography* (University of Wisconsin Press, Madison, 1957), vol. II, p. 414.

5 Information from Mrs Valerie Eliot.

6 Information from Moira Lynd.

7 V.S. Pritchett in the *New Statesman*, 1946.

8 *Journal*, 14 October 1921, p. 266.

9 J.M.M., *Katherine Mansfield and Other Literary Portraits* (Constable, London, 1959), p. 72.

Ken Arvidson, "Dancing on the Hand of God: Katherine Mansfield's Religious Sensibility"

The only religious event in Katherine Mansfield's life to attract much notice among such more interesting features of her life and personality as her early sexual promiscuity, her troubled relationship with John Middleton Murry, and her tragic death from tuberculosis, has been her brief interest in Roman Catholicism while at Ospidaletti and Menton in 1920. The entry in her journal for February 8 includes the declaration "I for the first time think I should like to join the Roman Catholic Church. I must have something." [1] This was in the middle of the period from September 1919 to April 1920 when, as Vincent O'Sullivan observes, ". . . she touched bottom in the despondency and antagonisms that were part of her disease."[2]   The context is enlarged by Mansfield's friend Ida Baker, who describes in her memoir Mansfield's father's London cousin Connie Beauchamp staying not far distant from Ospidaletti in Menton with her friend the "mesmeric" Jinnie Fullarton,[3] two very devout and ardent converts to Catholicism years before, who earnestly tried to bring Mansfield to their persuasion. Mansfield's emotional instability at the time clearly assisted them for a while. As she wrote in a letter she placed for Baker to find and read when alone, "This afternoon when we were lying on the hills . . . I knew there was a God. There you are . . .

> One day (before we go back to England, I hope), I mean to be received into the Church. I'm going to become a Catholic. Once I believe in a God, the rest is so easy. I can accept it all *my own way* —not 'literally' but symbolically: it's all quite easy and beautiful. But unless one believes in a God even though it is tempting to have that great inward gate opened—it is no good. [4]

These were not feelings that lasted long, or not at any rate in relation to Catholicism. In the course of a letter to Murry just a month later she wrote

> Yes, it's true about Catholics: their world is not our world—my *duty* is to *mankind*—theirs is to a personal deity—a really-living KING with a flashing face who gives you rewards. I read a panegyric by a Jesuit t'other day which did astonish me—"God shall be our most passionate love. He shall kiss us with the kisses of his mouth" and so on. It disgusted me. They horribly confuse sexuality and the state of beatification—I know really a good deal about Catholics now—Of course there's no doubt Jinny is a saint . . . But it has *warped* her—even her . . . [5]

How much of this came from Mansfield's offended sensibilities and how much from her desperate hope that through seeming to share an opinion[6] of Murry's she might consolidate her relationship with him, unstable to her great distress in the preceding months, is inevitably uncertain. But from this time on Catholicism seems to have lost its brief attraction for her completely.

No religious denomination ever did possess her fully for long, not even the Church of England she grew up in. "Although there were many times throughout her life when K.M. felt the need for some kind of spiritual peace," as Gillian Boddy has written, "it was not to be through conventional religion."[7] It is a view shared by Mansfield's biographer Anthony Alpers, who remarks cryptically "The Church of England played scarcely more part in her life than it had in her father's . . ."[8] But it is certain just the same that she was religiously inclined, and in this brief essay I will try to outline this aspect of her personality, her sense of there being a God to whom she stood in some kind of relationship. The evidence of the journal and the letters that she did have such a sense is so explicit and so abundant that such an outline requires no particular justification or special pleading. Her religious sense was as much a part of her personality as her sense of the beauty of the world, or her sense of her own being. And my aims are modest: scarcely more than to indicate how much it was habitual for her to think religiously in her personal writings; and to reflect finally on some implications I find in her last two stories, "The Fly"and "The Canary". I do not intend to go into her association with Gurdjieff and the quasi-religious Institute for the Harmonious Development of Man that occupied the final months of her life, as that gets extensive treatment in biographies.

Katherine Mansfield's early years were spent in the quiet enough environment of orthodox New Zealand Anglicanism. For two and a half years from the time she was eleven she attended Miss Swainson's School in Fitzherbert Terrace, where the Head of the Day School, Mrs Henry Smith, was a cousin of the Victorian churchman, historian, and novelist, Charles Kingsley. Something of Charles Kingsley's muscular variety of Broad Church Anglicanism can be sensed perhaps in Mansfield's comment, inscribed in her prayer book late in 1901, "I am going to be a Maori missionary."[9] No doubt Mrs Henry Smith's advice was involved in Mansfield's father Harold Beauchamp's decision to select Queen's College in Harley Street for the education of his older daughters from 1903: Queen's College had been founded by Charles Kingsley in 1848, with the Christian Socialist Frederic Denison Maurice, whose anti-dogmatic liberalism, like Kingsley's own, was to give such concern to the ritualistic John Henry Newman, who had become a Roman Catholic in 1845.

This hint of the milieu of her high school years makes it possible I think to adopt a simple rule-of-thumb when trying to assess the early religious passages in Mansfield's journal. The passage in the very first entry (January 1, 1904) reads like an authentic personal record with its focus on the morality of self-improvement:

> The church looked truly very fit for God's house tonight. It looked so strong, so hospitable, so invincible. It was only during the silent prayer that I made up my mind to write this. I mean this year to try and be a different person, and I wait at the end of this year to see how I have kept all the vows that I have made tonight. So much happens in a year. One may mean so much and do so little . . . What a wonderful and what a lovely world this is. I thank God tonight that I *am.* [10]

There are only three further entries to October 1906. The last of these, though it has the form of a scene observed, reads like an early mood-piece, a vignette in the manner of a prose poem:

> And now I pass through the narrow iron gate up the little path and through the heavy doors into the church. Silence hung motionless over the church; the shadow of her great wings darkened everything. Through the gloom the figures of the saints showed dimly. The high altar shone mystical—vision-like. A nun came and sat beside me. She raised a passionless, expressionless face—and the rosary shone like a thread of silver through her fingers.[11]

This is not, one feels, a recorded personal experience. It seems imagined in the way recalling Tennyson and the Pre-Raphaelites with its emphasis on the church and the religious life as vaguely other than normal, shadowy and mystical and transcendentally "passionless, expressionless." The experience is literary and aesthetic.

In the first five pages of the Journal then, two powerful aspects of Mansfield's religious sensibility are markedly apparent, one her recognition of a link between religion and ethics, the other her sense of an aesthetic dimension to religious experience. In between those two passages, a third is of interest also. This entry, dated simply 1906, has a title in German, Die Wege des Lebens; the Way of Life.[12] The title is religious in its connotations: the passage itself is totally humanistic, being a compendium of 18 or so short passages from Oscar Wilde, Montaigne, Marie Bashkirtseff, George Eliot, John Stuart Mill, Ibsen, and others, including KM herself: "To acknowledge the presence of fear is to give birth to failure;" and again, "Happy people are never brilliant. It implies friction." If one were to select a keynote from these aphoristic maxims, it would be Wilde's "If you want to mar a nature, you have merely to reform it." A Wildean subversiveness, almost Nietzschean, thus takes its place from the outset amongst the ethical and the aesthetic aspects of religion. The three are by no means incompatible or mutually exclusive. But often enough one or the other will seem to be trying to gain supremacy.

One of the surprises in reading Mansfield's journal and letters, considering how she is ordinarily represented as a woman for whom the visible world alone had much meaning, is how often and how very much as a matter of course she turns to God in one way or another; sometimes in invocation, sometimes in exclamation, often in praise, often in an attempt to reach some kind of self-understanding. Such an attempt seems to have been behind her journal entry for Good Friday 1909, not long after her absurd non-marriage to George Bowden, and in the toils of the fear of pregnancy to Garnet Trowell

> It is the evening of Good Friday; the day of all the year, surely, the most significant. I always, always, feel the nail-prints in my hands, the sickening thirst in my throat, the agony of Jesus. He is surely not dead, and surely all we love who have died are close to us. Grandmother and Jesus and all of them. Only lend me your aid. I thirst too—I hang upon the Cross. Let me be crucified—so that I may cry 'It is finished.'
>
> > I could find no rest.
> > Tossed and turned, and cried aloud 'I suffer'.
> > In my tortured breast
> > Turned the knife, and probed the flesh more deeply.
> >
> > Life seemed like a wall.
> > Brick and fouled and grimed
> >
> > Oh delicate branches,
> > Reaching up for the sun!
> > The plants on tiptoe, stretching up to the light.
>
> I cannot say it now. Maybe I shall be able to; much later.[13]

The risks of self-dramatisation here are considerable. But Mansfield's obvious loneliness and insecurity, the memory of her grandmother Dyer dead some 16 months, the clumsiness of the contrast between the suffering and the imperfection of human life and the light-seeking disposition of nature all modulate the passage to a simple enough cry from the heart, from one for whom Christ crucified has come to be the type or symbol of suffering human kind. The imaginative identification with Christ is something to which she will return in later years.

Most references to God in the journal and letters are so casual in themselves, taken one by one, that they do not at first thrust themselves into prominence as significant. It is only perhaps when a small selection is gathered together that the habitual cast of mind becomes apparent. Observing an ordinary enough street scene from her window in 1914 and clearly delighting in the human activity there she remarks "It is as though God opened his hand and let you dance on it a little, and then shut it up tight—so tight that you could not even cry."[14] On March 24, 1914, "Thank God! There's a sprinkle of sun today."[15] On April 5, 1914, "No bird sits a tree more proudly than a pigeon. It looks as though placed there by the Lord. The sky was silky blue and white, and the sun shone through the leaves. But the children, pinched and crooked, made me feel a bit out of love with God."[16] More enigmatically, on August 30, 1914, "Tell me, Is there a God? I do not trust Jack. I'm old tonight."[17] On January 11, 1915 "It is a bright, winking day. Oh my God, my God, let me work, . . .Wasted! Wasted!"[18] In December 1915, while suffering the "rheumatic" pains (caused as she later learned by gonorrhea) that affected the action of her heart: "Today I am hardening my heart. I am walking all round my heart and building up the defences. I do not mean to leave a loophole even for a tuft of violets to grow in. Give me a hard heart, O Lord! Lord, harden thou my heart!" [19]

In February 1916, five months after her brother Leslie's death in France, she records that her brother had called to her the night before; she had obeyed and gone upstairs:

> But then, when I leaned out the window I seemed to see my brother dotted all over the field—now on his back, now on his face, now huddled up, now half-pressed into the earth. Wherever I looked, there he lay. I felt that God showed him to me like that for some express purpose, and I knelt down by the bed. But I could not pray. I had done no work. I was not in an active state of grace. So I got up finally and went downstairs again. But I was terribly sad . . .[20]

It was around this time, early 1916, that Mansfield also wrote the poem "To L.H.B.",[21] in which she and her brother walked in a dream in the landscape of their shared childhood, by a stream "fringed with tall berry bushes, white and red." The poisonous berries—"We called them Dead Man's Bread"—are offered to Mansfield by her now dead brother:

> By the remembered stream my brother stands
> Waiting for me with berries in his hands . . .
> 'These are my body, Sister, take and eat.'

The fact that the poem takes a version of the Eucharist as its image for the poet's empathetic communion with the dead brother is as interesting, in its own right, as the poet's psychological acknowledgement that there could be risks for her in her emotional reliance on him. As in the small selection I've made of passages from the journal, the striking thing is the naturalness with which Mansfield allows her mind to engage with the supernatural, whether in grief or in delight or in praise: as she wrote to Anne Estelle Rice Drey in 1920 from Menton, remarking wryly on the restrictions her illness placed upon her, "I'll never be able to climb trees or run or swim again. Isn't that a bit steep of Almighty God. I'm always praising him too, but there you are . . ."[22]

For all this, it is true that her way of seeing God began to change from the time early in 1918 when she realised that she had tuberculosis. It is not so much her concept of God that began to change, as the way she began to see herself in relation to him. Ill in body, not whole, she came to see herself as lacking a real unity of personality or soul as well, and her endeavours were from then on increasingly in pursuit of wholeness and harmony of being. To put it at its reductive simplest, but very appropriately to the Broad Church environment of her early years, she wanted to have a "mens sana in corpore sano," a well mind in a well body. God, or rather her relationship with Him, began for the time being to take second place to the immediate end of self-restoration. This I think is why, on occasions in the five years of her worsening illness, she can seem to deny the very existence of God. "No, one can't believe in a God," she wrote to Murry in May 1921:

> But I must believe in something more nearly than I do. As I was lying here today I suddenly remembered that: 'Oh ye of little faith!' Not faith in a God. No, that's impossible. But do I live as though I believed in anything? Don't I live in glimpses only? There is something wrong: there is something small in such a life. One must live more fully and one must have more power of love and feeling.[23]

What is primarily at issue in this and many similar passages is less the reality of God than the limitations of one's inherited construction of him, and the slowness with which that may change to accommodate one's changing understanding of life and experience.

From the time Mansfield became aware of the magnitude of her illness, her links with aestheticism began to loosen, and in no respect more significantly than in her growing conviction of the need to gain a wholeness of being. The abundance, the variety of potentials in her own personality had early recognised the force of the rationale for trying as many masks as possible that she found in Wilde and to a lesser extent in Pater. It was a rationale in which "insincerity", a maximum diversification of personality, was the cardinal virtue.

By 1920 it is clear that this cult of personality and the "Truth of Masks" had begun to wear thin. In a journal entry in which she meditates on the mystery of Self, she notes ironically the boredom of once finding Polonius's "To thine own self be true" written so often in autograph books: but she goes on, "True to one's self! Which self? Which of my many—well, really, that's what it looks like coming to—hundreds of selves."[24] She has come to feel, she writes, like "the small clerk of some hotel without a proprietor, who has all his work cut out to enter the names and hand the keys to the wilful guests." And she goes on to reflect on the inner compulsion to believe in "a self which is continuous and permanent," one that we encounter only through shedding the trappings of personality, in "the moment of direct feeling when we are most ourselves and least personal." Three months later, in December 1920, at a time when her physical suffering was compounded by the psychological agony caused by Middleton Murry's love affair with Elizabeth Bibesco, she meditates on suffering in a way recalling Hopkins's sonnet on suffering, "No worst, there is none; pitched past pitch of grief / More pangs will, schooled at forepangs, wilder wring." "There is no limit to human suffering," she wrote; "when one thinks Now I have touched the bottom of the sea—now I can go no deeper, one goes deeper . . . suffering is boundless, it is eternity. One pang is eternal torment,"[25] and so on. She declares her belief that suffering can be overcome, but not "by passing beyond it;" rather:

> One must submit. Do not resist. Take it. Be overwhelmed. Accept it fully. Make it part of life. Everything in life that we really accept undergoes a change. So suffering must become Love. This is the mystery. This is what I must do. I must pass from personal love which has failed me to greater love. I must give to the whole of life what I gave to him. The present agony will pass—if it doesn't kill.

And she goes on to acknowledge Doctor Sorapure and Tchekov as her mentors and models, for their "purity of heart." The allusive analogies here with the sufferings of Christ will be clear; perhaps modulated by Mansfield by this time in a humanistic manner much as Ludwig Feuerbach had mediated the Christian model for George Eliot; but distinctly Christian in form and paradox: if you would gain your life you must first lose it.

The religious tendency of thought continues through 1921. Two passages from Tolstoy's *War and Peace* take their place in her Credo early in the year: "Life is everything. Life is God . . . To love life is to love God." And "A spiritual wound that comes from a rending of the spirit . . . only heals inwardly by the force of life pushing up from within." [26] "That is true, Master," is her assenting comment. Later in the year, still pursuing her need "to learn to forget herself", she notes "Oh God! I am divided still. I am bad. I fail in my personal life. I lapse into impatience, temper, vanity, and so I fail as thy priest."[27] A month later, in November 1921, trying to grapple with a new story in which it seems the Thorndon Baths were to feature, she prays "May I be found worthy to do it! Lord, make me crystal clear for thy light to shine through."[28] In a sense a "prayer" of this kind could be accounted for by reference to the nineteenth century Religion of Art, so relevant to the aestheticism of the end of the century. But the primary function of the prayer is, I believe, religious. Mansfield was by late 1921 a good distance along the way to disengagement from her aesthetic roots, as a conscious part of the more instinctive disengagements from the world that she undertook as her life progressively turned towards death. And the conscious part of these disengagements took the form, as I've tried to suggest, of a radical quest for integrity, the quest for the one inalienable inner self that could be found only by losing the lesser selves of personality, the masks.

For this reason, the last two stories she wrote, "The Fly", and "The Canary" do not spring from the same set of ideas about art that engendered the stories up to 1922. They seem to me to amount in some measure to a critique of the earlier aesthetic. The Boss in "The Fly", is very clearly an instance of the Artist as the God of Creation transposed into a human context. And his killing of the fly is equally clearly an image of the indifference of the creative mind, for which its ends are their own justification. The Boss is a dark manifestation of an aesthetic truism. But what gives the Boss his malignity is not simply his killing of the Fly. It is that in conjunction with his inability to remember his dead son, buried in France. The indifference of the act combined with the indifference of his memory mark him as irresponsible. Mansfield herself I believe confronted in this story the responsibility in personal terms of her own artistic treatment of the childhood memories triggered by the death in France of her brother Leslie; and the self-image she saw was one that disturbed her.

"The Canary" again examines a version of the artist in the image of the canary, "little actor", singer, healer of human fears and pains. The artist here is seen in an obviously benign light. But the artist is no longer a God of Creation. It is small and dependent, circumscribed by its cage, vulnerable to death. Humanity, in the figure of the lodging house woman, gains no enduring consolation from it; at best the artist leaves behind a sharper sense of "the still, sad music of humanity" as Wordsworth too had intuited in the "Tintern Abbey" ode. Mansfield's "The Canary" is a bitter-sweet variant on her earlier satiric picture of the garret-dwelling artist in "Feuille d'Album", and has its source in a cultural sphere Mansfield had once had much experience of, the music hall. Its source is not in the high aestheticism of the 90s, but in a popular song of that period, "I'm only a bird in a gilded cage." It was Mansfield's last creative comment on the mystique of art before her last attempt to achieve the peace of mind she needed.

Katherine Mansfield Centennial Conference (paper), Victoria University of Wellington, New Zealand, 12-15 October 1988.

---

[1] John Middleton Murry ed., *Journal of Katherine Mansfield 1904 - 1922,* (London: Hutchinson, 1954), Auckland: Hutchinson (NZ), 1984, p. 198.

[2] Vincent O'Sullivan and Margaret Scott eds. *The Collected Letters of Katherine Mansfield ,* Volume Three, Oxford: Oxford University Press, 1993, Intro. p. ix.

[3] Ida Constance Baker, *Katherine Mansfield: The Memories of LM,* (London: Michael Joseph, 1971), London: Virago Press, 1985, p. 149.

[4] *Memories* p. 149; and *Letters* 4 March 1920, p. 240.

[5] *Letters* 4 April 1920, p. 271.

[6] *Letters* 4 April 1920, n. 3, p. 272.

[7] Gillian Boddy, *Katherine Mansfield: the Woman and the Writer,* Ringwood, Victoria: Penguin Books, 1988, p. 127.

[8] Antony Alpers *The Life of Katherine Mansfield,* New York: The Viking Press, 1980, p. 19.

[9] *Life,* p. 20.

[10] *Journal* p. 3.

[11] *Journal,* p. 4.

[12] *Journal,* pp. 2-4.

[13] *Journal,* pp. 38-39.

[14] *Journal,* p. 51.

[15] *Journal,* p. 56.

[16] *Journal,* p. 59.

[17] *Journal,* p. 61.

[18] *Journal,* p. 67.

[19] *Journal ,* p. 91.

[20] *Journal,* p. 95.

[21] Vincent O'Sullivan (ed.), *Poems of Katherine Mansfield,* Auckland: Oxford University Press, 1988, p. 54.

[22] *Letters* p. 250.

[23] Vincent O'Sullivan (ed.), *Katherine Mansfield: Selected Letters,* Oxford and New York: Oxford University Press, 1990, p. 214.

[24] *Journal,* p. 205.

[25] *Journal,* p. 228.

[26] *Journal,* p. 246.

[27] *Journal,* p. 269.

[28] *Journal,* p. 271.

Judith Dale, "Performing Katherine Mansfield"

The notion of 'performing Katherine Mansfield', or Katherine Mansfield in performance, has several possible interpretations and all of them interesting. Mansfield was a good comic performer and supplemented her income when she returned to London by hiring herself out as an entertainer, writing and acting in her own skits and sketches.[1] She was unusually fond of the working-class entertainment of Edwardian music-halls and this provides the idea for Vincent O'Sullivan's new playscript *Jones & Jones* which picks up the nicknames Mansfield invented for herself and Ida Baker and recreates them as a performing duo. Mansfield was also given to 'putting on a performance' in a more ordinary sense. The construction and reconstruction of her life has occupied biographers since her death but the woman born Kathleen Mansfield Beauchamp was her own lifelong fictionaliser and we see her, and see her *as* 'performing Katherine Mansfield' from her earliest years.

Through the *Journal* there emerges Mansfield's developing understanding of the 'self' as a series of masks and faces, (re)constructions and performances. The image of Katherine Mansfield in dinner suit and tails which comes to mind from *Jones & Jones* or Cathy Downes' solo piece *The Case of Katherine Mansfield* is doubtlessly historically inaccurate, but there's no doubt that in the performance of her life as of her art Mansfield explores (what we now identify as) the social constructions of gender. Her instinct was to try on, to pick up, to unpick and refurbish, the various societal garbs and garments around her, and she even went so far as to identify as her 'philosophy'—'the defeat of the personal'. The critic Kate Fullbrook claims that the ideas underlying Mansfield's statements about consciousness and identity 'need to be seen in terms of the symbolist theory of the mask. . . . She conceived of self as multiple, shifting, non-consecutive, without essence, and perhaps unknowable.'[2] This in turn becomes characteristic of her writing: the voicing of the roles and guises of one fictionally constructed character after another; the conflating of a series of perceptions of consciousness; indeed, the loss of a clearly identified single narrating subject altogether.

Although Mansfield didn't write plays, dramatists today can find in her thinking a model for deconstructing what constitutes a gendered self, in the uniquely provocative modes of theatre. Cathy Downes' *Case*, O'Sullivan's *Jones & Jones* and above all, Alma de Groen's *The Rivers of China* explore the phenomena of roles, masks and constructs of selfhood in entirely theatrical terms. *The Rivers of China* at one point quotes the Shakespearean epigraph Mansfield had used for her story "This Flower", which Murry subsequently inscribed on her tombstone.[3] Hotspur, gallant, swaggering and soon to die, blurts out in the course of a soliloquy, '. . . but I tell you, my lord fool, out of this nettle, danger, we pluck this flower, safety.' These three Mansfield plays construct theatrical images and narratives around a sense of danger in the postures of personhood, as the ebullient Hotspur of a Mansfield did herself.

If theatre does things other art forms don't, prose fiction does things that theatre cannot. So what does one want from a short story read aloud? The Concert Programme ran a comprehensive series of talks on Mansfield including stories read as illustration, and other stories were read in full, giving radio listeners the pleasure of Mansfield's prose more or less straight—a rather more successful endeavour than some of the gimmicky 'dramatisations' they also offered.[4] In the latter case, different actors were allocated for each 'speaking part', the narrator was removed and extra dialogue was invented when characters' thoughts or reactions needed to be communicated. In a kind of momentary 'soliloquy' for externalising stage directions, emotion or desire was heard in a husky whisper: 'Oh Pearl, Pearl Fulton' (the Concert Programme's "Bliss"). Other readings maintained the narrator for all but direct speech, allocating that to actor-characters who then inhabit a different reality from the narratives. These characters were also used to say things which do not come from their mouths, yet are not in the idiom of the narrator either. This is one of Mansfield's most developed literary characteristics, sometimes called 'free indirect discourse': neither indirect speech nor directly transcribed interior monologue, it is neither, or both—undecidedly.

'And after all the weather was ideal. They could not have had a more perfect day for a garden party if they had ordered it.' Who is speaking here? The best of the performed readings of Mansfield stories realised this 'shifting voice', the absence of a fixed subject position or narrating subject, by moving flexibly even in mid-sentence between empathy with the subject and detachment from it, something in fact very difficult to achieve in performance.

There have been several attempts to dramatise Mansfield stories for the stage. The older *Today's Bay* by Craig Thaine (1983) is a play about a group of students themselves writing a play based on "At the Bay", intertwining the two narratives to productively foreground a number of social and political questions about sexuality, personal dreams and family expectations.[5] *Bright Birds* by Elizabeth O'Connor (1988) came into existence as a tribute from the Court Theatre for the centenary and dramatises the Edwardian world in which Kathleen Beauchamp grew up, using characters and story-lines from "The Garden Party", "Bliss", "Marriage à la Mode" and "A Cup of Tea", transposing them all to Wellington and conflating their plots.[6] The result is doubtless attractive enough as an evening out (I haven't seen it) but does nothing either for the stories or for theatre.

The most evident aspect of the birthday year was the retelling and revisioning of 'the Life' and much of this had an element of performance—Lady Reeves opening the Birthplace Trust, the Prime Minister launching the National Library's bibliography of Mansfield holdings, other book-launches and several academic conferences. The Concert Programme offered twenty 50-minute readings of the 1980 Alpers' biography using a female narrator (which distressed Antony Alpers), other actors for Mansfield and her contemporaries, and also various actors for opinions quoted indirectly, thus transforming them into direct speech too. [7] It made for compelling radio listening. The use of a male narrator would have appropriated Mansfield's story differently, and in fact the range of female voices replicated, even if unintentionally, Mansfield's own narrative stances; the radio biography had been cross-pollinated by radio versions of the stories.

Something similar happened with Gillian Boddy's and Julianne Stretton's documentary film *A Portrait of Katherine Mansfield*.[8] The primary decision to use as presenter à la Kenneth Clark or Allan Whicker the actor Catherine Wilkin who had played Katherine Mansfield in Brian McNeill's *The Two Tigers* in Wellington meant that for me the identification was inescapable, and perhaps it was intentional. In a lavender-blue, vaguely twenties fashion, longish skirt, a jacket for Europe in winter, short sleeves for the coastlines of childhood and summer, Wilkin came to represent the presence of Mansfield embodied anew for the purposes of cinematography. A voice-over presentation might have avoided the uneasy sense of capture that Wilkins' most reverent tones did not assuage; however a male presenter or an academic one would have suggested different kinds of appropriation. These are hazards that seem inescapable since *A Portrait* was entirely intended as a widely available, informative documentary made in preparation for the centenary. In fact, it was awarded a Golden Apple prize in America for the best educational film of the year, from a field of thousands. (An earlier Mansfield movie, the fictional *Leave All Fair* begins with the frankly exploitative idea of a plot featuring John Gielgud as the aging Middleton Murry; problems of the male subject-position and the annexation of the female as object are discussed by Sophie Tomlinson in *Landfall* 156.)[9]

Two plays by Brian McNeill also use Mansfield's life as their starting-point. *The Two Tigers*, the earliest of the Mansfield performance pieces, was first done in Auckland in 1973, and then rapidly became successful elsewhere. That the centenary did not see it revived is perhaps surprising since it is strongly written and could take a more acerbic or sceptical production than it is usually given. The play has one line which McNeill says 'should echo on down through the play as a shout of anguish'—'Lo, I have made of Love all my Religion.'[10] In the play this is Murry's line not Mansfield's, and the sequel *The Love and Ladies Man* is entirely about Murry and Murry's (and Lawrence's) ideas on sex and communism, Love, Religion, Liberation and so on; appearing in the centennial year here, the Mansfield connection is certainly stretched very thin.[11]

Three major theatre pieces seen in Wellington in 1988 all used a version of the Mansfield 'life' as their point of departure but thereupon departed in three very different directions; the genesis of each of these plays tells us much about them. *The Case of Katherine Mansfield* was devised as a solo performance piece arising out of Cathy Downes' work on her role for *The Two Tigers* at The Four Seasons, Wanganui, in 1977. She wanted to create a 'coherent kaleidoscope' of Mansfield's ideas on life and death, and this became the piece first performed in Utrecht, then Amsterdam in 1978, in London in 1979 and then at the Edinburgh Festival. There was a brief New Zealand tour in 1980, the first full season in 1985, and the show was performed again last year in an extended national tour for the Mansfield centennial; altogether Cathy Downes estimates she has given about 500 performances.[12] The text is entirely from Mansfield's writing. The shifting tones of letters, journal entries and stories are dramatised into a piece that is both urbane and sophisticated—what K.M. describes as 'ultra modern'—but also thoughtful and moving, weaving 'confessional' extracts, witticisms, snide social comments together with several stories or parts of stories. I've seen this show three times in ten years and in Wellington early in 1988 I found it even more accomplished than when I first saw it. Downes offers a marvellous projection of the varnished veneers of mask, role and (self)-(re)-presentation, from her opening lines in an arch pseudo-third-person narrative: 'Let me take the case of Katherine Mansfield. She has led, ever since she can remember, a very typically false life.'[13] This 'falsity' is as much the subject in search of a self as the writer/performer inscribed by her roles; it is K.M.'s famous response to Polonius' line 'To thine own self be true'—Ah, but to which self? Downes' strategy towards her audience is equally multifarious: Mansfieldiana for school parties, deconstructionist theatre for those who want it, a splendid performance for herself, dramatic entertainment for everyone.

Downstage however is a commercial theatre and simply wanted something successful for the centenary of New Zealand's best-known literary 'son'. Mansfield's feminism and Mansfield's usefulness for feminist discussion is only now become available (with, for instance, the Tomalin biography or Kate Fullbrook's critical work) which means that the Mansfield corpus is as likely to be annexed by feminist writers as any others; the current debate on Mansfield's stature as, or as not, lesbian is a case in point. So the capture of Katherine Mansfield for Downstage's theatrical calendar in 1988 simply reflects what goes on all the time. In fact the two pieces playing in repertory had very different origins. Vincent O'Sullivan's *Jones & Jones* was commissioned by Downstage specifically because of the centenary, an excellent move since O'Sullivan is an established Mansfield scholar and editor, also a playwright, and his earlier fiction and poetry show an appropriate disrespect for sacred cows. *Jones & Jones* is a play with musical interludes plagiarizing the tunes and parodying the words of the sort of music-hall songs Mansfield enjoyed.[14] Among the sacred cows tilted at—quixotically speaking—are Lawrence emerging grimy and brawny from a stage trapdoor with a very thick accent, Frieda as an almost life-sized rag doll used to perform extraordinarily phallic gestures with her arms and legs (it was Mansfield who suggested the Lawrences call their cottage 'The Phallus', after all), Bertrand Russell in plus-fours on a bicycle, Aleister Crowley cross-dressed, Lady Ottoline literally on a pedestal, and John Middleton Murry with a cardie drooping below his jacket and stacks of library books, entering on roller skates. (One sacred cow surprisingly left unmilked is Mrs. Woolf: who's afraid?) In addition there is a touching montage of Mansfield's life in London: the importance of her writing, Chummie's death, the last illness, all cheerfully interspersed with adapted versions of Edwardian music-hall songs which destabilise any sense of a 'subject' at all, just as the title does.

The Downstage production with its beautiful Raymond Boyce set makes it hard to imagine this piece done elsewhere, though doubtless it will be. Future versions might aim for a sharper musical focus, but I wonder if any other production will recapture the entirely unexpected pleasure of the first *Jones & Jones*, in Robyn Malcolm's Ida Baker. Ida Baker was Katherine Mansfield's lifelong friend; they met at school at 15 and were in continual contact until Mansfield's death. Mansfield's interest in Oscar Wilde and her acquaintance with the bisexuality of the Bloomsbury set, as well as her own early lesbian experiences (and her mother's appalment) and the sexual ambiguity of several of her stories (notably "Bliss", "Carnation", and two stories with intriguingly ungendered narrators, "The Young Girl" and the newly published story "Leves Amores")—all attest to a bisexuality on Mansfield's part even if acknowledged only within certain limits.

Of the nature of her relationship with 'L.M.' not a lot is known since Mansfield at one stage asked Ida Baker to destroy a large proportion of her (Mansfield's) letters to her, but that it was one of lifelong intimacy and, on Baker's part at least, lifelong devotion is not in doubt. The script of *Jones & Jones* avoids offence to both the pro- and anti-lesbian lobbies by its own episodic structure, by treating its materials cleverly as light entertainment, and by the displacement of any single centre-stage subject: both Mansfield *and* Ida Baker become 'Jones'. If these strategies avoid serious consideration of Mansfield's sexuality, they are also very funny: Baker opens the show, for example, lugging heavy suitcases and disclosing: 'I've got very strong wrists, everyone says that. . . . Once she bit my wrist and I said, "Yes, Katie, bite me if you want to". . . . So instead I carried her suitcases for eighteen years.' Robyn Malcolm's interpretation of her role at Downstage gave Ida Baker a rich, warm characterisation which she found in the text to be sure but developed to the extent of more than sharing centre-stage with Mansfield; for many viewers in fact she up-staged the comedy entirely. If *Jones & Jones* annexes Mansfield for showbiz, Mansfield's friend Jones, Ida Baker alias 'Lesley Moore', here offers to become more than the sum of her parts.

The Rivers of China has different origins but a similar complex relationship with its Mansfield material. Alma de Groen grew up in New Zealand but settled in Australia where she began writing plays under the influence of the new theatre movement there in the late sixties. *The Rivers of China* was workshopped at the 1986 (Australian) National Playwrights' Conference and premiered in Sydney; in 1988 it received productions in Auckland and Wellington. [15] The Mansfield materials are here so entirely integral to the playscript that if they didn't exist de Groen would have had to invent them: a woman writer whose death is imminent and whose writing life was spent seeking an understanding of 'self'. All this is interspliced with the story of a feminist regime in which futuristic men are oppressed and their writings forbidden. One anonymous man among many is hospitalised after a suicide attempt and is 'rebuilt' by a radical doctor (Rahel). Unhappy with the regime's repression of all that is male and utilising her feminist skills of hypnosis ('the Look . . . an evolutionary leap', p. 36)[16] as well as her skills in plastic surgery and her interest in literature, she invests the man, her patient, with the conscious mind and memory of the 100-years-dead Katherine Mansfield. The play joins these sequences to the portrait of a Gurdjieff as entirely sexist as St Augustine—'*Lidia*: He says that . . . for a woman to progress in the Work she must have a man beside her.' (p.41) '*Gurdjieff*: Woman is from ground. Man has aspiration to find heaven because has possibility for immortality. But such aspiration poison for woman . . .' (pp.51-2). This identifies very clearly what the new regime calls 'the Horror'—patriarchal supremacy in short—but it also problematises Rahel's resistance to the anti-male stance of her society. Her action in deliberately inserting a woman's mind into a man's body is individual and ineffectual, but it is clear that she would not wish to return to the Horror: 'I created a man who could be an equal, without being a danger' (p.54). The play destabilises both positions, by balancing Rahel's resistance to female hegemony with Katherine's resistance, (to what this play presents as) Gurdjieff's male supremacism, her early feminism in fact, thus the play deconstructs the categories of gendered power. In addition there is the split presence of Mansfield on stage provided by Katherine in the 1923 Gurdjieff scenes along with the unnamed man who inhabits, or is inhabited by her consciousness in the futuristic scenes, and this brilliantly displaces any sense of a unified self, especially in those scenes which theatrically foreground both acting areas at once. '*Rahel*: I gave him her thoughts and feelings, not her physical decay. But when he woke up, he knew more than I'd given him'. (p. 54).

Clearly *The Rivers of China* makes no claims as a work of Mansfield scholarship (though the Gurdjieff scenes are suggestive) since its theatrical strategies are entirely directed to theatrical and feminist ends.   There are, however, other relevancies for our present discussion. '*Gurdjieff (to Katherine)* : Everything you think you know about Katherine Mansfield is false. You are series of imaginary events. . . . You have dozens of selves, all calling themselves "Katherine Mansfield". Perhaps many as one thousand' (p. 22). True enough.

On November 9th, 1988, in the foyer of the National Library in Thorndon very close to the birthplace, a small crowd of Wellington's lunch-hour passers-by gathered to watch Alison Holst, widely known as a media cooking demonstrator, introduce an item from the Katherine Mansfield Notebook 1914-15 (qMS 1246)—a recipe for Marmalade Pudding, modified for the microwave. With her was the actor Kate Harcourt who read Mansfield snippets about food. At the end, cadenza, coda, and finale, was "Prelude".

> The dinner was baking beautifully on a concrete step. She began to lay the cloth on a pink garden seat. . . . There were three daisy heads on a laurel leaf for poached eggs, some slices of fuchsia petal cold beef, some lovely little rissoles made of earth and water and dandelion seeds. . . . But someone called from the front of the house and the luncheon party melted away, leaving the charming table, leaving the rissoles and the poached eggs to the ants and to an old snail who pushed his quivering horns over the edge of the garden seat.

Concluding with "Prelude" is to be reminded that when any performance comes to an end there is still the text—of a story, a recipe, a playscript, a life—which remains to be read afresh with every performing, performed anew by every reader.

Landfall, Christchurch: New Zealand, vol. 43, no. 4, 1989, 172 pp. 503-511.

---

[1] The texts for some of these dramatic sketches were first published in *The New Age* between 1911 and 1917 and have recently been reprinted in *Katherine Mansfield: Dramatic Sketches*, ed., David Drummond (Palmerston North: Ngaere Press, 1988). They are also to be found in the chronological order of their first publication in *The Stories of Katherine Mansfield*, ed., Antony Alpers (London: Oxford University Press, 1984).

[2] Kate Fullbrook, *Katherine Mansfield* (London: Harvester Press, 1986), pp.16, 17.

[3] Although "This Flower" does not appear in Alpers' 'Definitive Edition' (1984), it may be found in the *Collected Stories of Katherine Mansfield* (London: Constable, first published 1945).

4 Radio New Zealand Concert Programme, "The New Zealand Stories of Katherine Mansfield", radio talks with associated readings adapted for radio and other adaptations and dramatisations, approximately 18 stories in all.

5 Craig Thaine, *Today's Bay* (Wellington: Playmarket, 1983).

6 Elizabeth O'Connor, *Bright Birds* (Wellington: Playmarket, 1988).

7 Radio New Zealand Concert Programme, dramatised readings in 20 parts from Antony Alpers, *The Life of Katherine Mansfield* (New York: Viking Press, 1988).

8 *A Portrait of Katherine Mansfield*, a film written and researched by Gillian Boddy, directed by Julianne Stretton, Marigold Productions, 1986.

9 Sophie Tomlinson, "Mans-field in Bookform", *Landfall*, 156 (December, 1985), pp. 465-473.

10 Brian McNeill, *The Two Tigers* (Wellington: Price Milburn, 1977), p.10.

11 Brian McNeill, *The Love and Ladies Man* (Wellington: Playmarket, 1988).

12 I owe the information in this paragraph to personal conversations with Cathy Downes.

13 A cassette type of *The Case of Katherine Mansfield* made from an amalgam of recordings from the ABC and from London performances is available from Cathy Downes, 51 Ferry Road, Days Bay, Wellington.

14 Vincent O'Sullivan, *Jones & Jones*, Wellington, 1988; premiered at Downstage Theatre, Wellington, 30 September 1988.

15 Alma de Groen, *The Rivers of China* (Sydney: Currency Press, 1988); opened at Downstage Theatre, Wellington, 7 October 1988.

16 All page references are to Alma de Groen, *op.cit.*

Shifen Gong, "Katherine Mansfield: A Chinese Perspective"

In a recent article exploring the reason for Ibsen's powerful influence on modern Chinese drama, the Chinese critic Yi Xinnong argued that a 'universal law' governed the influence of a writer on another culture:

> Any significant influence that a foreign writer exerts on another country is chiefly determined by the necessity of its social and literary development.[1]

Although this formulation—with its vocabulary of 'universal law(s)', determinism and necessity—is heavily infected by what would now be called vulgar Marxism, there is no doubt that the social and literary context of the 'host' country *is* a significant factor in the reception of a foreign author. As has been pointed out, Mansfield attracted the interest of Chinese translators, critics, readers, and fiction writers at two key points of momentous social, political and cultural change in China. The first occurred at a time of general opening up of Chinese culture to the West in the early decades of the century, after several centuries in which a closed, decaying imperial order had carried with it an entrenched, rigid and rule-bound literary classicism that tended to stifle individuality or originality. The second occurred, in the 1980s, at a similar time of general awakening to foreign culture after several decades of equally entrenched, rule-bound, officially-promoted and officially-enforced socialist realism.

Such large-scale cultural shifts undoubtedly provided a necessary context in which interest in Mansfield might occur, but on their own they do not take us very far in explaining why, amongst the many hundreds of foreign authors who were translated, she was amongst those who attracted more interest than others. In the earlier period, for example, statistics reveal that more than 600 novels were translated between 1875 and 1911, and Lin Yutang has identified, between 1911 and 1934, almost 200 British, French, Russian, German, Japanese and American authors whose work was translated into Chinese.[2]

One factor in the special prominence of Mansfield—at least in the earlier period—was the key role of Xu Zhimo in introducing and promoting her work. Because of his importance in Chinese literary culture in the 1920s and early 1930s—as a leading writer in contact with other writers, and as a central figure in the promotion of modern Chinese literature—his championship of Mansfield in such unreserved terms (as 'one of the most important writers at least of the twentieth century'[3]) clearly carried a persuasive force with potential readers, which less well known translators of other foreign authors lacked. The dispersed effects of Xu Zhimo's early influence, on Xiao Qian and others, can be seen in the activities of some of the leading figures involved in Mansfield's rediscovery in the 1980s: Tang Baoxin, Wen Jieruo and Li Zi, and Feng Zongpu, for example.

Even so, such personal connections do not, I think, exhaust the reasons why Mansfield has exerted such a powerful attraction for Chinese readers. Over and above the role she played, alongside many other Western writers, in the specific political and cultural shifts of twentieth century China, and the championship of her work by individuals, there seem to be qualities in her sensibility and her writing which appealed deeply to aspects of the Chinese imagination, which were felt to connect with aesthetic values deeply rooted in China's own complex literary traditions. Her physical image, her temperament, the nature of her aesthetic interests, and the lifelong intensity of her search for stylistic integrity tapped into cultural values, perceptions and attitudes which many Chinese readers continue to think of as deeply and quintessentially Chinese. There is a continuity in this respect between Xu Zhimo's influential early portrayal of Mansfield's physical image and personality, and the way he characterizes her aesthetic preoccupations, and the approach of important 1980s critics like Fang Ping, with his suggestions of a link between Mansfield's sensibility and the sensiblity of Cao Xueqin's Lin Daiyu, and Feng Zongpu, with her careful exploration of Mansfield's art in terms of traditional Chinese philosophical concepts.

Lin Daiyu, the heroine of Cao Xueqin's novel *A Dream of Red Mansions* (1754-1791), in fact crystallized a romantic stereotype of the female artist in China—a woman with an acutely refined sensibility and intellect combined with extreme physical fragility and delicate, ethereal beauty—which had often appealed to the Chinese imagination at various times in the past and continued to do so into the twentieth century. Despite the tragedy of her life, and her early death from consumption, Lin Daiyu is not an idealized figure of passive feminine suffering. She is highly intelligent, witty, deeply aware of her female status as a 'second-class citizen', and she struggles throughout the novel to articulate a metaphysical philosophy that incorporates her profound sense of alienation, of transience, and of the betrayals and selfishnesses that seem inevitable in human relationships. Xu Zhimo's portrayal of Mansfield's personality in his famous essay of 1923 (which was learnt by heart by some of his contemporaries, so strong was its emotional impact) appealed precisely to the main elements of this traditional stereotype, emphasizing the tragedy and pathos of Mansfield's life, her fragile beauty, the strength of her intellect, and the purity of her commitment to the values of art and imagination.

'Purity', a term regularly used by Chinese critics in relation to Mansfield's sensibility and art, also carries resonances very different from its conventional associations in English usage. Its origins lie deep in the traditions of oriental mysticism, and in the aesthetics that flow from those traditions—identified, in a recent study of the characteristics of oriental aesthetics by Lin Tonghua, as primitive simplicity, mysticism, intuitiveness, implicitness, metaphysical gracefulness and the interdependence of life and art.[4] At the core of these aesthetic principles is the mystical concept of a unity composed of 'Yin' (the feminine or negative principle) and 'Yang' (the masculine or positive principle), from which derives the notion of 'Xu' (void) and 'Shi' (substance). Feng Zongpu drew strongly on the two latter concepts in her discussion of Mansfield's fictional techniques. The spiritual plenitude of the 'void' is presented as a state of 'Kongling' (crystallized emptiness) in Chinese art and literature, a state of 'perfection'—another term regularly applied to Mansfield's art—much sought after by Chinese artists and writers, as it was by Lin Daiyu. Mansfield herself, when she used the term 'purity' to describe her aspirations, in life and art, never provided any detailed explanation, for in its primary sense it was beyond language: a highly spiritual, crystalline, empty, and mysterious state, free of any taint of materialism or self-interest.

Little attention is devoted to this aspect of Mansfield's thinking in contemporary Western criticism, but it is a recurrent aspiration, taking different forms during the course of her life—hinted at, perhaps, even in an early teenage diary entry like the following:

> I should like to write something just a trifle mysterious—but really very beautiful and original.[5]

Perhaps, also, it lies behind her well-known comment in 1916, after her brother's death, in which she vows her determination to pay a 'debt of love' to her brother and direct her imagination to the country of her birth:

> I want for one moment to make our undiscovered country leap into the eyes of the Old World. It must be mysterious, as though floating. It must take the breath. It must be 'one of those islands'. I shall tell everything, even of how the laundry-basket squeaked at 75. But all must be told with a sense of mystery, a radiance, an afterglow. . .[6]

To a Western reader, the wish for imagination to create a 'mysterious' image, 'as though floating', itself seems mysterious—certainly something other than a conventionally romantic or sentimental or exotic revisiting of the country. To a Chinese reader familiar with the oriental aesthetics of lyric poetry and landscape painting, her utterance seems quite precise.

To Chinese readers, also, the fact that Mansfield turned to an Eastern-derived practical philosophy, in the extremity of the last months of her life, seeking to find a cure for her bodily disease by attending to the inner life of the mind and soul, does not seem in the least to conflict with habits of thought and belief that are seen as deeply embedded in almost all her writing, and in her lifelong effort to purify her motives and aims as a writer.

Lin Tonghua, in his accent on oriental aesthetics, also drew attention to the 'intuitiveness' and 'implicitness' of much traditional Chinese art: to the *expressive* silences of Eastern art, conveying the significance of what is unstated, compared with the 'strikingly conspicuous' *presence* of language in Western art, 'gaudy and lavish'.[7] The use of blank space in traditional Chinese landscape painting demonstrates this characteristic of oriental art, where with only a few simply drawn strokes, a substantial inner world of emotional and mental experience is intuitively evoked. For Chinese readers this quality is everywhere apparent in Mansfield's later stories: in the typical beginnings of her stories, which leave unstated the kinds of background 'explanation' of character, event, and setting that might be expected in conventional cause-and-effect narratives; and in the typical endings of her stories, which refuse to offer explicit resolutions, allowing 'significance' to be intuitively apprehended by readers. There is hardly a story without resonances of this kind: Else's simple statement about the lamp at the end of "The Doll's House", which is so much more than a mere statement of fact; Laura's unanswered question about life (and death) at the end of "The Garden Party"; the intensity of the feeling of 'bliss' and its opposite ('despair' or 'disillusionment') in "Bliss", neither of which can be directly articulated by Bertha except in relation to a richly-blossoming pear-tree in her garden. These were amongst the most often translated of all Mansfield's stories, perhaps for their distinctly Chinese qualities of 'implicitness' as much as for their potential to be read as social fables about bourgeois society. "Bliss", in particular, might be imagined as a sequence of two Chinese paintings suggesting the extremes of bliss and despair, with its central elements abstracted—woman, pear-tree, garden—and its human context, of betrayal, briefly evoked as background.

Like Chinese paintings, Chinese lyric poems, as Ezra Pound noted, also possess the quality of never directly stating their meanings. In an article of 1918 entitled 'Chinese Poetry', he commented:

> It is because Chinese poetry has certain qualities of vivid presentation; and because certain Chinese poets have been content to set forth their matter without moralizing and without comment that one labours to make a translation.[8]

And he went on to single out five distinctive qualities of Chinese poetry (they are remarkably similar to Lin Tonghua's list of the features of oriental aesthetics): 'obscurity', 'clarity and simplicity', 'mysticism', 'the human', and—especially— the use of nature as an equation for moods:

> Especially in their poems of nature and of scenery they seem to excel Western writers, both when they speak of their sympathy with the emotions of nature and when they describe natural things.[9]

It is this *Chinese* sense of the poetic that underlies the description of Mansfield's art as 'poetic' in some Chinese criticism. The Chinese use of the term, that is, is not simply a passive imitation of a Western critical commonplace, but an active reading of her work in Chinese terms. This Chinese 'poetic' quality can be illustrated from poems like the following, in Arthur Waley's *One Hundred & Seventy Chinese Poems*, a volume which Mansfield herself read and greatly liked.[10] With their rapid contrasts of times and places and seasons with images of permanence, the two poems convey profound human feelings, the former melancholy and the latter ecstasy. But neither poet explicitly speaks such feelings.

Climbing a Mountain

> High rises the Eastern Peak
> Soaring up to the blue sky.
> Among the rocks—an empty hollow,
> Secret . . .
> Bringing to my life ceaseless change?
> I will lodge for ever in this hollow
> Where Springs and Autumns unheeded pass.

Sailing Homeward

> Cliffs that rise a thousand feet
> Without a break,
> Lake that stretches a hundred miles
> Without a wave,
> Sands that are white through all the year . . .
> Trees that for twenty thousand years
> Your vows have kept,
> You have suddenly healed the pain of a traveller's heart,
> And moved his brush to write a new song.[11]

Such poems also illustrate the quality which Lin Tonghua called 'metaphysical grace', a difficult concept to grasp in Western terms, and one which Pound does not directly identify, though something like it might be implied in his discussion of Chinese poetry's distinctive orientation towards nature. In Chinese terms 'metaphysical grace' is the product of a particular kind of harmony between art and nature. In some comparative aesthetics, such harmony in Western poetry is seen as dynamic, sublime, fraught with tension, and immediate, whereas its counterpart in the East is distinguished by opposite qualities: static equilibrium, calmness and remoteness.[12] Mansfield's relationship to the landscape includes both kinds of feeling. The wind, in "The Wind Blows", signifies an increasingly turbulent inner agitation in the protagonist—an equation for a mood—which finds no resolution in a 'static equilibrium' or feeling of remoteness. What *is* significant, however, not only in many of the stories but also in her journals, scrapbook and letters, is their constant, detailed responsiveness to nature in terms of inner-directed states of feeling, and moods prompting self-analysis. Again, although such nature-consciousness has a long Western tradition behind it, and specific Romantic antecedents as far as Mansfield is concerned, it also carried powerful associations for Chinese readers in relation to Chinese literary traditions. And in some scenes in her fiction—the opening dawn scene of "At the Bay" which inspired so fine a translation by Tang Baoxin, or Linda's abstracted moonlight vision of the aloe as a ship with lifted oars riding the 'wave' of the grassy bank, transporting her to a remote world 'more real' than the actual world in which she feels trapped—the power of the writing to evoke a sense of mystery and remoteness is remarkably close to the effect of traditional Chinese landscape painting, to 'metaphysical grace' in Lin Tonghua's terms. Like such painting, the opening scene of "At the Bay" is still yet varied, irregular yet rhythmical, magnified yet far-away. Cloaked with sea-mist, and with silence reigning, the scene—prior to the eruption of the familiar sights and sounds of waking life—creates a mood of primordial tranquillity and mysterious remoteness: the rich plenitude of the void, into which all things return in the story's brief final section:

> A cloud, small, serene, floated across the moon. In that moment of darkness the sea sounded deep, troubled. Then the cloud sailed away, and the sound of the sea was a vague murmur, as though it waked out of a dark dream. All was still.[13]

Chinese literature has had numerous movements—in reaction to periods when classical values have solidified into a rigid, rule-bound formalism—when the values of lyrical beauty, of an aesthetics not primarily driven by a didactic or instrumental purpose, were asserted. The lyric verse of the late Tang Dynasty and throughout the Song Dynasty (from about 820 to 1279 A.D.) first represented in Waley's translations was the product of one of these aesthetic movements. One school within this movement, whose main lyricists were Wen Tingyun, Yan Shu, Qin Guan, and Li Qingzhao, was later named 'Wan yue pai' (the 'School of Grace and Implicitness') because of the refinement and delicacy of its style. Its modern version, in the art of the short story, is represented in the 1920s and 1930s by 'Gui xiu pai' (the 'Boudoir School') of Bing Xin, Ling Shuhua, and others. Mansfield's influence on such writers was thus not simply the imposition, from outside, of a wholly new direction on their art. Her role was more that of a catalyst.

In the initial stage, it is true—especially in the early work of Xu Zhimo, Xiao Qian and Ling Shuhua—influence manifested itself primarily as imitation. But as their art developed, the appropriate term to use is borrowing. Mansfield herself went through this development, it might be argued, in relation to Chekhov: in which an initial phase of imitation gives way to an active process of learning, studying, assimilating, involving a recognition of common ground. Influence, in this sense, is never simply a one-way process; it is part of a much larger process of cultural exchange. In learning from Mansfield, Chinese writers, as well as translators and critics, it might be argued, were rediscovering, and reasserting, values which connected deeply with their own cultural history.

What were Mansfield's own responses and attitudes to oriental art and literature? Like a chameleon, her identity has been constructed and deconstructed in numerous ways by Western criticism, from the 1920s through to the theory-conscious 1980s. Would she recognize herself in yet another identity proposed for her here, which links her writing and sensibility to aspects of the Chinese imagination? As far as one particular feature of her reception in China in the twentieth century is concerned the political appropriation of some of her work—one can be certain that her reaction would be similar to her view of Amy Lowell's misappropriations of Chinese poetry: "That's not the thing!"[14] Perhaps Xu Zhimo might have the last word, recalling Katherine Mansfield's own warmly responsive comments about Chinese culture during the brief meeting he had with her:

> She told me that she had just come back from Switzerland, where she had lived close to the Russells. They often talked about the merits of the East. She had always had a respect for China, and now she found herself becoming one of its warm admirers. She said that what she like best was Chinese poetry in the translations of Arthur Waley. She thought that the Chinese art of poetry was a wonderful revelation to the West.
>
> I told her that I might translate some of her stories and that I would like to ask her permission first. She seemed delighted, and agreed readily to my proposal. But at the same time she doubted if they were worth the trouble.[15]

Unpublished doctoral thesis for the Degree of Doctor of Philosophy in English, University of Auckland, New Zealand, 1993.

---

[1] Yi Xinnong, 'Yi bu sheng he zhong guo xian dai wen xue' ('Ibsen and Modern Chinese Literature'), *Bi jiao wen xue lun wen ji (A Collection of Essays in Comparative Literature),* by Zhu Weizhi, Fang Ping, and others, Tianjin: Nankai University Press, 1984, p.186.

[2] Lin Yutang, *Wu guo yu wu min (My Country & My People),* Shanghai, Shi jie xin wen chu ban she (World News Publishing Company), Vol. 2, 1938, pp. 355-366. See also Zhao Xiaqiu and Zeng Qingrui, *Zhong guo xian dai xiao shuo shi (The History of Modern Chinese Fiction),* Beijing: Chinese People's University Press, pp. 122-123; and Yang Jialuo, *Min guo yi lai chu ban xin shu zong mu ti yao chu bian (A Comprehensive Catalogue of Books Published Since the Founding of the Republic),* Zhong guo xue dian guan fu guan chuo bei chu (The Preparatory Committee of the Chinese Publication Storehouse), 3rd edition, Taipei, 1972, p. 892.

[3] Xu Zhimo, 'Zai shuo yi shuo man shu fei er' ('Another Talk on Mansfield'), *Xiao shuo yue bao (The Short Story Magazine),* Vol. 16, No. 3, 1925, p. 6.

[4] Lin Tonghua, 'Lüe lun dong fang mei xue de te zheng' ('A Talk on the Characteristics of Oriental Aesthetics'), *Wen yi yan jiu (Art and Literature Studies),* Beijing, No. 6, 1990, pp. 4-11.

[5] Katherine Mansfield, *Journal of Katherine Mansfield,* ed. John Middleton Murry, London: Constable & Co. Ltd, 1954, p. 8.

[6] Ibid., p. 94.

7 Lin Tonghua, 'Lüe lun dong fang mei xue de te zheng' ('A Talk on the Characteristics of Oriental Aesthetics'), p. 7.

8 Ezra Pound, 'Chinese Poetry', *To-Day* III, April-May, 1918, pp. 54-57, 93-95. Quoted in Hugo Witemeyer, *The Poetry of Ezra Pound*, California: University of California Press, [1969], 1981, p. 147.

9 Ibid., pp. 149-50.

10 In a letter to John Middleton Murry on June 5, 1918, she wrote, of Waley's translation: "Oh, how lovely these Chinese poems are. I shall carry them about with me as a sort of wavy branch all day to hide behinda fan . . ." See *The Collected Letters of Katherine Mansfield*, ed. Vincent O'Sullivan with Margaret Scott, Vol. 2 (1918-1919), 1987, p. 220.

11 *One Hundred & Seventy Chinese Poems*, translated by Arthur Waley, London: Constable, first edition 1918, reprinted 1942, pp. 81-82.

12 Lin Tonghua, 'Lüe lun dong fang mei xue de te zheng' ('A Talk on the Characteristics of Oriental Aesthetics'), p. 9.

13 *The Stories of Katherine Mansfield*, ed. Antony Alpers, p. 469.

14 Xu Zhimo, 'Man shu fei er' ('Mansfield'), *Xu Zhimo quan ji: san wen ji (jia, yi) [Collected Works of Xu Zhimo: Collected Prose (A, B)]*, Hong Kong: The Commercial Press, 1983, p. 19.

15 Ibid., pp. 19-20.

Witi Ihimaera, "Dear Katherine Mansfield" from *Dear Miss Mansfield: A Tribute to Kathleen Mansfield Beauchamp*

Dear Katherine Mansfield,

On the occasion of the hundredth anniversary of your birth, may I offer you this small *homage* as a personal tribute to your life and your art. Throughout the past year many, many people from all over the world have wished to say 'thank you' for illuminating our lives and our literature. Mine is but a single token of aroha and respect.

Miss Mansfield, we in New Zealand have laid proud claim to you because you were born and brought up a New Zealander. Although you spent most of your adult years in England and the Continent, you always looked back to these southern antipodean islands as the main source for your stories. On our part, we have long since acknowledged that New Zealand could not fulfil your expectations of Life, Art, Literature and Experience. The world was waiting in England, Germany, Switzerland, Italy and France. And out of all those restless voyages of the intellect, mind, heart and soul, out of that singular life, came the stories. Better people than I have praised their fine art, their subtle craft and their focus on inner truth. They are stories spun sometimes from gossamer, at other times from strong sinew, sometimes kept afloat by a strength of voice, at other times by a mere thread of breath. Near the end, they were stories grabbed from out of the air at great cost. They have kept you in our memory over all the years since you have gone.

It is the modern way, Miss Mansfield, for us to have become as much fascinated with your life as with your stories. I myself have always wished to write about your Maori friend Maata and why, if she had indeed possessed a novel you had written, she may have chosen not to part with it. The novella "Maata" is my attempt to provide a Maori response to this question. But the main part of this collection, Miss Mansfield, comprises an equally Maori response, not to the life but to the stories.

Like most New Zealanders, Miss Mansfield, I came to know the stories during my school years. My first acquaintance was as a young Maori student, struggling with English, at Te Karaka District High School. This was in 1957 and the story was "The Fly". At the time I resisted anything compulsory and I did not really grow to love and appreciate your art until I had left school behind. I can remember, one sunlit afternoon in Wellington, reading "At the Bay" again, surely, for the fourteenth time. What had simply been words suddenly sprang to life and *there* it all was, happening before me—the sleepy sea sounding Ah-Aah!, the flock of sheep rounding the corner of Coronet Bay, and then Stanley Burnell racing for dear life over the big porous stones, over the cold, wet pebbles, on to the hard sand to go Splish-Splosh! Splish-Splosh! into the sea. It was all such a revelation to me and I leapt up and down as if I had suddenly discovered a pearl of inestimable value. Does it happen like this for others?

Dear Miss Mansfield, my overwhelming inspiration and purpose comes from my Maori forebears—they are my source as surely as New Zealand was yours. The art of the short story, however, has taken its bearings from your voice also. I do hope that the variations on your stories find some favour with you. They are stories in themselves, some Maori and some with European themes, recognising the common experiences of mankind. But they found their inner compulsion in my wish to respond to your work.

Ah, New Zealand, New Zealand. One hundred years on, Miss Mansfield, and it has changed beyond your recognition. Life, Art, Society—all can be had here now. There is not as much need to make those forays, as you did, to seek it elsewhere. And when we do, it is merely to satisfy our island urgings to go plundering and raiding the world's riches and retreating with them to our island fortress. In the process of exploration within and without, the literary legacy of the New Zealand short story has been greatly enriched. These are the years of fulfilment—of Janet Frame, Patricia Grace, and Keri Hulme among others.

Please accept, Miss Mansfield, my highest regard and gratitude for having been among us and above us all.

Witi Ihimaera
New York, July 1988

Dear Miss Mansfield: A Tribute to Kathleen Mansfield Beauchamp, Auckland, New Zealand: Penguin, 1989, pp. 9-10.

Select Bibliography

Bibliographical

Bardas, Mary Louise, "The State of Scholarship on Katherine Mansfield, 1950-1970", *World Literature Written in English,* XI Arlington, Univ. of Texas, 1972, pp. 77-93.

Dowling, David, "A Katherine Mansfield Bibliography", *Australian and New Zealand Studies in Canada*, No. 2, London, Ontario, Fall, 1989.

Kirkpatrick, B.J., *Bibligraphy of Katherine Mansfield*, Oxford, Clarendon Press, 1989.

Mantz, Ruth Elvish, *The Critical Bibliography of Katherine Mansfield*, London, Constable, 1931.

Meyers, Jeffrey, "Katherine Mansfield: A Bibliography of International Criticism, 1921-1977", in *Bulletin of Bibliography and Magazine Notes*, vol. 34, 1977, pp. 53-67.

Meyers, Jeffrey, "Katherine Mansfield: A Selected Checklist", *Modern Fiction Studies* XXIV, Lafayette, Ind., 1978, pp. 475-477.

Sturm, Terry (ed.), "Katherine Mansfield 1888-1923", *The Oxford History of New Zealand Literature in English,* Auckland, Oxford University Press, 1991, pp. 680-687.

Wattie, Nelson, "A Bibliography of Katherine Mansfield References 1970-84", in *Journal of New Zealand Literature*, no. 3, Victoria University of Wellington, 1985.

Biographical

Alpers, Antony, *The Life of Katherine Mansfield*, London: Cape; New York: Viking; Toronto: Clarke Irwin, 1980.

Baker, Ida, *Katherine Mansfield: The Memories of LM*, London: Joseph, 1971 and London: Virago, 1985.

Beauchamp, Sir Harold, *The Reminiscences of Sir Harold Beauchamp*, New Plymouth, New Zealand: T Avery & Son, 1937.

Boddy, Gillian, *Katherine Mansfield: The Woman and the Writer*, Ringwood, Victoria: Penguin, 1988.

Boon, Kevin, *Katherine Mansfield* [for 9-13 year olds], Petone, New Zealand: Nelson Price Milburn, 1991.

Crone, Nora, *A Portrait of Katherine Mansfield*, Ilfracombe, Devon: A.H. Stockwell, 1985

Curnow, Heather, *Katherine Mansfield*, Wellington: Reed, 1968.

Hanson, Clare and Andrew Gurr, *Katherine Mansfield*, London: Macmillan, 1981.

Mantz, Ruth Elvish, & John Middleton Murry, *The Life of Katherine Mansfield*, London: Constable, 1933.

Meyers, Jeffrey, *Katherine Mansfield: A Biography*, London: Hamish Hamilton, 1978.

Phillimore, J., *Katherine Mansfield* (Life & Works Series) Hove, England: Wayland, 1989.

Tomalin, Claire. *Katherine Mansfield: A Secret Life*, London: Viking, 1987; Knopf, 1988.

Books

Berkman, Sylvia, *Katherine Mansfield: A Critical Study*, New Haven: Yale University Press; Christchurch: Whitcombe & Tombs, 1951; London: Oxford University Press, 1952.

Caffin, Elizabeth, *Introducing Katherine Mansfield*, Auckland: Longman Paul, 1982.

Carco, Francis, *Souvenirs sur Katherine Mansfield*, Paris, 1934.

Carswell, John, *Lives and Letters: A.R. Orage, Beatrice Hastings, Katherine Mansfield, John Middleton Murry, S.S. Koteliansky:1906-1957*, London: Faber & Faber, 1978.

Chatterjee, A.C., *The Art of Katherine Mansfield*, New Delhi, India: S. Chand, 1980.

Clarke, Isabel C., *Katherine Mansfield: A Biography*, Wellington, N.Z.: Beltone Book Bureau, 1944.

Daly, Saralyn, *Katherine Mansfield*, Twayne's English Authors Series, New York: Twayne, 1965.

Davin, Dan, *Katherine Mansfield in Her Letters*, Wellington: School Publications Branch, Department of Education, New Zealand, 1959.

Eustace, Cecil J., *Infinity of Questions*, Ayer Co., (Essay Index Reprint Ser.), 1946.

Fine Instrument, The: Essays on Katherine Mansfield, ed. Paulette Michel and Michel Dupuis, Sydney: Dangaroo Press, 1889.

Foot, John, *The Edwardianism of Katherine Mansfield*, Wellington, New Zealand: Brentwood's Press, 1969.

Friis, Anne, *Katherine Mansfield: Life and Stories*, Copenhagen: Einar Munksgaard, 1946.

Fullbrook, Kate, *Katherine Mansfield*, Brighton: Harvester Press, 1986.

Gordon, Ian A., *Katherine Mansfield*, [Writers and Their Work Series, no. 49], London: Longman's Green, 1954; revised edition 1963.

Gurr, Andrew, *Writers in Exile: The Literary Identity of Home in Modern Literature*, Brighton, Sussex: Harvester Press, 1981.

Halter, Peter, *Katherine Mansfield und die Kurzgeschichte: zur Entwicklung und Struktur einer Erzählform*, Bern: Francke Verlag, 1972.

Hankin, Cherry, *Katherine Mansfield and her Confessional Stories*, London: Macmillan, 1983.

Hayman, Ronald, *Literature and Living: A Consideration of Katherine Mansfield and Virginia Woolf*, [Covent Garden Essays, no. 3], London: Covent Garden Press, 1972.

Hormasji, Nariman, *Katherine Mansfield: An Appraisal*, Auckland: Collins, 1968.

Johnson, Elizabeth (comp.), *Katherine Mansfield: An Exhibition*, University of Texas: H. Ransom Ctr., 1975.

Kaplan, Sydney, Janet, *Katherine Mansfield and the Origins of Modernist Fiction*, Ithaca, N.Y.: Cornell Univ. Press, 1991.

Katherine Mansfield: In From the Margin, ed. Roger Robinson, Baton Rouge and London : Louisiana State Univ. Press, 1994.

Kobler, Jasper F., *Katherine Mansfield: A Study of the Short Fiction*, (Twayne's Studies in Short Fiction, no.14), Boston: Twayne, 1990.

Lawlor, P.A., From *The Loneliness of Katherine Mansfield*, (monograph) Wellington, New Zealand: Beltane Book Bureau, 1950.

Magalaner, Marvin, *The Fiction of Katherine Mansfield*, Carbondale: Southern Illinois University Press, 1971.

Mattei, Anna Grazia, *L'architettura e i frammenti: Tre racconti lunghi di Katherine Mansfield*, Pisa: ETS, 1984.

McNeish, Helen (ed.), *Passionate Pilgrimage: A Love Affair in Letters*, Auckland: Hodder & Stoughton; London: Michael Joseph, 1976.

Morrell, Ottoline, Lady, *Dear Lady Ginger*, ed. Helen Shaw, Wellington, New Zealand: Auckland Univ. Press/Oxford Univ. Press, 1983.

Morrow, Patrick D., *Katherine Mansfield's Fiction*, Bowling Green, Ohio: State Univ. Popular Press, 1993.

Murray, Heather, *Double Lives: Women in the Stories of Katherine Mansfield*, New Zealand: University of Otago Press, 1990.

Murry, John Middleton, *Between Two Worlds: An Autobiography*, London: Jonathan Cape, 1935.

Murry, John Middleton, *Katherine Mansfield and Other Literary Portraits*, London, Peter Nevill Ltd., 1949.

Murry, John Middleton, *Katherine Mansfield and Other Literary Studies*, London: Constable, 1959.

Nathan, Rhoda B, (ed.), *Critical Essays on Katherine Mansfield*, [Critical Essays on British Literature series, Gen. Ed. Zack Bowen], New York: G.K. Hall & Co./Macmillan; Ontario: Maxwell Macmillan Canada Inc., 1993.

O'Connor, Frank, *The Lonely Voice: A Study of the Short Story*, London: Macmillan, 1963.

O'Sullivan, Vincent, *Katherine Mansfield's New Zealand*, Auckland: Golden Press, 1974; London: Frederick Muller, 1975; repr. Auckland: Viking, 1988.

O'Sullivan, Vincent, "Finding the Pattern, Solving the Problem: Katherine Mansfield the New Zealand European", an inaugural address delivered on 11 October 1988. Wellington, New Zealand:Victoria University Press, 1989.

Parkin-Gounelas, Ruth, *The Female Self*, London: Macmillan (Academic & Prof.), 1991.

Rohrberger, Mary, *The Art of Katherine Mansfield*, Ann Arbor, Mich.: University Microfilms Inc., 1977.

Sewell, Arthur, "Katherine Mansfield, A Critical Essay", Auckland, New Zealand: Unicorn Press, 1936, pp1-32.

Wattie, Nelson, *Nation und Literatur: eine Studie zur Bestimmung der nationalen Merkmale literarischer Werke am Beispiel von Katherine Mansfield's Kurzgescchichten*, Bonn: Bouvier, 1980.

Worlds of Katherine Mansfield, ed. Harry Rickets, Palmerston North, New Zealand: Ngaere Press, 1991.

Essays and Articles

Adelphi, The, vol. I, No. 8, London: Jan. 1924.

Aiken, Conrad, "The Short Story as Colour", in *The Freeman*, 5, June 21, 1922, pp. 357-358. (Reprinted in *A Reviewer's ABC: Collected Criticism*, New York: Meridian Books, 1958).

Aiken, Conrad, "Your Obituary, Well Written", in *Costumes by Eros*, London: Jonathan Cape, 1929, pp. 9-33.

Allen, C. R., "The Katherine Mansfield Legend", in *The Christchurch Press*, October 24, 1951.

Allen, Walter, "Katherine Mansfield", in *The Short Story in English*, Oxford: Oxford University Press, 1981, pp. 165-175.

Alpers, Antony, *Katherine Mansfield*, Wellington: School Publications Branch, Department of Education, New Zealand, 1947.

Anon. Review of "In a German Pension", in *The New Age*, Dec.21.1911, p.188.

Anon. Review of *Bliss and Other Stories* in *The Athenæum*, January 21, 1921, p.67.

Anon. "Katherine Mansfield's Stories", *Times Literary Supplement*, London: March 2, 1946, p. 102. Also in *Listener*, London: July 4, 1946.

Arvidson, K.O., "Dancing on the Hand of God: Katherine Mansfield's Religious Sensibility", at Katherine Mansfield Centennial Conference, Victoria University of Wellington, New Zealand, 12-15 October 1988.

Athenaeum, The, April 4, 1919.

Athenaeum, The, February 11, 1921.

Baldeshwiler, Eileen, "Katherine Mansfield's Theory of Fiction", in *Studies in Short Fiction*, 1970, 7: pp. 421-432.

Bates, H.E., "Katherine Mansfield and A.E. Coppard", in *The Modern Short Story: A Critical Survey*, London, Thomas Nelson , 1941, pp. 122-133.

Bateson, F.W. and B. Shahevitch, "Katherine Mansfield's "The Fly", *Essays in Criticism*, January 1962, 12: pp. 39-53.

Beachcroft, T.O., "Katherine Mansfield's Encounter with Theocritus", *English ,* XXIII, Spring 1974. 115: pp. 13-19

Beauchamp, Harold, "Katherine Mansfield's Career", *Saturday Review of Literature*, 10, September 30, 1933, p. 144.

Blunden, Edmund, "A Prose-Writer's Poems", review of *Poems* in *The Nation & The Athenæum*, January 26, 1924, 34: p.609.

Bogan, Louise, "Childhood's False Eden", *Selected Criticism*, New York, 1955, pp. 186-188.

Bowen, Elizabeth. "A Living Writer", *Cornhill Magazine*, no. 1010, Winter 1956-7, pp. 118-134.

Brophy, Brigid, "Katherine Mansfield", *The London Magazine*, vol. 2, no. 9, (December 1962), pp41-47.

Brophy, Brigid, "Katherine Mansfield's Self-Depiction", *Michigan Quarterly Review*, 5, Spring 1966, pp. 89-93.

Brophy, Brigid, "Don't Never Forget", *Collected Views and Reviews*, London: Jonathan Cape, 1966.

Brown, Sally, "Hundreds of Selves: The British Library's Katherine Mansfield Letters", *The British Library Journal*, vol. 14, August 1988, 2, pp. 154-164.

Busch, Frieder, "Katherine Mansfield and Literary Impressionism in France and Germany", *Arcadia* V,1970, pp. 58-76.

Carter, Angela, "The Life of Katherine Mansfield", *Nothing Sacred*, London: Virago, 1982, pp. 158-161.

Cather, Willa, "Katherine Mansfield", in *Not Under Forty*, London: Cassell & Co. Ltd., 1936, pp. 139-166.

Cazmian, Louis, "D.H. Lawrence and Katherine Mansfield as Letter Writers", *The University of Toronto Quarterly*, 111, April 1934, pp. 286-307.

Clarke, Brice, "Katherine Mansfield's Illness", in *Proceedings of the Royal Society of Medicine*, 48: pp.1029-1032, April 1955.

Cowley, Malcolm, Review of *Bliss* in *Dial* September, 1921, p. 365.

Cowley, Malcolm, "The Author of 'Bliss' ", *Dial*, August 1922, 73, p. 230.

Cox, Sydney, "The Fastidiousness of Katherine Mansfield", *Sewanee Review*, XXXIX (1931), pp. 158-169.

Daiches, David, "The Art of Katherine Mansfield" in *New Literary Values* (Studies in Modern Literature series), Oliver & Boyd, 1936, pp.83-114,

Daiches, David, "Katherine Mansfield and the Search for Truth", *The Novel and the Modern World* , Chicago: University of Chicago Press, 1939, pp. 65-79.

Dale, Judith, "Performing Katherine Mansfield", *Landfall*, vol.43 4, Christchurch, New Zealand: 1989, 172: pp. 503-511.

Dunbar, Pamela, "What Does Bertha Want?: A Re-reading of Katherine Mansfield's 'Bliss' ", *Women's Studies Journal*, 4:2, December 1988, pp. 18-31.

Else, Anne, "Limitation, Selection and Assumption in Antony Alpers' *Life of Katherine Mansfield*", *New Zealand Women's Studies Journal*, August 1984, pp. 86-102.

Gillet, Louis, "Katherine Mansfield", *Revue des deux mondes*, December 15, 1924, 24, pp. 929-941.

Gordon, Ian A., "Katherine Mansfield, New Zealander" (*New Zealand New Writing*,), Wellington: New Zealand, 1943.

Gordon, Ian A., "The Editing of Katherine Mansfield's Journal and Scrapbook", in *Landfall* XIII, Christchurch: New Zealand, March 1959, 1: pp. 62-69.

Gubar, Susan, "The Birth of the Artist as Heroine:(Re)production, the Kunstlerroman Tradition, and the Fiction of Katherine Mansfield", in *The Representation of Women in Fiction*, Baltimore: Johns Hopkins University Press, 1983, pp. 19-59.

Gurr, Andrew, "The Question of Perspectives in Commonwealth Literature", in *Kunapipi*, vol. 6, 1984, 2: pp. 67-80.

Hankin, Cherry, "Fantasy and the Sense of an Ending in the Work of Katherine Mansfield", *Modern Fiction Studies*, XXIV, 1978, pp. 465-474.

Hardy, Linda, "The Ghost of Katherine Mansfield", *Landfall*, 43:4 December 1989, pp. 416-432.

Hubbell, George Shelton, "Katherine Mansfield and Kezia", *Sewanee Review*, XXXV, 1927, pp. 325-335.

Hynes, Sam, "Katherine Mansfield: The Defeat of the Personal", *South Atlantic Quarterly*, October 1953, pp. 555-560.

Ihimaera, Witi, "Dear Katherine Mansfield" from *Dear Miss Mansfield: A Tribute to Kathleen Mansfield Beauchamp*, Auckland, New Zealand: Penguin Books, 1989, pp. 9-10.

Isherwood, Christopher, "Katherine Mansfield", *Exhumations: Stories, Articles, Verses*, London: Methuen, 1966, pp. 64-72.

Journal of New Zealand Literature, The, [special Mansfield edition], no. 6, Palmerston North: Massey University, 1988.

King, Russel S., "Katherine Mansfield as an Expatriate Writer", *The Journal of Commonwealth Literature*, Vol. VIII, no. 1, June 1973, pp. 97-109.

Kaplan, Sydney Janet, "Katherine Mansfield's 'Passion for Technique'", *Women's Language and Style*, ed. Douglas Buttruff and E.L. Epstein. *Studies in Contemporary Language*, no. 1, Akron, Ohio: University of Akron, 1978, pp. 119-131.

Landfall 172; (Katherine Mansfield Special Edition), Christchurch, New Zealand, vol. 43, no. 4, December 1989.

Mais, S.P.B., "Katherine Mansfield" in *Some Modern Authors* , London: Grant Richards Ltd., 1923, pp. 108-113.

Mantz, Ruth Elvish, "Katherine Mansfield—Tormentor and Tormented". *Katherine Mansfield Exhibition Catalogue*, Austin: Texas University Press, 1975, pp 5-7, reprinted in *Adam*, no. 370-375, 1972-3, [Katherine Mansfield Anniversary Issue].

Meyers, Jeffrey, *Married to Genius*, London: London Magazine Editions, 1977.

Meyers, Jeffrey, "Katherine Mansfield's 'To Stanislaw Wyspianski'' in *Modern Fiction Studies*, XXIV, 1978, pp. 337-41.

Meyers, Jeffrey, "Murry's Cult of Mansfield", *Journal of Modern Literature*, 1979.

Modern Fiction Studies: Katherine Mansfield Special Issue, vol. 24, no. 3 (Autumn 1978).

Morrow, Patrick, "The Idea of the Perfect Short Story", in *International Literature in English: Essays on the Major Writers*, ed. Robert L. Ross, New York: Garland, 1991.

Mortelier, Christiane, "The Genesis and Development of the Katherine Mansfield Legend in France", *AUMLA*, XXXIV, Christchurch, New Zealand: pp. 252-263. Also published in French, *Etudes Anglaises* XXIII, 1970, pp. 357-368.

Mortimer, Raymond, Review of *The Dove's Nest, and Other Stories*, in *The New Statesman*, 21, July 7, 1923, p. 394.

Murry, John Middleton, "In Memory of Katherine Mansfield", *The Adelphi*, January 1924, 1, pp. 663-665.

Neaman, Judith S., "Allusion, Image, and Associative Pattern: The Answers in Mansfield's 'Bliss' ", *Twentieth Century Literature* no. 2 September 1986, pp. 242-254.

Nebeker, Helen B., "The Pear Tree: Sexual Implications in Katherine Mansfield's 'Bliss'", *Modern Fiction Studies*, vol 18, no. 4, Winter 1972-73.

Olgivanna [Mrs Frank Lloyd Wright, née Lazovich], "The Last Days of Katherine Mansfield", *Bookman*, New York, March 1931, 73, pp. 6-13.

Orr, Bridget, "Reading with the Taint of the Pioneer: Katherine Mansfield and Settler Criticism", *Landfall*, 43:4 (December 1989), pp. 447-461.

O'Sullivan, Vincent, from "The Magnetic Chain: Notes and Approaches to K.M." in *Lanafall* V 29:2, June 1975,114: pp. 95-131.

Porter, Katherine Anne, "The Art of Katherine Mansfield", in *The Nation*, 145, October 23, 1937, pp. 435-6, reprinted in *The Days Before*, New York: Harcourt Brace, 1952.

Pritchett, V.S. Review of *Novels and Novelists*, in *The Spectator*, 145, September 6, 1930, p. 315.

Rhythm, I-II (Summer, 1911-March, 1913).

Schirmer, Ruth, "Nachwort" des Katherine Mansfield's *Erzählungen und Tagebücher*, Zurich: 1974, pp. 437-458. Reprinted from *Neue Zürcher Zeitung*, 7 January 1973, pp. 41-42.

Schneider, Elisabeth, "Katherine Mansfield and Chekhov", in *Modern Language Notes* vol. 50:6, June, 1935, pp. 394-7.

Scott, Margaret, "The Extant Manuscripts of Katherine Mansfield", *Etudes Anglaises*, XXVI, 4, 1973, pp. 413-419.

Signature, The, I (October 4-November 1, 1915).

Sitwell, Edith, "Three Women Writers", *Vogue*, London, October, 1924, p. 83.

Stead, C.K., "Katherine Mansfield and the Art of Fiction" in *The New Review*, 4, no. 43, September 1977, pp. 27-36, [reprinted in *In the Glass Case:Essays on New Zealand Literature*, Auckland, New Zealand: Auckland/Oxford University Press, 1981, pp. 29-46].

Sullivan, J.W.N., Review of "Je ne parle pas Français", in *The Athenæum*, April 2, 1920, p. 447.

Tomalin, Claire,. "Maria La Vida secreta de Katherine Mansfield", *Quimera: Revista de Literatura*, 1990, 96, pp. 12-21.

Tomlinson, Sophie, "Mansfield in Bookform", *Landfall*, 156 (December, 1985), pp. 465-473.

Uglow, Jennifer, "Publicizing the Private", *Times Literary Supplement*, October 17, 1980, p. 1166.

Wagenknecht, Edward, "Katherine Mansfield", *The English Journal*, April 1928, 17, pp. 281-282.

Waldron, Philip, "Katherine Mansfield's *Journal*", *Twentieth Century Literature*, 20, 1974, pp. 11-18.

Waldron, Philip, "A Katherine Mansfield Poem Printed Incomplete", *Notes and Queries*, XXI 1974, pp. 365-366.

Waldron, Philip, "Katherine Mansfield's Journal", *Twentieth Century Literature*, XX, 1974, pp. 11-18.

Walker, Nancy, *Stages of Womanhood in Katherine Mansfield's "Prelude"* (Diss.), University of Massachussetts, 1976.

Wattie, Nelson, "Katherine Mansfield: Was She 'a New Zealand Writer'?" *New Zealand Headlines*, (Bonn) 29 (March 1975), pp. 7-13.

Webby, Elizabeth, "Katherine Mansfield: Everything and Nothing", *Meanjin*, 41, no. 2, (1982), pp. 236-243.

West, Rebecca, Review of "The Garden Party" in *The New Statesman*, 18, March 18, 1922, p. 673.

Wevers, Lydia, "How Kathleen Beauchamp Was Kidnapped", *Women's Studies Journal* 4:2 (December 1988), pp. 5-17.

Whitridge, Arnold, "Katherine Mansfield", *The Sewanee Review*, XLVIII, April-June 1940, pp. 256-272.

Woolf, Virginia, "A Terribly Sensitive Mind", in *New York Herald Tribune*, September 18, 1927, p. 1. (Reprinted in Virginia Woolf, *Collected Essays I*, London: The Hogarth Press), 1925 (1966), pp. 356-358.

Wright, Celeste T., "Genesis of a Short Story", in *Philological Quarterly*, XXXIV, I, January 1955, pp. 91-96.

Zinman, Toby Silverman, "The Snail Under the Leaf: Katherine Mansfield's Imagery", *Modern Fiction Studies*, XXIV, 1978, pp. 457-464.

Index

About the Editor

JAN PILDITCH is a Lecturer in the Department of English at the University of Waikato in New Zealand.